Praise for *The Congressional Experience, Fourth Edition*

"There is no one who combines the practical and scholarly understanding of Congress as well as David Price. At a time when too many Americans have all but given up on the first branch of government as a source of fixes for the nation's biggest problems, the 16-term North Carolina lawmaker and political science professor reminds us why it still matters. He conveys the reality of the legislative experience, explains what it can do when at its best, and suggests remedies that ultimately point to us, America's citizens."
—**Judy Woodruff**, Anchor and Managing Editor, The PBS NewsHour

"David Price was one of the foremost scholars of Congress before he became a member of the House. *The Congressional Experience* was a goldmine for students of Congress when it first came out, combining in a unique way the best of political science with the invaluable insights of an ultimate insider. Every edition since has been more enriching. This fourth edition, filled with insights of how our politics more broadly, and those of Congress itself, have changed over the past sixteen years, and notably since Donald Trump became president, is the best yet, an extraordinary treat for anyone interested in how Congress works, what motivates its members, and how it can be better."
—**Norman Ornstein**, resident scholar, The American Enterprise Institute

"Three cheers for this new edition of *The Congressional Experience!* With deftness and thoughtfulness, David Price carries the story through the ups and downs, budgetary traumas, nasty polarization and the rest up through Obama and Trump, not to mention Covid-19. The book is illuminating on congressional structure and what to do about its difficulties. I haven't seen a better discussion of how to be a responsible legislator."
—**David R. Mayhew**, Sterling Professor of Political Science Emeritus, Yale University

"Congressman David Price has written a compelling and intellectually stimulating book on Congress from the perspective of one of its members. But Congressman Price is also Dr. Price, a political scientist, and the book is not simply a narrative of his experiences, but a scholarly contribution to our understanding of the nuances, changes, and inner-workings of the institution. In these polarized times, this book provides a window into the effects of that polarization on the workings of one of our most important government institutions."

James B. Duke Distinguished

"To invoke an overused word, David Price really is unique. No one else brings his breadth of experience and learning to the study of the Constitution's first branch of government. He is, at once, a distinguished political scientist, a former state party chair, and a House member who has won election after election. He not only understands politics from the inside out but also brings to it the instructive distance of an intellectual who sees things whole. It's a great blessing that he has given us a new edition of *The Congressional Experience*."

—E.J. Dionne, Jr., author, *Code Red* and *Our Divided Political Heart*

The Congressional Experience

Congressman David E. Price is uniquely qualified to guide readers through the labyrinth of Congress, to portray honestly its strengths and failings, and to illuminate the forces transforming the institution. As a trained political scientist, he connects the practical politics on the Hill with the theories of the discipline. He is equally focused on the ethics of public service at a time when politics seem to have reached a new low. Through it all, he conveys a clear sense of the challenges, disappointments, elations, and deep concerns implicit in serving as a member of Congress—especially at a time of national and international fragility.

New to the Fourth Edition

- Covers the Obama and Trump presidencies, three turnovers in House leadership, and growing party polarization and its effects.
- Provides a stronger emphasis on foreign policy, including the House Democracy Partnership's work with parliaments in emerging democracies, the House's role in Middle East diplomacy, and the unique challenges to the "Article One" branch of government posed by the Trump presidency.
- Compares and contrasts the Clinton and Trump impeachments.
- Expands the treatment of America's broken and besieged electoral system and the path to reform.

David E. Price is U.S. Representative (D-NC) for North Carolina's Fourth District. He received his undergraduate degree at UNC-Chapel Hill and went on to Yale University to earn a Bachelor of Divinity as well as a Ph.D. in Political Science. Before he began serving in Congress in 1987, Price was a professor of political science and public policy at Duke University. He is the author of four books on Congress and the American political system. Price is North Carolina's only member of the House Appropriations

Committee and serves as the Chairman of the Transportation, Housing and Urban Development Appropriations Subcommittee. He is a recognized leader on foreign policy, serving as Chairman of the House Democracy Partnership and an outspoken advocate for Middle East peace. He received the Hubert H. Humphrey Award from the American Political Science Association and the William Sloane Coffin Award for Peace and Justice from Yale Divinity School.

The Congressional Experience
An Institution Transformed

Fourth Edition

David E. Price

Routledge
Taylor & Francis Group

NEW YORK AND LONDON

Fourth edition published 2021
by Routledge
52 Vanderbilt Avenue, New York, NY 10017

and by Routledge
2 Park Square, Milton Park, Abingdon, Oxon, OX14 4RN

Routledge is an imprint of the Taylor & Francis Group, an informa business

© 2021 Taylor & Francis

First edition published by Westview Press, 1992

Second edition published by Westview Press, 2000

Third edition published by Westview Press, 2004 and by Routledge, 2018

Library of Congress Cataloging-in-Publication Data
Names: Price, David Eugene, author.
Title: The congressional experience: an institution transformed /
David E. Price.
Identifiers: LCCN 2020035052 (print) | LCCN 2020035053 (ebook) |
ISBN 9780367627072 (Paperback) | ISBN 9780367626938 (Hardback) |
ISBN 9781003110347 (eBook)
Subjects: LCSH: Price, David Eugene. | Legislators–United
States–Biography. | United States. Congress. House–Biography. |
United States–Politics and government–1989- |
North Carolina–Politics and government–1951- |
Politics, Practical–North Carolina. | Politics,
Practical–United States.
Classification: LCC E840.8.P65 A3 2021 (print) |
LCC E840.8.P65 (ebook) | DDC 328.73/092–dc23
LC record available at https://lccn.loc.gov/2020035052
LC ebook record available at https://lccn.loc.gov/2020035053

ISBN: 978-0-367-62693-8 (hbk)
ISBN: 978-0-367-62707-2 (pbk)
ISBN: 978-1-003-11034-7 (ebk)

Typeset in Sabon
by Deanta Global Publishing Services, Chennai, India

For Charlie, Maggie, and Genevieve

Contents

List of Figures and Table

Figures

Table

Preface to the Fourth Edition

The cover of this book features the majestic U.S. Capitol, seat of the Article One branch of government, but with storm clouds looming overhead. The symbolism seems apt. As the book went to press, the turbulent and fateful 2020 elections were unfolding, the coronavirus was threatening the country's health and economic well-being, and a powerful movement for racial justice, sparked by a brutal police killing in Minneapolis, was sweeping the country with demands for change.

Even before this dramatic convergence of events, however, it was evident that writing the fourth edition of *The Congressional Experience* would pose special challenges. Sixteen years had passed since the last edition, a long time to cover in the history of the institution and my place within it. These were not tranquil years; they saw heightened political conflict and polarization, three turnovers in House leadership, and significant changes in how, and how well, the institution functioned. Add to that the erratic and norm-shattering quality of the Trump presidency, and the challenge becomes clear: at what point can one take a snapshot and claim to have a definitive picture of how the system works? Or of the character of the congressional experience?

I do not offer this book as such a steady-state portrayal, but as an account of life in an institution in transition. This edition contains far more new material and revised interpretations than previous editions—a function of the passage of time and of the roles I have assumed as a senior member, but also of the changes that have occurred and are still in progress within the institution and in the broader political environment. I have felt strongly motivated to take stock of these changes and put a revised account together and am indebted to many people who have helped me see the project through.

Jean-Louise Beard, my former chief of staff, has taken the manuscript from scrawled legal pads to page proofs, jogging and correcting my memory and offering helpful suggestions and insights all along the way. For critical readings of specific chapters, I am indebted to Sean Maxwell, Jackson Tufts, Katelynn Vogt, and Justin Wein. The narrative draws on articles that

Asher Hildebrand and Tommy Ross helped me write. For helping me get the story straight on specific episodes and processes, I thank Nora Blalock, Joe Carlile, Sawyer Hackett, James Hunter, Mary Lou Leiser-Smith, John Lis, Mac McCorkle, Darek Newby, Gloria Nlewedim, Kate Roetzer, Eric Sapp, Samantha Schifrin, Laura Thrift, Anna Tilghman, and Janssen White. Richard Kogan and Walter Oleszek directed me to valuable data. Nadia Alston, Sonia Barnes, Tracy Lovett, Dave Russell, and Robyn Winneberger furnished useful accounts of constituent-service interactions.

It has been a pleasure to work again with Jennifer Knerr, Senior Editor at Routledge, who has encouraged and facilitated this project throughout, just as she did twenty-eight years ago when Westview published the first edition. I appreciate the good work of editorial assistant at Routledge, Jacqueline Dorsey, and project manager at Deanta Global, Sarah Silva, and remain indebted to Larry Dodd, who first encouraged me to write the book and was the series editor for earlier editions.

I am once again grateful to my wife Lisa for her understanding and support both of what service in the House requires and of my determination to write about it. She and I have experienced a transition of our own since the last edition—the arrival of our wonderful grandchildren, Charles Albert, Margaret Elizabeth, and Genevieve Annalise. I dedicate this book to them with love and hopeful anticipation.

David E. Price
July 2020

1 Introduction

On November 4, 1986, I was elected to the U.S. House of Representatives from the Fourth District of North Carolina, a five-county area that included the cities of Raleigh, Chapel Hill, and Asheboro. Many thoughts crowded in on me during election night, but one of the most vivid was of a spring evening in 1959 when I had first set foot in the part of North Carolina I was now to represent. At the time, I was a student at Mars Hill, a junior college in the North Carolina mountains a few miles from my home in Erwin, a small town in East Tennessee. I had taken an eight-hour bus ride from Mars Hill to Chapel Hill to be interviewed for a Morehead Scholarship, a generous award that subsequently made it possible for me to attend the University of North Carolina (UNC). I was awed by the university and nervous about the interview. Thinking back on some of the answers I gave ("Would you say Cecil Rhodes was an imperialist?" "I believe so."), I still marvel that I won the scholarship. But I did, and the next two years were among the most exciting and formative of my life.

I went north in 1961 to divinity school and eventually graduate school and a faculty appointment in political science, all at Yale University. But the idea of returning to the Raleigh–Durham–Chapel Hill area of North Carolina continued to tug at me, particularly as I decided on a teaching career and thought about where I would like to put down personal and academic roots. Fortunately, my wife, Lisa, also found the idea agreeable, despite her budding political career as a member of the New Haven Board of Aldermen. Therefore, when I received an offer to join the political science faculty at Duke University and help launch what is now the Terry Sanford School of Public Policy, I jumped at the opportunity. In mid-1973, we moved with our children (three-year-old Karen and one-year-old Michael) to Chapel Hill. Though we were delighted with the community and the job and saw the move as a long-term one, I would have been incredulous at the suggestion that within fourteen years I would represent the district in Congress.

The Fourth District has been redrawn six times since I was first elected, after the three decennial censuses and three additional times ordered by the courts. As I will elaborate in Chapter 3, North Carolina has become a poster child for partisan gerrymandering. In the last decade, this has given my district some bizarre configurations but has also made it more solidly Democratic—designed not for my benefit, but in order to make the surrounding districts more Republican. The district has included as many as seven and as few as three counties; overall, I have at some time represented all or part of twelve counties, a large swath of central North Carolina.

North Carolina, and our part of the state especially, have grown and diversified greatly over these three decades. The state's congressional delegation has grown from eleven to a projected fourteen after the 2020 census. The five-county area I first represented now contains enough people to populate almost three congressional districts.

The Fourth District has always centered on the cities of Raleigh, Cary, Durham, and Chapel Hill in some combination and has included all or parts of Research Triangle Park, a monument to synergy among high-tech large and small businesses, research universities, and the state and federal governments. Rapid growth has produced widespread suburbanization and, more recently, extensive downtown renewal, although small-town and rural areas remain. African Americans have comprised between 20–32 percent of the drawn and redrawn district, and increasing numbers of people with Chinese, Indian, Middle Eastern, and other ethnic backgrounds have been drawn to the area. The Latino population is approaching 11–12 percent and has increased at least tenfold over my time in office.

Politically, my present district is 48 percent Democratic by voter registration, 24 percent Republican, and 28 percent "unaffiliated." Hillary Clinton received 68 percent of the district's vote for president in 2016. During my early years in office, as Chapter 2 will amply demonstrate, the Fourth was a "swing" district, a partisan battleground in national, state, and many local elections. The addition of Durham County to the district in 1997 increased its Democratic tilt, but this was largely offset when the more Democratic parts of Raleigh and Wake County were transferred to neighboring districts. Republican control of the General Assembly after the 2010 census brought extreme gerrymandering and the "packing" of the Fourth District with many more African Americans and Democrats.

Several of the district's counties were represented in the distant past by Nathaniel Macon (1791–1815), North Carolina's only Speaker of the U.S. House of Representatives. The district sent two Chatham County populists, William F. Stroud and John W. Atwater, to the House during that movement's ascendancy in North Carolina in the 1890s, but again elected a Democrat in the White supremacy campaign of 1900. For the first two-thirds of the twentieth century, the eastern part of the present Fourth District was represented by two men: Edward W. Pou (1901–1934), who chaired the House Rules Committee, and Harold D. Cooley (1934–1967), flamboyant chairman of the House Agriculture Committee. Carl Durham, who represented the district's western counties from 1939 until 1961, chaired the Joint Committee on Atomic Energy.[1] Such extended periods of service, with attendant seniority in the House, became less common in our part of North Carolina after the departure of Durham and Cooley. Heightened partisan competition produced more frequent turnovers in congressional seats. Members also became less intent on House careers, sometimes resigning to seek other political offices. And the drawing and redrawing of district lines following the Supreme Court's redistricting decisions destabilized traditional electoral coalitions and rendered elections less predictable. When I was sworn in on January 6, 1987, I became the Fourth District's third representative in as many terms. Now, it is hard for me to comprehend that I am on track to match Pou's and Cooley's terms of service!

By the time I ran for Congress, I had amassed a good deal of political experience. Senator E. L. ("Bob") Bartlett (D-Alaska) hired me as a summer intern in 1963, and I returned to his staff as a legislative aide for the four succeeding summers, eventually doing interviews out of his office for a doctoral dissertation on the Senate. After moving back to North Carolina, I worked actively in local politics, managed a couple of congressional districts (including the Fourth) in Jimmy Carter's 1976 presidential campaign, and took leaves from Duke in 1980 and 1984 to serve as executive director and then chairman of the North Carolina Democratic Party. But these were diversions, albeit increasingly serious ones, from a primary career in teaching and research. By 1986, I had studied, taught, and written about Congress, among other subjects, for twenty years.

Among some voters—and occasionally among congressional colleagues—my academic background has been a barrier to be overcome. But not for most. My district has one of the highest numbers of Ph.Ds. per capita of any comparable area in the country. Representing an area that boasts multiple institutions of higher education, the Research Triangle Park, and retirement communities populated by people with distinguished careers, I have remarkably literate constituents. I sometimes reflect ambivalently on this as I contemplate the volume of well-reasoned correspondence on every conceivable issue that comes into my office! Yet the electoral advantages are considerable. During my first campaign, we polled to test public reactions to my academic affiliation and background, expecting to downplay them in the campaign. Instead, we found highly positive associations and ended up running a television ad that featured me in the classroom!

The growth of the Research Triangle area has brought economic and political strains along with increased prosperity and diversity, and the benefits have not been equally enjoyed. The district's median household income is around $70,000, some 34 percent above the median income statewide. But around 12 percent of our residents live below the federal poverty level of $26,200 for a family of four. Downtown and inner-suburban redevelopment has produced gentrification and displacement of lower-income residents, creating pressures to preserve housing diversity and promote transportation alternatives.

It was, I suppose, in light of my dual background as an academic and a political practitioner that I was asked to contribute reflections on my first term in office to the 1989 edition of *Congress Reconsidered*.[2] I was reluctant at first, pressed for time and uncertain of the value of the exercise, but I was challenged by the idea of giving an account of congressional operations that would combine personal experience with the sort of generalization and analysis characteristic of political science. My story and the stories of other people and events would be told not mainly for their own sake but as a way of showing how the U.S. Congress works. The article that I produced formed the core of the first edition of this book, which extended through the midpoint of my third term (1991–1992). The second edition took the story forward to the 106th Congress (1999–2000), the third edition to the 108th (2003–2004), and the current edition to the 116th (2019–2020), with many years and monumental changes to cover, adding up to a substantial transformation of the institution. The chapters to follow will address getting elected (and unelected and then reelected); adjusting to life in Congress, finding a niche and later assuming leadership in the House; varieties of policy entrepreneurship; the evolving politics of appropriations, the budget, and foreign affairs; party operations and the effects of increasing polarization; and communicating with and serving the district.

Topics that were familiar to me as an academic—the place of religion in politics, the ethics of public service, the critique of Congress as an institution, and political reform—have taken on particular interest during my years in office, and in later chapters I will offer some reflections on them. These are areas where ideas are often used as weaponry more than as a means to enlightenment, and I will try to nudge these discussions in a more productive direction.

The period covered in this volume was a contentious and challenging time for Congress and the country, never more than at present. It extends from the waning of Ronald Reagan's presidency to the advent of Donald Trump. It was a time of momentous change in world politics, spanning the end of the Cold War and the collapse of communism in Russia and Eastern Europe; allied interventions in Bosnia and Kosovo; two U.S.-led wars against Iraq, the terrorist attacks of September 11, 2001, and the subsequent offensive against al Qaeda and international terrorism; successful diplomatic efforts to prevent Iran's development of nuclear capacity, followed by Donald Trump's deliberate blowing up of that agreement; and the further disruption under Trump of American alliances and diplomacy. At home, it was at first a period of tepid economic performance and a deepening recession (1990–1991), followed by a decade-long economic boom, an economic downturn that culminated in the great recession of 2007–2008, and a slow and steady, if somewhat uneven, economic recovery unexpectedly derailed by a global pandemic. Intertwined with these trends as both cause and effect were federal budget deficits of $250 billion "as far as the eye could see" giving way in the mid-1990s to modest budget surpluses but then, after 2001, abruptly returning to red ink and mounting debt. The comprehensive budget deals which had facilitated the fiscal turnaround of the 1990s became ever more elusive in the face of partisan polarization. This reduced the country's readiness for the economic impact of the coronavirus, which nonetheless had to be countered with massive rescue and recovery expenditures.

It was also a period of political turbulence, with neither party clearly dominant, in North Carolina or the nation, and citizens expressing considerable dissatisfaction with politics and politicians. Democrats controlled the House, Senate, and White House for two unstable periods (1993–1994 and 2009–2010), as did the Republicans after the 2002 and 2016 elections. But the norm during these years was divided party control. Republican presidents faced Democratic control of one or both houses of Congress through the 1980s to 1992 and after the 2006 and 2018 elections; Democratic presidents faced opposition control after wave elections in 1995–2000 and 2011–2016. During the sixteen terms covered in this volume, I served under seven House Speakers—Democrats Jim Wright, Tom Foley, and Nancy Pelosi, and Republicans Newt Gingrich, Dennis Hastert, John Boehner, and Paul Ryan. Wright and Gingrich resigned amid ethics charges and Boehner was driven from office by dissidents from his own party during a period that also spanned President Reagan's Iran–Contra scandal and the impeachment of two presidents.

The reputation of Congress, never Americans' favorite political institution, reached historic lows during these years, and House members often found it politically profitable to run for Congress by denigrating and running against the institution. Gingrich and his self-styled Republican revolutionaries came to power in 1994 largely on the strength of a harsh institutional critique. They in turn became the targets of public cynicism and distrust as their revolution overreached and began to falter. "Congress bashing" has continued unabated, often crowding out more reasoned and relevant judgments about individual and institutional performance. My hope in this book is to encourage and facilitate more useful assessments by conveying a sense of how Congress works and beginning to raise some of the right evaluative questions.

But first things first. Recalling the dictum of former House Speaker Tip O'Neill that "all politics is local"[3] (except when it isn't, I might add, in light of 1994 and subsequent wave elections), I will begin with an account of how I came to run for Congress and managed, with the help of a great many people, to get elected.

Notes

1 See David E. Price, "Roll Call: A Congressman Looks Back at Those Who Went Before," Raleigh *News and Observer*, July 30, 1989, p. 1D.

2 David E. Price, "The House of Representatives: A Report from the Field," in Lawrence C. Dodd and Bruce I. Oppenheimer, eds., *Congress Reconsidered*, 4th ed. (Washington, DC: Congressional Quarterly Press, 1989), chap. 17.
3 Thomas P. O'Neill, *Man of the House* (New York: Random House, 1987), chap. 1. "You can be the most important congressman in the country, but you had better not forget the people back home. I wish I had a dime for every politician I've known who had to learn that lesson the hard way. I've seen so many good people come to Washington, where they get so worked up over important national issues that they lose the connection to their own constituents. Before they know it, some new guy comes along and sends them packing" (p. 26).

2 Campaigning for Congress

The University of North Carolina at Chapel Hill has an elaborate student government and a tradition of lively campus politics. The years I was there, 1959–1961, were particularly active because of the civil rights movement. The sit-ins that began at a Greensboro lunch counter in February 1960 rapidly spread across the state, and many students became involved in efforts to desegregate restaurants, theaters, and other public accommodations. The movement awakened my political consciousness and channeled my campus involvement. I was president of the Baptist Student Union at a time when campus religious groups were among the most active proponents of change, and my main achievement as a member of the student legislature was the narrow passage of a resolution urging Chapel Hill merchants to desegregate their businesses.

I knew a number of campus politicians who were reasonably certain that they would someday be governor, senator, or at the very least a member of Congress. I did not regard such expectations as realistic for myself and had other career interests I wanted to pursue. But those years were politically formative in a number of respects. I began to realize that, by conviction, I was a Democrat, despite an East Tennessee background that predisposed me in the opposite direction. I came to admire political leaders like Adlai Stevenson, John F. Kennedy, and North Carolina's young governor, Terry Sanford. Most of the new ideas and responses to social problems seemed to be coming from Democrats; the Eisenhower era Republican Party, by contrast, seemed cautious and complacent. Like others in my student generation, I discovered that communities and political institutions could respond positively to pressures for change. It was a mere three years after our efforts to integrate the theaters in Chapel Hill that I was witnessing the passage of the Civil Rights Act of 1964 from the Senate gallery. A spark was lit that later led me, in addition to whatever else I was doing, to involve myself in local politics and community affairs.

During my years of graduate study and teaching in New Haven, my political activities ranged from canvassing for the Johnson-Humphrey ticket in 1964, to returning to Tennessee in 1970 to organize campus groups and get-out-the-vote operations in Sen. Albert Gore Sr.'s last reelection campaign, to helping my wife Lisa win a seat on the New Haven Board of Aldermen.[1] On returning to North Carolina in 1973, she and I became active with the Democratic Party. Today, when someone gives me the line about how closed and conspiratorial politics is, I sometimes respond with a description of our first party precinct meeting, shortly after arriving in Chapel Hill. Lisa emerged from that meeting as precinct chairwoman and I as a member of the precinct committee—an outcome that said more about the state of local party organization than about anything we said or did.

I had already ventured into North Carolina politics from a distance the year before, working with a friend from the Gore campaign to lay the groundwork for Senator Edmund Muskie's presidential primary effort in the state. I still regard the collapse of the 1972 Muskie campaign as especially unfortunate and fateful, considering the directions in which George McGovern's nomination took the Democratic Party and Richard Nixon's subsequent election took the country. In 1976, after I had permanently returned to North Carolina, friends from the Muskie campaign recruited me to manage two congressional districts (including the one I now represent) in Jimmy Carter's bid for the presidency. In 1980, I was asked to take a year's leave from my teaching position at Duke University to serve as executive director of the North Carolina Democratic Party. This tour of duty put me in the thick of statewide politics and introduced me to state senator Russell Walker of Asheboro, who was serving as state party chairman and who became my mentor and role model in politics.

During these years, I also became a friend and political ally of North Carolina's governor, Jim Hunt, a young progressive whose main causes were education and economic development. Hunt also took an active hand in party affairs. In 1981, he was named by the Democratic national chairman to head the party's Commission on Presidential Nomination, charged with undertaking a complete review of the nomination process and devising needed changes in party rules.[2] Hunt recruited me as his staff director. The assignment struck me as both politically important and academically interesting, offering an opportunity (realized only in part) to alter the "reformed" Democratic presidential nomination process in ways that might strengthen the organized party and its ties to its elected officials. What I did not foresee was how this stint in Washington and the acquaintances I struck with party leaders would prove useful if I decided to run for office myself.

In 1984, Hunt asked me to take another leave from teaching to return to the state Democratic Party, this time as full-time chairman. I accepted readily, for this was the event we had all been waiting for—the marathon Senate race between Hunt and incumbent Sen. Jesse Helms, the television commentator–turned–politician who was the Senate's most visible champion of right-wing causes. Many had thought, quite justifiably, of the 1970 race between Gore and William Brock as a momentous one with national implications, but it paled in comparison to the Hunt–Helms contest. The 1984 race produced expenditures of $26.4 million (Senator Helms's $16.9

million campaign was the most expensive Senate campaign in U.S. history until he broke his own record in 1990) and focused national and international attention on North Carolina. Our state party spent an unprecedented $2 million and organized a massive voter-contact and mobilization effort.

The results were bitterly disappointing. Helms, aided by Ronald Reagan's national landslide, won with 52 percent of the vote. This "sent a signal throughout the world," the senator told his supporters on election night, "that North Carolina is a God-fearing, conservative state."[3] Behind these code words, I saw a devastating setback for the hopes and aspirations that had first brought me into politics and for the progress we had begun to make in North Carolina.

Our Senate loss was compounded by the loss of the governorship and three Democratic House seats. One of these was in the Fourth District, where six-term Democratic incumbent Ike Andrews was defeated by Bill Cobey, a former athletic director at the University of North Carolina who had close ties to Helms's organization, the National Congressional Club. I was deeply stung by these defeats and in the following weeks thought a great deal about how they might be reversed. For the first time, I seriously entertained the prospect of becoming a candidate myself. By spring, I had made my decision: I was running for Congress.

The First Campaign

It was my work as state party chairman that first led others to think seriously of me—and led me to think of myself—as a potential candidate. The job's traditional organizational aspects put me in touch with hundreds of party activists, and the position attained a new level of public visibility as I held dozens of press conferences and took the lead in challenging and refuting the opposition. It was no longer only a behind-the-scenes job, and the experience and exposure it offered were ideal preparation for a congressional candidacy.

Still, I had not expected the Fourth District seat to turn over, and it took a while for me to get comfortable with the idea of actually running instead of supporting another candidate, or making politics a full-time vocation rather than a sporadic engagement. My wife, Lisa, became more and more enthused at the idea. Her political interests had always been strong. She grew up in a family of New Deal Democrats in the Washington suburbs, and her college experience with civil rights was similar to my own. When I first met her during one of my Washington summers, she was a social worker in a War on Poverty job training agency. Later, she was elected to the Board of Aldermen in New Haven and shared my political interests in North Carolina.

To run for Congress in what was certain to be an expensive, difficult race gave us both pause, and I had seen enough political families to know that I would never run without my wife's full support. We had searching conversations with friends and family and two congressional couples whom we respected. Our teenage children were growing increasingly independent, and I had earned a sabbatical year at Duke; this would let me draw half my salary and (barely) get by financially. But the ultimate question was whether we wanted to do this, knowing how much work and sacrifice it would require but also sensing how exciting and rewarding it could be. Without too much agonizing, we decided that the answer was yes. It was a commitment my wife took very seriously, and she has been intensely active, both behind the scenes and in public, in each of my subsequent campaigns.

Our discussions also involved a group of friends who, once the decision to run was made, became the "Wednesday night group," an inner circle that remained central to the entire effort. We met weekly to discuss campaign strategy, parcel out key contacts and tasks, and bolster one another's morale. This group was a fertile source of campaign ideas, good and bad. (One scheme for bringing attention to my race, mercifully abandoned, would have had me staging a Lawton Chiles–style walk from Liberty in the western part of the district to Justice, a community in the east!) Our group included several young attorneys with whom I had been associated in politics, a government affairs official from Duke, and a college friend at Mars Hill and his wife, who was an active local realtor. The campaign manager was Randolph Cloud, a veteran of several local campaigns who had worked with me as get-out-the-vote coordinator for the state party in 1984. We later added a deputy manager, Michelle Smith, who, despite limited political experience, proved to be an exceptionally quick study. This was fortunate, for the leadership of the campaign was thrust on her when Cloud left after the primary.

My decision to run was prompted in part by the realization that 1986 represented a window of opportunity that might not open again. The odds nationally of defeating an incumbent were low; the general election success rate for incumbents seeking reelection had fallen below 92 percent only once since 1966. But North Carolina had been something of an exception to this pattern. Close contests and incumbent defeats had become fairly common since the 1960s, particularly in western districts (where both parties historically had strong bases) and in Piedmont and urban–suburban districts (where split-ticket voting was on the increase, with GOP candidates often benefiting from national trends). My district, the Fourth, had displayed considerable volatility—voting for Governor Hunt over Senator Helms by 14,282 votes in 1984, for example, but at the same time giving President Reagan a 46,552-vote margin in his victory over Walter Mondale. Congressman Andrews had lost to Bill Cobey by fewer than 3,000 votes.

The district's volatility and Cobey's narrow win suggested that he could be beaten in 1986. I felt that he had won because of factors peculiar to 1984—the presidential landslide and Andrews's personal vulnerabilities—and that Cobey's beliefs and background put him considerably to the right of modal opinion in our part of the state. The Fourth District was by no means "Helms country," despite the fact that the senator lived in Raleigh. Yet Cobey stood out, even in comparison to the other North Carolina Republican members, in his ties to the Helms organization and in his decision to firmly align himself with the most conservative group of House Republicans, the Conservative Opportunity Society, once he got to Washington. He seemed an uneasy fit for the district and was likely to be especially vulnerable in 1986, his first try for reelection—before he had a chance to fully reap the advantages of incumbency and in a year when there would be no Republican presidential coattails.

In firming up my decision to run, I talked with a number of elected officials and other political leaders in the district, including several who, I thought, might consider running. Some had advantages that I lacked, such as living in Wake County (the district's largest), enjoying greater name recognition, having stronger financial ties, and so forth. I was surprised, and a bit unsettled, by the strong aversion most of them expressed to such a venture. But they gave me some encouragement, and I decided I should move ahead with a firm announcement of my intent to run, which I did at the time of the county Democratic conventions in April, over a year before the May 1986 primary. Although this probably helped limit the proliferation of candidates, the primary field eventually expanded to four. Wilma Woodard, a well-known state senator from Wake County, was generally considered to be the front-runner.

Most members of our Wednesday night group had worked together in the Hunt campaign and had taken from that experience the idea of blending the "old" politics and the "new." We believed strongly in the politics of personal contact; I began to steadily call on people who could be helpful and to attend every party gathering or community function I could find. Since traditional voter-contact and fundraising functions now required high-tech backup, we moved early to establish a computer capability and to contract for direct mail services. We also assumed from the beginning (long before we had the money to pay for it) that we would have an extensive media campaign. Hard-hitting television ads had come early to North Carolina, thanks largely to Senator Helms and the National Congressional Club, and had reached saturation levels in 1984. Television had been a major factor in Cobey's unseating of Andrews, and we assumed more of the same would be necessary if we were to shake loose the new incumbent.

We decided to seek outside professional assistance in three areas: media, polling, and out-of-district fundraising. My status as a challenger having no money and facing three primary opponents meant that the better-known Washington consultants took little interest in me. But I had my own prejudices against these operators in any case, stemming from my experience with the Hunt campaign. I had heard far too much pontification from media and polling experts based, it seemed to me, on thin survey data and a deficient "feel" for the state. I felt at the time that if I ever ran, I would want consultants who were young and lean and hungry and wanted to win as badly as I did. So, we looked to smaller, independent operators who seemed personally compatible and likely to give my campaign their personal attention. Fortunately, we found a team that was willing to work with us during the lean times with confidence that better-funded campaigns might follow.

As media consultant we chose Saul Shorr of Philadelphia, whose use of humor and instinct for the clever counterpunch especially appealed to me. I am still working with Saul, who has gone on to become a preeminent consultant to prominent Democrats. For polling we engaged Mark Mellman and Ed Lazarus, who had gotten their start in 1982 as Yale graduate students helping elect Bruce Morrison to Congress; by 1985 they were well on their way to being established nationally. For fundraising we chose Linda Davis, a North Carolinian who was successfully freelancing in Washington as head of her own small consulting firm. This proved to be a compatible team and a durable one as well, holding together through 1986 and several subsequent elections.

I maintained my full teaching schedule through the end of 1985 while campaigning extensively. I scheduled dozens of meetings with political and community leaders, as attested to by a couple of notebooks filled with descriptions of these personal conversations. I considered it a major breakthrough when people such as the preeminent Democratic fundraiser in my district and a respected Black city council member in Raleigh agreed to help me. I also attended countless community functions and visited the small-town business districts and suburban malls, ideally with a local supporter to introduce me. But a rude awakening came in February 1986, when we could finally afford to take our first poll. Despite a year of personal campaigning and considerable prior exposure as state party chairman, my name recognition among Democrats had reached only 11 percent. I was headed for a second-place primary finish.

What changed all that was television. Face-to-face campaigning was not sufficient to reach the people I needed to reach—a matter not merely of numbers but of how many were newcomers or did not have deep community roots or political ties. Most people received most of their political information through television. Fortunately, four out of my five counties were in a single media market, but the market was the second most expensive in the state, and my campaign was struggling financially.

By April 1986, we had raised $155,000, a sum that, though respectable for a challenger running in a contested primary, was inadequate to run an extensive television campaign. I did, however, have some fundraising advantages. I had more contacts and more credibility in Washington circles than would have been true for most challengers, and I cultivated potential donors carefully, calling on them personally and sending them a steady flow of information about the campaign—particularly coverage suggesting I might win. Yet these efforts would not fully pay off until I had proved myself in the primary. I received early endorsements and contributions from a number of labor organizations, which had reasons to oppose both the incumbent and my major primary opponent. An endorsement by Raleigh's major Black political organization was critical organizationally but less so financially. Other groups, like doctors and teachers, contributed to my main primary opponent because of help she had given them in the state legislature. Mainly, the organized groups and political action committees (PACs) stayed out of the primary. Their rule of thumb is generally to support incumbents if they have been reasonably receptive to the group's concerns. After all, the percentages suggest that the incumbents will survive, and their organization will need to deal with them in the future. But even issue-oriented, Democratic-leaning PACs that had good reason to like me and oppose the incumbent were unwilling to help me until I had survived the primary and could show that I had a good chance to win in November.

I have undertaken few ventures as difficult and discouraging as raising money for the primary campaign. Our trademark became "low–dollar" fundraisers, to which a host or group of sponsors would invite their circle of friends and associates. These events were profitable politically as well as financially, but with net receipts per event of $500 to $2,500, the dollars added up slowly. (I seldom had the heart to tell sponsors of such events that their labors would underwrite the purchase of *one* primetime, thirty-second television spot.) We sent mail appeals to party activists and to lists of donors from the 1984 Senate campaign and then periodically resolicited those who had already given. I spent a lot of time approaching potential large contributors personally or by phone, with mixed success. My wife and I shed our inhibitions and contacted our Christmas card lists from years past, our professional colleagues at home and across the country, and far-flung family members. Finally, we did what we had said we would never do—we took out a $45,000 second mortgage on our home.

With all of this, the campaign was able to buy $75,000 worth of television time during the three weeks before the May primary, going $80,000 in debt. We also spent $20,000 on radio spots, an underestimated medium that boosts name familiarity (especially when one can play on a name like Price). Our sixty-second "name familiarity" radio ad mentioned my name no less than fifteen times:

[Background: Marching band music throughout]
WOMAN: What's the cheering about?
MAN: Oh ... Price for Congress.
WOMAN: There's a price for Congress?
MAN: (Laughing) No ... not *a* price for Congress—*David Price* for Congress.
WOMAN: Oh ... *David* Price.
MAN: Yeah, David Price. He's putting some real decency back into North Carolina politics.
WOMAN: No mudslinging or name-calling?

MAN: Uh-uh, not David Price. Just straight talk about the issues ... like improving education, reducing the federal deficit.
WOMAN: Hey, this Price is going up in my book.
MAN: Come on! Listen to David Price's background. He's been an educator most of his life, like his parents; he was a Morehead Scholar at Carolina, earned a divinity degree, and later his Ph.D. in political science.
WOMAN: Sounds priceless.
MAN: David Price teaches government at Duke University. He's a nationally known expert on how Congress works. Price was chairman of North Carolina's Democratic Party, and Jim Hunt chose him to direct a national committee to reform the presidential nominating process. He's really experienced!
WOMAN: Hmm? That's quite a Price.
MAN: An honest Price.
WOMAN: David Price ...
MAN: for Congress.

Needing to make a forceful impression in a fluid primary situation on limited resources, we decided to produce three low-budget television ads. One featured quotes from my recent endorsement by the Raleigh *News and Observer*, the district's most prominent newspaper. The two ads that we ran most heavily showed me talking about one major theme: the need to straighten out North Carolina politics, stop mudslinging, and deal with the real issues again. We knew from polling and campaign experience that this was a powerful theme, drawing on people's negative memories of the 1984 Senate race and their reactions to the nasty 1986 Senate Republican primary then underway. But it wasn't until our primary results came in that we realized just how right we had been. I received 48 percent of the vote, and Senator Woodard, who polled 32 percent, elected not to call for a runoff.

Fundraising for the general election was a continuing struggle but paid richer dividends. We spent $550,000 in the fall campaign, including $300,000 for television airtime. This permitted a more diversified ad campaign: "soft" biographical spots in September and more forceful, issue-oriented spots in October. Some of the issue ads dealt with the incumbent's record: I had to take him on directly to give voters sufficient grounds for distinguishing between the two of us, but in a way consistent with my own injunctions about getting North Carolina politics on a more positive, issue-based footing. The ads therefore focused on three areas—Social Security, African famine relief, and farm credit—that illustrated the incumbent's isolation from mainstream members of both parties in terms of his roll call voting and featured me looking into the camera and saying that I would have voted differently.

We were able to afford more polling after the primary. The most important message the polls conveyed concerned the incumbent's vulnerability: although he enjoyed considerable personal popularity, there was a sizable gap between the number of voters who recognized his name and those who gave him a high job performance rating or were firmly committed to vote for him. The early "horse race" numbers were inconclusive, primarily measuring the gap in name familiarity, but they documented a narrowing of that gap over the months of the campaign; the incumbent's lead dropped from 21 percentage points in July to 10 points on October 4 and 1 point on October 26. But the only poll that actually showed me ahead was the election itself, when I received 56 percent of the vote—the highest percentage by which any challenger in the nation defeated an incumbent in 1986.

Television was the major factor in this result, but other campaign efforts played a part as well: organizing and personal campaigning in small towns and rural areas, voter-contact and turnout operations undertaken in conjunction with party and other organizations, and canvassing and literature drops that utilized hundreds of volunteers and helped raise the campaign's visibility. Cobey was damaged when the press headlined a "Dear Christian Friend" letter he had sent to individuals on a mailing list compiled by the religious right, encouraging the faithful to support him lest he be replaced by "someone who is not willing to take a strong stand for the principles outlined in the Word of God." Although our polling did not detect any measurable impact from this letter, my surmise is that it helped by generally raising the visibility of the race and framing a key issue for some groups (e.g., white-collar suburbanites) that I needed to reach. Finally, we were helped by the year's electoral trends—the absence of presidential coattails and a return to the fold by enough Democrats to produce senatorial victories across the South, including former governor Terry Sanford's win in North Carolina.

I will never forget the exhilaration of election night 1986, and neither will my family and the friends who had lived and breathed the campaign for almost two years (see Figure 2.1). My father, who had been featured in one of Saul Shorr's best spots, came from Tennessee to help work the polls and was shocked to be greeted on election night as a television celebrity. We had talked a great deal during the campaign about "recapturing our politics" and "turning North Carolina around," and on that night, it seemed to have happened, dispelling the dark clouds of 1984. We also felt we had succeeded in our announced strategy of combining the old and new politics, integrating traditional organizing techniques and lots of personal campaigning into an effort that was well financed, professionally managed, and media smart. We felt confident about the future, but if we thought it would be ours without a fight, we had the election night comments of the state Republican chairman to ponder: the Fourth District, he opined, had just elected another one-term congressman!

Getting Reelected

The Fourth District was bound to be a partisan target in 1988. Republicans by mid-1987 settled on my challenger: Tom Fetzer, a thirty-three-year-old

Figure 2.1 Election night, 1986. To my right is my nephew, Bob Shepherd, and concealed behind me are my sister, Mary Anne Combs, and her other son, Steven Shepherd. To my left are my wife, Lisa; my brother-in-law, Sam Combs; my son, Michael; my daughter, Karen; my father, Albert Price; Nell Benson; campaign manager Michelle Smith; and finance chairman Cliff Benson.

protégé of Senators John East and Jesse Helms who had spent virtually his entire working life as a political operative, including several positions with the National Congressional Club. I had mixed feelings about this. My district was relatively unsympathetic to Senator Helms, and a Congressional Club affiliation could be used effectively against an opponent. At the same time, I knew what having an opponent from that quarter was likely to mean in terms of the money he could raise and the negative tone of the campaign. As it turned out, I was correct on both counts.

In the early months of 1987, we retired the $80,000 debt from the previous year and began planning the 1988 effort. Fundraising was easier for me as an incumbent but was still a struggle, both because of the amounts required (my 1988 campaign eventually cost over $900,000) and my district's history of modest giving and the weakness of my ties to potentially large donors. I recruited as campaign manager an outside professional, Mike Davis, whom I had come to know well when he was deputy manager of Hunt's 1984 campaign. By the time we officially kicked off the campaign after Labor Day 1988, we had held dozens of organizational meetings and fundraisers, both in the district and in Washington, and campaign head-quarters had been open for four months, eventually accommodating a paid staff of seven and numerous volunteers.

Blessed for the first time with an adequate campaign budget, we aired television spots touting my work on consumer protection, education, home ownership, and other issues starting in September. Fetzer started with generic anti-Congress material, but we knew the main message was yet to come. On September 30 it arrived:

ANNOUNCER: Liberal politicians. False promises.
[Audio clips from Price appearances in 1986, identified by script on screen]
QUESTIONER: Mr. Price, under what circumstances would you support a federal tax increase?
DAVID PRICE: [1.] I would not support a federal tax increase, and I've said repeatedly that I would not ....
[2.] I do oppose a tax increase ...
[3.] We're not going to reduce that deficit by tax increases ...
ANNOUNCER: False promises. In his first year David Price voted to increase taxes four different times.
[Visual: newspaper headline, "Democrats Seek Billions in New Taxes"]
DAVID PRICE: False Promises. Liberal Votes.

Our counterpunch was already taped, and we had it on the air in a day:

ANNOUNCER: In recent days, we've seen TV ads that distort the record of our congressman, David Price. We know the ads are paid for by the Tom Fetzer Campaign....
But who is Tom Fetzer?
[Script on screen, synchronized with audio]
Tom Fetzer has spent most of his adult life working for Jesse Helms's Congressional Club or its candidates.
In fact, Fetzer actually headed the Club's operations.
We've seen Congressional Club tactics before ...
The distortions ...
The negative campaigning ...
The mudslinging.
[Audible stamp of universal "NO" symbol (circle and slash) on these words]
Will we allow ourselves to be "Clubbed" again?

Subsequently, although my negative ratings went from 9 percent to 15 percent, Fetzer's negatives increased far more, from 12 percent to 31 percent. He had run mainly negative material, first against Congress and then against me, thereby failing to identify himself positively and leaving himself vulnerable to my definition. Our ads "framed" his ads, so that when viewers saw the latter, they got not only a negative message about me but also a negative impression of him, his right-wing associations, and his tactics.

Fetzer aired several variations of his message on taxes in early October, a message reinforced by the "no new taxes" pledge featured in George H.W. Bush's presidential campaign. Eventually, he relied on ten-second zingers:

> *ANNOUNCER:* [Script on screen synchronized with audio]
> How liberal is David Price?
> He voted to increase taxes an average of $700 per family.
> Too liberal—that's David Price.

Naturally, I found all this highly frustrating, and my first impulse was to run an ad that set the record straight. We therefore cut a spot that featured me looking into the camera and saying:

> I'm David Price. My opponent, Tom Fetzer, is distorting my record.
> But the facts are clear. I have never voted to raise your tax rates.
> Tom Fetzer is actually criticizing me for supporting a bipartisan deficit reduction agreement that closed tax loopholes and cut spending by more than 36 billion dollars.
> President Reagan asked me to vote for it.
> Tom Fetzer is assuming voters won't know the difference between increasing taxes and tightening loopholes.
> Let's stop the distortion and stick to the facts.

As it turned out, we never ran this ad. Despite my impulse and the urgings of supporters to answer my opponent's charges, I became convinced that it would play into his hands. We would then be debating his issue. He might excerpt a clip from my ad and do a response to the response, appearing to refute it. Viewers might then perceive a bewildering array of charges and countercharges that seemed somehow to implicate me. And in the meantime, my own positive message would have been lost.

Consequently, we settled on a second "framing" ad, one that rolled a long list of issues down the screen. It reminded viewers that Fetzer had run an almost totally negative campaign, distorting my record but not telling them where he stood on much of anything. This kept the focus on his campaign tactics while reinforcing the Congressional Club association, without moving the campaign to his chosen turf—taxes. Meanwhile, all through October, we continued to mix in my positive ads on education, housing, and so forth. The strategy worked very well; our late October polls showed my favorability ratings again picking up, and I finished with a 58 percent win.

It was reassuring to me and my campaign staff to be able to neutralize the well-financed attack ads that we had known were coming. Our confidence had been shaken by the failure of the Hunt campaign to mount an effective defense in 1984 and by Michael Dukakis's stunning helplessness against George Bush's prison furlough/pledge of allegiance campaign in 1988. But we prepared carefully and developed a strategy that, at least in 1988, proved quite effective: (1) Lay out a compelling positive message, focusing on issues or character traits that voters care about, and never let yourself get more than temporarily diverted from that message. (2) Make campaigning itself an issue, tapping into the negative feelings that most people have about distortions and personal attacks (regardless of the fact that those same people may also be influenced by such ads). (3) Frame the opposition's ads, so that when viewers see them they are drawing as many conclusions about your opponent as about you. (4) Do not let damaging attacks go unanswered, but beware of answering point for point in a way that puts you on your opponent's turf. (5) Do all this in a straightforward and truthful manner, so that you are not and do not appear to be descending to your opponent's level.

That formula, however, was severely tested in my next campaign. What changed was not the negative attacks—I have yet to draw an opponent who ran more than a few scattered positive ads—but the political context. As public cynicism about politics and politicians deepened, it became more difficult to move public opinion with positive messages or neutralize an opponent's negative characterizations. My 1990 campaign thus posed challenges that went beyond the lessons of 1988 and raised warnings of more serious problems to come.

My challenger was John Carrington, a wealthy, self-made businessman who had won self-financed Republican primaries for lieutenant governor in 1984 and secretary of state in 1988. He came close to winning in the 1988 general election, aided by a strong Republican showing at the top of the ticket. He was actively embraced by the Republican Party organization for the first time in 1990. They had no one else to run against me, and in Carrington they saw a candidate who would pay his own way and might win or at least rough me up considerably.

It is disconcerting to run against a self-financed opponent. The cues one would normally get from a candidate's Federal Election Commission (FEC) reports, indicating breadth of support and the likely scale of the campaign, are useless. Carrington's reports revealed very little public support, but his campaign potential was nonetheless immense, limited only by his willingness to spend. As it turned out, the $500,000 he had given to each of his previous campaigns was not a very reliable guide to what he was willing to do in 1990; he eventually contributed over $800,000 toward total campaign expenditures of $891,000.

My hopes for a less elaborate and expensive campaign were largely frustrated by Carrington's willingness to spend and a negative political climate—exacerbated by a protracted budget battle between President Bush and the Democratic Congress—that gave his attack ads more traction. We invested as much in polling as we had in the previous two campaigns combined—a fortunate decision that helped us spot trouble early and step up our campaign efforts accordingly. In the end, we spent a total of $698,000 and bought as much television time as we had in 1988.

Carrington switched from generic anticongressional ads to spots attacking me personally in late September. His most persistent theme was that I was in the pocket of the savings and loan (S&L) industry and was to blame for a debacle that was going to cost every American taxpayer thousands of dollars. My 1987 vote in the Banking Committee for one short–term recapitalization plan for the S&L insurance fund rather than another was portrayed as a capitulation to the industry that brought about the entire disaster. My overnight trip to address the southeastern S&L trade association on a consumer protection bill that I was pushing through the Banking Committee was presented as a reward for my vote—a "paid vacation on Captiva Island." One ad even featured an unflattering picture of me with dollar signs superimposed over my eyes.

Drawing on our 1988 experience, our first response ad attempted to frame Carrington's message, reminding viewers of the kind of tactics he had used in his past failed campaigns:

> *ANNOUNCER:* John Carrington has a track record.
> [Copy on screen tracks audio, with newspaper editorials in background]
> When John Carrington ran for secretary of state, and lost, an editorial said, "John Carrington's campaign has spent a fortune on mean-spirited commercials."
> When John Carrington ran for lieutenant governor, and lost, an editorial said, "John Carrington's campaign has consisted largely of negative commercials that unfairly distort the record of his opponent."
> Now against David Price, John Carrington is at it again with the same negative campaign tactics.
> [On screen: "The Carrington record speaks for itself."]
> You'd have thought that John Carrington would have learned by now.

But 1990 was not 1988. The political climate was far more hostile to incumbents, and negative attacks were harder to discredit. Carrington's unfavorability numbers, already relatively high, continued to rise in early October, but my vote-to-reelect and job performance numbers were eroding more rapidly. Clearly we needed to fight back with something more potent. In particular, we needed to deal with the S&L accusations, and my impulse to rush out and set the record straight was even stronger than in 1988. However, we still understood the pitfalls of a point-for-point response and instead decided on an ad that drew on a local newspaper editorial and showed that I had answers to the charges. More importantly, it let me tell of the initiatives I had taken to address the S&L problem:

> *ANNOUNCER:* [Copy of editorial on screen] John Carrington is distorting David Price's record on savings and loans. A recent editorial called Carrington's charges "ill-founded."

DAVID PRICE [Into camera]: Let's get to the facts. I wrote the law that prevents corrupt savings and loan executives from writing themselves big bonus checks, and I sponsored legislation to require the attorney general to go after the savings and loan crooks.
ANNOUNCER: A clean campaign. A congressman fighting for you. Reelect David Price.[4]

The more direct, forceful ad helped stop the slippage our October 17 poll had revealed. Within a week, the horse race numbers had leveled off at around 43 percent for me and 25 percent for Carrington. But my favorability and job performance ratings continued to slip. Though we knew this was as much the function of the negative media coverage Congress was then getting as of Carrington's ads, we also recognized the continuing need to frame his message. He gave us an unexpected assist as we were preparing copy for our late October ads, acknowledging to a reporter that his attack ads were "a garbage way of running a campaign."[5] We were on the air within three days, first with an ad documenting via newspaper copy what Carrington had said about his own campaign and then with an ad that featured me looking at one of his ads on a television monitor and turning to comment on it:

[Clip from Carrington ad on TV monitor]: "David Price voted to let them keep gambling with your money."
ANNOUNCER: Here's what John Carrington says about the TV ads he's running: "This is a garbage way of running a campaign, but it's the only way." [Quote superimposed on screen, with monitor still showing]
DAVID PRICE [pointing to monitor, then looking into camera]: Mr. Carrington calls his own ads garbage, but he's wrong to think this is the only way to run a campaign. For four years now we've shown that a positive, clean campaign can address real issues.
Please join me in saying no to John Carrington's distortions.

Our successive efforts to neutralize Carrington's attacks represented a modification of our 1988 approach necessitated by the huge quantity of his ads, the sharply personal nature of his attacks, and the stormy political climate that threatened damage to all incumbents. We also modified our positive ads, still stressing my work on middle-class issues like education and housing but dropping the pictures of me at work in Washington. We rather hearkened back to my first campaign when, as a challenger, I set out to "turn North Carolina politics around," even patching a clip from an early 1986 spot into my first 1990 ad.

Our October 27 poll confirmed that the turnaround we had detected on October 22 was genuine; my vote-to-reelect numbers were on the way back up, and Carrington's unfavorable numbers had actually overtaken his favorables. I finished with a 58 percent win, closely replicating our 1988 result. Our team felt hugely relieved and vindicated on election night, although the occasion was marred when Harvey Gantt's spirited challenge failed to unseat Senator Helms.

For the moment, we had defied a national trend that saw the average victory margin of incumbents decline by almost 5 points. For fifty-three members, their 1990 reelection margin was their lowest ever, and for another fifty-seven it was their lowest since their first election.[6] Nationally, six Democratic members and nine Republican members were defeated by challengers; those numbers would have been higher had the parties anticipated the strength of anti-incumbent sentiment in time to recruit stronger teams of challengers and finance them well. But the trend was unmistakable, fueled by increasingly negative public perceptions of Congress and frustrations at the governmental gridlock and partisan wrangling exemplified by the protracted 1990 budget battle. Because control of government was divided between the parties and the blame for failure diffused, these sentiments were limited in their electoral impact. It would not be until 1994, when they found a clear partisan target, that their devastating potential, both for me and for the Democratic Party in the House, would become fully evident.

Defeat and Comeback

The 1992 election proved to be the lull before the storm in the Fourth District and across most of North Carolina. Nationally, the anti-institutional sentiment and anti-incumbent voting evident in 1990 intensified. This was effectively promoted by Newt Gingrich, whose election as House Republican whip in 1989 had heralded a newly confrontational style of minority leadership. Gingrich had relentlessly pressed the case against Speaker Jim Wright, forcing his resignation amid ethics charges. Although the so-called House Bank scandal, which identified a few members abusing the banking services of the House payroll office while many more got burned by its lax accounting practices, involved members of both parties, Gingrich and the self-styled Gang of Seven conservative Republicans used it in the period leading up to the 1992 election to indict "corrupt" Democratic leadership.

To these anti-institutional stirrings were added the effects of the post-1990 congressional redistricting and the discontent stirred up by a weak economy. The result was the departure of the largest number of House incumbents since 1948. Fifty-two members, many of them anticipating electoral trouble, retired; nineteen were defeated in primaries, and sixteen Democratic and eight Republican incumbents were defeated in the general election.[7] The partisan impact was blunted. Divided government still presented multiple targets for voter ire, and Bill Clinton's strength in the presidential race helped hold the net Democratic loss of House seats to ten. This hardly provided a mandate to Democrats as they assumed control of both the presidency and Congress for the first time in twelve years, but it fell short of the Democratic losses many had anticipated.

Very little of this turbulence was immediately apparent in the Fourth District. The main impact of redistricting in North Carolina was the election of two African American members, the first since the turn of the century (see Chapter 3). Several traditionally Democratic districts were weakened by the removal of loyal partisan voters to the new minority districts, but the effects would not be evident until 1994. The Fourth District was made marginally more Democratic when it was pared from five counties to three, although the loss of traditionally Republican Randolph County to the west was soon to be offset by Republican gains in the fast-growing Raleigh suburbs. Republicans, however, mounted only a token effort, and I secured 65 percent of the vote.

Election night was again marred by a Senate loss, as Terry Sanford fell before the sharp attacks of Lauch Faircloth. (Ominously, Faircloth carried Wake County, which made up 83 percent of my district.) But North Carolina's House delegation reached a high-water mark of eight Democrats and four Republicans. This set the stage for what I experienced as one of my most enjoyable and productive (if also most contentious) terms in office. But it was not to last; in fact, the 8 to 4 ratio was precisely reversed as North Carolina's House delegation, largely insulated from the turbulence of 1992, felt the full force of the gathering storm in 1994.

One of the earliest and surest signs that the 1994 campaign season was going to be different was the growing anger and disruption at my community meetings. The mix of issues ranged from gays in the military to abortion to taxes and spending. But the anti-Clinton, anti-Democratic, and antigovernment rhetoric reached an intensity that I had never experienced and was not certain how to handle. Some of this was organized by local religious right and anti–tax groups, and many were clearly utilizing information picked up from talk radio, which was attracting a larger and larger audience. My staff (and my wife) began to question whether we should continue to hold open meetings. But I disliked the idea of letting our adversaries shut us down. I was concerned that these raucous sessions were leaving me looking beleaguered, but I was also drawing considerable praise from many of those attending the meetings and from the press for continuing to hold open discussions and not responding in kind. We began asking local law enforcement to cover the meetings, modified the format (not very successfully) to gain more control over the agenda, and forged ahead with a full schedule. We thus had a constant reminder of the hostility toward Clinton and the Democratic Congress that was rising across the country and ample evidence that incumbents like me were unlikely to escape the anti-institutional ire.

It soon became clear that the Republicans were going to contest the Fourth District seat more strongly than they had in 1992. Growing Republican organizational strength was evident in 1993, as my opponent from 1988, Tom Fetzer, was elected mayor of Raleigh in a well-funded campaign. A group of Republican leaders announced that they had recruited a young businessman, Rob Romaine, to run against me, but their plans were upended when Raleigh's retiring police chief, Fred Heineman, decided to seek the GOP nomination. Heineman was a native of New York City who had put in twenty-three years on the NYPD before Raleigh recruited him as its chief in 1979. He ran into some turbulence in his later years as chief, particularly in relations with the Black community, and plotted a retirement strategy that included switching his party registration to Republican in 1993 and entering the race for Congress. Mainly by virtue of his name recognition, Heinemann defeated Romaine by 243 votes in a low-turnout primary that gave little indication of the Republican mobilization to come.

My benchmark poll, taken in late June, contained clear warning signs. President Clinton, who won 47 percent of the district's presidential vote in 1992 (compared to George Bush's 39 percent and Ross Perot's 14), had slipped in popularity; he now polled below Senator Helms, for whom the Fourth had always been a problem. The percentage of voters rating me favorably had drifted to 47, while my "unfavorables" had jumped to 27 percent and my job rating was relatively weak. These numbers clearly reflected the more general negative assessments voters were giving Congress and incumbent officeholders, but that offered little reassurance. In fact, it pointed out the obstacles my campaign and I were likely to face in trying to turn them around single-handedly.

The "horse race" numbers were 46 percent for Price, 32 percent for Heineman, and 22 percent undecided, reflecting slippage in the number of voters committed to my reelection as well as the fact that Heineman was better known than any of my previous opponents. When respondents were given personal profiles and sample campaign pitches from the two of us, the gap narrowed further. And when they were asked what issues concerned them most, government waste and crime trumped education, home ownership, and transportation, the issues with which I was most strongly identified.

In the meantime, the 103rd Congress had grown more and more contentious. Republicans unanimously opposed and relentlessly criticized Clinton's 1993 deficit reduction plan, portraying it as a massive tax increase. Throughout 1994, leaders of the GOP and the religious right activated their electoral base with issues such as abortion and gay rights. Meanwhile, Democrats struggled to move Clinton's complicated, comprehensive national health care plan, ultimately failing to do so. With the administration's crime bill we succeeded, but in the messiest possible way, whipsawed among the death penalty, the assault weapons ban, and other inflammatory issues. Overall, Republicans found "that it was virtually impossible to overreach in attacking Washington or the federal government."[8]

It was at first unclear how much Heineman would be able to capitalize on the national turmoil. His fundraising got off to a slow start, and national and state GOP leaders regarded the Fourth District as a second-tier race, surpassed by four other North Carolina seats as a pickup prospect. But toward the end of the campaign, as it became clear that a national victory might be in the offing, the national party put some $60,000 into Heineman's campaign. Overall, he raised $265,000, a modest amount for a challenger but enough to be on television for most of October and, under the circumstances of 1994, to solidify his name recognition as a crime fighter and catch the wave of anti-Washington, anti-Democratic sentiment.

Our fundraising, which eventually produced $676,000, was well underway by the time I kicked off my campaign officially with the usual cross-district tour on September 7. After the Democratic leadership gave up on getting anything more from the 103rd Congress and adjourned on October 8, I had almost five weeks to campaign full-time in the district.

We planned four weeks of television ads, but faced unsettling challenges in formulating a message. The profile and the positions I had featured in past campaigns were devalued in the context of 1994, as were the district-related benefits I had managed to secure on the Appropriations Committee. Our challenge was to relate to the values and concerns on voters' minds while maintaining continuity with my past appeals and denying Heineman the ability to define the agenda. My biographical ad, for example, featured photos of my parents and captions pointing out that I was "the son of two small-town schoolteachers" and had earned a divinity degree. "My parents taught me to do my best and to do my part," I said in a script that I wrote personally, to show the moral context in which I placed public service:

> Lisa and I have stressed hard work and personal responsibility with our own children. Our country still depends on strong faith and strong families. And while government can open up opportunities, we won't solve our problems until people take responsibility for their own actions and each one of us pitches in and does our part.

The greatest challenge was the crime issue, which was clearly on voters' minds. I had supported the 1994 crime bill but had not made it a personal priority. On specific provisions where Heineman and I differed (e.g., community policing and the assault weapons ban), he had shifted away from his earlier support and the public seemed to agree with me. We therefore produced an ad that put me on camera pointing out these differences and noting that Heineman's "own police force has failed to endorse his candidacy." The ad's captions referenced the endorsements I had received from the local and national Fraternal Order of Police. Heineman responded with an ad featuring a retired police officer attesting to his character and protesting that police departments did not endorse candidates. Although I had not said that they did, I regretted giving him the opening. And we had ample reason to reflect on whether we should have raised the crime issue in the first place; it was clearly Heineman's turf. His identification as police chief and the negative publicity surrounding the Clinton crime bill put him in a strong position to ridicule the bill and my support for it (another of his ads featured much-maligned "midnight basketball" recreation programs for at-risk youth) and to slough off criticisms of his specific positions.

Heineman, like my previous opponents, failed to run biographical or other positive ads. But the omission hurt him less because he was reasonably well known and the political climate was not conducive to positive messages. His ads attacked me on issues ranging from the death penalty to health care to the line-item veto. The ads frequently linked me to Clinton and always contained a tag line tying me to the unpopular institution of Congress. For example, one zinger managed, in ten seconds, to distort both my position on Clinton's health care plan and the plan's effects:

> Congressman Price supported Clinton's health care plan to increase spending and taxes.
> [On screen: revolving pictures of Clinton and Price, then captions: $700 BILLION SPENDING; 27% TAX INCREASES]
> To change Congress, you've got to change your congressman. Vote Heineman for change.
> [On screen: picture of Heineman with captions: FOR CHANGE. HEINEMAN FOR CONGRESS]

We became sufficiently concerned about Heineman's last-minute ads and mailings to add a refutation of his charges on Social Security and the balanced budget amendment to our mix of ads in the campaign's last week.

Heineman signed onto Newt Gingrich's much-touted platform, the Contract with America, but said little about it. He was nonetheless in a position to benefit from Republicans' successful "nationalizing" of the election as a protest against Democratic liberalism and all things governmental. The advent of unified Democratic control of Congress and the White House had provided a clear partisan target for the voter anger that had been building since 1990.[9] I began hearing alarming reports from Democratic colleagues across the country and from my media consultant, Saul Shorr, and others working with imperiled candidates. A tidal wave was coming. The only question was how large and encompassing it would be and what, if anything, campaigns like mine could do about it.[10] Heineman's television message was less pervasive, with fewer dollars behind it, than Carrington's had been in 1990, but we had similar worries about a political climate that made it difficult to get my message through and neutralize my opponent's attacks. We took hope when our late October polls seemed to show my vote solidifying and Heineman's attacks not moving my "favorables" down very much. But election day told another story. The tidal wave swept across North Carolina with special severity, and in the Fourth District I fell short by 1,215 votes.

Turnout was exceptionally low, even for a nonpresidential year. Heineman and I together received 17,000 fewer votes than I alone had received in 1992. The main effect of the antigovernment fever and the negative tone of the campaign was not the mobilization of hitherto inactive voters but rather voter apathy and withdrawal. Heavily Democratic areas were particularly affected. The 1990 redistricting, which contributed to North Carolina's other three Democratic House turnovers, had an indirect effect on my race: Raleigh's African American representative in the state House had been placed in a safe, single-member district. Republicans had the good sense to refrain from filing an opponent against either him or Wake County's popular Black sheriff, thus making it more difficult to mobilize voters in those precincts. The absence in North Carolina of a Senate or other major competitive statewide race was also important; nationwide comparisons suggested that this not only depressed turnout but also helped make NC House Democrats the victims of voter ire that otherwise might have been directed at more prominent targets.[11]

I greeted voters until the polls closed and approached election-night headquarters with an ominous feeling. Turnout was especially low in central Raleigh and Chapel Hill precincts, and poll workers reported seeing busloads of voters brought in from conservative churches. It became apparent as the first returns came in that I was in trouble, running well behind in suburban precincts where I had once lost narrowly or broken even. Orange and Chatham County numbers trickled in later, but they were not enough to make up the difference.

I had already begun to formulate what I would say if I lost. As the results became clear, my family and I went to the hotel ballroom, which offered a funereal contrast to the joyous election nights of years past. "We have fought the good fight," I said to assembled friends and campaign workers. "We can be proud of what we have stood for, and nothing that has happened tonight should lead us to cynicism or despair." I tried hard that night and in the ensuing weeks to follow my own advice.

The nationwide results were stunning, with thirty-four House Democratic incumbents defeated and an additional net shift of eighteen open seats to the Republicans. North Carolina was hit especially hard, with party control of one-third of our twelve U.S. House seats turning over and Republicans gaining control of the state House of Representatives. Lisa and I became accustomed to being called or stopped on the street by people expressing their shock and chagrin, some admitting they had not voted and a few even telling me that they had voted Republican as a protest but would not have done so had they known I was in trouble! I also received hundreds of supportive letters. Despite the feeling they sometimes prompted that I was reading my own obituary, I will forever treasure them. They helped me determine to stay in the fight.

My staff and I had to pull ourselves together quickly. We returned to Washington for a brief lame-duck session and to pack up eight years' worth of papers and records. Within two months, I was back in the classroom at Duke University. I felt warmly welcomed and valued the chance to get back in touch with my former career and friends I had seen too infrequently. I was determined to find time for reflection, but I knew that I would need to make and announce a decision about my political plans within a few months. I engaged in considerable soul-searching, analyzed the loss, and sought advice about how it happened and whether I should try to reverse it.

I closely followed national and local political developments and discussions. They left little doubt that 1996 would be a hard-fought election, determining whether 1994 was an aberration or whether it marked a longer-lasting partisan and ideological realignment. Whatever hopes Democrats had for a comeback would depend critically on districts like the Fourth.

During the spring and summer of 1995, I moved steadily toward a decision to run. I found that the determination and defiance I had felt during the congressional struggles of 1993–1994 did not fade. If anything, they intensified. I was at the peak of my capacity to serve, and it seemed unthinkable to let 1994 be the last word personally or politically. Lisa strongly agreed with these sentiments.

Because my defeat had been so unexpected and so close, I faced no opposition within the Democratic Party and benefited from the widespread expectation that I could reverse the outcome. I was not so sure, as I witnessed the extraordinary energy and discipline with which the new House majority enacted most elements of the Contract with America. Nonetheless I firmed up my decision to run, and as both the House leadership and Heineman began to stumble, that began to look more and more like a winning proposition.

The first Republican blunder to gain widespread attention in my district was the attempt to gut environmental regulation by attaching seventeen legislative "riders" to the Fiscal 1996 Veterans Administration, Housing and Urban Development, and Independent Agencies (VA-HUD) appropriations bill. The bill proposed to cut Environmental Protection Agency (EPA) funding by 33 percent and limit the agency's authority to regulate matters such as emissions from industrial facilities and oil refineries, raw sewage overflows, arsenic and radon in drinking water, and cancer-causing substances in processed foods. The GOP leadership was embarrassed on July 28, 1995, when fifty-one Republicans joined with most Democrats in deleting the riders. Republican leaders managed to reverse the vote three days later, but the episode left an impression of environmental extremism and created "a wedge issue Democrats would use through the 1996 campaign."[12]

Heineman had already received publicity in the district for his uncritical support of Gingrich's Contract (ranking first in the North Carolina delegation) and for his overnight reversal on the question of cop-killer bullets on the Judiciary Committee, supposedly at the behest of the National Rifle Association via the Republican leadership. He took a harder hit on the environmental issue, since the VA-HUD bill he supported not only contained the EPA cuts and antiregulatory riders but also omitted funding for a new EPA research center in the Research Triangle Park, which I had helped get off the ground and which he had claimed credit for supporting (see Chapter 5).[13]

None of this compared, however, with the criticism and ridicule that followed a comment he made to a Raleigh *News and Observer* reporter in an interview for an October 21 feature story. Following up on a remark Heineman had dropped in an earlier discussion with the newspaper's editorial board, the reporter asked where his congressional salary and police pensions (totaling some $184,000 per year) placed him on the income scale. Heineman responded:

> That does not make me rich. That does not make me upper-middle class. In fact, that does not make me middle class. In my opinion, that makes me lower-middle class....
>
> When I see a first-class individual who makes $80,000 a year, he's lower middle class. When I see someone who is making anywhere from $300,000 to $750,00 a year, that's middle class. When I see anyone above that, that's upper middle class.[14]

My first reaction to the comments was bewilderment. But the next day, at neighborhood gatherings I had scheduled to talk politics and explore my candidacy, I found people talking of little else. Biting editorials and editorial cartoons soon appeared; a local radio station ran a "Hiney-thon," inviting listeners to fax dollar bills to their impoverished congressman. Democrats from minority leader Dick Gephardt on down had a field day on the House floor, purporting to find in Heineman's remarks "a unique window onto the Republican worldview."

In the meantime, I had announced my firm intention to run. Plotting my course with Mac McCorkle, a close friend and an original member of the 1986 Wednesday night group who was now in business as a policy and message consultant, I began in midsummer to schedule neighborhood gatherings, asking friends to invite neighbors of all political persuasions to meet for open-ended discussions. I gained a great deal of insight from these meetings as to how Washington appeared from the Fourth District and how the new House leadership was misreading its mandate. I declared my candidacy in early October in a letter to 8,000 supporters and contributors. This letter brought in an astounding $80,000 in contributions, three times more than I had ever raised with a single mailing. I also began spending numerous hours each week in a small campaign office calling larger donors. Here too the response was encouraging; by the time I filed in January, I had raised $215,000 and was well on my way to what became a $1.17 million campaign.

I engaged a new polling firm and enlisted Joe Goode, a senior analyst with Greenberg Research who was in North Carolina because of his wife's graduate study, as campaign manager. In some ways it felt like the first campaign. I was on the trail every day after my teaching duties ended in May; this time it was Heineman who was alternately stuck in Washington or catching grief at town meetings, trying to persuade voters that his party really wasn't cutting Medicare. I was well aware of the incumbency advantages that he now enjoyed, but I found it liberating and invigorating to be the challenger again. I was less defensive, more adversarial, free to go on the offense in developing and delivering a message. I also had far more time and energy for retail politics. We held dozens of low–dollar, friends-and-neighbors functions that were as much outreach events as they were fundraisers, and my door-to-door neighborhood walks became a hallmark of the campaign.

I was relieved to find, when I took my benchmark poll in January, that I led Heineman in the horse race numbers, 47 to 38 percent. The result owed more to negative views of Heineman than to positive views of me, but on other measures, my numbers were considerably better than his (I had a 45–32 positive-negative rating, for example, compared to Heineman's 38–40 and Gingrich's 32–57). Still, we knew we had a great deal of work to do.

In early September, when Heineman was already running television ads and I was set to begin my own, two events occurred that altered both the pace and the content of the campaign. Heineman suffered a perforated intestine and underwent emergency surgery. And Hurricane Fran hit central North Carolina, creating widespread devastation and displacing politics with more immediate concerns. We canceled most campaign events for two weeks, pitching in with community relief and cleanup efforts. Heineman briefly cut back on his ads, which at that point were attacking me on the Medicare issue. I delayed the beginning of my television campaign by a week and then ran only an introductory biographical spot that stressed my educational background and advocacy.

We knew, however, that I could not safely let Heineman's attacks go unanswered, and we were well aware of his greatest point of vulnerability. Therefore, during the last week in September, with Heineman out of the hospital and his ad campaign back in full swing, we unveiled "Earth to Fred":

> *MISSION CONTROL:* Earth to Fred. Come in, Congressman.
> [Video shows flight through space, passing by planets and stars]
> *ANNOUNCER:* It's amazing. Fred Heineman actually said "middle-class" people make between $300,000 and $700,000 a year.
> [Text with *Business Week* citation superimposed on space shots]
> *MISSION CONTROL:* Fred, are you there?
> *ANNOUNCER:* And Heineman claims his $180,000 a year income makes him, quote, lower middle class.
> [Text with *USA Today* citation superimposed]
> *MISSION CONTROL:* Earth to, ah, Fred, over.
> *ANNOUNCER:* Fred Heineman: He's out of touch with average families here. Way out. [Video of space flight continues]
> *MISSION CONTROL:* Earth to Fred. Come in!

This ad effectively countered everything Heineman threw at me. His Medicare ad featured a film clip from my cable show that cut me off in midsentence and left the impression that I was eager to cut Medicare. But his main efforts to bring down my numbers reached back to the anti-institutional and antitax themes of 1994. His ads not only attacked me for raising taxes, raising my own pay, and "bouncing checks in the bank scandal" but also accused me of breaking promises or lying about each. "Now you remember why we voted him out," one of them added. And then the tag line that almost all of Heineman's ads contained: "David Price. Too liberal then. Too liberal now."

As in previous races, we polled carefully and wrestled with the dilemma of whether and how directly to respond. We cut an ad directly addressing the House bank allegations but elected not to run it when a late poll showed Heineman's ad doing less damage than we feared.[15] We ran ads criticizing Heineman's votes on Medicare and the anti-environmental riders, with frequent references to "Newt Gingrich's Congress" and "Newt Gingrich's plan." But nothing worked as well as "Earth to Fred." It is the only ad I ever ran that drew viewer complaints when we took it *off* the air. We returned to the ad and to a variant that linked his views on the income scale to his willingness to cut student loans ("It's not just what Heineman says. It's how he votes.") throughout October.

I ended up spending more than $455,000 on television airtime over a seven-week period, and Heineman spent a like amount from his overall budget of $980,000. There was a strange contrast between his pervasive presence on television and his virtual absence from the campaign trail. North Carolinians were familiar with this pattern from Jesse Helms's Senate campaigns, but in Heineman's case it was difficult to know how much was deliberate strategy and how much the result of his illness. Despite a dozen or more invitations, we never had a debate or joint appearance. He began in October to attend fundraisers and Republican meetings but declined all opportunities to engage face-to-face. "We just don't have enough time to prep the chief [the title Heineman preferred]. He doesn't have time to study," said his campaign spokesman in an ill-advised explanation of his boss's cancellation of a TV debate. This selectivity in scheduling led to widespread editorial criticism and, in several cases where the sponsor chose not to cancel the forum, gave me the opportunity to present my policy views and make a point about responsiveness and open campaigning.

My election-day margin of 54–44 percent (with 2 percent going to the Libertarian candidate) varied little from the polls we had taken in January and throughout the year. As in 1994, there was a great deal of oppositional voting; just as Heineman had persuaded voters to "fire Congress" and me in the process, a number of voters had now elected to fire him. Among those who voted for me, 51 percent described their vote as mainly pro-Price, 30 percent as mainly anti-Heineman, and 19 percent as both or not sure. Anti-Heineman voters reported a strong receptivity to portrayals of the incumbent as both "out of touch" and "too close to Newt Gingrich and his extremist agenda." Among Heineman voters, 54 percent described their vote as mainly pro-Heineman, 29 percent as mainly anti-Price, and 17 percent as both or not sure, and our poll suggested that Heineman's portrayals of me as dishonest and "too liberal" had taken their toll. It had been a rough campaign in which getting any traction with a positive message was difficult; it left both of us bruised and me with the challenge of solidifying my positive credentials in the eyes of my constituents as I returned to office.

Beyond the Fourth District, election night revealed mixed results. Bob Etheridge, formerly North Carolina's Superintendent of Public Instruction, recaptured the neighboring Second District for Democrats, but the other two House seats that had turned over in 1994 remained in Republican hands, leaving our delegation divided 6–6. Harvey Gantt's second attempt at unseating Senator Helms failed, and President Clinton lost North Carolina while winning nationally, although both Gantt and Clinton narrowly carried the Fourth District. Nationally, the 1996 election continued a pattern of what James Ceaser and Andrew Busch called "losing to win": Republicans winning Congress in 1994 by virtue of their loss of the presidency in 1992 and Democrats winning the presidency in 1996 largely in reaction to their congressional loss of 1994 and what it produced.[16] Although the Republicans lost ground in the House, they did not lose control. I was one of sixteen Democrats defeating a Republican incumbent; in too many cases, Gingrich's stumbles and the show of Republican vulnerability had come too late for Democrats to recruit strong challengers. Overall, the net Democratic gain was only nine seats, with most of the 1994 Republican freshmen hanging on and the GOP picking up a number of conservative districts, especially in the south, where senior Democrats had retired. This left the House narrowly divided at 228–206 (plus one independent) and guaranteed another intense battle for control two years hence.

The 1996 campaign was our strongest grassroots effort since 1986, and our election night celebration was the largest and most raucous since that first win. The outcome was never in doubt. Turnout, boosted by the presidential race, was relatively high all over the district and the early returns from Wake County precincts showed me running far ahead of 1994. I ended up with a 51.2 percent win in Wake, which I had lost with 45.1 percent in 1994, and I scored 56.7 percent in Chatham County and 68.4 percent in my home county of Orange. In acknowledging victory, I held up a well-worn shoe as a symbol of our grassroots campaign and gave my heartfelt thanks to family, staff, and volunteers for a wonderful team effort that had accomplished exactly what we set out to do.

In Clinton's Shadow

In anticipating the next election cycle, three things were immediately clear. I was still a Republican target, and there was a candidate waiting to take me on: Tom Roberg, a software executive who had been chairman of the Wake County Republican Party during its 1994 heyday and had considerable potential to finance his own campaign. It was also clear that I would be defending a substantially redrawn Fourth District. The North Carolina General Assembly was required to re-draw the Black-majority Twelfth District, which the Supreme Court had found unconstitutional, in advance of the 1998 election (see Chapter 3). The fact that Durham County, surrounded on three sides by the Fourth District, was at the heart of the legal challenge—in addition to the political calculations of key state legislators—made it quite likely that Durham would be added to the Fourth. I began moving around the county on that assumption.

The assumption proved correct as all of Durham County was added to the Fourth and some 44 percent of Wake County was taken away, including the state Capitol complex and the Democratic-leaning precincts where many of my loyal voters and volunteers lived. Durham was a compatible addition that largely compensated for the loss, though not without hard work. I knew Durham County well from living next door, teaching at Duke University, and working in the Democratic Party. Durham residents had seen my television ads and my cable call-in show for years, and I already had a modest contributor base there. The city included a large and relatively well-organized African American community that ended up welcoming me warmly. Yet it was a challenge to touch the bases and establish a level of comfort and confidence, particularly in the context of the politics of impeachment, which came to dominate much of 1998.

We planned a campaign comparable to 1996 in both financing and structure. I again brought in a campaign manager from outside, Chris Chwastyk, who had successfully managed Chet Edwards's (D-Texas) 1996 campaign, and we set and eventually raised a campaign budget of $1.2 million. We were also aware of the parallels with 1994: another nonpresidential election year with the potential for depressed turnout, with the outcome determined by the most angry or intense voters. But we also understood the pitfalls of "fighting the last war" when circumstances in fact had changed.

Between 1994 and 1996, we had found voters shifting less in their *level* of discontent or their tendency to opposition voting than in the *object* of their discontent, with Newt Gingrich and the Republican Congress becoming a major target. But by 1998, when we asked our constituents the standard question as to which way they thought the country was heading, 53 percent said the right direction, with only 29 percent disagreeing—compared to 28 percent right direction and 53 percent wrong just two years before! We also found that education was back in its accustomed position as the Fourth District's top-rated issue, although the linkage between me and that issue in the voters' minds was relatively weak. These findings helped shape our media strategy: we would frame a positive message, highlighting my educational background and specific recent achievements such as the Education Affordability Act (see Chapter 5).

Roberg went on the air in early August with a standard-issue message. "At home David Price talks like a moderate," the main television ad began, "but in Washington, Price votes with the liberals." In the meantime, President

Bill Clinton acknowledged his relationship with Monica Lewinsky before a Washington grand jury. On September 9, Independent Counsel Kenneth Starr delivered his report recommending impeachment to the House. Within a few days, Roberg had a centerpiece for his campaign:

> *ANNOUNCER:* Where do you stand, Congressman Price?
> [Video: picture of Price with text superimposed]
> Bill Clinton has admitted lying to us.
> [Clinton picture appears alongside Price]
> Leading newspapers, including the *Durham Herald-Sun*, *USA Today*, and the *Winston-Salem Journal*, have called for Bill Clinton's resignation.
> [Banners from these papers swoop up, covering Price picture]
> And Tom Roberg has called for Bill Clinton's resignation.
> [Color photo of Roberg covers Clinton]
> This is not the time to be silent, Mr. Price. Where do you stand?
> [Price photo, text superimposed]
> Tom Roberg for Congress, for conservative leadership.
> [Text on screen]

We viewed Roberg's attack with trepidation, for I was picking up a great sense of anger and disillusionment with the president, not only from expected sources but also from Democrats, even at my own fundraisers. My September poll confirmed that Clinton's positive-negative numbers had taken a tumble and mine with them. At the same time, most voters agreed with the approach I was taking: expressing my moral outrage at Clinton's behavior while recognizing the need to reserve official judgment until all the facts were in and chastising Roberg for using the situation for his own political gain. I decided to begin my television campaign as originally planned, with an engaging "School Play" ad featuring children and conveying information about education legislation I had pushed. Despite the Clinton mess, voters were still basically in an optimistic mood and receptive to a positive message, and the need we had earlier identified to link me more strongly to education remained. "School Play" did this quite nicely while giving viewers a respite from the television clutter surrounding other campaigns and the Lewinsky scandal.

A major test loomed, however, as the House prepared to vote on October 8 on whether and in what fashion to carry the impeachment inquiry forward. Republicans proposed an open-ended inquiry in both content and duration, while Democrats wished to limit the inquiry to the material referred by Starr and end it by December 31. This vote (unlike the impeachment votes to follow) was hardly a matter of high principle. But it seemed to offer a stark choice: if, after the Democratic alternative predictably failed, I then voted against the Republican plan, it would be portrayed by my opponents as opposition to any inquiry whatsoever. The poll we took as the vote approached merely underscored my dilemma: almost half of the electorate could be influenced in their vote by how I voted on the impeachment inquiry. This group was equally divided; half would be more likely to vote for me and half less likely, no matter how I voted!

As the hour of the vote approached, I became more and more convinced that after voting for the limited inquiry, I should then vote against the open-ended version. The more I thought about it, the less I wanted to be fighting on two fronts simultaneously. Roberg and other opponents of the president would attack me in any case. Did I really want to have to defend myself among loyal Democrats and supporters of the president as well? I gave particular attention to Durham in this connection and consulted with leaders there—not just because a large number of Durham voters opposed impeachment, but because these were new constituents who were taking their measure of me and whose wholehearted support I very much needed.

Almost immediately I came to see the vote as both right on the merits and more helpful than harmful politically. I felt comfortable and confident in explaining it and was put on the defensive far less than I expected. As anticipated, Roberg reacted quickly with a radio ad: "Congressman Price stood up for Bill Clinton and voted against an impeachment inquiry." But he got little traction from the issue, as my next poll (and no doubt his as well) showed. Opinions as to whether Clinton should resign had actually shifted in the president's favor, and when respondents were asked whether Price or Roberg could be better trusted "to do the right thing when it comes to Bill Clinton," my earlier 32–28 advantage increased to 39–30, with a particularly dramatic shift among White independent voters. We thus continued to run positive ads, adding to our education message a testimonial from a breast cancer victim required to leave the hospital immediately after her mastectomy (which the Patient's Bill of Rights would change) and a "protect Social Security" message featuring senior citizens. Our only ad "answering" Roberg did not deal with the president at all but placed Roberg's positions on school construction and HOPE scholarship tax credits in juxtaposition with mine.

Roberg's campaign budget of $453,000, to which he personally contributed $180,000, was not as large as we had expected. But with the help of the National Republican Congressional Committee (NRCC), he was able to buy $354,000 worth of over-the-air and cable television time and another $52,000 on radio. This compared favorably with my $427,000 media budget, almost all of it spent on over-the-air television. Still, his message did not work. He never bothered to introduce himself and what he was for; he spread his ads over thirteen weeks, often in buys too scattered to penetrate; and his attempt to tie me to Clinton's troubles was not well-received by most voters. After that fizzled, he had very little message left.

My victory margin was 57–42 percent. Durham performed impressively at 67.8 percent as did my home county of Orange at 70.2 percent, but I was just as proud of almost breaking even in the Fourth District portion of Wake County (48.2 percent), given the hand I had been dealt in redistricting. Election night brought a strange mixture of exhilaration and relief, for this had been a campaign of ups and downs, and we had often felt at the mercy of events beyond our control. The dreaded repeat of 1994, which for a time the president's troubles seemed likely to produce, did not materialize. Turnout rebounded from the abnormally low levels of four years before, from 38 percent of registered voters in 1994 to 45 percent in 1998, although it was still far below presidential-year levels. This helped boost my numbers, but my share of the vote improved overall. The precincts gained through redistricting were slightly more favorable than those I had lost, but my greatest relative gain came in communities like Cary, common to the old and new districts, where my percentage went from 41.7 in 1994 to 49.4 in 1998.

Nationwide, the 1998 elections produced little change in the margins of party control in Congress but a much greater upheaval politically, because Democratic performance far exceeded predictions and expectations. North Carolina delivered an important Senate turnover for Democrats as John Edwards narrowly defeated Lauch Faircloth, but the 55-45 Republican advantage in the Senate remained unchanged. In the House, only six incumbents were defeated, but five of these were Republicans; eleven open seats turned over, of which Democrats won six.[17]

While this left Democrats on the short end of a 223–211 alignment in the House, we came within six seats of gaining control. Not since 1934 had the party holding the White House gained seats in a midterm election, and not since 1822 had this happened during a president's second term. Clearly Republican reliance on Clinton's problems—particularly the decision by Gingrich and the NRCC chairman to put almost $10 million into a media blitz highlighting the scandal during the campaign's last week—had been a major miscalculation. Three days after the election, Gingrich, facing a serious challenge within House Republican ranks, announced his resignation as Speaker.

As it turned out, the 1998 campaign was my last as a nationally targeted race. The 2000 presidential campaign was still very much "in Clinton's shadow," as Vice President Al Gore struggled both to capitalize on the achievements and popularity of the Clinton-Gore administration and to separate himself from Clinton's personal scandals. In the Fourth District, voters were generally upbeat about the economy and the country's direction, but expressed an early preference, 46–42 percent, for the Republican nominee, Governor George W. Bush, over Gore in the presidential race. My opponent, Jess Ward—a Cary councilman and the only African American general election opponent I have faced—failed to pick up support beyond the hard-core Republican base.

We raised $686,000 over the two-year cycle and again invested heavily in efforts to turn out African American and core Democratic voters. Our mail program and my personal schedule—still featuring door-to-door walks in suburban neighborhoods—also targeted swing voters and recent arrivals.

Our decision not to buy television time freed me to offer more financial help to congressional candidates in swing districts in North Carolina and elsewhere, as we struggled to regain the House majority. I won with 62 percent of the vote and Gore ended up carrying the district by three points while losing North Carolina overall. Nationally, the election was a virtual tie. The Senate was left divided exactly in half, a balance that tipped toward Democrats a few months later when Senator James Jeffords (R-Vermont) became an independent. Democrats netted two additional House seats but not the seven needed to regain the majority. And the presidential race went into overtime: Gore won the popular plurality by almost 540,000 votes, but the electoral vote was in doubt as recounts were started and stopped in Florida over a five-week period. Ultimately the U.S. Supreme Court intervened with a 5–4 ruling, cutting short a recount ordered by the Florida Supreme Court and handing Bush the presidency.

Securing the District

I had a new district to secure after the 2000 census, but its political contours were little changed. Any desire I had for a more Democratic district, and any inclination the Democrats who controlled the General Assembly might have had to draw such a district, were tempered by the realization that if the three Triangle area districts (Fourth, Second, and a new Thirteenth district) were each to have the prospect of electing a Democrat, none of us could be greedy. My 2002 margin of victory, 61 percent, tracked 2000, while the neighboring districts remained in the Democratic column as well. Bob Etheridge gained reelection in the Second, and Brad Miller, who had headed the redistricting effort in the North Carolina Senate, won in the new Thirteenth. This initiated an era when the three of us represented the Triangle in a cooperative and complementary fashion—until Etheridge was defeated in the turbulent election of 2010 and the congressional map was redrawn thereafter.

Nationally, the 2002 outcome again reflected the even partisan division of the electorate but was decisively influenced by the terrorist attacks of September 11, 2001. Senate control tipped back to Republicans, and the GOP added five seats to their House majority. This again broke from the historical pattern of midterm losses for the president's party. The Bush administration escaped the consequences of the slowing economy, and the financial scandals affecting Enron and other companies as the political focus shifted to national defense and foreign policy issues, where Republican credibility was stronger. As Gary Jacobson concluded:

> Had the terrorist attacks not occurred, Bush's overall approval rating would have remained much closer to his rating on the economy, and if standard midterm referendum models are to be believed, this alone might have cost Republicans control of the House.[18]

My 2002 campaign was the first managed by Anna Tilghman of Raleigh, and it also featured a new pollster, Fred Yang—both of whom I have worked with ever since. We had every reason to poll carefully: the national consensus that had formed around the post–9/11 antiterrorism offensive and the war in Afghanistan was beginning to fracture over the president's determination to invade Iraq.

The situation was reminiscent of 1998, when the pivotal House vote loomed on authorizing the impeachment inquiry; in 2002, the pivotal vote was an open-ended authorization for the president to employ military force in Iraq. As in 1998, there was an alternative resolution that I and many other Democrats supported: a proposal written by Rep. John Spratt (D–South Carolina) authorizing the president to use armed force to protect weapons inspectors and undertake U.N. enforcement actions but requiring him to come back to Congress if he wished to invade Iraq unilaterally. This vote was much more a matter of principal than the 1998 vote had been: after seeing the Spratt proposal fail, I would certainly oppose the main motion. As in 1998, however, our polling revealed political peril no matter which way I voted. Respondents divided closely (43 percent in favor, 46 percent opposed) on the question of a U.S. invasion to remove Saddam Hussein from power; the balance shifted to 77–17 if the United Nations supported the action. But when asked to choose between a hypothetical Democrat who opposed invasion "at this time" and a Republican who wanted to give President Bush the authority he requested, the opponent of invasion prevailed by six percentage points (47–41).

When the time came to vote on October 10, I chose to publicize my work with John Spratt on his alternative and my arguments for voting no on the main motion. Yang found a high awareness of my vote among my constituents, who favored by 55–40 percent the resolution I had opposed. But when given the gist of the Spratt resolution and told that I had supported it, 59 percent (including 31 percent of those who favored the president's request) expressed their approval. Meanwhile my positive "feeling thermometer" score went from 61 to 74 percent among Democrats, while my negative score went from 21 to 29 among undecided voters and 23 to 30 among independents. We concluded that, while the war vote had probably shaved my margin among these latter groups, it had also helped energize my Democratic base.

My vote has fallen below 60 percent only once since 1998, in the 2010 midterm election, two years into the Obama presidency. This election produced a net gain of sixty-three House seats for Republicans, bringing them back into the majority. It was this election that saw the emergence of libertarian "Tea Party" Republicanism, but I had had a foretaste of what was to come in my previous race against B.J. Lawson, a young medical software entrepreneur who set out to "redefine the Republican Party," in 2008.

Lawson's then-unfamiliar mix of positions—opposing the Iraq war, supporting civil liberties (except in the case of abortion), opposing "tax-payer bailouts of Wall Street," regarding most domestic federal programs as unconstitutional—attracted media attention and some support among unaffiliated voters and disaffected Democrats. I took the challenge seriously, raised $1.15 million, and prepared the first television ad I had cut in years, in case our polls suggested we needed to run it. But I had some wind at my back as the Obama presidential campaign targeted North Carolina, generating great excitement and mobilizing many new voters. My victory margin was 63 percent on a night that also saw Obama carry the state and NC Senator Kay Hagan defeat incumbent U.S. Senator Elizabeth Dole.

My 2010 rematch with Lawson was in a radically changed environment. I got an early inkling of what was to come when I encountered extreme anger and hostility at my town meetings early in 2009. Obama's agenda, even the anti–recessionary Recovery Act, met with unremitting hostility from Republicans. All of this conjured up memories of 1994, and I determined to leave nothing to chance. We raised almost $1 million (compared to Lawson's $473,000) and put three weeks of television ads and of Black-oriented radio ads on the air, in addition to extensive mailings to unaffiliated voters and turnout sweeps through African American precincts. Our "case" ad put Lawson in the dock for "extreme" positions: "eliminating all federal funding for medical research, even for cancer," favoring abolition of the Department of Education, and "making abortion illegal, even in cases of rape and incest." One of our mailers reprised "Earth to Fred": "Earth to Lawson ... come in B.J. ... Lawson's ideas are not just strange—they're way out there."

The campaign took a bizarre turn in its final days when Lawson aired a radio ad narrated by a voice which, while not identified, sounded like the actor Morgan Freeman. Lawson deepened the mystery when he claimed that the voice was indeed Freeman's and that his willingness to record the ad amounted to an endorsement. As fate would have it, one of my former staffers reached out to say he was the point person on all of Freeman's political work and confirmed that Freeman had not cut the ad. With his help, my campaign tracked down Freeman's agent, and within hours Freeman had issued an indignant and unequivocal public denial, which began: "These people are lying ... "

Lawson then claimed to have been misled by MEI Political, an advertising company that specialized in celebrity endorsements and ads using "voice doubles." This prompted a stern public response from the firm:

> We made it clear to the Lawson campaign that ... even though the ad was similar to Morgan Freeman in style and tone, the campaign should not represent it as the actor Morgan Freeman or as an endorsement by Mr. Freeman ... We regard the Lawson campaign's statement that MEI Political in any way misled the campaign as false and defamatory. We ask that the Lawson campaign issue an immediate apology and retraction.

Thus was whatever message Lawson had planned to close his campaign totally obliterated.

Given the scale of the midterm backlash, I wrote in my journal that my personal goal "was to break 55%." So I was pleased with the 57 percent result, including a 43 percent tally in the area that most worried us, the Republican-leaning precincts of western Wake County. I was shaken by Etheridge's narrow loss in the neighboring Second District; a gifted retail politician, he was nonetheless swamped by powerful national currents. The election also produced large Republican majorities in both houses of the North Carolina General Assembly, just in time to draw the congressional and assembly districts following the decennial census.

The North Carolina legislature proceeded in 2011 to draw the most radically gerrymandered congressional maps in the state's history (see Chapter 3). The Fourth District was splayed over seven counties and packed with the maximum number of African Americans (32 percent of the population and 50 percent of registered Democrats) and of Democrats (55 percent of registered voters), so as to make the surrounding districts safe for Republicans. I was personally pleased to get back many of the Democratic precincts in Wake County removed by the 1997 redistricting. But I was well aware that this was not done for my or my party's benefit. Quite the contrary: the North Carolina congressional delegation went from seven Democrats and six Republicans in the 112th Congress (2011–2012) to four Democrats and nine Republicans in the 113th and 3–10 in the 114th Congress.

Two interrelated trends—increased polarization of the parties' popular bases and more extreme partisan gerrymandering—have put more and more House members in skewed districts, where their main perceived electoral threat is not the opponent fielded by the other party but possible primary opponents within their own party—opponents frequently claiming to represent party ideology more purely. I experienced some of this in both 2006 and 2018—years of Democratic resurgence—and was able to fend off the primary challenges without great difficulty. But the threat posed by the 2011 redistricting was another matter entirely. The General Assembly, with what one imagines was fiendish delight, "triple-bunked" the three Democrats who had represented the Triangle during the past decade—Brad Miller of the Thirteenth district, Bob Etheridge, who had lost the Second district seat in 2010, and me. All of us found ourselves residing within the new Fourth District despite living in different counties.

In the months that followed the General Assembly's July 28, 2011, dropping of this bombshell, two things because increasingly clear: no legal challenges to the map were likely to succeed in time to affect the 2012 election, and Miller was strongly inclined to run in the new Fourth District. His reconfigured Thirteenth district was impossible for a Democrat to win. The new Fourth contained 31 percent of what had been the Thirteenth, and much of Fayetteville, the city where Miller had grown up, would now also be in the Fourth. But my claim was stronger: the new Fourth contained 33 percent of the old Fourth, and 73 percent of the district was from areas I had represented at some point, including sizable areas of Orange and Durham counties, which Miller had never represented. My best course, however, was not to rely on such arguments but to move energetically around the new territory and to raise funds in anticipation of—or as a deterrent to—a primary campaign. Even a long-planned beach vacation was not spared; my family recalls my frequent retreats upstairs to call key leaders in Fayetteville.

Miller and I had been friends and political allies for some thirty years, and our voting records in Congress were similar. Most ideological rankings gave me a slightly higher liberalism score—an important credential among primary voters—but it nonetheless became clear that Miller intended to run from my left, stressing our differences on trade and financial services regulation. In the meantime, I stepped up my visits to the district's three new counties and hired two campaign field staff with Fayetteville backgrounds. I intensified my fundraising—bringing in $122,00 for the third quarter of 2011 and $259,000 for the fourth, compared to a six-month total of $124,000 for Miller. Most importantly, we took—and leaked—a poll.

The mid-October survey was decisive: I prevailed over Miller in the trial test 46–25 percent. This was not merely a reflection of name familiarity—among respondents who said they knew us both, my margin increased to 50–28—and it extended to all parts of the district, including Fayetteville. Some 72 percent of voters favoring me described their support as "strong," compared to 42 percent of Miller's voters. "Many Triangle Democrats have supported both Price and Miller, and may do so again," concluded the Raleigh *News and Observer*'s senior political correspondent. "But Price has roots in the Democratic Party going back to the early 1980s and he seems to have first call on the loyalties of party activists."[19]

Miller and I talked less about our mutual dilemma than I would have liked, but in truth there was no win-win solution at hand. "Brad was left without good options," I noted in my journal, "and he certainly had no good ideas for me beyond retiring." On January 26, 2012, Miller announced that he would not be running, while noting "the important differences between us." Expressing disappointment that our mutual supporters seemed to "shrug off the differences," he acknowledged that there was little appetite in the Fourth District for an intraparty fight. I was of course hugely relieved and issued a statement sincerely praising Miller for his work on financial services and other issues and condemning General Assembly Republicans for drawing "unfair and illegal" maps that pitted member against member for partisan gain. It had been a difficult experience. There are few greater strains on a friendship in politics than being forced into an electoral showdown with a colleague, and I'm afraid that Miller and I failed to create an exception to that rule.

In the packed Fourth District I soared to general election margins of 74 percent in 2012 and 75 percent in 2014. In the meantime, the legal challenges to the map inched forward and the courts in 2015 ruled that the legislature had made an unconstitutional use of race in drawing the lines (see Chapter 3). The resulting new map, drawn in advance of the 2016 elections, cleaned up the racial numbers but remained a 10–3 political gerrymander, subject to a new round of challenges in court.

The Fourth District was made more compact, contracting from seven counties to three. It included my home county of Orange, but almost 80 percent of the voters were located in Raleigh and central Wake County—giving me even more of the territory I had formerly represented. I received 68 percent of the vote in 2016, an election that saw Donald Trump carry the state but our Democratic Attorney General, Roy Cooper, claim the governor's mansion. In the 2018 election, the highly energized anti-Trump midterm, with only a Supreme Court race at the top of the ticket in North Carolina, my margin was 72 percent.

My 2018 campaign budget was fairly typical of the campaigns we have run in the decade of extreme gerrymanders. I raised $920,000 for the cycle. About $138,000 of this went to primary expenses, including polling, radio, mailings, and social media. I ended up carrying every precinct but was taking no chances in a turbulent year. After the primary, I refocused on the team effort, giving $175,0000 to the Democratic Congressional Campaign Committee (DCCC) for targeted House races nationwide, $13,000 to Democratic House challengers in North Carolina and $21,000 to challengers and endangered incumbent nationwide, $50,000 for our state Democratic Party's unity campaign, $20,000 to the State House and Senate campaign committees, and $24,000 to county Democratic parties and affiliated groups running turnout efforts.

I do not begrudge such contributions to the team effort in the least. My nostalgia for the days when my own race was targeted is quite limited, particularly considering how much the cost of such races has escalated. I am more than happy to help those who have replaced me on the hit list. And as I frequently tell my constituents, even if I am the best qualified representative imaginable, my effectiveness is diminished if I am not part of a governing majority.

Send reinforcements! Fortunately, this message took hold in 2018 as it had in 2006, midway in George W. Bush's second term, again bringing Democrats to power to check a Republican administration that had lost favor. Our daughter Karen produced a feature-length documentary film about that earlier midterm, aptly titled "Housequake."[20] The Housequake of 2018 compared favorably to that of 2006—a net gain of forty Democratic seats compared to 31 in 2006. But in North Carolina, extreme gerrymandering produced some differences on both sides of the ledger. My 2006 margin of 65 percent, my high point for that decade, increased by seven percentage points. But the barricades held in the Republican districts. In 2006, Democrats turned over one North Carolina district and came within 328 votes of flipping another, but none of the spirited challenges of 2018 succeeded. Democrats won 49.7 percent of the votes for the U.S. House statewide, but still held only 23 percent of the seats.[21]

Nationally, the reaction and resistance to Donald Trump, much more intense than the forces behind the 2006 Housequake, were successfully translated into votes and seats. "The steady work of citizens who've been trying, over the last two years, to fight the civic nightmare of Trumpism bore fruit," observed Michelle Goldberg.[22] The 2018 election, political scientist Gary Jacobson concluded, was "the most partisan, nationalized and president-centered midterm ... on record." The congruence between voters' approval/disapproval of President Trump and their choice of the U.S. House reached 93 percent, an all-time high.[23]

The lead sentence of my 2018 stump speech was typical of Democrats across the country, articulating two basic goals: "I'm running for reelection to defend the values we share against an unfit and dangerous president and a compliant Republican Congress ... and to continue fighting for health care, education, and the progressive policies that matter to North Carolina families." That was the dual mandate that the 2018 election gave Democrats the opportunity and obligation to pursue. Ironically, we would almost surely not have won the House were it not for the election and subsequent malfeasance of Donald Trump. That was a frightful price to pay but one that Democrats were determined to redeem as we returned to Washington.

Notes

1 My experiences in Tennessee led to an effort to measure the electoral effect of voter-contact activities and a conviction that such activities should be an integral part of state and county party operations. See David E. Price, "Volunteers for Gore: The Evolution of a Campaign," *Soundings*, Spring 1971, pp. 57–72; and David E. Price and Michael Lupfer, "Volunteers for Gore: The Impact of a Precinct-Level Canvass in Three Tennessee Cities," *Journal of Politics*, 35 (May 1973), pp. 410–438.

2 *Report of the Commission on Presidential Nomination* (Washington, DC: Democratic National Committee, 1982), p. 1. For an account of the commission's efforts and rationale, see David E. Price, *Bringing Back the Parties* (Washington, DC: Congressional Quarterly Press, 1984), chaps. 6–7.

3 Quoted in William D. Snider, *Helms and Hunt: The North Carolina Senate Race, 1984* (Chapel Hill, NC: University of North Carolina Press, 1985), p. 203.

4 My first reference was to my amendment, initially added to the Financial Crimes Prosecution and Recovery Act of 1990 in the Banking Committee and eventually included in the Crime Control Act of 1990, to authorize regulators to disallow extravagant severance payments (golden parachutes) to the executives of failing financial institutions. The second reference was to the Savings Association Law Enforcement Improvement Act of 1990, an effort to step up prosecution of S&L fraud.

5 Van Denton, "Carrington Bombards Airwaves Hoping to Oust Price," Raleigh *News and Observer*, October 23, 1990, p. 1A.

6 *Congressional Quarterly Almanac*, 46 (Washington, DC: QC Press, 1990), p. 903.

7 The resulting 93 percent reelection rate for incumbents who were on the November ballot thus considerably "overstated the security enjoyed by

incumbents." See James Ceaser and Andrew Busch, *Upside Down and Inside Out: The 1992 Elections and American Politics* (Lanham, MD: Rowman & Littlefield, 1993), p. 144.

8 Dan Balz and Ronald Brownstein, *Storming the Gates: Protest Politics and the Republican Revival* (Boston, MA: Little, Brown, 1996), p. 253.

9 See the analysis in Gary C. Jacobson, "The 1994 House Elections in Perspective," in Philip A. Klinker, ed., *Midterm: The Elections of 1994 in Context* (Boulder, CO: Westview, 1996), chap. 1; and Jacobson, "Divided Government and the 1994 Elections," in Peter F. Galderisi, ed., *Divided Government: Change, Uncertainty, and the Constitutional Order* (Lanham, MD: Rowman & Littlefield, 1996), chap. 3.

10 "In this political season of voter discontent, the four-term congressman is running for re-election as if he has never run before, logging 12-hour days on the campaign trail.... 'Any candidate who is not polling, who is not working very hard, is divorced from reality,' Price said. 'This is a year when you have to watch it very carefully.'" James Rosen, "Dogged Price Does Homework, Pursues Goals," Raleigh *News and Observer*, October 29, 1994, p. 16A.

11 Robert E. Orme and David W. Rohde measured this at my suggestion and confirmed the predicted effects. "Presidential Surge and Differential Decline: The Effects of Changing Turnout on the Fortunes of Democratic House Incumbents in 1994" (prepared for delivery at the *Annual Meeting of the American Political Science Association*, Chicago, IL, 1995).

12 Linda Killian, *The Freshmen: What Happened to the Republican Revolution?* (Boulder, CO: Westview, 1998), p. 134; also see David Maraniss and Michael Weisskopf, *Tell Newt to Shut Up!* (New York: Simon & Schuster, 1996), pp. 91–93.

13 See, for example, the following editorials: "The Case of the 'Cop-Killer Bullets,'" *Washington Post*, June 17, 1995, p. A16; "Heineman's Peculiar Retreat," Raleigh *News and Observer*, June 21, 1995, p. A10; and "Environmental Setback," Raleigh *News and Observer*, August 8, 1995, p. A8.

14 James Rosen, "Heineman Says He's Not Middle Class," Raleigh *News and Observer*, October 21, 1995, p. A14. On the circumstances of the interview and subsequent reactions, see Rosen, "Heineman Comments Cause Flap," Raleigh *News and Observer*, October 26, 1995, p. 1A.

15 "Fred Heineman is not telling the truth," this ad stated. "As a newspaper 'ad watch' now confirms, David Price's checks did not bounce and David Price did not misuse any money at the House bank." For the ad watch cited, which dealt with various Heineman charges, see Joe Dew, "Heineman Hits Price over House Bank Scandal," Raleigh *News and Observer*, October 24, 1996, p. A3.

16 Ceaser and Busch, *Losing to Win: The 1996 Elections and American Politics* (Lanham, MD: Rowman & Littlefield), 1997, p. 145.

17 The 395 members returned to office in 1998 were the most for any midterm House election in history. The number of incumbents defeated (6) tied the record for least change in any midterm, and the total number of seats switching party control (17) set a new low. Incumbents in both parties enjoyed an average vote gain of 2.6 percentage points over 1996. "That voters did opt for the status quo in 1998 is beyond question." Gary Jacobson, "Impeachment Politics in the 1998 Congressional Elections," *Political Science Quarterly*, 114 (Spring 1999), p. 32. The results, Jacobson argued, were compatible with the election's underlying conditions—few exposed Democratic incumbents (thanks to earlier losses), a strong economy, and a Democratic president with high job-approval ratings: "about what we would expect if no one had ever heard of Monica Lewinsky," (p. 36).

18 Gary C. Jacobson, "Terror, Terrain, and Turnout: Explaining the 2002 Midterm Elections," *Political Science Quarterly*, 128 (Spring 2003), pp. 6–7.

19 Rob Christensen, "Poll Finds Price Favored over Miller," Raleigh *News and Observer*, October 30, 2011.

20 Roxanne Roberts and Amy Argetsinger, "Politicians and Their Auteur Daughters," The Reliable Source, *Washington Post*, October 20, 2009, p. 2C; Peter Baker, "Film Celebrates Emmanuel as Democrats' Dynamo," *New York Times*, October 22, 2009, p. A24. See also Naftali Bendavid, *The Thumpin': How Rahm Emanuel and the Democrats Learned to Be Ruthless and Ended the Republican Revolution* (New York: Doubleday, 2007).

21 In 2006, Democrat Heath Shuler defeated incumbent Republican Charles Taylor in the Eleventh district. Challenger Larry Kissell almost defeated incumbent Robin Hayes in the Eighth district, prompting a 2008 rematch with DCCC support which Kissell won. In 2018, our three best-funded challengers, all with DCCC support, fell short: Dan McCready by only 905 votes in the Ninth district, Kathy Manning with 45.5 percent in the Thirteenth, and Linda Coleman with 45.8 percent in the Second. The Ninth district result was not certified because of fraud on the Republican side, which resulted in a new election with a new Republican candidate, who won with 50.7 percent of the vote. Statewide, Democrats prevailed in electing Anita Earls to the NC Supreme Court and three judges to the state Court of Appeals, and in substantially reducing Republican majorities in the NC House and Senate.

22 Michelle Goldberg, "The Resistance Strikes Back," *New York Times*, November 11, 2018.

23 Gary Jacobson, "Extreme Referendum: Donald Trump and the 2018 Midterm Elections," *Political Science Quarterly*, 134 (Spring 2019), pp. 9–38. As E.J. Dionne commented, "Trump likes everything to be about him. The 2018 midterms really were," in *Code Red: How Progressives and Moderates Can Unite to Save Our Country* (New York: St. Martin's Press, 2020), p. 24.

3 Our Broken Electoral System

By the time Democrats regained control of the House of Representatives in 2019, our collective experience with extreme gerrymandering, the domination of campaign airwaves by unaccountable "independent" groups, widespread attempts to restrict and suppress the vote, abuses and incompetence in the management of elections, and evidence of foreign intrusion in the electoral process motivated us to designate comprehensive electoral reform as H.R. 1, giving it top billing in the new Congress. Introduced with 225 cosponsors on the first day of the session by Rep. John Sarbanes (D-Maryland) and vigorously promoted by Speaker Nancy Pelosi, the "For the People" Act passed on March 8, 2019, on a 234–193 party-line vote.

I participated actively in this effort, which I had anticipated in 2017, when, along with Senator Tom Udall (D-New Mexico), I introduced the "We the People" Act (H.R. 3848). The bill combined my own reform proposals—including the refurbishing of public financing for presidential campaigns, public financing through the matching of small contributions for congressional campaigns, forbidding coordination between supposedly independent political action committees (Super PACs) and candidates, modernizing disclosure requirements to include sponsors of paid social media ads and those aired by independent groups, and reforming the Federal Election Commission (FEC)—with several bills introduced by other members. This approach, which owed much to the expertise and strategic acumen of Democracy 21 President Fred Wertheimer, highlighted the interdependence of reform issues and the enormous backlog that had accumulated. In this chapter, I will reflect on the relevance of my own and my state's experience to key components of the reform agenda.

Drawing the Districts

Gerrymandering—the drawing of legislative districts, often in convoluted ways, for political advantage—is as old as the republic. The practice takes its name from Elbridge Gerry, who as Massachusetts governor signed a bill in 1812 that created a contorted district, designed to benefit his Democratic-Republican party, likened to a mythological salamander. For most of our country's history, in most states, the drawing of congressional districts has been the responsibility of state legislatures and has thus often displayed a partisan bias.

Gerrymandering has since the 1980s been under intensifying legal challenge from the Voting Rights Act (VRA) of 1965 and the equal protection clause (Amendment 14) of the Constitution—complementary standards that are sometimes in tension. North Carolina has been at the center of this litigation.

When I was first elected in 1986, the state's population was 22 percent African American, but the state's eleven-member House delegation was all White and had been since 1900. Congress had recently strengthened the Voting Rights Act, however, creating a "results" test whereby a districting plan that denied or abridged the voting rights of a minority could be challenged regardless of the legislature's express intent. A U.S. district court panel ruled in 1984 that the state's multimember General Assembly districts violated this standard, and their ruling was upheld by the U.S. Supreme Court in the landmark *Thornburg v. Gingles* decision. "As a result of the challenged practice or structure," the Court declared, "plaintiffs do not have an equal opportunity to participate in the political processes and to elect candidates of their choice."[1] The Court also laid down criteria to identify voter dilution under the amended VRA and to determine whether a minority group was sufficiently large and geographically concentrated to warrant the drawing of a district where that group could constitute a voting majority.

North Carolina legislators interpreted these criteria to require the drawing of at least one—and, under pressure from the Bush Justice Department, two—districts with Black majorities after the 1990 census. The new First district, which in 1992 elected Eva Clayton, included all or part of twenty-seven counties scattered across eastern North Carolina. The second and more controversial Twelfth district, which Mel Watt was elected to represent, extended 160 miles from Charlotte to Greensboro, Winston-Salem, and Durham, connecting Black urban areas across central North Carolina.

These changes altered the map, and ultimately the composition of our congressional delegation, in major ways, but at first the effect on the Fourth district was minimal. Population growth took the district from five counties to three, with no new territory (see Figure 3.1). But that was not to last, as challenges were mounted to the new map and to the Twelfth district in particular.

The case ultimately involved two 5–4 Supreme Court decisions, *Shaw v. Reno* and *Shaw v. Hunt*, which disallowed the Twelfth district as "racial gerrymandering" violative of the equal protection clause.[2] The court reasoned that although race could be considered in drawing district lines to facilitate minority participation and representation, its use carried a burden of proof as to whether there was a compelling state interest and the remedy was narrowly tailored to accommodate that interest. The Shaw dissenters

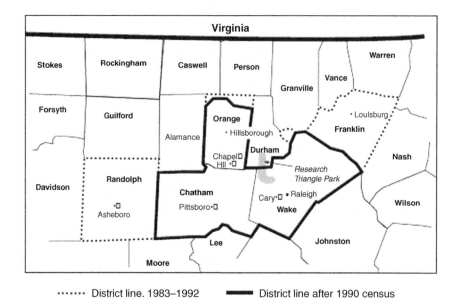

······· District line. 1983–1992   ▬▬▬ District line after 1990 census

Figure 3.1 North Carolina's Fourth Congressional District, 1983–1998.

saw districts like the Twelfth as legitimate, given the extent of past patterns of exclusion, but the majority saw the remedy as excessive and, in effect, ordered the district to be redrawn.

The legislature thus "fattened" the elongated Twelfth district somewhat, eliminating Durham County at its easternmost end, in advance of the 1998 election. Legal challenges continued, delaying the 1998 primary, but the new lines held in 1998 and 2000. They eventually were affirmed in yet another 5-4 Supreme Court decision, *Easley v. Cromartie*, which found the legislature's revised plan to be less determined by racial, as opposed to political, considerations.[3] The swing vote was Sandra Day O'Connor, whose majority opinion in the first Shaw case had called the Twelfth district "bizarre" in its configuration, likening it to "political apartheid," but who apparently now felt that an acceptable balance had been struck.

The politics of this protracted fight was complicated. The new majority-minority districts, in North Carolina and elsewhere, uniformly elected Democrats, and Democrats saw themselves as champions of the VRA and enhanced Black representation. But Republicans in many instances saw an opportunity for themselves: to the extent minority voters were concentrated into a limited number of districts, they would be removed from other districts, rendering those districts more Republican. Beginning in 1989, Republican national chairman Lee Atwater orchestrated a campaign to cement Black-Republican alliances, especially in the South, promoting the formation of majority-Black districts.[4] Not all Black leaders bought into this proposition. In North Carolina, the tradeoffs were recognized and led to considerable ambivalence about adding a second minority district. But two African American representatives would still represent only 16 percent of the delegation, compared to 22 percent of the population. I thus supported the fight for a majority-minority Twelfth district (after the "fattening," it was actually just under 50 percent Black), as did most Democrats. The changes increased the vulnerability of some Democratic districts, especially the Third, which was intertwined with the new First district. But the shift in the alignment of the state's delegation after 1994—from eight Democrats and four Republicans to the reverse—was mainly attributable to national forces, the anti-Clinton backlash, and the Gingrich revolution. We nonetheless received a foretaste of how more extreme efforts to "pack" Black voters into a few districts might be used to benefit Republicans—a possibility fully realized in North Carolina after the 2010 election.

The redrawing of the Twelfth district in 1997 in response to the *Shaw* decisions also prompted a major redrawing of the Fourth. Durham County, severed from the Twelfth, was added, while much of Raleigh and Wake County was taken away. This gave me approximately one-third new territory in 1998 (see Figure 3.2). The redistricting process interested me intensely, of course, but key legislators had their own ideas and interests to pursue, including satisfying the courts, and my influence was limited.

The next redistricting, which followed the 2000 census, offered more opportunities for input and involvement. I knew the Fourth would have to lose some 147,000 constituents because of population growth, and that a new Thirteenth district would be added, probably in our part of the state. This was a great development for the state, but having just resolved the 1990 redistricting, it created considerable uncertainty and anxiety, which was shared for various reasons by other delegation members.

Future Representative Brad Miller, then in the NC General Assembly, was chair of the Senate redistricting committee, and he took the lead on congressional redistricting. The challenge was to create a reasonably compact new district among those that were comparatively overpopulated without running afoul of either the Voting Rights Act or the *Shaw* decisions. That required making the surrounding Democratic districts more competitive and created uneasiness all around. In the end I was able to maintain the basic Fourth District configuration set in 1997 and to protect the ties I had developed in Durham County. And Miller succeeded in drawing a new Thirteenth district that was competitive for Democrats, ultimately running in and winning it himself.

Both in 1997 and 2001, with the General Assembly under Democratic control, party leaders and representatives from my part of the state were willing to listen to my suggestions and concerns. But they were in charge and had many additional factors to consider: the redrawing of their own districts; legal requirements and court decisions; local preferences and

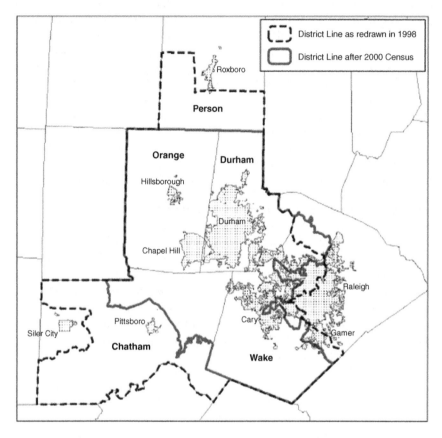

Figure 3.2 North Carolina's Reconfigured Fourth District. North Carolina's Fourth Congressional District, as redrawn in 1998.

loyalties; their own, and their friends', ambitions and plans, including congressional aspirations; and sometimes political debts or scores to settle of which I was barely aware. There were many reminders along the way that I was not in control of the process. But it produced districts where I could compete and win.

The districts that emerged were not highly gerrymandered by current standards, with the exception of the two majority-minority districts, which had their own rationale. Over the years 1992–2010, neither party ordinarily held an advantage of more than one or two seats statewide and many seats remained competitive. Certainly nothing that Democratic legislators did provided a barricade against the Republican sweep of 1994. Various tweaks and twists favored Democrats, but legislators often expressed wariness of voter reactions to districts that seemed unfair. And some of their tweaks reflected deals with Republicans, as when in 2001 a narrow peninsula of precincts assigned to the new Thirteenth district was drawn into Cary so as to include the home of a GOP state legislator who was considering a race for Congress and preferred not to run in the Fourth.

All of this changed radically when the Republican General Assembly elected in 2010 came to town. North Carolina was a prime target of the Redistricting Majority Project (REDMAP) of the Republican State Leadership Committee (RSLC), the largest caucus of Republican state leaders. The RSLC amassed large sums, taking advantage of campaign finance loopholes, to orchestrate "the most strategic, large-scale and well-funded campaign ever to redraw the political map coast to coast, with the express goal of locking in Republican control of the U.S. House of Representatives and state legislative chambers for the next decade or more."[5] It was a brilliantly conceived and coordinated campaign that utilized highly sophisticated mapping technology to produce maximally gerrymandered plans for state party and legislative leaders, all far from public view.

It was "a bad year to have a bad year," we Democrats grimly told one another in reflecting on the perfect storm we faced after 2010: a fierce Obama backlash, turning over both houses of the General Assembly, in the year that would determine the legislative lineup for redistricting. In North Carolina and across the country the effects were compounded by the sharp rightward and unaccommodating turn of Republican politics and the tools and tactical support supplied by REDMAP.

The new seven-county Fourth District concocted by the legislature— "long and thin, like a horse up on its front legs"—became a national symbol of extreme gerrymandering.[6] Thus began a decade of legal challenges that produced three contrasting versions of the district over five elections, from 2012 to 2020 (see Figure 3.3). The district drawn in 2011 was packed with African Americans (31 percent of registered voters) and Democrats (55 percent). But the First and Twelfth districts offered even more extreme examples, and it was these two districts on which the legal challenge focused.

Once again, the issue was racial gerrymandering and the balance to be struck between the VRA and the equal protection clause. Both districts had been drawn with less than 50 percent Black voting age population (BVAP) after the 2000 census and had continued to elect Black representatives by large margins. But Republican legislators, claiming that they otherwise might be accused of "diluting" the votes of African Americans under the VRA, moved sizable numbers of Black voters into both the First and the Twelfth, bringing their BVAPs to 52.7 and 50.7 percent, respectively. The Black voters who challenged the map countered that "dilution" could cut both ways: what was being diluted and diminished was their influence in *surrounding* districts. The VRA, in other words, was being used as a pretext for packing Black voters into a limited number of districts, rendering the surrounding districts more White (and more Republican).

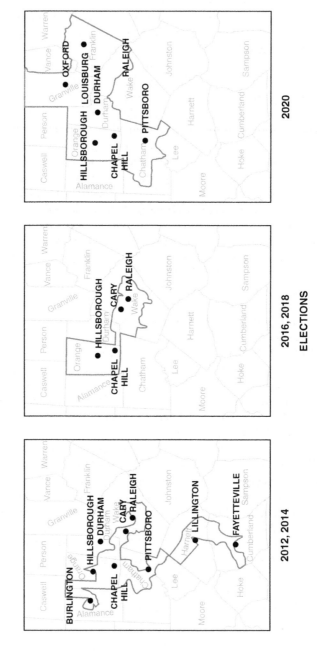

Figure 3.3 Successive gerrymanders of North Carolina's Fourth District, 2013–2022.

The Supreme Court determined that race had impermissibly predominated in the drawing of districts 1 and 12. Since the use of race was not required to meet the objectives of the VRA, it could not withstand the strict scrutiny that the 14th amendment required.[7] By the time the decision was rendered, the General Assembly had already drawn a new congressional map for the 2016 election, responding to the district court ruling which the Supreme Court affirmed. But while the new map adjusted the problematic racial numbers and improved its appearance by greatly reducing the number of split counties, it was equally gerrymandered, maintaining the lopsided 10R–3D partisan breakdown. The Fourth District became considerably more compact, going from seven counties to three, but it was still packed. Districts 1 and 12, also still packed, became the basis for a new round of litigation, based this time on *partisan* gerrymandering.

The spirit of the 2016 snap-redistricting was captured in a notorious quote from Rep. David Lewis, who led the effort in the NC House: "I propose that we draw the maps to give a partisan advantage to 10 Republicans and three Democrats, because I do not believe it's possible to draw a map of 11 Republicans and two Democrats."[8] Lewis was no doubt thinking of earlier court decisions that, in attempting to disengage racial from political gerrymandering, had implied that the latter was not constitutionally forbidden. But a series of legal challenges arising from states subjected to extreme gerrymandering after 2010 argued that the same constitutional considerations that applied to racial gerrymandering—the systematic dilution and diminishing of the electoral influence of a class of voters—should apply to the extreme segregation of voters into districts by party.

The North Carolina case, *Rucho v. Common Cause*, made it to the Supreme Court on appeal after the 2016 map was struck down by a three-judge district court panel. We became hopeful that the Supreme Court might at least try to define the outer limits of partisan gerrymandering when it combined *Rucho* with a Maryland case alleging extreme Democratic gerrymandering—an attempt, we speculated, at partisan balance.[9] But it was not to be. In a 5–4 ruling, the Court found that the case presented "political questions beyond the reach of the federal courts." Chief Justice John Roberts, writing for the majority, recalled the David Lewis quote and acknowledged that extreme partisanship in districting might "reasonably seem unjust." But he rejected the comparison to racial gerrymandering and concluded that remedies for political gerrymandering must be left to Congress and the states—a declaration of judicial impotence with regard to citizens' "most fundamental ... constitutional rights" that Justice Elena Kagan dissected in a scathing dissent.[10]

The *Rucho* outcome dashed, at least temporarily, hopes for a game-changing national verdict on political gerrymandering. But the long running North Carolina saga was not over. Reform advocates, bolstered by the leadership of the National Democratic Redistricting Committee, headed by former Attorney General Eric Holder, turned to the state courts for relief.

They were encouraged by favorable changes in the composition of the NC Supreme Court and by state-level developments elsewhere, including a 2015 decision by the Florida Supreme Court which struck down the state's congressional map. The Florida decision was based on a Fair Districts amendment in the state's constitution. North Carolina's constitution had no such specific provision, so the challenges turned to its Free Elections, Equal Protection, Freedom of Speech, and Freedom of Assembly clauses instead.

North Carolina's Chief Justice assigned the case to a three-judge Superior Court panel, which on October 28, 2019, five weeks before the beginning of the filing period for the 2020 elections, enjoined state officials from preparing to administer the elections under the 2016 map. The judges had incontrovertible evidence from REDMAP mastermind Thomas Hofeller's computer files (released by his daughter after his death) of "both the partisan intent and the intended partisan effects" of the 2016 redistricting exercise. In taking note of *Rucho*'s deference to the states, they argued that they were not bound by the same limitations in adjudicating "political questions" that Roberts had articulated. They found partisan gerrymandering—"seeking to diminish the electoral power of supporters of a disfavored party"—particularly vulnerable to equal protection claims. The judges therefore granted injunctive relief, anticipating that the challengers were likely to prevail on the merits eventually and preventing "irreparable loss" to them in the meantime.[11]

The legislature's Republican leaders, concluding that they could not ultimately prevail, convened as they had in 2016 for a snap redistricting session. They did the minimum they were obligated to do, drawing two new urban/suburban districts: district 2 within Wake County and district 6 in Greensboro/Winston-Salem. This prompted the retirement of the incumbent Republicans representing these districts, and set the stage for a likely 8–5 partisan lineup statewide. This still fell considerably short of reflecting the state's partisan division, and few if any seats were truly competitive. But the judicial panel, acknowledging the results were "not perfect," elected to let the filing for 2020 go forward under the new maps rather than delaying the primary elections.[12]

This process resulted in a radically reconfigured Fourth District, once again spread over seven counties and containing about 75 percent new territory (see Figure 3.3). The district again included Durham and most of Chatham as well as territory from northern Wake and Franklin counties I had represented in the more distant past. Granville County, extending to the Virginia state line, was totally new territory, as was a sliver of Vance County. The district was solidly Democratic, and I was well-received as I began the now-familiar process of moving around the new territory. But the decision by Republican legislative leaders to redraw the district so extensively was by no means required or even suggested by the court's decision; in fact, it flew in the face of many of the criteria—compactness, contiguity of territory, leaving "communities of interest" intact—often held up as marks of fair and sensible districting.

The best way to avoid what North Carolina has gone through in the past decade is to take redistricting out of the hands of partisan legislative majorities (the state constitution gives the governor no part in the process) and to entrust it to a nonpartisan commission. In doing this, we would join a growing list of some fourteen states.[13] We should also keep pushing for favorable federal and state court rulings. But even if those decisions provided a stronger constitutional or legal standard, partisan legislative majorities could still test their limits, provoking repeated challenges and court orders and redrawings of the lines that would take years to play out—and in the meantime cause great public confusion and distrust. It would be far better to have fair maps in the first place.

I included in my comprehensive We the People Act a provision long championed by Rep. John Tanner (D-Tennessee) to require each state to establish an independent commission to draw congressional districts. H.R. 1 contained a similar but far more prescriptive provision authored by Rep. Zoe Lofgren (D-California). The bill specified that plans should "permit racial, ethnic, and language minorities with an equal opportunity to participate in the political process and to elect candidates of choice" and otherwise comply with the Voting Rights Act. Given that compliance, state commissions would then be obliged to "respect communities of interest ... including but not limited to ethnic, racial, economic, social, cultural, geographic or historic identities, neighborhoods and potential subdivisions to the extent practicable." Excluded from consideration would be the residence of any incumbent member or candidate and the partisan affiliation or voting history of the residents.[14]

Many states have already formed redistricting commissions and are, in effect, testing the merits of various arrangements. Congress should evaluate the results and permit considerable latitude going forward. But it is time to establish nonpartisan congressional districting nationwide. This will not end legitimate debate; one question that intrigues me, for example, is whether a long-established district configuration might itself constitute a community of interest. There will still be a need for legislative oversight and judicial review. Nor should we conclude that all districting undertaken by partisan majorities has been unfair; despite what the cynics say, they don't "all do it." But the country—and certainly North Carolina—has had enough experience, particularly as partisanship has gotten more extreme, to know that we need a better way. Nonpartisan districting, carried out by independent state commissions, is an idea whose time has come.

Campaign Finance Reform

In beginning this book with accounts of my seventeen election and reelection efforts, I perhaps risked giving an impression of life in Congress as an endless sequence of campaigns. The remainder of the book will provide perspective on campaigning relative to other congressional duties. For all but about three months of the twenty-four-month election cycle, I am involved in congressional more than campaign activities. That, I believe, is how constituents prefer it, and most campaigns would be hard-pressed to improve on the typical non-campaign schedule maintained by members of Congress in their districts as a means of reaching out to voters and letting them know what the member is about.

Still, we are never far from the next election; I often tell supporters that they never need to remove their bumper stickers. Is the two-year term too short? It would be a rare House member who has not on occasion looked enviously at the Senate with its six-year terms. But the House is the body of government constitutionally designed to be most sensitive to currents of public opinion, and recent history has frequently seen voters applying what many saw as a "corrective" to presidential outcomes and policies in House races two years later: 1994 comes to mind, as do 1982, 2006, 2010, and 2018. I am not an unbiased observer. A trend of this sort in North Carolina in 1986, following the wipeout of Democrats in 1984, helped first elect me to the House, and I was again fortunate, in trying to recapture the Fourth District seat in 1996, to face a turnaround time of only two years.

The most serious criticism of the two-year cycle is that it requires nonstop fundraising. But that is less a criticism of two-year terms than it is of the financial demands of politics. It is not uncommon for House members in targeted races to raise and spend $5 to $10 million, to say nothing of what "independent" party and other organizations may spend on their behalf. Nor are senators spared by their longer terms: they often are as preoccupied as House members with the quest for dollars, and in contested races must raise millions through nonstop calls and receptions from coast to coast.

I am neither fond of nor particularly adept at fundraising, but I have outraised my opponents in every campaign except John Carrington's largely self-financed effort in 1990. I have needed this money (and obviously should have raised and spent more in 1994) to challenge two well-financed incumbents and to defend myself in a sometimes hostile national environment. In recent campaigns, I have also been increasingly obligated to help fund state and national party efforts.

The main factor driving these campaign expenditures is television. I have probably worked harder than most candidates at keeping the politics of personal contact alive. I believe in it and will continue to do it. But as I survey the vast, rapidly growing suburban tracts throughout my district and ask myself how I am going to reach them, there is no answer that does not lead back to television. Targeted mail is important, as are phone banks, field operations and, increasingly, social media. But television is the medium that most people attend to and their main source of political information. And the most effective format by far is the well-conceived, well-produced thirty-second ad, strategically placed on dominant local channels and on news and entertainment channels watched by targeted audiences as well.

This greatly complicates the task of controlling campaign costs. In a system biased in many ways toward incumbents, television is often the most effective tool that a challenger has. I share the misgivings that many have expressed about how much money a serious race for Congress requires, the good people that this eliminates from participation, and the constant preoccupation with fundraising it requires. But if we want campaigns that reach and raise the awareness of the vast majority of the community, we must come to grips with the unique power of television, and that requires significant resources.

There is a place in campaign reform for both contribution and spending limits to prevent excesses of the kind we have repeatedly seen in U.S. Senate races in North Carolina. But the *Buckley v. Valeo*[15] decision still is a formidable obstacle to expenditure limitations, and in any event, any limits would have to be high enough to permit full and effective campaigns. Various measures that might relieve fundraising pressures are worth considering—the restoration of tax credits or deductions for small contributions, for example, or requirements that a certain amount of television time be made available to candidates free or at reduced rates—but ultimately, the only solution that achieves the multiple goals of adequate but constrained funding, broad financial participation, and reduced reliance on large individual and corporate donors is *public* financing: the matching of small individual contributions with public funds up to a reasonable limit.

The United States has already demonstrated the viability of public financing in the presidential arena. The Federal Elections Campaign Act (FECA) Amendments of 1974, enacted in the wake of Watergate, established a federal match for contributions up to $250 for presidential primary campaigns and full federal funding of the general election campaigns. Every major-party nominee accepted public financing from 1976 until 2000, when George W. Bush opted out of the public system for the primary, and 2008, when John McCain opted out for the primary and Barack Obama for both the primary and the general election.

The system proved its worth over a thirty-year period, particularly benefiting long-shot candidates such as Jimmy Carter and Ronald Reagan (both in 1976), but it failed to keep pace with rising campaign costs and the earlier start of the primary season. In 2010, I introduced, with Chris Van Hollen (D-Maryland) and Mike Castle (R-Delaware) as cosponsors and in collaboration with Fred Wertheimer of Democracy 21, a bill to modernize public financing for presidential campaigns. But the shift to Tea Party-inspired Republican leadership in the House ended the prospect for bipartisan cooperation on this and other reform measures. The House voted along party lines to abolish presidential public financing entirely on December 1, 2011. Such efforts have never fully succeeded, but the system remains on life support. In 2016, Democrat Martin O'Malley was the only one of twenty-three initial primary contenders to seek public funding. In the meantime, I have reintroduced my modernization bill in every succeeding Congress, and it was incorporated in the Democratic omnibus reform measure, H.R. 1, in 2019.

Public financing for congressional campaigns was initially part of the FECA Amendments of 1974 but was eventually dropped. In 1992, both chambers, under Democratic leadership, passed legislation combining voluntary spending limits with public financing for general election congressional campaigns, but President George H.W. Bush vetoed the bill. In 2013, I first developed and included a congressional public financing proposal (H.R. 270) alongside, and largely modeled on, presidential public financing. The first $250 of a contribution to a House or Senate candidate would be matched by public funds at a 5:1 ratio. The contribution limit (then $2,500 per donor per election) would be cut in half, and only the first $250 would be eligible for a match. To protect candidates who might be deluged with spending from "independent" groups operating without limits, the parties would be authorized to spend unlimited amounts in coordination with such candidates, provided the parties were drawing on a designated fund that limited contributions to $1,250 per donor, per year.

I refined the proposal over succeeding congresses, and in 2019 it served as a partial basis, alongside a more elaborate proposal developed by Rep. Sarbanes, for the congressional public financing provisions in H.R. 1. The traditional financing mechanism for presidential public financing, a tax checkoff fund that relied on voluntary participation by taxpayers but still ultimately drew on the U.S. Treasury, was replaced by a Freedom from Influence Fund for both presidential and congressional elections, funded by an assessment on federal fines, penalties, and settlements for certain tax crimes and corporate violations.

The interest in campaign finance reform I brought with me from academia was sharpened by my early campaign experiences. Soon after my 1996 comeback, reform currents again began stirring in both houses. Legislation to close two major spending loopholes—eliminating "soft money," funds that the national parties could raise and spend without regard for federal limits; and reining in "electioneering communications," requiring unions, corporations, and nonprofits that run advertisements advocating the election or defeat of specific candidates within thirty days of a primary or sixty days of general election to pay for the ads with regulated PAC funds—finally passed in 2002. The Bipartisan Campaign Reform Act (BCRA) was commonly designated by the names of its lead sponsors, Chris Shays (R-Connecticut) and Martin Meehan (D-Massachusetts) in the House and John McCain (R-Arizona) and Russ Feingold (D-Wisconsin) in the Senate.

In 1998 and 1999, the Shays-Meehan legislation cleared the hurdles erected by the House Republican leadership and passed by substantial votes, only to fall to Senate filibusters. In 2001, President George W. Bush's opposition was added to the mix. But so was the collapse of the Enron

Corporation, amid revelations of the company's political contributions and influence. That was sufficient to prompt the necessary 218 members to sign a Discharge Petition, bypassing the relevant committees and forcing the bill onto the floor despite leadership opposition. Our margin of victory was 240–189, and this time the Senate went along, 60–40. The president signed the bill on March 27, 2002, pointedly refusing to stage the usual signing ceremony.

As the battle then shifted to the courts, I joined with Mike Castle in organizing a bipartisan group of twenty-five members to submit an amicus curiae brief defending the bill. We stressed the continuity of Shays-Meehan's loophole closings with past, legally sanctioned attempts at regulation and argued that reducing the parties to "mere conduits for the flow of big soft-money contributions" to be expended by candidates and their operatives, far from strengthening parties, "hollowed out" and marginalized their traditional organizational functions. Finally, in a 5–4 ruling on December 10, 2003, the Supreme Court upheld the major provisions of the law.[16]

I was able to add an amendment to the reform legislation which strengthened the "disclaimer" requirements whereby the candidates and organizations running ads were required to identify themselves but often did so with a postage stamp-size picture and tiny print on the screen. I first took on the disclaimer issue in 1997 (H.R. 227) when I introduced what I termed (with apologies to country music star Tammy Wynette and her signature hit, "Stand by Your Man") a "Stand by Your Ad" bill. The idea was to require candidates (or interest group representatives) to appear briefly, full-screen, identifying themselves and acknowledging that they approved and paid for the ad the viewer has seen or is about to see. This strengthened disclaimer would not regulate the content of the body of the ad but, in requiring a more explicit assumption of personal responsibility, could perhaps deter reckless charges and distortions.

The idea was hatched by Mac McCorkle, my Wednesday night group friend from 1986 who had helped engineer my 1996 comeback and had hung out a shingle as a policy consultant. McCorkle successfully promoted "Stand by Your Ad" at the state level, working with NC lieutenant governor Dennis Wicker; Jim Scott of the Virginia House of Delegates, a close friend of mine from UNC days, picked up on the idea as well. I worked with Shays and Meehan to include the proposal in their bill from 1999 through the 2002 House-Senate conference, and its major elements remained in the bill the president signed. We were careful to point out in our amicus brief that these provisions simply strengthened requirements already in law. The Supreme Court agreed, specifically upholding the enhanced disclaimer in its decision.[17] In the meantime, I took great satisfaction in seeing presidential candidates acknowledge that they had "approved this message" as they ran commercials in the 2004 campaign and thereafter.

The BCRA victory was short-lived, however. It was eclipsed in 2010 by another 5–4 Supreme Court decision, *Citizens United*, which gave corporations, unions, and associations a First Amendment right to raise and spend unlimited funds for or against specific candidates as long as they were operating "independently" of those candidates' campaign organizations. BCRA's "electioneering communications" restrictions were explicitly ruled out, while a related decision held that individual and corporate contributions to PACs that make only independent expenditures (but do not contribute directly to campaigns)—commonly called super-PACs—could not constitutionally be limited.[18] As a result, such PACs proliferated, and the floodgates of special-interest money opened wide. "The old corruption of soft money was replaced by the new corruption of super PACs," which in the next four elections raised nearly $5 billion in unlimited contributions—$1 billion from their top ten donors alone—to spend in federal elections.[19]

In the post-*Citizens United* decade, a combination of FEC rulings, court decisions, and congressional actions has opened the floodgates even wider. For example, the Supreme Court in 2014 invalidated FECA and BCRA limits on the total amount individuals could contribute to federal campaigns and committees over an election cycle.[20] Senate Majority Leader Mitch McConnell then took advantage of the pressures surrounding passage of the fiscal 2015 "Cromnibus" appropriations bill to insert a provision that greatly increased what individuals and PACs could contribute to national party committees. By this time, the flow of super PAC money was such that McConnell could rationalize increased contribution limits for the parties as a needed counterweight to newly empowered and less accountable groups.

The proverbial genie is obviously out of the bottle. HR 1, in its "findings" section, laid "tidal waves of unlimited and anonymous spending"—increasing nearly 900 percent between the 2008 and 2018 election cycles—at the feet of *Citizens United* and related decisions. The bill advocated both a constitutional amendment "so that Congress and the States may regulate and set limits on the raising and spending of money to influence elections" and the wholesale displacement of the present system by public financing of presidential and congressional elections. But it also assembled various less comprehensive reform proposals that in the meantime could increase the transparency and integrity of elections.

One such measure, the DISCLOSE (Democracy Is Strengthened by Casting Light on Spending in Elections) Act, had come close to enactment in 2010 immediately after the *Citizens United* decision, while Congress was still under Democratic control. The bill required super PACs and other groups making independent expenditures to make timely reports of those expenditures and their major donors. I worked with lead sponsor Chris Van Hollen on the bill and added a Stand by Your Ad provision to require the groups' leaders to appear in their ads and to show the top five donors who paid for the ads on-screen. The bill passed the House on June 24, 2010, but fell to a Republican filibuster in the Senate.

I introduced several additional measures in succeeding congresses and included them in my We the People Act in 2017:

- Stand by Every Ad, requiring personal disclaimers on paid internet ads and robocalls similar to those required for TV and radio.
- Replace the deadlocked and ineffectual FEC with a five-member Federal Election Administration with enhanced enforcement powers.
- Stop Super PAC-Candidate Coordination: shut down individual candidate super PACs—a self-contradictory concept—and tighten the rules that prohibit coordination between PACs making independent expenditures and the candidates and parties they support.

In 2018, working with Senator Jon Tester (D-Montana), I added to the list the Spotlight Act, which would void the Trump administration's reversal of a longstanding rule requiring non-profit political advocacy organizations to report donor information to the Internal Revenue Service (IRS). All of these proposals were included in some form in HR 1 when it passed the House in 2019.

Such proposals raise the possibility of incremental progress on discrete problems, even as we work long-term toward more sweeping reforms. For example, it is not only Democrats who risk losing control of their own message as independent groups enter the fray to "help" candidates or attack their opponents. Couldn't common ground be found on increased transparency for super PACs as well as rules to ensure their true independence? The bipartisanship of BRCA is long gone, and it is difficult to secure cooperation even on incremental reforms nowadays. HR 1 provides a menu of possibilities, however, and I intend to pursue them.

The Right to Vote—and to Have Every Vote Count

It did not take long. The Republican leaders of the North Carolina General Assembly were poised to act in 2013 when the Supreme Court voided key provisions of the Voting Rights Act. Passed in 1965 after "Bloody Sunday" in Selma, Alabama, had pricked the nation's conscience, the VRA had been regularly renewed by large bipartisan congressional majorities. But the Court in 2013 took aim at the "preclearance" provisions in sections 4(b) and 5 of the law, which required jurisdictions with a history of voting discrimination—including forty out of 100 counties in North Carolina—to get permission in advance from the Justice Department before making any changes in state law that affected voting. The law had blocked eighty-six prejudicial election law changes since 1998 and deterred hundreds more. But Justice John Roberts, writing for a 5–4 majority, ruled that the criteria for requiring preclearance were sufficiently outdated to amount to an unjustified denial of "equal sovereignty" among the states. Justice Ruth Bader Ginsburg dissented sharply: "To throw out preclearance when it has worked and is continuing to work to stop discriminatory changes," she wrote, "is like throwing away your umbrella in a rainstorm because you are not getting wet."[21]

Within two months, the North Carolina legislature had passed a comprehensive voter suppression law (HB 589) that surely would have failed preclearance. Texas moved even faster: within *two hours* of the Court's decision, Attorney General Greg Abbott announced that a tightened voter identification requirement for which the state had been seeking preclearance would take effect immediately. The North Carolina law, termed by the Brennan Center "possibly the most restrictive" in the nation, imposed requirements for a photo identification for voters from a limited list of acceptable documents; curtailed early voting; ended "same-day" registration, whereby early voters could register and vote at the same time; and ended "provisional" voting, which enabled voters who showed up at the wrong precinct to nonetheless complete a ballot and have it counted later for the races for which they were eligible to vote. By 2018, some twenty-three states had passed laws restricting voting rights—a result of post-2010 Republican dominance of state legislatures as well as of the Court's decision.[22]

Almost all of these voter suppression measures were immediately challenged in court, with mixed results. The U.S. Court of Appeals for the Fourth Circuit found that all of the key provisions of the North Carolina law "disproportionately affected African-Americans" and had in fact targeted them "with almost surgical precision." The Court thus ruled that the law violated both the Equal Protection clauses of the Constitution and Section 2 of the VRA (which had remained intact after the Supreme Court's 2013 decision).[23] As in the gerrymandering cases, the process across the country involved a constant back-and-forth between legislatures tweaking the laws and courts ruling on new rounds of challenges. The courts have at least delayed the most sweeping efforts at voter suppression, but lawsuits under Section 2 are no substitute for preclearance, which prevented discriminatory changes in law from occurring in the first place.

I included in my comprehensive We the People bill measures introduced by colleagues that targeted specific state suppression efforts—requiring same-day registration nationwide, for example, as well as the automatic registration of voters when they interacted with certain state agencies. In 2019, HR 1 added protections for provisional ballots, early voting, the rights of individuals with felony convictions to vote after completing their sentences, and against the premature purging of voter rolls. But the House took its most important step on December 6, 2019, when it passed HR 4, the Voting Rights Advancement Act, which revised and restored the preclearance provisions the Court had disallowed.

There had been much talk of restoring some form of preclearance immediately after the Court's 2013 decision. After all, the House had renewed the VRA, including preclearance, in 2006 by a vote of 360–33 (the Senate vote was 98–0). But increased partisan polarization, in addition to the fact that Republicans had developed a playbook for imposing state-level voting restrictions nationwide, made it impossible to secure bipartisan support for a robust VRA that would check state practices. Passage came only with the resumption of Democratic control of the House, on a mostly party-line vote (228–187) with the Trump administration threatening a veto and the Republican Senate unlikely to take up the legislation.

If the right to vote is threatened by continuing efforts to make voting more difficult and intimidating, it is also put in jeopardy by factors blocking the accurate and straightforward translation of votes into electoral results. The most formidable of these factors, of course, is the one embedded in the Constitution, the Electoral College. Two of the last five presidential elections have seen the electoral vote go to a candidate who lost the popular vote.

Such disparate outcomes have become more likely by virtue of the current political alignment of the states. Just as equal representation in the Senate gives voting power to small states—mostly located in the Great Plains and Rocky Mountain regions—disproportionate to their share of the population, the Electoral College (where each state's vote equals its total number of U.S. representatives and senators) displays the same bias. Because those states are heavily Republican at present, it has become fairly likely that a Democratic victory in the popular vote will be offset by a Republican victory in the Electoral College, as happened in 2000 and 2016. The increasing likelihood that the popular vote will be reversed is eroding the Electoral College's legitimacy, but in the near term it is also making it more difficult to achieve the bipartisan consensus that constitutional change would require.

Congress almost sent a constitutional amendment to the states after the 1968 election, which saw Richard Nixon almost lose the popular vote but win the electoral vote handily. The amendment to institute direct popular election passed the House with a bipartisan 339–70 vote on September 11, 1969, but fell to a Senate filibuster. Nothing has come nearly as close since then, even when President Jimmy Carter sent a proposal to abolish the Electoral College to the Congress. But the arguments once made for the arrangement as a guard against direct democracy or a protection of the states' electoral role have been rendered obsolete by the emergence of mass parties and the overall democratization of the system.[24] And surely the prospect of popular vote majorities being reversed with some regularity cannot be acceptable indefinitely in a democracy.

This is not to offer an obvious pathway to change. Even if one party or one group of states did not see an advantage for themselves in the working of the present system, securing constitutional change would be daunting. Efforts to modify the system without requiring an amendment have gained some traction. Currently fifteen states (plus DC) have joined the National Popular Vote Interstate Compact, pledging their electors to the winner of the national popular vote; this represents some 73 percent of the Electoral College majority of 270 required for the compact to take effect. But such efforts still face formidable political and legal obstacles.

It is important to distinguish the Electoral College debate from questions surrounding the presidential *nomination* process. Here, too, some have advocated for direct selection via national primaries: every state would vote on the same day, and every voter would have an equal say. Democratic principles do not require such a system, however, and in fact are better served by an iterative, state-by-state decision process that gives greater weight to grass roots politics and has a greater potential for self-correction.

There are many legitimate debates about the sequencing of the contests—the influence of the early bellwether states, for example, and the "front-loading" of the primary calendar—as well as the primary vs. caucus format. We thoroughly reviewed these arguments even if we did not totally resolve them on the Commission on Presidential Nomination Timing and Scheduling, which I co-chaired for the Democratic National Committee in 2005 (see Chapter 6). But none of this argues for a national primary, which would give big money and big media even more influence than they already have and would provide a less thorough consideration of candidates and certainly a less correctible, cumulative judgment as to their merits, than does our state-by-state system, whatever its flaws.[25]

Partly because of my political science background, I was drawn into congressional debate and media commentary on the workings of the Electoral College in the midst of the disputed 2000 Bush–Gore presidential election and the recount of the vote in Florida. In mid-November, when it seemed that Congress might be confronted with two competing sets of Florida electors sending conflicting electoral certificates to Washington, I introduced a resolution requiring the Archivist of the United States, the official responsible for coordinating the functions of the Electoral College, to inform the House of preparations he was making to receive lists of qualified electors from the states and any challenges to their legality.[26] I was appalled when the Supreme Court summarily cut off the Florida recount, and as the 107th Congress got underway, I resolved to salvage some election reform from the debacle.

Most reform efforts aimed at the immediate problems with voting equipment and election procedures that the Florida experience had highlighted. My contribution to this agenda was the Voting Improvement Act (HR 775), which I introduced with Steny Hoyer (D-Maryland), ranking Democrat on the Committee on House Administration, on February 28, 2001. The bill would have provided funds to states and localities to replace punch card voting systems, the least reliable among systems commonly in use, and proposed creation of a federal commission to develop a model election code for the states.

With memories of Florida still fresh, the possibilities for bipartisan cooperation were unclear, even to repair obvious flaws. Many Republicans were wary lest reform efforts shed a negative light on the 2000 outcome; Democrats had no desire to settle for halfway measures, which would imply the Florida problems and abuses were less than serious. Many of us criticized Speaker Dennis Hastert for refusing to appoint a special committee on reform equally divided between the parties, but his negative decision had a silver lining: it freed minority leader Dick Gephardt to appoint an all-Democratic committee that could be much bolder in its critique and its agenda for reform. I was named as one of eight vice chairs of the committee, which held six hearings across the country and issued a comprehensive reform proposal.[27]

In the end, election reform became one of the few areas of bipartisan achievement for the 107th Congress, largely through the efforts of Hoyer, Chairman Bob Ney (R-Ohio) of the Committee on House Administration, and their Senate counterparts. The Help America Vote Act (HAVA, HR 3295), signed by the president on October 29, 2002, retained the punch card machine buyout from the Voting Improvement Act, as well as the commission to oversee work on a model election code. In addition, it set some standards for national elections: states were required to provide voters with a means of checking and correcting errors in casting their ballots, for example, and provisional ballots were required when a voter's eligibility was in doubt (although a bipartisan compromise left a loophole whereby states could avoid counting the ballots). The bill also authorized grants to help states meet the new standards and replace obsolete equipment and created the Election Assistance Commission (EAC) to administer these funds.

Congressional appropriations to implement HAVA reached $1.5 billion in fiscal years 2003 and 2004 but declined rapidly thereafter. The security of the equipment being purchased was an issue from the start, leading Rep. Rush Holt (D-New Jersey) and others to push for years to require voting machines to produce a "paper trail" that voters could use in checking their individual ballots and that would permit a separate tally if needed to verify the result.[28] But much of the HAVA money to replace punch card and other obsolete systems was used to buy Direct Recording Electronic (DRE) systems whereby the voter touched a computer screen and the vote was displayed and stored electronically, usually without a paper record that could be used to back up the count if a computer malfunction or hacking was suspected.

I decided in the course of these debates that simpler was better: the "optical scan" systems in use in my district, whereby voters marked their choices on paper ballots and then inserted the ballots into an electronic device for storing and tabulation, had the advantages of simplicity, accuracy, security, and redundancy. Many jurisdictions across the country have come to the same conclusion over the past decade as security concerns have mounted, either switching to optical scanners or reconfiguring DREs to produce a voter-verifiable paper audit trail (VVPAT). Still, at least some jurisdictions in twenty-four states continue to use DREs as standard equipment, of which only 29 percent were equipped with VVPAT by 2016.[29]

Security concerns reached a new level, focused on foreign election interference, during and after the 2016 presidential elections. "The Russian government interfered in the 2016 presidential election in sweeping fashion," stated Special Counsel Robert Mueller in his report on the matter in early 2019. They did this, "principally through two operations:"

> First, a Russian entity carried out a social media campaign that favored presidential candidate Donald J. Trump and disparaged presidential candidate Hillary Clinton. Second, a Russian intelligence service conducted computer-intrusion operations against entities, employees, and volunteers working on the Clinton campaign and then released stolen documents.

The report also found that the Intelligence Directorate of the Russian Army (GRU) had "targeted" and "sought access" to the networks of state and local boards of elections and other entities administering elections, as well as private manufacturers of voting equipment. The Senate Intelligence Committee later confirmed that these efforts were extensive and largely undetected, reaching election systems in all fifty states. While there was no conclusive evidence Russian cyber actors actually altered voter data or election outcomes, the committee concluded that, at least in some places, they were in a position to do so.[30] To this day, we are uncertain whether Russian or other malign interference was a factor in serious election-day malfunctions in Durham, North Carolina, and other locations.

President Trump has remained defensive and in denial about Russian interference, obviously regarding it as a threat to his legitimacy. Congressional Republicans have to some extent followed suit. In late 2019, for example, Senator Michael Crapo (R-Idaho) blocked consideration of a bipartisan bill to establish sanctions for election interference, charging that it was "designed more to attack the Trump administration and Republicans" than to deter Russians or others threatening our elections.[31] But the 2016 experience nonetheless was a widely heard wake-up call, highlighting how the post-HAVA effort to modernize election systems had faltered and how exposed and vulnerable most jurisdictions were. The 2018 election experience, with a surge in turnout in an atmosphere of mistrust, only heightened the sense of an election system in crisis—not only because of foreign threats but because of a range of investments and reforms long deferred.[32]

Congress responded with increases in HAVA appropriations to $380 and $425 million for fiscal 2018 and 2020, respectively. The bills made clear that the purchase of voting machines that provided a paper trail, the conduct of post-election audits, and addressing cyber vulnerabilities would be favored uses of the funds. But the funding fell short of both previous HAVA levels and documented needs, and generally received only grudging Republican support. We Democrats therefore took advantage of our ascent to House leadership in 2019 to promote election security and integrity as part of the broader agenda of political reform.

HR 1 thus authorized higher HAVA funding levels. It required voting systems nationwide to use voter-certified paper ballots that could then be optically scanned or counted by hand. It required the Department of Homeland Security to provide timely assessment of threats to elections and election infrastructure. It expanded the responsibilities of the EAC significantly, from pre-election assessments of state readiness to post-election audits.

A separate election security measure, the SHIELD (Stopping Harmful Interference in Elections for a Lasting Democracy) Act, HR 4617, passed the House on October 23, 2019, on a party-line vote of 227–181, under threat of a presidential veto. The bill would create an affirmative duty on the part of a presidential campaign to report an offer of assistance from a foreign government and would forbid the sharing of non-public campaign data and information with such governments. It would strengthen disclaimer and disclosure requirements for anyone running online political ads and would strengthen FECA limitations on political spending by foreign entities.

Then came the coronavirus and another major shift in the context of the voting rights and election security debates. We were able to hold Super Tuesday primaries in North Carolina and other states on March 3, 2020, setting Joe Biden on a sure path to the Democratic nomination, barely before public activities, including elections, began to shut down. The Wisconsin presidential primary and judicial election on April 7 provided the nightmare scenario for both public health and democracy, with the help of yet another 5–4 Supreme Court decision.

Fifteen other states had postponed elections, and Wisconsin's Democratic governor tried to do the same or to shift to voting entirely by mail, but was rebuffed by the Republican-led legislature. In the meantime, requests for mail-in absentee ballots had flooded the system, and a federal district judge ordered that voters be given six additional days to receive and mail in their ballots and still have them counted. It was this order that the U.S. Supreme Court stayed in a stunning four-page unsigned opinion. The decision was reminiscent of *Bush v. Gore* in its partisan bias and of *Citizens United* in its cluelessness about its likely real-world effects. Justice Ginsburg made those implications clear in a stinging dissent:

> The question here is whether tens of thousands of Wisconsin citizens can vote safely in the midst of a pandemic. Under the District Court's order, they would be able to do so. Even if they receive their absentee ballot in the days immediately following Election Day, they could return it. With the [Court] majority's stay in place, that will not be possible. Either they will have to brave the polls, endangering their own and others' safety, or they will lose their right to vote through no fault of their own.[33]

Wisconsin voters thus went to the polls. Only five polling places (out of an ordinary 180) were open in Milwaukee because of an absence of poll workers. Voters, many wearing masks and practicing distancing, stood in line for hours. The two statewide judicial candidates whom Republicans were attempting to protect were defeated, but Democratic satisfaction was muted by realization of the price voters had to pay. Some seventy-one cases of COVID-19 among voters and poll workers were linked by Wisconsin health authorities to possible April 7 exposure.[34]

In the meantime, House Democrats were pushing for HAVA funding in the major pandemic relief package passed on March 26. The bill included $400 million in supplemental appropriations (down from a request of $2 billion) and specified that, in addition to the security measures envisioned in the 2018 and 2020 appropriations, states could use the funds to ensure that the right and ability to vote would not be impaired, regardless of the state of the pandemic come November. This mainly would require expanding the availability and ease of absentee voting by mail—"vote at home" we called it—but also could include expanded hours and locations for early voting; automatic, same-day, and online registration; and improved voter education.

As the pandemic continued and it became clear that many states were not prepared to avoid what had transpired in Wisconsin, Democrats continued to push for HAVA funding, reduction or removal of state matching requirements, and a vote-by-mail mandate nationwide. Republicans resisted; mail-in ballots "don't work out well for Republicans," Trump tweeted in the midst of the Wisconsin turmoil.[35] Added to the GOP's history of voter suppression in the states and seeming tolerance of the prospect of foreign interference, the pandemic crisis, rather than presenting a common threat calling for a common effort, seemed likely to deepen the partisan divide on questions of electoral reform.

The difficulty of overcoming such partisan divisions does not make the reform agenda—from fair rules for drawing districts, to financing elections in ways that avoid undue influence and serve the public interest, to ensuring the right to vote, the ability to vote under adverse circumstances, and the integrity of election processes—any less vital to the legitimacy of our political system and everything that it produces. The elements of reform are interdependent, and many of them have reached a crisis point. The post-2016 threats and dangers are especially urgent and severe, but dealing with them will inevitably direct attention to a broader range of reform challenges that have long been accumulating and are equally relevant to the health of our democracy.

Notes

1 478 US 30 (1986) at 44. The account that follows draws on L. Paige Whitaker, *Congressional Redistricting Law: Background and Recent Court Rulings*, Congressional Research Service, Library of Congress, March 23, 2017.
2 509 US 630 (1993) and 517 US 899 (1996).
3 532 US 234 (2001) at 258.
4 See David Daley, *Rat F***ked: The True Story Behind the Secret Plan to Steal America's Democracy* (New York: Liveright Publishing, 2016), pp. 35–38.

5 Ibid., p. xviii. On the North Carolina effort, see chap. 3.

6 Ibid., p. 41.

7 *Cooper v. Harris*, 132 S. Ct. 1455 (2017). Justice Elena Kagan, writing for the majority, recalled Rep. Mel Watt's account of what he told the NC senator in charge of redistricting: "I'm getting 65 percent of the vote in a 40 percent black district. If you ramp my [BVAP] to over 50 percent, I'll probably get 80 percent of the vote.... That's not what the [VRA] was designed to do." (fn.10).

8 Anne Blythe, "League of Women Voters Challenges NC Congressional Districts as Partisan Gerrymander," *Charlotte Observer*, September 22, 2016.

9 *Rucho v. Common Cause* and *Lamone v. Benisek*, 139 S. Ct. 2484 (2019).

10 *Rucho*, slip opinion at 2, 21, 30; dissent at 1.

11 *Harper v. Lewis*, North Carolina Superior Court, *Order* on Injunctive Relief, October 28, 2019, at 4, 8, 12, 14. For an overview of state initiatives in the wake of *Rucho*, see Sam Wang, "How We Can Still Prevent Gerrymandering," *New York Times*, July 14, 2019, p. SR-5.

12 Melissa Broughton, "State Court Cites Time Constraints in Approving Congressional Maps that Are 'Not Perfect,'" *NC Policy Watch*, December 2, 2019.

13 Arizona, California, Colorado, Michigan, New Jersey, New York, Hawaii, Montana, Idaho, Utah, and Washington utilize nonpartisan or bipartisan commissions to draw congressional maps initially. Ohio and Missouri use commissions to approve or revise plans. Iowa employs a nonpartisan Legislative Services Agency to draw districts according to strict criteria. Associated Press, "Number of States Using Redistricting Commissions Growing," apnews.com, March 21, 2019.

14 HR 1, 116th Congress, Section 2413.

15 424 US 1 (1976), Justice Byron White's lone dissent, finding limitations on campaign expenditures to be both "essential if the aims of the [Federal Election Campaign] Act were to be achieved fully" (p. 248) and capable of withstanding First Amendment scrutiny, is still convincing, but it represents a minority judicial view.

16 Reps. Castle and Price et al., Brief of *Amici Curiae, Mitch McConnell et al. v. Federal Election Commission et al.*, US Supreme Court, August 5, 2003, pp. 15–16. The decision may be found at 540 US 93 (2003).

17 Castle and Price Brief, pp. 26–30; *McConnell v. FEC* at 147, upholding section 311 of the law.

18 *Citizens United v. Federal Election Commission*, 558 US 310 (2010); and *Speechnow.org v. Federal Election Commission*, 599 F. 3d 686 (DC Cir. 2010).

19 Fred Wertheimer, "The Legacy of *Citizens United* Has Been Destructive; We Need Campaign Finance Reform," *Washington Post*, January 20, 2020.

20 *McCutcheon v. Federal Election Commission*, 572 US 185 (2014). The $2,700 limit on what an individual could contribute to individual campaigns was left intact. For an overview of other liberalizing measures, see R. Sam Garrett, "The State of Campaign Finance Policy: Recent Developments and Issues for Congress," Congressional Research Service, Library of Congress, December 13, 2018.

21 *Shelby County v. Holder*, 570 US 529 (2013) at 554, 593. See www.brennancenter.org, "How We Can Restore the Voting Rights Act," August 6, 2018, (excerpted from Brennan Center for Justice's Solutions 2018 Democracy Agenda, eds. Wendy Weiser and Alicia Bannon); and Wendy Weiser and Max Feldman, "The State of Voting 2018," June 5, 2018, Brennan Center for Justice at New York University School of Law.

22 www.brennancenter.org, "The Effects of *Shelby County v. Holder*," August 6, 2018.

23 *NC State Conference of the NAACP v. McCrory*, 831 F. 3d 204 (4th Cir., 2016) at 214, 219. The US Supreme Court denied certiorari in 2017 without ruling on the merits of the case.
24 To say nothing of the constitutional scheme's link to slavery. "In a direct election system, the North would outnumber the South, whose [half-million] slaves ... of course could not vote. But the Electoral College... instead let each southern state count its slaves, albeit with a two-fifths discount, in computing its share of the overall count." Akhil Reed Amar, "The Troubling Reason the Electoral College Exists," *Time*, November 26, 2018.
25 David E. Price, "The Way We Choose Presidential Nominees: Problems and Prospects," in Jack Citrin and David Karol, eds., *Nominating the President* (New York: Rowman & Littlefield, 2009), p. 142.
26 H. Res. 667, 106th Congress. See the accompanying remarks in *Congressional Record*, daily ed., November 14, 2000, pp. E2101–02.
27 Special Committee on Election Reform, Democratic Caucus, *Revitalizing Our Nation's Election System* (Washington, DC, 2001).
28 Matthew Murray, "Holt's Rush to Fairer Elections," *Roll Call*, June 25, 2007.
29 Arthur L. Burris and Eric A. Fischer, *The Help America Vote Act and Election Administration: Overview and Selected Issues for the 2016 Election*, Congressional Research Service, Library of Congress, October 18, 2016, p. 13.
30 Mueller, *Report on the Investigation into Russian Interference in the 2016 Presidential Election* (Washington, DC, 2019), pp. 1, 50; David E. Sanger and Catie Edmondson, "Russia Targeted Election Systems in All 50 States, Report Finds," *New York Times*, July 25, 2019.
31 Jordain Carney, "GOP Senator Blocks Bill Aimed at Preventing Russia Election Meddling," *The Hill*, December 10, 2019. The bill was the DETER (Defending Elections from Threats by Establishing Redlines) Act, S 2313, sponsored by Chris Van Hollen (D-Maryland) and Marco Rubio (R-Florida).
32 Mike McIntire, Michael Wines, and Alan Blinder "An Election Grid Rife with Flaws Shows Them All," *New York Times*, November 18, 2018, p. 1.
33 *Republican National Committee et al. v. Democratic National Committee et al.*, 589 US____(2020); Ginsburg slip opinion at 6. The majority's opinion, longtime student of the Court Linda Greenhouse observed, gave "barely a hint... of the turmoil in the country." "The Supreme Court Fails Us," *New York Times*, April 9, 2020.
34 madison.com, May 16, 2020.
35 Quoted in Greenhouse, "Supreme Court Fails Us."

4   At Home in the House

"It was like being dropped into the jungle and having to learn to survive," a freshman senator told Richard Fenno after his first year in office. "Gradually, you cut out a little place for yourself, a clearing in which you can live."[1] I would not have given quite as dramatic a description of my first year, perhaps because my staff work in the Senate, my years of studying congressional policymaking, and my previous work in national politics had taught me what to expect. Still, the adjustments confronting any new member are profound: from campaigning to organizing legislative and constituent services offices, from the expectations and demands of one job or profession to those of another, from hometown family life to the bifurcated existence of an airborne commuter.

I will describe some of these transitions in the present chapter as well as the further task identified by Fenno's senator: securing a niche within the institution, cutting out and cultivating "a clearing in which you can live." The immediate challenge is to secure a desirable committee assignment—a challenge heightened by both the knowledge that it can decisively shape one's subsequent career and uncertainty as to how the assignment decisions are going to be made. It is a rapid and jarring transition, from the electoral areas to the arena of House politics—equally political, equally challenging, but often quite dissimilar in the skills it requires and the behavior it rewards.

Setting up Shop

My experience in Senator Bartlett's office, where the needs of Alaskans were attended to diligently, impressed on me the importance of having a competent, energetic staff and a well-managed office. I learned the same lesson in a less positive way through campaign experiences with a couple of senators who had reputations for poor constituent services and slack staff operations—reputations that proved hard to shake and very damaging politically. I therefore devoted a great deal of time to staffing decisions in the three months following my election.

I decided to ask my campaign manager, Michelle Smith, who also had some Hill experience, to come to Washington as my chief of staff. She and

I were given a tiny cubicle in which to interview prospective aides and handle calls and letters until permanent office space was made available on the first day of the new congress. We immediately confronted thousands of pieces of mail that had accumulated since the election, with no possible way of responding until mid-January. Two items—requests for me to back an American Airlines application for a London gateway from Raleigh-Durham Airport and letters opposing the start-up of a nuclear power plant in my district—had arrived in such volume that we decided to use an outside mail house to send these responses before we set up our office. Unfortunately, the mail house confused the two lists, sending several hundred power plant responses to people who had written about the airport! Consequently, we were more than ready to get our own house in order when the day finally came to move into my assigned office.

Freshmen are at the bottom of the list when it comes to selecting offices, which are assigned on the basis of length of service in the House, regardless of party. I ended up in the Longworth House Office Building, the middle of the three House office buildings in terms of location and age. The main drawback of my office was that its three rooms were not adjacent; the third room was an annex on another floor. We lived with this space and another divided Longworth office until I was able to choose a unified space at the beginning of my third term. This contrasts markedly with my present office in the Rayburn building with a beautiful Capitol view—a location I finally attained after 13 terms!

I deployed my staff in a fashion that is typical of the House, setting up three district offices and locating most constituent service functions there. My main district office has always been in Raleigh, with smaller constituent service offices located initially in Asheboro and Chapel Hill and later in other places as the district's configuration changed. Total district staff has numbered six to ten, including field representatives, who stay in touch with a range of local organizations and agencies and help me get around, and casework specialists, who assist constituents in dealing with federal agencies.

Our Washington staff operations have changed more over the years. Gene Conti, a longtime friend with experience at the Office of Management and Budget and the Treasury Department, became chief of staff in mid-1987 when Michelle Smith left for law school; he served for seven years. He was initially assisted by an office manager, who also handled my personal schedule; a legislative director, who focused on my committee work; a press secretary; a computer operator; a receptionist; and three legislative assistants, who covered specific issue-areas and helped us cope with the flood of mail.

My allowance for staff salaries in 1987 was just over $400,000. I was well aware of the need to hire relatively senior people with Washington experience for the top positions. For most other staff positions I hired younger people hoping to gain in experience and exposure what I couldn't pay them in dollars. Most had helped in some fashion with the campaign and were invested in my success by virtue of that experience. Although I did not make it an absolute condition, every staff member, as it developed, had some past or present North Carolina connection.

My appointment to the Appropriations Committee in 1991 required a major reorganization of staff responsibilities. It also entitled me to an additional allowance for staff, which I used to add a staff member and also, for the first time in four years, to give the staff decent raises in pay. My fourth term brought further changes as I gained appointment to the Budget Committee, along with an additional staff allowance. I also attained enough seniority to move into the Rayburn Building, an early-1960s behemoth that a leading critic once called "the biggest star-spangled architectural blunder of our time."[2] Rayburn was indeed the least attractive of the three House office buildings externally, but it had larger suites that were more easily outfitted with modern office equipment.

I had remarkably little staff turnover during my first four terms, but after my 1994 loss, staff members moved, retired, or took other positions. I was able to bring back several key staff members when I returned to the House in 1997, but three-quarters of my staff were new. As chief of staff I chose Billy Moore, who had held that position for Jim Chapman (D-Texas), a colleague from the class of 1986 who had just retired. I brought eight people onto the Washington and district staffs who had proved their mettle during the 1996 campaign. My seniority (I was considered a fifth-term member for purposes of office selection) still entitled me to a Rayburn suite, but my Appropriations slot no longer brought with it any additional staff allowances. The Republicans, on assuming control of the House in 1995, had eliminated the second of the add-on staff positions for appropriators, which was a reasonable cost-cutting move. But they had also denied the first add-on staff position to those on the bottom third of the committee's seniority ladder, which did not make sense, since we were the members who had least access to subcommittee staff and thus needed extra help the most.

When Billy Moore left for the private sector after the 2000 election, I asked Jean-Louise Beard, who had worked her way up from computer operator to senior appropriations aide, to succeed him as chief of staff. She oversaw our adjustment to the post 9-11 era, as security concerns brought changes in the day-to-day operations of individual member offices, and managed our reallocation of staff resources as I assumed leadership positions on Appropriations and the House Democracy Partnership. She also concentrated on adjusting to my ever-shifting district lines—particularly the addition of Fayetteville in 2011—and improving Washington-district coordination. Upon her retirement in 2015, I appointed another longtime staff member, Asher Hildebrand, to the top position. He has been my only chief of staff to reside in the district, dividing his time between Raleigh and Washington. This arrangement worked by virtue of his long experience on the DC staff and our reliance on an able deputy chief of staff to handle day-to-day Washington operations. I returned to a DC-based chief of staff in

2019, when Hildebrand took a teaching position at Duke's Sanford School of Public Policy and was succeeded by Justin Wein.

Overall, my staff of seventeen full-time members and one who divides her time between congressional and campaign offices is about the same size as the one I had in 1987, but it is more experienced, more focused on appropriations and foreign policy, and faces a far heavier and more varied communications load and a transformed media environment (see Chapter 9). Our district office caseload has also grown larger, with veterans affairs and immigration being the main areas of growth.

My current staff is also somewhat better paid; total compensation for 2020 was $1.18 million, a variable amount that must now be carved out of an overall office expense allocation, plus an Appropriations allowance of about $173,000. Still, my office, like most others, manages much of its workload with younger staffers for whom pay is not the job's major attraction. We have tried to maintain a strong ethic of responsiveness to constituents in dealing with both legislative inquiries and casework, and have utilized an annual all staff meeting, regular weekly staff meetings, weekly reports, and other devices to foster accountability and communication among our three (sometimes four) offices. The "mission statement" we formulated in 1999 encapsulates the goals that successive chiefs of staff, district managers, and I have pursued through sixteen terms:

> I want to help build a community—in North Carolina and the nation—where people have a sense of expanding opportunity and common purpose, nurtured in high-quality schools, safe neighborhoods, good housing, accessible health care, and security for old age.

> I want to help make government an instrument of our common purpose by being an activist legislator, encouraging staff entrepreneurship, developing and pushing clear funding priorities, actively engaging my constituents, advocating for those who need help, and conducting myself and running our office in a way that builds confidence and solidifies support.

Transitions

As my wife Lisa and I first weighed the decision to run, we talked with two couples, who described the quite different ways they had coped with the demands congressional life placed on their families. One family lived in Washington, and the member made sporadic weekend trips back to the district; the other family lived in the district, to which the member returned every weekend. Although each couple claimed that their arrangement worked satisfactorily and though we knew that roughly equal numbers of members chose each pattern, we never doubted what would be best for us: to keep our main residence in Chapel Hill. This decision spared us the rigors of the Washington real estate market and the family upheavals attendant to moving. I rented an apartment on Capitol Hill, walked to work, and settled into a pattern of heading for the airport after the final vote was taken on the House floor each week, usually late on Thursday or Friday afternoon. We chose this option partly because of the easy commute—less than three hours door to door, with several nonstop flights each day—and because my status as a freshman from a swing district required maximizing my presence at home. It also suited our family situation, since a move would have been difficult for our teenage children. Although relocating to the Washington area would have been relatively comfortable for Lisa, who grew up there, she preferred the idea of frequent visits to the capital rather than moving our primary residence. As it turned out, the visits were not so frequent, thanks to the soaring cost of airline tickets and to her demanding jobs, first as assistant to the mayor of Chapel Hill and then as executive director of North Carolinians Against Gun Violence.

The fact that we already were familiar with Washington and had a number of friends in the area made our decision easier, for we had less to lose by not electing to live there. We have missed out on a certain amount of social and family contact with my colleagues. But even members who live in Washington travel to their districts frequently, and there is far less weekend socializing than there used to be. And the wear and tear of weekly commuting is not overwhelming, once a routine is established. In fact, I have found that compartmentalizing my life works rather well. When I am in Washington, usually Monday through Thursday or Tuesday through Friday, I generally work twelve-to-fifteen-hour days, often staying at my office into the night. But when I head for home, I concentrate on district matters and family life. I can't imagine that it would have worked as well in reverse: dragging home late when Congress is in session and then heading for North Carolina on the weekends, leaving the family behind. But these are highly personal decisions, and if our children had been at a different stage or if my commute had required multiple connecting flights, the options might have looked very different.

Becoming a member of the House also alters the roles and routines associated with one's previous career. I took a special interest in Fenno's interview with a freshman senator who had been a college professor. "Life in the Senate," he said, "is the antithesis of academic life."[3] I would not put it quite that way, since this viewpoint both exaggerates the orderliness and tranquility of modern academic life and underestimates the extent to which one can impose a modicum of order on life in the Congress. Still, few jobs present as many diverse and competing demands as does service in Congress.

Consider, for example, my schedule for four typical days in May, 2019, reprinted here with a few explanatory notes (see Table 4.1). This was a time of year when appropriations markups were getting underway. I thus spent some ten hours in full committee markups and at least six hours with staff going over our draft T-HUD bill line by line. The week also included two

Table 4.1 Member's Typical Daily Schedule

Tuesday, May 7, 2019
10:00 Adjutant General Greg Lusk, NC National Guard Headquarters
12:30 Flight to Washington
 3:00 Azerbaijan Ambassador Sulemanov
 3:30 Executives from Aireon, Inc.
 4:00 Representatives of NC Emergency Management Association
 4:30 NC Board members, Environmental Defense Fund
 5:00 T-HUD staff re-prepare bill for markup
 6:30 First votes of week, House floor
 7:00 Pre-markup meeting, State and Foreign Operations (SFOPS) Appropriations
       Subcommittee Democrats
 7:45 Dinner with Israeli Rabbi Michael Melchior, hosted by Center for Middle
       East Peace

Wednesday, May 8, 2019
 8:00 Democratic Policy Group
       Guest: former Census Bureau Director Robert Groves re. 2020 Census
 9:00 Democratic Caucus
 9:45 NC representatives, American Council of Engineering Companies
10:00 Pre-markup meeting, Appropriations Democrats
10:45 Appropriations Committee markup
       Labor-Health and Human Services-Education (LHHS) [continues to 5:00 P.M.]
 2:30 IBM executives from NC
 3:00 Moldova Ambassador Balan
 6:00 Reception: Science Coalition—Introduce Rep. GK Butterfield for award
 7:00 Reception: Environmental Defense Fund
 7:30 Democratic Caucus Dinner at the home of Rep. Rosa DeLauro
       Guest: Susan Glasser of *New Yorker*

Thursday, May 9, 2019
 8:00 Aspen Institute Breakfast
       Topic: Tomorrow's Infrastructure with Marianne Kah, Center for Global
       Energy Policy, Columbia University
 9:00 Board meeting, Open World Leadership Center, Library of Congress
10:00 Pre-markup meeting, Appropriations Democrats
10:30 Appropriations Committee markup: Legislative Branch
11:30 Appropriations Committee markup: Military Construction-Veterans
       Administration (MilCon-VA) [continues to 3:00 P.M.]
 1:00 Group of 14 Oak Scholars, NC State University
 3:00 T-HUD bill preparation
 4:00 Task Force on House Chaplaincy
 5:00 Congressional App Challenge: Demonstration Day for district winners
 6:00 NC delegation leads moment of silence on House floor for victims of UNC-
       Charlotte shooting
 7:00 T-HUD bill preparation

Friday, May 10
 8:00 SFOPS Appropriations Subcommittee markup
 9:00 Help manage floor debate on HR 2157, Disaster Supplemental
       Appropriations
12:30 T-HUD bill preparation
 2:30 American Public Media phone interview
 4:15 Flight to Raleigh-Durham (delayed)

---

ambassadorial appointments related to the work of the House Democracy Partnership (HDP) and three forums described later in this chapter: the Democratic Policy Group (DPG), a Rosa DeLauro dinner, and an Aspen breakfast.

This week was somewhat past the peak season for North Carolina groups making their annual visits to Washington, but I saw several such delegations either in my office or in a side-room during committee markups. Since assuming T-HUD leadership, I have taken more meetings from organizations and local governments with a stake in our bill, and I still try to meet with most groups registering general policy concerns as long as a representative from my district is in the group. In order to accommodate all these meetings, I have reconfigured my office, splitting the traditional member's office in half to create space for a conference area. This permits us to schedule two meetings at once and for me to alternate between them.

This schedule lists only events and meetings I actually attended. Others were covered by staff when I was in committee meetings or on the House floor. The schedule does not capture trips to the floor for votes or the phone calls, media interviews, and staff conferences scattered throughout the day. Unfortunately, it is typical in one additional respect: my return flight home was delayed three hours!

This sheer busyness in Washington, as well as at home, surpasses what almost all members experienced in their previous careers and requires specific survival techniques. Most important, you must set priorities—separate matters in which you want to invest considerable time and energy from those you wish to handle perfunctorily or not deal with personally.[4] Confronted with two or three simultaneous subcommittee hearings, a member often has a choice: pop in on each of them for fifteen minutes or choose one and remain long enough to learn and contribute something. It is also essential to delegate a great deal to staff and to develop a good mutual understanding within the office about what requires the member's personal direction and attention.

Still, there are no management techniques that can make a representative's life totally predictable or controllable or that can convert a congressional office into a tidy bureaucracy. A member (or aide) who requires that kind of control—who cannot tolerate, for example, being diverted to talk to a visiting school class or to hear out a delegation of homebuilders or social workers—is in the wrong line of work. Fortunately, House offices are small enough to permit a flexible mode of operation. My previous managerial experience with the North Carolina Democratic Party was on a similar scale. I was also influenced by my time in Senator Bartlett's office, including recollections of how much personal recognition from the senator or inclusion in key meetings boosted my morale. I therefore tried to strike a balance that achieved a measure of efficiency and order, enabled senior staff to effectively direct and mentor younger staff, and yet was conducive to informal brainstorming and non-hierarchical personal interaction.

My academic career influenced my adaptation as a member of Congress in other ways as well. Certainly my previous study and staff experience gave me an inclination toward "policy entrepreneurship" and some understanding of how to undertake it (see Chapter 5). I naturally gravitated toward major domestic issues—education, housing, transportation, research—and eventually foreign policy, and felt well equipped by both background and temperament for work on the Appropriations and Budget Committees. Stylistically, I have been fastidious about what goes out of the office under my name. I spent far more time than the average member reviewing and editing mail and press statements, especially in my early years, and sometimes have found it difficult to delegate speechwriting to staff. Some of this stems from knowing I have a relatively well-informed and demanding constituency, but the habits and standards (and the streak of compulsiveness) I developed during my years in academic life are no doubt also partly responsible.

My background also has predisposed me toward an activist, but selective and specialized, legislative style. Speaker Sam Rayburn famously distinguished "show horses" from "workhorses" in the House, while expressing his clear preference for the latter. Today, the norms of specialization, apprenticeship, and deference that once held show horse behavior in check have weakened considerably, and even self-effacing workhorses must pay more attention to courting the media and building public support. But the rough stylistic distinction still holds, and the workhorse label is one that most Appropriations members would claim for themselves and would apply to the committee.[5] This has been my own preferred style. There is still something of the student in me, with an urge to master the assignment at hand, and although the committee system is not what it used to be, it continues to encourage and reward this sort of behavior. In my early terms, I concentrated on a limited number of initiatives, mostly in my committee areas, on which I could work in a concerted fashion. This was a sensible strategy for a junior member, but it also stemmed from my preference, rooted in prior experience, to focus on a manageable number of projects and operate from a substantial base of knowledge. I later channeled more and more of my policy work through the Appropriations Committee where, most of the time, value is still placed on the workhorse virtues of careful preparation, practicality, and a spirit of accommodation.

My academic background and inclinations have also led me to seek out serious policy discussions beyond standard caucus and committee fare. Early on, I began attending the Wednesday morning sessions of the Democratic Budget Group (DBG), an informal discussion group first organized in 1983 by two freshman Democrats, Buddy MacKay of Florida and Tim Penny of Minnesota, as the Reagan-era budget deficits began to mount. I have cochaired the group since 1989. We still focus on budget and economic issues, but also venture into foreign policy and other current topics, with recent guests ranging from former Secretary of State Madeline Albright to former Transportation Secretary Anthony Foxx, Federal Commissions Commissioner

Jessica Rosenworcel, former Federal Reserve Chairman Ben Bernanke, and national columnists David Brooks and E.J. Dionne. In 2019, we renamed the forum the Democratic Policy Group (DPG) to reflect this broader focus.

I have also greatly valued the Thursday morning sessions of the Aspen Institute's Congressional Program, founded by former senator Dick Clark (D-Iowa) and currently led by former representative Dan Glickman (D-Kansas). These bicameral, bipartisan discussions usually focus on foreign policy and draw on a variety of academic specialists and veteran governmental and diplomatic leaders. Three or four times a year, Aspen also organizes overseas trips premised on a highly successful formula: convene twenty House members and senators with interest or expertise in a particular issue, organize sessions with an array of outside experts, and expect four days of undivided attention to topics ranging from political Islam, to Russian and European relations, to the U.S.-China relationship. I have attended one or two of these conferences annually during most of my time in Congress and have found them absolutely invaluable in deepening my policy understanding and in building working relationships with members on both sides of the aisle. Several of these trips were cancelled in 2020 when the coronavirus struck, but Aspen proved remarkably fast on its feet, organizing frequent Zoom meetings for members with outstanding speakers on public health, foreign policy, and other topics.

Other such opportunities abound for members inclined to seek them out. The Library of Congress, underwritten by Carlyle Group founder David Rubenstein, has for several years hosted bicameral, bipartisan dinner discussions in the Library's Great Hall featuring astute interviews by Rubenstein of biographers and other authors on significant figures and movements in American history. We Democrats are also indebted to our colleague Rosa DeLauro (D-Connecticut) for a long-running series of dinner discussions at her home on Capitol Hill, featuring talks by a variety of guests elucidating major issues and political challenges.

Finally, in addition to transitioning from one career and lifestyle to another, every member must also make the sometimes jarring transition from campaigning to governing. This transition is perhaps better seen as a balancing act, since it recurs every two years and requires constant adjustment.

For me, the shift from campaign trail to congressional life was emotionally dramatic but not especially problematic, particularly as I began to develop a legislative record that squared with my campaign themes. I never got myself into the kind of binds some of my colleagues did when, in the course of their campaigns, they got pressed into taking "the pledge" to never, ever raise anyone's taxes or to take other absolute positions. In my early terms I was especially wary of votes that might be construed as reversals of position or might otherwise provide material for thirty-second ads. Concerning "hot button" issues, I was often reminded of the dictum, "If you have to explain it, you're already in trouble." But I gradually got more relaxed about this, realizing that no amount of caution can prevent an opponent's media consultants from finding something on which to base an outrageous ad, that these ads can often be effectively countered, and that it is simply intolerable to have one's life and work dominated by memories of the last (or fears of the next) campaign. Admittedly, having an increasingly Democratic district has facilitated my attitude adjustment.

As I will argue later in this book, maintaining continuity—between campaigning and governing linking what I say on the campaign trail to what I do in office—is not merely a tactical challenge for a politician. It is a democratic necessity, and the yawning gaps that we have increasingly seen threaten both public trust and accountability.

The tension between campaigning and governing has some positive aspects, however. We rightly decry campaign appeals and tactics that deceive and distract, making responsive governance less rather than more likely. But the sensitivities and skills developed in campaigns often are of continuing use in the Congress, prompting proactive efforts to interpret and engage. I found that my campaign experience—and the realization that another campaign was soon to come—sometimes acted as a counterweight to my inclination simply to do a workmanlike job on the task before me.

Traditional congressional norms, reinforced in my case by my career background, encourage members to choose a few matters for specialization and to work persistently, mainly out of the limelight, to shape policy or obtain funding in these areas. But constituents expect their representatives to be their voices and votes on the full range of policy matters, and members cannot realistically expect constituents to understand and appreciate their policymaking efforts if they do not make the effort to interpret, even dramatize, them. Such interpretation, moreover, cannot simply be a policy dissertation; it must show empathy and connection with larger values and goals. In these respects, the sensitivities and skills acquired in the campaign are of constant relevance.

That, at least, is the way it has worked for me. My background in teaching and research has proved serviceable in many ways. Fortunately, I was forced out of those routines for a demanding twenty-month campaign and developed the broad-gauged knowledge of national issues, the sensitivity to constituency needs and views, and the ability to communicate that were required by that effort. This does not mean that I want or need a mudslinging campaign every two years! But I believe that, for much of what the contemporary member of Congress needs to do, the experience and exposure offered by recurring campaigns, far from being diversions, are absolutely essential.

Securing a Niche

My first extended conversation with the new Speaker of the House, Jim Wright, occurred during orientation week, one month after the 1986 election. We met to discuss committee assignments, officially the purview of the party's 33-member Steering and Policy Committee, but in reality heavily influenced if not controlled by the Speaker—particularly a Speaker as assertive as Jim Wright.

Wright had visited my district once during the campaign. My memory of the visit was mainly of the relief I felt when it was over. Wright's staff had told us on very short notice that he would be coming on a Saturday afternoon, when, as luck would have it, both the University of North Carolina and North Carolina State had home football games. Our thought, in throwing together a fundraising barbecue, was less of the money we could raise than of how we could get enough people together to convince our guest we were not dying on the vine. We erected a Potemkin Village facade, complete with haystacks and a bluegrass band. After the event, I spirited Wright off to the airport, but en route, he punctured his leg on a wire protruding from the seat of my well-worn station wagon. My embarrassment exceeded his injury, but it was the kind of day that seems much funnier in retrospect than it did at the time.

Memories of this encounter notwithstanding, Wright was cordial but noncommittal about my prospects when we met in December. I approached the conversation with some trepidation. I knew better than to request one of the three "exclusive" committees—Appropriations, Ways and Means, and Rules, termed exclusive because their members were required to drop all other standing committee assignments—for they were virtually off-limits to first-term members. There was intense competition for these powerful positions, and party and committee leaders ordinarily wished to take the measure of a member before placing him or her in such a critical spot. A story had circulated among our class about a freshman who had been filmed for a television feature as he made his initial rounds. He had told Speaker O'Neill of his desire to be appointed to Appropriations, Ways and Means, or Rules, and the camera had caught the Speaker as his eyes rolled heavenward. So I knew what not to request. But the assignment I most wanted—to the Energy and Commerce Committee—also seemed likely to be out of reach, and I was uncertain how hard to press my case before falling back on a second choice.

I had a particular personal interest in Energy and Commerce. My time with Senator Bartlett had involved extensive work with the Senate Commerce Committee, of which he was a senior member, and my academic work had included a general study of both the House and Senate Commerce Committees and an examination of the House Committee's oversight role.[6] The Energy and Commerce Committee, moreover, had an exceedingly broad jurisdiction—health, communications, energy, the environment, consumer protection, transportation, and securities and exchanges—much of it vitally important to North Carolina and to my district in particular. Former North Carolina representatives James Broyhill, a Republican, and Richardson Preyer, a Democrat, had risen to ranking positions on the committee, but by 1987 the state had no Energy and Commerce member and had not had a Democratic member for six years.

All this was to no avail. Energy and Commerce was on its way to becoming a fourth exclusive committee by virtue of the increasing salience of its jurisdiction and the success of its chairman, John Dingell (D-Michigan), in carving out an assertive and expansive role. I received no encouragement from Wright, suggesting that the rumors were probably true that he and Dingell were prepared to endorse three members, none of whom was a freshman, for the available Energy and Commerce slots. I soon decided it was time to shift to plan B, to settle on a realistic backup choice and let my alternative preferences be known.

As I surveyed the available alternatives and considered the interests of North Carolina and my district, I decided to pursue assignments on the committees on Banking, Finance, and Urban Affairs (now called Financial Services) and on Science, Space, and Technology. With the crucial help of my regional representative on Steering and Policy, Butler Derrick (D-South Carolina), I secured both assignments. I also received an appointment to the Small Business Committee, along with other freshmen for whom party leaders presumably thought the assignment would be politically helpful.

This was as strong a combination as I could realistically have hoped for, and I made good use of each assignment. The Banking Committee presented the greatest challenge in several respects: the complexity of its subject matter; the number of major policy questions on the agenda; the intricacy of committee politics, both internal and in relation to outside groups; the depth of its leadership difficulties, which continued despite a change in committee chairs in 1989; and, as my 1990 campaign demonstrated, the political perils associated with the policies under its care, especially savings and loan (S&L) regulation. To my surprise, however, the Banking Committee provided most amenable to my own legislative projects, as I will elaborate in the next chapter.

The Science and Small Business Committees were less torn by conflicting interests than was Banking. Their histories featured promotion and advocacy for American scientific leadership and the well-being of small businesses, missions that often attracted like-minded members to the committees and helped mute partisan conflict. Especially on the Science Committee, however, this tradition of advocacy began in the 1980s to run up against the painful choices imposed by budget constraint. The space station, the ill-fated superconducting supercollider, healthy National Science Foundation budgets—the Science Committee historically and often effectively had said, "We want it all." The trade-offs were difficult to make, and as the committee faced the necessity of setting priorities, its bipartisan promotional consensus came under increasing strain.

On both Science and Small Business, I concentrated initially on securing compatible subcommittee assignments, preferably under young, aggressive subcommittee chairmen who would pursue an expansive agenda and would welcome my participation. I gained the cooperation of Chairman Doug Walgren (D-Pennsylvania) in bringing our Science, Research, and Technology Subcommittee to my district for a day of hearings on workplace literacy and then in developing a legislative proposal to improve curricula and teaching methods in advanced technical training in community colleges (see Chapter 5). On Small Business, I convened hearings in my district on government and military procurement, asking how small, local, and minority businesses could be included in that process more effectively. This too proved to be of lasting importance: I helped secure a full-time Small Business Administration procurement officer for the state, began working with federal installations on the transparency and openness of their procurement operations, and instituted periodic day-long "Marketplace" procurement workshops in the district, which have continued ever since.

As my third term approached, I faced a choice: settle in on Banking and Science and begin to accumulate seniority, or get on the seniority ladder of one of the exclusive committees, where I hoped to serve long-term.

I was inclined toward the latter course, but Energy and Commerce had become an even more unlikely prospect, partly because several intervening appointments had weakened our region's claim for more seats. In the meantime I had shifted my sights toward Appropriations as a more likely assignment and one that ultimately promised more influence over a wide range of critical issues. Our state already had a senior Appropriations member—Bill Hefner, chairman of the Military Construction Subcommittee—but considering the critical balance among Steering and Policy regions, my argument was very strong: we had only two members.

Late in 1988, Derrick, Hefner, and I went to talk with Speaker Wright about my prospects. Wright was not inclined to leave Steering and Policy decisions (or much of anything else) to chance. He had already let it be known that he wanted one of the two Appropriations Committee slots coming open at the beginning of the 101st Congress to go to his fellow Texan, Jim Chapman, and we knew that the second was bound to go to the New England region. We assured the Speaker that we had no desire to challenge his decision, but indicated that I would be seeking the next Appropriations seat that came open. As it turned out, by the time the next Democratic vacancy occurred in March 1990, Wright was no longer Speaker, and the new speaker, Tom Foley, was less inclined than Wright to dictate Steering and Policy decisions, at least on midterm appointments like this one.

The result was a wide-open race for the seat. I decided to run and run hard, for in addition to filling the vacant seat, the race was likely to establish a presumption as to who might get future seats, based on a show of strength this round. A number of other members saw it the same way, including some who were senior to me (Marcy Kaptur of Ohio, Pete Visclosky of Indiana) and some from my own class (David Skaggs of Colorado, Nancy Pelosi of California). I systematically made the rounds among Steering and Policy members, with reactions ranging from pledges of first-ballot support, to promises of later-ballot support, if preferred candidates were eliminated, to a senior member who assured me he had "nothing against me" and seemed to think I should be relieved to hear it.

Kaptur won the vacant seat, benefiting from an effort by Midwestern members (anticipating a loss of seats in the 1991 reapportionment) to shore up their representation and from a concern that Appropriations had very few women members. It was a close contest that required four ballots. My six first-ballot votes were enough to put me in second place, and I held that position throughout, surviving until the last ballot. It was a stronger finish than most had predicted, and I felt encouraged because I had strengthened my position for the next round at the beginning of the 102nd Congress.

Running for Appropriations was an intense and, on the whole, enjoyable experience. I got to know a number of senior members better, and a good deal of camaraderie developed among most of us who were competing. We mostly knew what commitments of support each other had, and what we did not know before the balloting we figured out by comparing notes afterward. Most Steering and Policy members had been careful in what they promised, but for those who had made inconsistent promises to several of us or who had not delivered on their pledges, the secret ballot concealed very little.

Resignations produced two Democratic vacancies on Appropriations for the 102nd Congress, and the slight shift in the balance of party strength in the House produced by the 1990 elections let the leadership add two more Democratic seats. This resulted in four Democratic vacancies—good news for those of us lining up for the race. Party leaders, not particularly pleased with the outcome of the midterm contest—the winner had bucked them on a critical pay raise/ethics vote—were now inclined to make their preferences for Appropriations and other top committee assignments known, and I made it onto their list.

The Steering and Policy decisions were made during the pre-session organizational meetings in December 1990. Larry Smith (D-Florida), a late entry who was beginning his fifth term, led the balloting. I was second, followed by Pelosi and Skaggs. Visclosky fell short with a fifth-place finish, but the leaders promised him their support for the next vacancy to occur. It was therefore a happy outcome, accommodating all of us who had made a serious run for the midterm vacancy. Having survived a rougher than expected 1990 reelection contest, I was gratified to see this exercise in internal House politics turn out successfully as well.

Appropriations subcommittee selection came next. The committee's work is subcommittee-centered, and senior members jealously guard their positions on these panels. Subcommittee chairmanships on the Democratic side (Republicans have different procedures) are based on subcommittee (rather than full committee) seniority, and members are allowed to lock in or "grandfather" two of their previous subcommittee assignments as each new Congress begins. The number of slots is sufficient to allow only relatively senior members to gain seats on a third subcommittee. "Bidding" for vacant subcommittee positions proceeds among new members and any returning members who have given up seats hoping to better their situation. In 1990, we new members at first feared we would have little to choose from, but the addition of a slot to the Defense Subcommittee induced a middle-ranking member to give up his grandfathered rights in order to claim it. This set up a chain reaction down the seniority ladder, with each new member being able to bid successfully for a seat on one of the more sought after subcommittees.

The other new members and I gathered all the information we could and carefully plotted how the bidding for slots was likely to go. My first choice was the Subcommittee on Veterans Affairs, Housing and Urban Development, and Independent Agencies (VA-HUD), which appropriated in both the housing and National Science Foundation areas where I had worked hardest for the past four years. Higher-ranking committee members were unlikely to drop their assignments for this vacancy, but Marcy Kaptur, who ranked just ahead of our group in committee seniority, would likely claim it. As I considered the available vacancies and the likely preferences of those ahead of me in the order of bidding, it became clear that I could secure a seat on the Subcommittee on Transportation and that a seat on Agriculture and Rural Development would still be available to me in the second round of bidding. Additional possibilities opened up in the 103rd Congress: I elected to hold on to Transportation, where I was gaining seniority rapidly because of retirements, and picked up a new second subcommittee with an expansive jurisdiction, Commerce, Justice, State, and the Judiciary (C-J-S).

With the support of party and committee leaders, I also gained assignment in 1993 to one of the Budget Committee seats reserved for Appropriations members. This was one of the few second assignments members of the "exclusive" Appropriations and Ways and Means Committees could hold; the architects of the budget process had provided for such representation as a way of limiting the independence of the Budget Committee. I welcomed the assignments as a way of combining macro- and micro-economic approaches to the budget and expanding my reach as a junior member.

By 1994, I was poised to become third in seniority on the Transportation Appropriations Subcommittee. But I lost my bid for a fifth term, and Democrats lost the House. As I contemplated a comeback effort, I felt that a return to Appropriations had to be part of the equation. I sought and received assurances from the minority leader, Dick Gephardt of Missouri, as well as other party leaders, that I would be first in line. I was well aware that my appropriations accomplishments had been devalued in the political context of 1994, when government was demonized and all spending caricatured as "pork barreling." We had filmed an ad touting my achievements for the district but barely ran it. I also watched with dismay as Speaker Gingrich and the Republic leadership pressed the Appropriations Committee into service of the "revolution," demanding deep funding cuts and insisting that legislative riders be included on appropriations bills.[7] This threatened the tradition of bipartisan comity that had given the committee solidarity, credibility, and strength, both in the House and in relation to the executive. But Appropriations retained more autonomy than most committees in the Republican-controlled House and was still one of the better places for a minority member to be.

Seven Democratic Appropriations slots were opened up by retirements in 1997, more than enough to accommodate me and the five Democrats who had served a term on the committee in 1993–1994 but had been bumped when the shift in party control reduced the number of Democratic seats. Although the number of vacancies removed any potential conflict between me and the members who had been waiting during the previous Congress to reclaim their seats, it did not resolve a more subtle question: what seniority ranking would we have within the committee? This was important in determining the order in which we would bid for subcommittees. In promising displaced members a speedy return to the committee, party leaders apparently didn't consider the possibility that a member like myself, with four years of committee service compared to two years for the others, might return at the same time.

I naturally argued that my four years should trump their two, and I had strong supporters on the Steering Committee.[8] But that view did not prevail, so I ended up five slots below where I would have been had I headed the new cohort and eleven slots below my former position.

In the short run, ironically, this situation led to an improved subcommittee assignment. I had assumed that I would get back on Transportation; there were three vacancies, and it seemed likely that one would be left even when the bidding got around to me. But as the bidding proceeded, one member after another chose Transportation, shutting out that possibility. As I anxiously scanned the board to see what alternatives remained, I was astounded to find that a slot on VA-HUD was still available. This was the subcommittee I had most wanted six years before, relevant to strong district interests in housing, veterans affairs, and the EPA lab under construction in Research Triangle Park (see Chapter 5). I claimed the slot gleefully.

With the reduced number of seats for the minority and my reduced seniority, I had no hope of reclaiming C-J-S as my second subcommittee. I thus chose Treasury-Postal Service instead and decided to stick with the choice in the two succeeding Congresses. This was partly because of its interesting jurisdiction, which included most Treasury Department and White House operations, but also because of the subcommittee's small size, which let members like myself gain seniority and the potential for leadership relatively quickly.

As it turned out, this strategy failed, for reasons I could hardly have anticipated. In the aftermath of the 9/11 terrorist attacks, twenty-two federal agencies were gathered into the new Department of Homeland Security (DHS). In 2003, at the beginning of the 108th Congress, a new Homeland

Security Appropriations Subcommittee was formed to conform with the change. The Treasury-Postal and Transportation Subcommittees, both of which had lost major pieces of jurisdiction to the new subcommittee, were combined into a new Transportation-Treasury Subcommittee.

In the meantime, I had been preparing to serve as ranking Democrat on Treasury-Postal while Steny Hoyer (D-Maryland) took a leave from that position to become Democratic whip. While the normal Democratic practice was to honor subcommittee seniority, the full committee's ranking Democrat, Dave Obey (D-Wisconsin), decided that the members of the Treasury-Postal and Transportation Subcommittees should be placed in a single pool and allowed to bid, in order of full committee seniority, for slots on either of the two new panels. This placed me at a decided disadvantage, compounding the effects of the decision on my full committee ranking made six years earlier. I ended up as second-ranking Democrat on Homeland Security, behind Martin Sabo (D-Minnesota). This was a desirable assignment but a disappointment in terms of my earlier expectation to be a ranking member.

Moving into Leadership

Four years later, the situation changed drastically: I not only became the top Democrat on the Homeland Security Subcommittee upon Sabo's retirement, but became chairman, as Democrats assumed House leadership. This confirmed the wisdom of having chosen the second slot on Homeland Security rather than the fourth slot on Transportation in 2003. Homeland still was not a top choice for many members, but with the consolidation of scattered agencies into a major new department and the national preoccupation with its subject matter, it was receiving increasing budget allocations and participating in wide-ranging and consequential policy debates. Moreover, to be chairman, even of a less sought-after subcommittee, puts one in the ranks of committee leadership. It provides leverage over an important area of national policy and go-to status among fellow members, beyond what secondary membership, even on the most desirable subcommittees, can offer.

I was delighted to take on the job. The Homeland Security Department was ably led by Secretary Michael Chertoff, who understood the necessity of securing cooperation with the new Democratic majority. As detailed in the next chapter, we pushed the administration in major areas—insisting on a more targeted approach to immigration enforcement, for example, and requiring justification for each segment of the Bush administration's proposed border fence. Immigration was our most contentious issue, but not as polarizing as it was later to become; Chertoff, in fact, led the administration's ill-fated 2007 push for bipartisan comprehensive immigration reform.

Dave Obey again became chairman of the full Appropriations Committee. He had leapfrogged over more senior members to become chairman upon Chairman Bill Natcher's (D-Kentucky) death in 1994, but was relegated to the Ranking Member position by the 1994 election. Obey sat *ex officio* on all subcommittees and retained appointment powers over all Democratic staff. But Homeland was not one of his main policy interests, and in any event he honored the tradition of giving subcommittee chairs wide leeway in running their operations.

Beverly Pheto, who had been Sabo's aide in the minority, was appointed "chief clerk," the top subcommittee staff position. She was a strong choice, combining deep budgetary expertise with keen political instincts. She assembled a strong professional staff of five and developed an ambitious agenda of agency hearings—the preparation for which became a crash course for me in the full range of the subcommittee's jurisdiction. I appointed a member of my personal staff, Darek Newby, to work alongside the professional subcommittee staff with a particular eye on North Carolina impacts and connections to my other policy interests.

The election of a Democratic president in 2008 brought a new Homeland Security Secretary, former Arizona Governor Janet Napolitano, and an opportunity to work cooperatively on revamping the Federal Emergency Management Agency (FEMA), still reeling from harsh criticisms of its response to Hurricane Katrina in 2005, and on refining the use of executive discretion in immigration enforcement, necessitated by fading prospects for congressional action on comprehensive reform. Obey, meanwhile, tapped Beverly Pheto to be the full committee's new chief clerk; we replaced her on Homeland with an able veteran from our professional staff, Stephanie Gupta.

The ranking Republican member during my chairmanship was Hal Rogers (R-Kentucky), previous subcommittee and future full committee chairman. Behind him was future subcommittee chair John Carter (R-Texas). We enjoyed cooperative working relationships and generally brought our bills to the floor with bipartisan support. The immigration issue was becoming more divisive, however. After Republicans regained control in 2011, I worked, as ranking Democrat, with Chairman Carter to report bipartisan bills only to have them blown up on the floor in both 2012 and 2013 by extreme anti-immigration amendments that the Republican leadership either could not or would not deflect.

I served four more years as ranking member on Homeland after my chairmanship ended in 2011. But I was biding my time on my second subcommittee, Transportation-HUD (T-HUD), which since 2003 had been led on the Democratic side by members who had been placed ahead of me on the full committee seniority ladder in 1997. My chance came in 2015 with the retirement of T-HUD ranking member Ed Pastor (D-New Mexico). I relinquished the ranking position on Homeland to Lucille Roybal-Allard (D-California). I remained on the subcommittee, however, retaining a strong interest in FEMA and in Department of Homeland Security's research and public health operations. The assignment assumed greater policy importance and a heightened level of conflict with the advent of the

Trump administration and its draconian immigration policies (see Chapter 5).

Assuming leadership on the T-HUD subcommittee took me back to the housing and transportation issues on which I had concentrated during my early years in Congress and which remained vitally important to my district. These are also areas of essential national investment, subject to greater partisan differences than most components of Homeland Security (except immigration). These differences were enshrined in the ten-year spending caps contained in the Budget Control Act (BCA), enacted after the return of the House to Republican control in the 2010 elections (see Chapter 7). It was impossible to get bipartisan support for T-HUD bills which adhered to these caps. During the years of Republican leadership, 2011–2018, we depended on biennial bipartisan budget agreements to lift the caps above BCA levels and let us write our bills to more workable numbers.

While these adjustments in top-line numbers typically came late in the appropriations cycle, accompanied too often by government shutdowns, threatened shutdowns, or other sorts of political drama, we usually proceeded cooperatively once the adjustments had been made. This was facilitated by the fact that the subcommittee chairman, Mario Diaz-Balart (R-Florida), displayed a cooperative style and represented an urban district with pressing transportation and housing needs. I also benefited from a cooperative relationship with Nita Lowey (D-New York), ranking member of the full committee, and from a superb professional staff headed by Kate Hallahan and Joe Carlile along with my in-house T-HUD aide, Sean Maxwell.

In my first term as ranking member, I had the advantage of serving under a Democratic president with outstanding secretaries—Anthony Foxx, from my home state, at Transportation, and Julián Castro at HUD. These relationships became more challenging and, particularly at HUD, sometimes seriously strained under the Trump administration. But we avoided the kind of severe conflict and noncooperation some subcommittees and the departments and agencies under their jurisdiction suffered. In both fiscal years 2018 and 2019, once a budget agreement was reached, Diaz-Balart and I were able to write bills that rejected the administration's deep cuts and elicited widespread bipartisan support.

Then came the 2018 election and my assumption of the chairmanship. We Democrats bypassed the BCA charade and marked up our bills to top-line numbers close to what we assumed another bipartisan budget agreement would eventually produce. Lowey was now full committee chair and Shalanda Young, whose first appropriations job had been with me at Homeland Security in 2007, became chief clerk. They made sure that the allocation given our subcommittee was relatively generous; both parties, after all, had promised to make infrastructure a priority. I was thus able to report a fiscal 2020 bill that built nicely on the advances we had made in 2018 and 2019, fully funding transit "new starts" and rental assistance vouchers, putting additional resources into intercity rail and airport improvements, and stepping up new construction of housing for the elderly and for people with disabilities (see Chapter 5). Diaz-Balart cooperated in assembling this bill, which passed the House on June 26, 2019. But the Republican conference withheld their votes on all appropriations bills in the absence of a budget agreement, and the Republican Senate declined to act as well. When the two-year agreement finally came in August, it required us to cut back on the T-HUD total by some $1.4 billion, but I was able to protect most of our priorities in the final omnibus bill and in the bill we wrote for fiscal 2021 as well.

In 2017, I also gained membership on the State Department and Foreign Operations (SFOPS) subcommittee. By then I had enough seniority not only to get a seat on a third subcommittee but also to bid successfully for SFOPS, which was much sought after. My foreign policy involvement had steadily increased, mainly by virtue of my leadership of the House Democracy Partnership. Membership on SFOPS gave me the opportunity to secure support for HDP, our partner countries, and democracy promotion in general (see Chapter 8). As was the case with Homeland Security, the policies of the Trump administration often cast me and other Democratic SFOPS members in oppositional roles as we defended global health programs and other foreign aid, Middle East diplomacy, and the work of international organizations against draconian cuts and other hostile policies.

Informal Groups and Caucuses

Although members give primary attention to their committee assignments, most also affiliate with a number of the caucuses and other informal member organizations that have proliferated since the mid-1970s. The number of such groups in the House has grown from almost 100 when I was first elected to about 700 today. They reflect the array of interests and constituencies with which members are dealing and the need to find outlets and form alliances beyond the committee and party systems.[9]

When Republicans reorganized the House after the 1994 election, they took aim at these caucuses, particularly the twenty-eight designated legislative service organizations (LSOs) that were allowed to pay staff with moneys transferred from members' office accounts and, in many cases, to occupy space in House office buildings. Critics, with considerable justification, saw partisan motives in the abolition of LSOs. Speaker Gingrich and the new majority were trying to consolidate power and shut down alternative sources of information and advocacy; the most dramatic effect was on the Congressional Black and Hispanic Caucuses, both predominately Democratic in membership. Although a number of LSOs were weakened, only three disbanded entirely and most were reconstituted as congressional member organizations (CMOs), which meant that members' aides could still work part-time on caucus matters. Most of the growth since then has been of smaller caucuses more narrowly focused on specific policy interests or constituencies. These groups of members may seldom meet, but they can be instantly alerted and sometimes mobilized when a policy intervention is called for or a special occasion arises.

Some of these affiliations were of considerable importance to me as I got started. The Congressional Sunbelt Caucus, for example, was a regional, bipartisan LSO, unfortunately destroyed by the "reforms" of 1995, that provided an important outlet for my interests in workplace literacy, infant mortality, and other issues of special relevance to the South. Under the direction of Rep. Hal Rogers (R-Kentucky) and myself, the Caucus's affiliated think tank, the Sunbelt Institute, commissioned a study on workforce needs in the region and the education and training programs required to meet them—important groundwork for my bill establishing the Advanced Technological Education program at the National Science Foundation.[10]

One of the most rapidly growing groups of caucuses in recent years has been those devoted to U.S. relations with specific countries. My first affiliation of this kind was with the Congressional Study Group on Germany, a bipartisan, bicameral organization which I helped found in 1987 and chaired in 1990. I also helped start the House Caucus on India and Indian Americans, encouraged in part by the interests of the growing number of Indian Americans in my district, and participated in the inaugural exchange between the House and India's Lok Sabha in 1999. Subsequently, I have joined a number of caucuses dedicated to strong relations with our HDP partner countries, but have thought it best not to chair or co-chair any one of them. I have, however, co-chaired the Moldova Caucus by virtue of North Carolina's sister state relationship with that country.

Among the most prominent caucuses are those within the two parties, from the GOP's Freedom Caucus to the Progressive Caucus on the Democratic side. I am not a member of any of these groups and am ambivalent about their impact on the congressional parties. For a number of terms, however, I affiliated with the New Democrat Coalition (NDC) and its predecessor, the Mainstream Democratic Forum, caucuses loosely tied to the Democratic Leadership Council (DLC)—a national group of elected officials and other Democratic leaders which attempted to inspire serious policy debate within the party and maintain its broad middle-class appeal. The DLC was chaired by Governor Bill Clinton in 1990–1991 and greatly shaped his agenda as president.[11] I chaired a North Carolina DLC chapter in the early 1990s, mainly using it to organize much-needed discussions of policy and messaging among all the elements of the state party. But I never got fully engaged with the House NDC, and in the early 2000s, as I got busier with leadership responsibilities and underwent some changes in my district's politics and my own views, I let my affiliation lapse.

The largest group of caucuses, sometimes called "personal interest" organizations, enable members to show support for specific issues and groups and to advocate for desired policy and funding outcomes. I have joined many of them and for several congresses have paired with a Republican colleague to co-chair four: the Multiple Sclerosis (MS), Vision, Humanities, and National Service caucuses. In 2019, I joined Rep. Don Young (R-AK) in launching a new America's Languages Caucus to promote the study of world languages. Each of these positions influences my policy and funding advocacy, creates a mutually supportive relationship with advocates organized around these causes, and places me in forums ranging from the American Academy of Arts and Sciences' Commission on the Humanities and Social Sciences to local vision screenings and events honoring AmeriCorps volunteers. In 2020, Doris Matsui (D-CA) and I, as co-chairs of the National Service Caucus, joined with Senator Chris Coons (D-DE) to lead the legislative effort to mobilize and expand AmeriCorps to meet a range of front-line needs created by the COVID-19 pandemic.

Finally, a word about our state delegation. North Carolina's House delegation has for most of the past decade consisted of three Democrats and ten Republicans, a monument to extreme partisan gerrymandering. I became our "dean," or most senior member, upon the retirement of Greensboro Republican Howard Coble in 2015. We have occasionally convened delegation meetings to share information—most often when dealing with a natural disaster—and I have more often called meetings of Democratic members to discuss redistricting and other home-state political and legislative matters. The delegation meets with the governor, state cabinet secretaries, university presidents, and other state leaders when they come to Washington. We frequently come together for breakfasts or luncheons organized by groups such as community college trustees, independent insurance agents, and county commissioners.

Our Democratic delegation has met with some frequency among ourselves and with Clinton and Obama administration officials to discuss federal appointments, particularly over the six years (1993–1998) when the state had no Democratic senator. With or without formal meetings, I see North Carolina colleagues, particularly Democratic colleagues, on the floor daily, exchange information and opinions with them, learn how they are inclining on matters before us, and discuss projects in which we are jointly involved.

Sometimes all members from the state or a region within the state join to express an opinion or make a request—for example, urging the Pentagon to leave the Army Research Office in the Research Triangle Park or backing a bid for an international route by an air carrier from one of the state's major airports. Our staffs worked with the governor's Washington office and with each other to coordinate requests to various agencies for relief and repair after Hurricanes Fran in 1997, Floyd and the attendant floods in 1999, Matthew in 2016, and Florence in 2018. We have frequently counted on well-situated members to carry the ball for the rest of us, for example, Transportation Committee members trying to secure a more favorable formula for the return of Highway Trust Fund moneys to the state;

Agriculture members seeking a fair pricing policy for dairy farmers in our region; or appropriators obtaining funding for harbor dredging, rail corridor improvements, wilderness area purchases, or other projects of statewide significance. I have increasingly played this role in recent years as the state's only appropriator from either party.

The state delegation's role as a reference group is especially important in roll call voting. The party cue is often compelling, of course, and on some votes a member may want to know how other members from the committee of jurisdiction are voting, how members identified as experts on the issue are inclined, and so forth. But on any vote involving a significant division of opinion, I generally check the voting board to see how at least some of my North Carolina Democratic colleagues are recorded. That is a way of double-checking my intended vote, looking for an impact on the state or another consideration that I may have missed.

During my sixteen terms, the collegiality of the North Carolina delegation has fluctuated. I will later describe (see Chapter 5) a rift that occurred in 1993, when our new senator decided to oppose a major federal project in Research Triangle Park (RTP) that had hitherto enjoyed bipartisan support. I also noticed a decline in collegiality on returning to the House in 1997. This was partly a function of the reduction of our Democratic contingent and the departure of several colleagues from both parties with whom I had undertaken common projects. It also reflected the greater polarization in the House as a whole and the decline of moderation in Republican ranks.

While these trends have continued, we have for the most part maintained cordial personal relations and an ability to work together on matters of interest to the state. In early 2020, for example, I joined with two Republican colleagues, Sen. Thom Tillis and Rep. Richard Hudson, in sending a letter to the Trump administration regarding North Carolina's urgent need for more testing kits for coronavirus. There is no denying the political interests and beliefs that divide us, which often discourage efforts to persuade or even to communicate on divisive issues. But we know that no one understands or cares about home like one's home state colleagues and that cordial, cooperative relationships within a delegation can be an important resource for the members and an asset for the state.

Notes

1 Richard F. Fenno Jr., "Adjusting to the U.S. Senate," in Gerald C. Wright Jr., Leroy N. Rieselbach, and Lawrence C. Dodd, eds., *Congress and Policy Change* (New York: Agathon, 1986), p. 142.

2 Ada Louise Huxtable, "Complaints Grow on New House Office Building," *New York Times*, March 20, 1965, p. 32.

3 Fenno, "Adjusting to the U.S. Senate," p. 126.

4 On this point, Fenno's ex-professor seems to agree: "You need to establish a set of priorities.... Don't let yourself be a piece of cloth pulled at from every side. Don't let yourself unravel." "Adjusting to the U.S. Senate," p. 128.

5 For an attempt to operationalize the show horse–workhorse typologies and discuss the conditions of their occurrence, see James L. Payne, "Show Horses and Work Horses in the United States House of Representatives," *Polity*, Spring 1980, pp. 428–456. Payne found that the orientations are indeed distinctive, with few members ranking high on both "legislative work" and "publicity" indexes. He also found evidence that "being a show horse pays off electorally" and is far less costly than it once was in terms of advancement within the House.

6 David E. Price et al., *The Commerce Committees* (New York: Grossman, 1975); Price, "The Impact of Reform: The House Commerce Subcommittee on Oversight and Investigations," in Leroy N. Rieselbach, ed., *Legislative Reform: The Policy Impact* (Lexington, MA: Lexington Books, 1978), chap. 11.

7 See David Maraniss and Michael Weisskopf, "*Tell Newt to Shut Up!*" (New York: Simon & Schuster, 1996), chap. 7; and John H. Aldrich and David W. Rohde, "The Republican Revolution and the House Appropriations Committee," *Journal of Politics*, 64 (February 2000), pp. 1–33. Aldrich and Rohde documented the tactics Republican leaders used to gain control of the appropriations process, the increased partisan polarization of committee markups and floor proceedings, and the continuing tensions among Appropriations leaders, Republican Party leaders, and conservative members of the GOP Conference. They failed to note, however, that even in 1995 and certainly thereafter, most Appropriations subcommittees still assembled their bills with substantial bipartisan input.

8 Democrats split the Steering and Policy Committee into two committees in 1995, with the Steering Committee in charge of committee assignments. Minority leader Nancy Pelosi rejoined the two in 2003.

9 Sarah Eckman, "Congressional Member Organizations and Informed Member Groups: Their Purpose and Activities, History, and Formation," Congressional Research Service, Library of Congress, January 23, 2019; Sarah Mimms, "Congress Has a Caucus for Everything," *The Atlantic*, April 18, 2014.

10 Richard A. Mendel, *Workforce Literacy in the South* (Chapel Hill, NC: MDC, 1988).

11 Al From, *The New Democrats and the Return to Power* (New York: Palgrave McMillan, 2013). The DLC closed its doors in 2011, but its mission has in part been picked up by the think tank, Third Way. In the meantime, the House NDC has shown renewed vitality under the successive chairmanships of Ron Kind (Wisconsin), Jim Himes (Connecticut), and Derek Kilmer (Washington) and now claims 103 members.

5 Policy Entrepreneurship

"Policy entrepreneurship" is not what it used to be. I coined the term in my doctoral dissertation to describe what I observed and experienced among senators and their aides in the mid-1960s.[1] Their collective impact ran counter to what had almost become conventional wisdom: "The President is now the motor in the system," asserted a distinguished political scientist, "the Congress applies the brakes."[2] But in examining the roots of major bills reported by the Senate committees, I found the congressional role in legislation to be significant, even for major administration initiatives at the height of President Lyndon Johnson's Great Society program.

In seeking an explanation, I identified the emerging phenomenon of "entrepreneurship" among senators and their aides, an orientation that began to alter the cultures of committees like Commerce and Labor and Public Welfare.[3] Institutional folkways that had inhibited legislative activity down through the ranks of the Senate came under increasing strain as senators sought to exert greater policy influence and often found a receptive public when they did. A new breed of activist senators exemplified by Hubert Humphrey, Joseph Clark, Philip Hart, Edmund Muskie, and Jacob Javits began to make their mark. They were often reinforced by entrepreneurship on their staffs—a continual search for policy gaps and opportunities, a job orientation that stressed the generation and promotion of policy initiatives designed to heighten the public visibility of the senator and his or her leadership role in the chamber.

Policy entrepreneurship was slower to emerge in the House, where the size of the body placed greater restrictions on most members' independence and impact. Their electoral fortunes turned more on constituent services and district relations and less on media exposure than was true for most senators. But House members also faced a changing political environment that increasingly left them on their own electorally. Members faced voters who were less inclined to support them on partisan grounds alone, just as party organizations were becoming less effective in communicating with and mobilizing the electorate. Party decline, together with the rise of television as the dominant news and campaign medium, thus gave members incentives to seek a higher public profile. For many representatives, especially those from districts where public awareness of and concern for national policy questions were high, policy entrepreneurship was a promising means to that end.

The desire for a more prominent policy role was a powerful motivation behind the House reforms of the 1970s, which for the most part parceled out authority and resources to subcommittees and individual members. These changes, in turn, encouraged policy initiatives down through the congressional ranks. The fragmentation of power, ironically, also made it more difficult for the House to handle conflict and bring legislative initiatives to fruition and thus prompted renewed calls for stronger party leadership (see Chapter 6).

Entrepreneurial activity had waned significantly by the time I came to the House. During the first two years of the Reagan administration, for example, the number of public laws enacted dropped to 473, the lowest since World War II. The volume of committee hearings tapered off somewhat after the peak years of the 1970s and reached a postwar low in 1986.[4] A number of factors contributed to this decline—shifts in the political climate that seemed to reduce public support for legislative activism, the advent of an administration hostile to much policy innovation, and constraints imposed by the perceived budget crisis on new policy departures, especially those that cost money.

Still, the distribution of authority and resources in both the House and Senate gave large numbers of members opportunities for legislative entrepreneurship, and I was strongly inclined to seek an active policymaking role. This was influenced by my earlier study and staff experience (I had handled the Radiation Protection Act of 1967 for Senator Bartlett, who was its chief Senate sponsor) and by my conviction that my competitive district would reward such endeavors. At the same time, I faced certain constraints, first as a junior member expected to concentrate on my committee assignments and defer to committee leaders and later as a member of the Appropriations Committee ineligible for a seat on an authorizing committee. I will discuss in this chapter several initiatives that I managed, under contrasting circumstances, to push to passage, both within and beyond my committee assignments, and then give an account of the policy leverage that membership—and leadership—on Appropriations provide.

Legislating from Committee[5]

My arrival on the Banking Committee with an eye out for entrepreneurial opportunities coincided with the rise of home equity loans as a hot new financial product. The Tax Reform Act of 1986 had terminated income tax deductibility for interest on most consumer loans and credit card accounts, but it had left deductibility in place for loans secured by one's home. In response, home equity loans—second mortgages that ordinarily had a variable interest rate and an open line of credit up to a substantial portion of the value of the house—were vigorously marketed, and many consumers (including me) found them attractive and advantageous. This aggressive marketing and the possibility that, with a rise in interest rates, borrowers might find themselves in over their heads with their homes at risk made certain basic consumer protections desirable. Yet these loans were subject to few advertising or disclosure requirements. My committee assignment gave me a good opportunity to work on a remedy that would subject home equity loans to disclosure requirements as stringent as those that applied to other mortgages.

Having discovered a promising policy gap and feeling anxious lest other members might be getting similar ideas, I hurried to draft a bill and to circulate a "Dear Colleague" letter inviting other members to join me as cosponsors. My staff and I solicited suggestions from several consumer and banking groups and, most importantly, from the staff of the Federal Reserve Board, which was already working on new regulations for the timing and content of disclosures for adjustable-rate mortgages.

One critical early decision was to make this primarily a disclosure bill. Although it went beyond what most industry associations preferred, it also fell short of the consumer groups' wish lists. I made this decision on the merits of the case. I did not want to place regulations on home equity loans that went far beyond what was required of comparable products; nor did I want to see these loans increased in price or made less available. This approach had the advantage of broad bipartisan appeal, but it risked criticism from the "left"—which materialized in a more intrusive bill introduced to the applause of some consumer groups by Rep. Charles Schumer (D-New York), then an ambitious, middle-ranking Banking Committee member. From the "right" there was the danger of unified lender opposition, particularly if my bill were amended to include interest rate caps or other restrictions proposed in the Schumer bill. As it turned out, with the help of committee leaders from both parties, I was able both to maintain my bill's approach and to keep my name on it as prime sponsor.

The Banking Committee's Subcommittee on Consumer Affairs and Coinage held a day of hearings on the bill on October 6, 1987. I used the subcommittee markup to strengthen the bill in various ways—by tightly restricting the lender's right to call in a loan or change its terms, for example—but our negotiations grew quite contentious. We got the revised bill reported out of subcommittee only by promising all concerned that they would get another crack at it before the full committee undertook its final revisions.

In the meantime, the Senate Banking Committee's Subcommittee on Consumer Affairs used my bill and Schumer's as the basis for a day of hearings on home equity loans. The committee leadership later decided to append a home equity disclosure provision to their bill repealing the Glass-Steagall Act and expanding bank powers—Senate Banking's most ambitious legislative project in the 100th Congress—which passed on March 30, 1988. Home equity loans were an afterthought for the Senate, and their provision was hastily drawn. Nonetheless, this temporary shift to the Senate of the negotiations among industry and consumer groups served us well on the House side: the prospect of immediate floor action forced everyone to reveal their bottom lines in short order, and we were able to use the Senate language to resolve several difficult issues that were slowing our progress toward full committee markup in the House.

The House Banking Committee approved the Home Equity Loan Consumer Protection Act by a unanimous vote on May 19, 1988, and the House passed the bill by voice vote on June 20. Although I had been happy to see the measure pass the Senate expeditiously as part of the bank powers legislation, I wanted to pass it as a separate bill in the House, where the prognosis for the bank powers bill was far less hopeful and home equity's prospects could be harmed if it became entwined in the conflicts surrounding the broader measure. This strategy, supported by the bipartisan leadership of our committee, preserved both options—taking home equity to a House-Senate conference as part of the larger bill or passing it as a freestanding measure if the bank powers bill failed.

This proved to be a wise strategy, for the bank powers legislation ran into major obstacles in the House. However, both the chairman and the ranking Republican of the Senate Banking Committee, who were also the chief proponents of the bank powers bill, were reluctant to pass home equity separately because they believed it enhanced the broader bill and improved their chances for getting it approved. It was only after the prospects for bank powers were seen as completely hopeless that separate passage of home equity could even be discussed. By then, time was so short that the only feasible approach was for the Senate to pass the House's freestanding home equity bill and send it directly to the president, thus making further House action or a House-Senate conference on the bill unnecessary.

My legislative director, Paul Feldman, and I spent many hours during the closing days of the session working with allies that included several House members and aides as well as industry and consumer lobbyists, trying to secure Senate passage. The task was complicated by the fact that the Senate was conducting its business essentially by unanimous consent in the waning hours. Any one member could block approval, and several placed holds on the home equity bill, hoping to use it as a vehicle or bargaining chip for proposals of their own. The Senate committee staff worked all day on October 21 to accommodate as many of these members as possible and finally, at 2:00 A.M., got home equity to the floor as part of a package of three bills. With one hour remaining before final adjournment of the 100th Congress, the Home Equity Loan Consumer Protection Act passed the Senate by voice vote and was on its way to the White House!

I was ecstatic at this success, not simply because of its policy impact and political benefits, but as the realization of a role I had come to Congress hoping to play. I also had some wind at my back, favorable conditions that made success more likely—conditions more common in 1987 than they are today.

The committee environment, for example, was relatively hospitable. The House Democratic leadership was friendly to consumer protection initiatives, but partisan differences were not as sharply defined as they later became. Republican cooperation was easier to secure. Moreover, committees like Banking exercised more independence in developing their agendas than is now the case. Not all policy areas were the same with respect to either partisan conflict or the involvement of House leadership. But consumer protection was not a highly charged issue, and the effective decentralization of both the committee and the House fostered member entrepreneurship and gave it a fair chance of success.

The political conditions surrounding the home equity issue were also favorable.[6] The bill spoke to a problem of growing public salience, one that promised recognition and reward to legislators who addressed it, and it was not saddled with the kind of debilitating conflict that would have discouraged legislative involvement. The relevant outside groups and agencies had good reasons for adopting a constructive, cooperative posture, although it was by no means always certain that they would do so. The Federal Reserve Board, having acknowledged the need for home equity loan regulation and having begun its own rule making, needed to ensure congruence between congressional action and its own. Industry groups recognized that the price of noncooperation might be a more punitive and less workable bill. This led to a rather grudging decision by the American Bankers Association not to oppose the bill actively, as well as to more positive collaboration by other industry groups. Some of the consumer lobbyists were inclined to push for "their bill or none," to test the limits of the developing consensus. But others, most notably the American Association of Retired Persons (AARP), needed to deliver a bill to their constituents, and their allies on the committee let them know that they would not back an absolutist stance.

These conditions facilitated a successful initiative but did not ensure it. Successful entrepreneurship requires members and their aides to push continually and push hard. Furthermore, an initiative must be shaped to make the most of favorable conditions. In the home equity case, this meant taking full account of the Federal Reserve's preferences as the bill was drafted and refined. It meant consulting with and deferring to the committee leadership. It meant drafting the bill to attract bipartisan support, seeking that support, and insisting that all the major players be brought along at each successive stage. It meant working hard to keep the intergroup negotiations on track. And right up to that last hour, there were many signs that even all this might not be enough!

My second term on the Banking Committee was dominated by the main issue that had attracted me in the first place, housing. But we initially had to deal with the collapse of the savings and loan industry and legislation to recapitalize the insurance fund and revamp regulation of the industry—the Financial Institutions Reform, Recovery, and Enforcement Act (FIRREA). The three amendments I added to this bill as it made its way through the Financial Institutions Subcommittee set the pattern for more extensive attempts a year later to modify and augment the National Affordable Housing Act. This legislation established the HOME program, a new framework for housing partnerships among the Department of Housing and Urban Development (HUD), state and local governments, nonprofits, and the private sector.

The offering of amendments in committee is still the most common sort of legislating that House members individually undertake, although markups of major bills have become less expansive and more dominated by party leadership. Also increasingly rare are committee field hearings, but my involvement in shaping the housing bill and my public identification with the issue were greatly facilitated when Chairman Henry Gonzalez (D-Texas) scheduled such a hearing in Raleigh in early 1990. The hearing helped provide a basis for later cooperation with the bipartisan group of three colleagues who made the trip—and let me call witnesses to support several amendments I was working on.

I used the field hearing, for example, to highlight the success of "soft second" mortgages in financing local affordable-housing developments. In this financing arrangement, a bank loaned a borrower approximately 70 percent of the home's value. A local government or nonprofit organization made a second loan—the soft second—to the borrower for the remaining percentage of the home's value. Principal and interest payments on the second mortgage were deferred for several years or until the house was sold again. Such schemes, several witnesses testified, were bringing monthly mortgage payments within reach for home buyers of modest income. However, the resources for such financing were limited; "the problem," said one mayor, "is now that we know this works, we don't have the resources to replicate it."[7]

Providing second-mortgage resources seemed to be a feasible federal role, a way of stimulating substantial public and private investments in affordable housing with a relatively modest federal contribution. (In fact, it later became a familiar feature of HOME projects.) I proposed that we set up a demonstration program at HUD that would allow local governments and nonprofits to apply for funds for soft second mortgage financing. After a good deal of discussion, mainly at the staff level, Chairman Gonzalez agreed to include a modest authorization as part of his home ownership title in the "chairman's mark," the revised draft of the bill offered to the subcommittee for markup.

Another of my amendments loosened the so-called federal preference eligibility rules for public housing and rental assistance projects. By law, 90 percent of such units had to go to families in the preference categories—families who were paying more than 50 percent of their income in rent, had been involuntarily displaced, or were living in substandard housing. The Bush administration defended such targeting as a way of giving priority to the most needy, but the people who actually had to administer these developments told a different story. "The concept of dealing only with the neediest of the poor ... was well intended," the director of the Raleigh Housing Authority told our subcommittee, but as a result,

> we have driven the low-income working families out of our public housing and we have driven the role models out, we have driven the two-parent households out and [have helped create] much of the negative environment that we are now being criticized for in public housing.[8]

Rigid preference rules meant that public housing was not working as a community, for the neediest or for anyone else.

I therefore proposed that up to 30 percent of the slots in public and assisted housing could go to persons who met the income eligibility requirements but fell outside the federal preference criteria. The amendment drew skeptical responses from liberal Democratic members like Gonzalez and Joe Kennedy (D-Massachusetts), as well as administration partisans on the Republican side. But members like Schumer and Steve Bartlett (R-Texas), who knew a great deal about how housing programs actually worked, came to the amendment's defense, and in the end the subcommittee adopted it by voice vote.

My additional four amendments ranged from increasing the maximum value of a home eligible for Federal Housing Administration (FHA) mortgage insurance to modifying the conditions under which landlords should be permitted to exit federal rent subsidy programs. All six amendments survived in House-Senate conference, although I was not there to defend them in person—partly because of my junior status but also because Gonzalez did not take his disagreements with me and others lightly when he recommended names to the Speaker for appointment.

My amendments reflected the sources from which legislative initiatives may flow—agencies, advocacy groups, constituency complaints, one's own ideas and experiences, discomfort with the existing alternatives. Like the home equity bill, they demonstrate the centrality of creative and persistent staff work to successful entrepreneurship and the importance of agency and group support. They also show that the Banking Committee, despite a reputation for arbitrary leadership and persistent conflict, remained relatively permeable in terms of members' ability to shape its legislative product. Its patterns of conflict were sufficiently fluid to permit the assemblage, from issue to issue, of all sorts of coalitions, often across party lines. Today, that process has been rendered more difficult both by the hardening of party lines and the increased centralization of committee and party leadership.

Finding Policy Gaps

While the Banking Committee provided a positive setting for my early entrepreneurial efforts, the issue that came most naturally to me was education. My mother was a high school English teacher; I have early memories of former students coming up to her on the street, recounting what she had done for them, and sometimes, to my amazement, thanking her for demanding so much. My father taught biology and served as high school principal until the needs of our growing family forced him to take a job with more adequate pay. Education opened up the wider world to me, and it probably surprised no one that I chose teaching as a career. When I ran for Congress, both my personal credentials and the preoccupations of my district dictated that the need to support and improve education would be a central campaign theme.

From my earliest months in the House, I was looking for a fit between my education interests and my committee assignments. This helped attract me to the Science Committee and to Science, Research, and Technology (SRT) as the subcommittee most attuned to education policy. Fortunately, the subcommittee had a generous and accommodating chair, Doug Walgren (D-Pennsylvania), who had pushed for years to get the National Science Foundation (NSF) to use methods successfully employed at other educational levels to improve advanced technology curricula and teaching methods at community colleges. He welcomed my interest and scheduled a field hearing in Research Triangle Park (RTP) ten months into my first term. This allowed me to assemble a stellar cast of North Carolinians, including the president of the community college system, the general manager of IBM, and other business, education, and civic leaders, and to stake out training for the workplace and strengthening community colleges as education issues I intended to pursue.[9]

I also made good auxiliary use of the Sunbelt Caucus (see Chapter 4), co-chairing (with Hal Rogers [R-Kentucky]) a task force and commissioning a study on workplace literacy. I then organized a literacy summit in RTP which carried forward some of the interest and enthusiasm generated in our 1987 hearing.

By mid-1989, I was ready to introduce my own bill. I retained the basic thrust of Walgren's earlier proposal: individual project grants from NSF to community colleges to support meritorious training programs and the creation of ten "centers of excellence" among these colleges to serve as national clearinghouses for best practices in technical training and/or science and mathematics education. I added sections authorizing a focus on curricular revision and the development of innovative instruction technologies. Before introducing the bill, I carefully assembled a bipartisan group of cosponsors, including Rogers and Sherwood Boehlert (R-New York), ranking Republican on the SRT Subcommittee, as well as Walgren and Robert Roe (D-New Jersey), chair of the full Science Committee.[10]

The SRT hearing on October 31 was an upbeat affair, with a number of members participating and former (and future) North Carolina governor Jim Hunt serving as leadoff witness. But NSF continued to drag its feet. Out of a budget approaching $3 billion, NSF acknowledged spending only $4 million annually on two-year institutions, with most of that going for instrumentation and laboratory equipment. The foundation insisted that it needed no new statutory authority to do what the bill envisioned and that these kinds of training programs would be best handled by the Education and Labor Departments.[11] This attitude changed somewhat in the ensuing months. When NSF Director Erich Bloch made a rare joint appearance with Secretary of Education Lauro Cavazos before our subcommittee on February 28, 1990, he identified "adult science and technical training" as an area that was "falling through the cracks" between the two agencies—an admission I immediately seized on as a demonstration

> that strengthening NSF's ... support for the development of exemplary technical training programs ... might not be quite as distant from NSF's mission as some have suggested in the past.[12]

We were not able to move the bill in the 101st Congress, a disappointment to me as I prepared to leave the Science Committee for Appropriations. But we had made some headway, not only in softening NSF and Bush administration opposition but also in mobilizing the national community college associations and institutions in the districts of key members. This was sometimes harder than it should have been, reminding me of a phenomenon Senator Ralph Yarborough (D-Texas) first described to me in connection with his Cold War GI Bill in the mid-1960s. He found himself lobbying the lobbyists, pushing veterans' groups to give his bill higher priority as they contacted their supporters. Sometimes, one of his aides observed, "the echo creates the yell."[13]

Election night 1990 brought unwelcome news of Walgren's defeat, but the accession of my North Carolina colleague Tim Valentine to the chair of the Subcommittee on Technology and Competitiveness provided an opportunity to give the bill an added boost. On reintroducing the bill, I secured a referral to Valentine's subcommittee as well as SRT. An October hearing which Valentine then convened helped propel the bill to the full Science Committee, where it was marked up on March 18, 1992, with particular attention to the concerns of NSF.[14]

The Science Committee reported the bill to the House on April 30, but floor consideration was delayed while the staff of the Education and Labor Committee, to whom it had been jointly referred, scrutinized its provisions. They eventually agreed, after minor changes, to release the bill; the House passed it without dissent on August 10 and sent it to the Senate. This would have been impossibly late in the session had the Senate been required to consider the House bill de novo. Fortunately, however, Senator Barbara Mikulski (D-Maryland) and her staff had been working with community college leaders and my staff on a companion bill. House passage of my bill enabled Mikulski to put her proposal on a fast track; the Senate passed it by voice vote on October 2, and the next day the House gave its final approval. On October 23, President Bush signed what was now called the Scientific and Advanced-Technology Act of 1992—establishing the Advanced Technological Education (ATE) program at NSF—into law.

In the meantime, I was pursuing a second major education initiative outside of committee boundaries—what became the Education Affordability Act, eventually passed in 1997. The initial idea came from Martin Lancaster, a friend and fellow member of the class of 1986 who represented eastern North Carolina's Third District. We jointly offered a bill to restore income tax deductibility for interest on student loans (which had been removed by the Tax Reform Act of 1986) and to make scholarships and fellowships tax-exempt. We promoted the bill year after year to anyone who would listen, interrupted only by the elections of 1994, when we both lost our seats. Certainly the idea was well-received at home: heads invariably nodded in community meetings when I expressed the view that if you could deduct the interest on the mortgage on your home (or even on your second home at the beach!), you surely ought to get a break on something as basic as an educational loan.

It was (and is) extremely difficult to pass tax bills individually because of their budget impact. They are generally wrapped into omnibus bills, often in the context of budget "reconciliation" or another comprehensive agreement (see Chapter 7). I finally found such a vehicle after I returned to the House in 1997—the Taxpayer Relief Act, part of a deficit reduction package under negotiation between the president and the leadership of Congress. I added to the student loan deductibility proposal a section permitting the drawdown without penalty of individual retirement account (IRA) savings for educational purposes. I then sought inclusion in the list of tax breaks certain to be included in the overall package. President Clinton made clear that HOPE Scholarships (tax credits for tuition expenses) and other initiatives for higher education were at the top of his priority list. And although most of the 58 sponsors of the bill were minority Democrats, our ideas were also being pushed by several key Republicans. If this meant that credit for the final outcome would be more widely shared, it also increased the chances that that outcome would be favorable.

Throughout the budget discussions, I maintained communication with congressional and administration leaders who were in a position to shape the final product and helped higher education representatives do the same. I particularly wanted to make certain that the support of Democratic leaders for such measures as HOPE Scholarships and expanded Pell Grants (which I shared) did not displace support for my proposal. The five-year cost of the student loan and IRA components ($690 million and $812 million, respectively) was low relative to many other proposals under discussion. This made it easier to include them, but the danger remained that negotiators might drop them as they balanced the numbers and fine-tuned the package.

There was never much doubt that the IRA drawdown provision would make it. The president included it in his proposed budget, and it was included in both the Senate and House versions of the Taxpayer Relief Act.

But we had a harder time with the interest deductibility proposal. It was omitted from the Republican bill, initially passed by the House, and I failed to get it included in the Democratic alternative. We knew its prospects were better in the Senate, and as I lobbied administration officials and House conferees, I was assured by Treasury Secretary Robert Rubin that interest deductibility was a personal favorite of the president and he was pushing for its inclusion. In the end, both the IRA drawdown and a modified version of our interest deductibility proposal (available for five years per student, for joint filers with incomes up to $60,000) were included in the conference agreement, passed overwhelmingly by both houses on July 31. These Education Affordability Act provisions were hardly noticed amid the hoopla surrounding the conclusion of the budget deal, but I was not inclined to complain: I knew that their significance would later become evident and that they hardly could have been passed any other way.

Education initiatives have continued to figure prominently on my legislative agenda. Beginning in 1999, for example, I proposed categorial federal support for state fellowship programs for prospective teachers, modeled on the Teaching Fellows program established by the North Carolina General Assembly in 1986 (which Republicans repealed upon taking control in 2011). I persuaded Mike Castle (R-Delaware), chairman of the relevant Education and the Workforce subcommittee, to convene a field hearing in Raleigh which we utilized to familiarize the subcommittee with the workings of the North Carolina program and to plant the idea that teacher recruitment might suggest a "new area of policy direction" for an expanded Elementary and Secondary Education Act (ESEA).[15]

My press secretary earned his pay on February 27, 2001, the day we unveiled a new and improved Teaching Fellows Act for the 107th Congress. We staged the announcement in North Carolina State University's empty football stadium, attracting an array of curious television crews as I pointed out that we could fill every seat in sight, in addition to every seat in the basketball arena next door, and would still fall short by 6,000 of the 80,000 new teachers North Carolina needed to recruit in the next decade (see Figure 5.1)! But despite the incoming George W. Bush administration's much-touted emphasis on ESEA reauthorization (aka "No Child Left Behind"), their proposal focused on standards and accountability, and the Education Committee was inclined to consolidate and block-grant "teacher quality" programs rather than add a new categorical program of the sort I had proposed.

I thus began to look for another legislative vehicle; the obvious candidate was the Higher Education Act (HEA), up for renewal in 2003–2004. I was able to enlist a particularly important additional cosponsor, Cass Ballenger (R-North Carolina), with the help of a mutual friend who was on the board of the North Carolina Teaching Fellows program. A senior member of the Education Committee, Ballenger helped persuade committee leaders to include programmatic elements from our bill in the teacher preparation

Figure 5.1 Press conference announcing Teaching Fellows Act, Carter-Finley Stadium, February 27, 2001. Photo by *Raleigh News and Observer*.

portion of the HEA—scholarships for high school seniors and/or college sophomores; scholarships and institutional support for community colleges; extracurricular enrichment and professional development activities; and an obligation for recipients to teach in a public school for the term of their scholarship plus one year.

While this outcome was not what I had originally sought, I regarded it as a positive achievement in a difficult political environment. I was careful, with a detailed statement on the House floor, to provide a legislative history—an account of how the elements we had added to the bill would cohere in a functioning program.[16] But our efforts came to naught as HEA reauthorization languished in the Senate.

I tried again in 2008, when the HEA was next reauthorized, this time under Democratic leadership. Committee leaders included a new Teacher Quality Partnership (TQP) program in the HEA, reauthorizing and streamlining previous teacher recruitment and training activities. While this approach did not allow for the kind of categorical program I had in mind, it created an opening for state, local, and university-based scholarship programs for beginning teachers to receive federal support. I thus declared victory and have concentrated on pressing subsequent administrations to implement such programs and Congress to fund TQP generously.

Not all legislative efforts are so protracted. In 2016, for example, I was able to enact a major revision in the distribution formula for the Housing Opportunities for People with AIDS (HOPWA) program within a few months as a bipartisan amendment to a major housing bill.[17] North Carolina and many other states had strong claims based on the current distribution of AIDS cases, but we faced resistance from areas in California and New York that had been the early centers of the epidemic and were represented by influential members. Aided by an entrepreneurial staff member, Laura Thrift, I was able to line up advocates and representatives from areas that stood to gain—a large majority—in favor of a revised formula. It was also critical to minimize the negative tradeoffs for areas losing funding, which I achieved through a parallel effort on my T-HUD appropriations subcommittee to increase the overall amount of HOPWA funding available for distribution.

A comparable target of opportunity was spotted in 2017 and pursued relentlessly by another entrepreneurial staffer, Nora Blalock. I had long supported robust finding for the Department of Education's Foreign Language Assistance Program (FLAP), the only federal program that supported language education in elementary and secondary schools. When the Obama administration and Republican appropriators agreed to merge FLAP with other funding streams, I was not pleased, accurately anticipating a decline in emphasis and support. In 2015, I introduced a new programmatic authorization with Rep. Don Young (R-AK) and other colleagues. We tried to get the bill included in the reauthorization of the ESEA later that year but did not succeed.

This disappointment led me, in collaboration with foreign language advocacy organizations, to consider a different approach for the next Congress. Focusing on the national security and readiness aspects of language education, we decided to seek inclusion in the annual National Defense Authorization Act (NDAA). What finally did the trick was Democratic control of the House, although even then the road to passage had many twists and turns. Our shift to the NDAA in 2017 initially failed, partly because the chair of the Education and the Workforce Committee, to which the bill had been jointly referred, refused to grant a waiver. Our 2019 efforts with the House Armed Services Committee (HASC), now under Democratic control, also fell short at first. But I was able to get Rules Committee approval to take an amendment to the floor, which passed with HASC acquiescence.[18] Our provision was not in the Senate NDAA bill, and getting it accepted in conference required another major effort. But the provision was accepted with modifications to make its defense relevance clearer by limiting eligibility for language education funding to school districts that hosted J-ROTC programs and to schools serving defense bases. This gave us a foot in the door. I was happy to declare victory, at least temporarily, and to begin pursuing funding in the Fiscal 2021 Defense Appropriations bill.

There are times when my policy initiatives have received an unaccustomed boost: the intervention of the House Speaker in 2005 to pass the resolution establishing the House Democracy Partnership (see Chapter 8), and the inclusion of several of my political reform proposals in 2019 in H.R. 1, a high-profile leadership package (see Chapter 3). Ordinarily, however, members who wish to take on major policy issues had best prepare for a long slog. Consider these three longstanding initiatives of mine:

- The MEJA (Military Extraterritorial Jurisdiction Act) Expansion and Enforcement Act. This bill would subject to U.S. criminal law all private security and other contractors working for the U.S. government worldwide. Prompted by the widespread use of private security forces in Iraq and Afghanistan, I first sought to address the gap in MEJA coverage in 2004, in collaboration with Chris Shays (R-Connecticut). The bill was propelled to House passage in 2007 when Blackwater security guards employed by the State Department opened fire in Nisoor Square in Baghdad, killing 17 Iraqi civilians.[19] But the bill never made it out of the Senate, and we have struggled to get both houses and subsequent administrations on the same page ever since.

- The SCORE (Standardization of Collegiate Oversight of Revenues and Expenditures) Act. The bill would require universities, athletic conferences, and tournaments, through the National Collegiate Athletic Association (NCAA), to make standardized public reports of all receipts and expenditures for their athletic programs. I first introduced the bill in 2014 amid ongoing scandals and inquiries, convinced that greater transparency and accountability were sorely needed and would then provide a sound base of knowledge for farther-reaching reforms. I drew both inspiration and ideas from the Knight Commission on Intercollegiate Athletics, of which UNC President William Friday had served as Founding Co-chairman (1989–2005), and from other reform advocates.

- The SWINE (Swine Waste Infrastructure and Natural Environment) Act. The bill would authorize ongoing research on environmentally sound technologies for the management and disposal of waste from large hog farms, and would provide tax and other incentives for the replacement of current lagoon and spray-field systems with these technologies. Beginning in the 1990s, I secured appropriations earmarks for North Carolina State University (NCSU) researchers to develop new disposal technologies; the situation's urgency became more apparent in 1999 when Hurricane Floyd destroyed some 50 lagoons, flooding nearby waterways and communities with untreated waste. Still, various efforts to induce growers and packers to put their operations on a more sustainable footing met with stiff resistance, and with the advent of Republican control in Raleigh and Washington in 2011, they ground to a halt. I first introduced the SWINE Act in 2016 to demonstrate the kind of comprehensive approach that this environmental disaster was going to require and am pursuing it more hopefully under Democratic leadership.

It is important to take note of such bills, the ones that have *not* been enacted, as well as the ones that have, in any account of policy entrepreneurship. For me and my staff, they represent as much or more exertion, and often bolder legislative ambition, than enacted bills. They are instructive in terms of the pressures and problems that give rise to them and the strategies by which one attempts to get them, or pieces of them, enacted. But they also illustrate, even more than the convoluted case histories of enacted bills, how many hurdles must be cleared and how many obstacles often confront even the best-crafted proposals. The vitality and effectiveness of Congress still depend on members' willingness to invest time, energy, and staff resources in policy initiatives, but the incentive to seek such a role has become weaker and the path to success more difficult in the modern House.

The Appropriations Arena

Ever since I first gained appointment to the House Appropriations Committee in 1991, that has been my main arena for policy initiation. Most of my funding projects have been modest in scope and oriented toward my district's and North Carolina's needs. But some, most notably the Environmental Protection Agency (EPA) laboratory in Research Triangle Park and the headquarters building for North Carolina's National Guard and Office of Emergency Management, were major undertakings. Appropriations bills also offer an opportunity to exert policy leverage, beyond funding, on matters large and small. As I have moved into leadership positions on homeland security, transportation, and housing, I have increasingly focused on these broader policy priorities and concerns.

In shifting from Banking and Science to Appropriations, I encountered marked differences in committee organization and procedures which influence the way policy entrepreneurship works. Most authorizing committees, including Science and Banking, have devolved significant decision-making power to subcommittees, but none more than Appropriations. The most opportune time to get an item into an appropriations bill is when the subcommittee is preparing it for the full committee, and the most important players are the subcommittee chairman and his or her staff. The "chairman's mark," a document of considerable importance on most committees, is even more important on Appropriations. The chairman, ranking minority member, and their staffs assemble and evaluate myriad member requests and incorporate many of them, in some fashion, in the draft bill. Special consideration is often given to requests from subcommittee members and full committee and party leaders. Under both Democratic and Republican regimes, there has been variation among subcommittees as to the bipartisanship of this process, ranging from full collaboration to giving the ranking minority member a quick look before bringing the mark to the subcommittee. In general, the decision process on Appropriations is less partisan than on most authorizing committees, and the chances for minority members to have significant input are much greater. In recent years, the ability of subcommittees to develop consensual products has depended greatly on whether there has been a prior bipartisan budget agreement. Expansive topline numbers make possible the kind of win-win outcomes that appropriators like best.

The starting point for the subcommittee chairman's mark is the administration's budget request, which has been presented and defended by agency heads in subcommittee hearings. Members are furnished documents showing how the chairman's draft differs from the administration's request on each item. The differences are often substantial, particularly when different parties are in charge of the two branches or in the case of a president like Donald Trump, whose budgets often seem to come off the shelf at the far-right Heritage Foundation. In any event, the bill is reviewed item by item and given the subcommittee's imprint.

The layout of the room used for full committee hearings and markups is distinctive (see Figure 5.2), suggesting collegiality and a lack of hierarchy. But while full committee markups often elicit widespread participation from members of both parties, major changes in subcommittee-reported bills are rare. In the past that was often attributable to a bipartisan closing of the ranks around a subcommittee product; that can still happen when bills have

Figure 5.2 Managing the markup of the Transportation-HUD Appropriations bill, June 4, 2019.

Photo courtesy of Gloria Nlewedim.

had the benefit of a bipartisan budget agreement. But members are also constrained by rules that require spending increases to be offset by decreases elsewhere in the bill—a requirement Democrats found impossible to meet when Republicans were marking up bills at sequestration-level aggregate numbers (see Chapter 7).

Many amendments therefore concern not spending levels but the addition or subtraction of policy "riders" to the bills. The rules permit the addition of policy provisions only when they impose conditions on actual spending, but members sometimes offer legislative language despite the fact that it would require a waiver of the rules to be in order on the floor. Under Republican leadership (2011–2018), subcommittee chairs often added controversial riders to their bills to accommodate their members, and many of the amendments proposed by Democrats in full committee markup sought to remove these provisions. More rarely, we Democrats sought to add provisions of our own. Therefore, in contrast to the bipartisan accommodation often in evidence when the bills were originally assembled, markups often featured up-or-down party line votes and very little accommodation.

I failed to break the mold in 2018, when I offered an amendment during markup of the Financial Services bill to deny funds to the Federal Communications Commission (FCC) to implement its reversal of the "net neutrality" rule adopted during the Obama administration. The previous rule, which provided that all content traveling over the internet should be treated equally by internet service providers, had widespread public support; I had received more communications asking me to defend it than I received on any other issue during the 115th Congress.

My amendment, like most others offered that day, failed on a 22–29 party line vote. But it brought to mind a more successful effort fifteen years earlier that had first impressed on me the political resonance FCC rulings could have. The issue was media concentration—a phenomenon for which I had an instinctive distaste by virtue of one of my first jobs, as an announcer at WEMB, a 1,000-watt station in my home town. Ironically, local radio was the first medium to undergo widespread consolidation and conglomerate control. In 2003, the issue was to what extent television companies should be limited in the number of stations they could own in a single market or as their share of the national market.

FCC Chairman Michael Powell was preparing a far-reaching ruling. But he had a formidable opponent in Democratic commissioner Michael Copps, who was opposed to further deregulation and offended that Powell had scheduled only one public hearing on the matter. I had an equally formidable Raleigh media executive urging me on, James Goodmon, who as CEO of the family-owned firm that dominated TV ratings in the Triangle, was something of a contrarian in the industry.

Copps convened unofficial hearings around the country during the spring, the first of which I helped him stage at Duke University. We were astounded at the enthusiastic response. Media concentration clearly resonated across the political spectrum, from family values advocates disturbed that "reality" television shows demeaning marriage were being foisted by networks on their local affiliates, to Dixie Chicks fans appalled that the group was being removed from a radio conglomerate's playlist because of their outspoken opposition to President Bush.

An appropriations amendment was not the ideal way to head off an FCC ruling.[20] It would only be operative for the next fiscal year, and in order to escape an adverse parliamentary ruling, it could only forbid the expenditure of funds appropriated by the bill to implement one or more of the FCC rules. House Republican leaders were certain to object to waiving House rules, which a farther-reaching amendment would require. But an appropriations strategy also had major advantages: the Commerce-Justice-State (C-J-S) bill, which included FCC funding, was must-pass legislation, and the Appropriations Committee markup offered an opportunity to force a simple up-or-down vote which Republican leaders could not block.

As the July 16 markup approached, I worked with Rep. Dave Obey (D-Wisconsin), the full committee's ranking Democrat, to prepare an amendment withholding funding for the new FCC rules. We decided to focus on the rule which would increase a company's permitted national market share from 35 to 45 percent, calculating that this was the element of the FCC decision we had the best chance of blocking. Assisted by a diverse array of supportive groups, we lobbied our colleagues intensively. By the time the committee voted, all Democratic members were in their seats voting aye, and we were joined by eleven Republicans. The 40–25 vote was a stunning rebuke to the FCC, the White House, and the House GOP leadership.

As it turned out, that was the high point of our effort. Maurice Hinchey (D-New York) and I barely fell short of passing an additional amendment on the floor to block funding for the remaining FCC rules, involving cross-media ownership and local ownership concentration. Still, our committee amendment on national market share remained in the bill.

The Senate bill contained a similar provision, but as the beginning of the new fiscal year came and went, the C-J-S bill got caught up in efforts to combine all remaining bills into an "omnibus." This gave Republican leaders and the administration the chance to modify our amendment. Their "compromise" raised the 35 percent cap, which we had sought to preserve, to 39 percent, high enough to accommodate CBS and Fox, the networks that had already exceeded the 35 percent ownership limit. "The Republicans went into a closet, met with themselves and announced a 'compromise,'" explained Sen. Ernest Hollings, ranking Democrat on both Commerce and the C-J-S Appropriations Subcommittee. "We weren't a part of it whatsoever."[21]

The media concentration amendment to the C-J-S bill thus fell short of a total victory: it reached only one of the FCC rules, and that only in part. Still, it serves as an example of how an appropriations provision can reduce agency discretion or block implementation of an agency ruling, offering a way around the conventional legislative process.

Appropriations also offers opportunities to launch innovative programs, usually through the funding of a specific project but sometimes through the creation of new funding categories. An example of the first type is the earmark mentioned earlier to support research on swine waste utilization and disposal at NCSU. During my term on the Agriculture Subcommittee, I began discussing the project with NCSU administrators and scientists, who understood the challenge of controlling poultry and swine waste and the potential of converting it to value-added products long before waste became a headline issue in North Carolina and the nation. I obtained $888,000 for facility construction in fiscal 1993, $414,000 for research operations in 1994, and annual appropriations ranging from $300,000 to $500,000 for a dozen years thereafter. These funds were at times supplemented by funding from industry and other sources. The result has been the development of effective and economically feasible technologies which have brought the kind of waste management envisioned in my SWINE Act within reach—despite the unfortunate fact that industry still insists these technologies are unaffordable.

Sometimes what appears to be a minor adjustment to an appropriations bill can have significant consequences. For example, I and my staff were approached in 2016 by advocates and researchers concerning the absence of federal funding for the treatment of Hereditary Hemorrhagic Telangiectasia (HHT), a hereditary blood vessel disorder afflicting some 75,000 Americans. UNC-Chapel Hill was the site of one of the 25 HHT Centers of Excellence in the U.S. and Canada, but it was obvious that both research and clinical outreach would be enhanced by increased funding and coordination with related medical operations. We thus devised a pilot program to take advantage of the network of 130 Hemophilia Treatment Centers (HTCs) already in existence. By adding only $100,000 to the HTC account in the Labor-HHS appropriations bill, we could co-locate three HHT and HTC centers, enabling them to take advantage of shared facilities and teams of providers. The experiment was implemented in fiscal 2017 and 2018, and every indication was that it provided a model for the future.

Another example of program innovation was the appropriations equivalent of my soft second mortgage amendment to the 1990 Housing Bill. The idea was to encourage home ownership among low-income borrowers by making credit from private institutions more available to them; the device was HUD grants to nonprofits, usable for capital reserves, to help them create a secondary market for these mortgages.

I had been impressed by the success of the Center for Community Self-Help, a community development financial institution (CDFI) in Durham, in pioneering a secondary-market demonstration that encouraged lenders to serve persons who had hitherto been considered high risk and, with counseling and good management, kept default rates low. I was pleased to find, as Self-Help shopped its idea of a HUD secondary-market demonstration in anticipation of FY 1998 appropriations, that their prior reputation gained them a respectful hearing among Republican as well as Democratic staff.

Still, this was a much more ambitious venture than beefing up appropriations for existing programs or earmarking a specific project. We were creating authority for a new housing program, however small and experimental, on an appropriations bill. HUD administrators, while not absolutely opposed, were unenthused, and we faced possible parliamentary objections from Banking, the authorizing committee. But VA-HUD chairman Jerry Lewis (R-California) and ranking Democrat Louis Stokes (D-Ohio) and their staffs were receptive to my idea and found a place for it in the bill. We settled on a $10 million set-aside in the HOME account, which was already being increased by $191 million over the administration's request.

The secondary market provision was still vulnerable to a point of order on the House floor. To try to head that off, I enlisted the help of Mel Watt (D-North Carolina), a Banking Committee member who at that time represented Durham, knew Self-Help well, and had considered offering its proposal on his own committee. We spoke selectively with members and staff, not wishing to call more attention to this rather obscure provision than it had already attracted. But we did not know until the moment of floor consideration whether any Banking member would appear to object. As the bill title containing HOME was considered, Watt stood at one door to the chamber and I at the other. The member we most feared would offer objections finally appeared, but only after the title was closed and objections were not in order. We are not certain to this day whether he was late inadvertently or was deferring to our request.

In any event, the bill was passed on July 16, 1997, with the secondary market demonstration intact, and the provision survived in conference. HUD did not implement the new program with great dispatch. After considerable goading, including my sharp exchange with Secretary Andrew Cuomo in subcommittee hearings, the department finally issued a notice of funding availability on March 10, 1999. The program then got underway, and Self-Help received one of two $5 million grants awarded in 1999. It leveraged the grant at a 20 to 1 ratio in just one year, financing $100 million in loans. This allowed 1,800 families who fell outside the traditional underwriting criteria to buy their first homes and demonstrated to participants in the secondary market how opportunities for home ownership might safely be extended to hundreds of thousands more families of modest income.

Such projects have become much more difficult by virtue of the double whammy appropriations suffered under Republican leadership: unrealistic caps on domestic discretionary spending imposed by the 2011 Budget Control Act, and the disallowing of congressionally directed spending, or earmarks, that same year. I will elaborate in Chapter 9 on the use I made of earmarks to benefit North Carolina and the Fourth District. I frequently reminded my staff that every earmark needed to be something we would be proud to have announced on the front page of the Raleigh *News and Observer* the next day, and I don't believe we ever violated that standard. But self-styled reformers in both parties, especially Republicans, succeeded in stigmatizing earmarks as invitations to abuse and grossly exaggerating their impact on the federal budget.

Dubious projects such as a "Bridge to Nowhere" serving a sparsely populated island in Alaska and the defense contractor deals for which Randy "Duke" Cunningham (R-California) went to prison were portrayed as typical earmarks. Democratic appropriators, during our years (2007–2010) in leadership, responded by instituting reforms that made the requesting and securing of earmarks far more transparent and accountable—more so, in fact, than the remaining 98 percent of federal discretionary spending. As Jonathan Rausch concluded in 2009,

> If you wanted to create a non bureaucratic, transparent system of rapid-response grants for pressing local concerns, you'd come up with something very much like today's earmarking system (and you'd call it "reinventing government").[22]

The earmark ban was nonetheless imposed as the Republicans regained control. Today, at least in private, it is hard to find a member of Congress who believes the ban has worked, even among its original advocates.[23] Spending has not been reduced, but the authority to allocate spending has been massively ceded to the executive branch. The ban is extreme: it applies not only to the addition of discrete items to appropriations bills, but also to the upward adjustment of proposed funding levels for public works, military construction, or other projects. If I judge the administration's proposed funding for dredging the harbor at Wilmington, NC, to be inadequate, for example, I cannot request an increase in the relevant bill. This denies appropriators the tools we need to do our jobs and reduces the value of our committee assignment for ourselves and our constituents.

The Big Projects: EPA and the National Guard

My most ambitious appropriations initiative remains the construction of a new research facility for the Environmental Protection Agency (EPA) in RTP. This saga shows how appropriations efforts—normally local in orientation, muted in partisanship, and of limited complexity—can break out of that mold. This fight drew in authorizers as well as appropriators, opened up deep partisan and political divisions, and carried broader implications for not only the location but also the scale of the nation's environmental research. The EPA laboratory was an undertaking of national significance, backed by successive administrations. But it remained a year-to-year congressional struggle, dependent to a surprising degree on the initiative and ingenuity of North Carolina politicians to make or break it. In fact, much of what I did along the way would today be forbidden earmarks!

The founders of RTP regarded federal labs as potential tenants from the beginning. A series of North Carolina governors, congressional representatives, and business leaders set out to lure EPA's predecessor agency and the National Institute of Environmental Health Sciences (NIEHS; founded in 1966 and the only National Institutes of Health (NIH) institute located outside of Washington, D.C.) to North Carolina. In 1968, the Research Triangle Foundation set aside 509 acres for eventual occupation by federal environmental labs. In 1971, shortly after its reorganization as an independent agency, EPA opened a research center in rented space in RTP. NIEHS moved to its permanent RTP site in the early 1980s, but by 1991 EPA had not even designed its permanent facility. In the meantime, its lab operations had spread to twelve locations, with rental and associated costs of about $15 million annually.

I got to know administrators at EPA and NIEHS during my first term. They proved responsive to my concerns about procurement opportunities for small and/or local businesses and provided me a quick education on their needs for modernized and expanded lab space. Before I was appointed to the Appropriations Committee, I was able to earmark a $1.7 million planning grant, which led to construction on the UNC-Chapel Hill campus of a human studies laboratory to be leased and operated by EPA. Appointment to the committee put me in an improved position to promote NIEHS requests for lab expansion ($42 million from 1992–1995) and to get planning and design work underway on the long-deferred EPA project in RTP.

I worked with Tim Valentine (D-North Carolina), a member of EPA's authorizing committee (the main research facilities were then located in Valentine's district), successive VA-HUD Subcommittee chairmen Bob Traxler (D-Michigan) and Louis Stokes (D-Ohio), and EPA officials in North Carolina and Washington to secure planning funds in fiscal 1992 and succeeding VA-HUD appropriations bills. We made some headway, but with $5 million in 1992 and $5.5 million in 1993, we seemed destined to spend five years piecing together the planning budget for a project already long overdue. I was not on the VA-HUD Subcommittee, and both the administration and the subcommittee seemed unlikely to propose larger amounts. But we knew that the General Services Administration (GSA), the agency charged with overseeing federal construction, would eventually be involved with the project, and we had a supportive colleague in Steny Hoyer (D-Maryland), chair of the subcommittee that appropriated for GSA. We therefore devised a plan. For fiscal 1994, $8.8 million for the design of the EPA building would be included in the GSA budget, along with another $3 million in the EPA budget. This brought the planning and design total to $22.3 million and enabled us to complete the funding in three years rather than five. It also speeded up the interagency "value engineering" process, which in early 1994 produced a revised cost estimate for the project, $231.9 million, down 12 percent from earlier projections.

In the meantime, Lauch Faircloth replaced Terry Sanford as North Carolina's junior senator. Sanford, who as governor had helped recruit EPA in the 1960s, had been a valuable partner in our funding efforts. But I had reason to expect Faircloth to be helpful; during his earlier years as a Democrat, he had been state commerce secretary and an energetic promoter of economic development. It soon became clear that I was totally mistaken. Faircloth lost little time in expressing his disdain for the EPA and declaring that reducing federal spending should start with this project (despite estimated thirty-year savings of $166 million compared to rental costs). Faircloth brought along Senator Helms, who had hitherto been a supporter but now told the press that he would rather see EPA housed in Quonset huts than increase the national debt.

Faircloth sat on the Public Works Committee, which authorized for the EPA. He used a hearing on May 12, 1993, at which the new EPA administrator, Carol Browner, was testifying, to announce his opposition to the RTP project. He and Helms then got the 1994 planning funds deleted from both the GSA and EPA bills in the Senate. Thanks to Democratic control in both houses, we got the full $11.8 million restored in conference, but a fresh peril awaited: GSA's work required authorization before it could be fully executed. This placed the project back before the Senate Public Works Committee, where Faircloth resolved to defeat it. Valentine and I enlisted the help of Bill Hefner, a North Carolina colleague and senior appropriator, and Governor Jim Hunt, an energetic promoter of RTP. We coordinated with Administrator Browner, lobbying the Public Works senators one by one before their scheduled January 27, 1994, meeting. Even among Democrats, we were concerned about the senatorial custom of deference to a colleague about a project in his or her state, to say nothing of those who coveted EPA funds and facilities for their own states. Harry Reid (D-Nevada) voted with Faircloth, no doubt mindful of likely future votes on the placement of a repository for high-level nuclear waste in his state. But the other Democratic senators held firm, enabling us to defeat Faircloth on his own committee by a single vote (8–9).

Then came the 1994 election, which put Faircloth in the Senate majority and replaced Valentine (who retired) and me with two declared opponents of the EPA building. But the project survived. The election seemed to call the Republicans' bluff: faced with the potential finally to kill the project, they chose not to do so. Fred Heineman had opposed the project during the campaign, but in an offhand way. EPA officials brought him around to a position of support within a few months, and he in turn helped persuade Faircloth. On May 20, 1995, the two jointly announced their change of position, claiming credit for the cost reductions in the earlier value engineering study. In the meantime, the Clinton administration requested $50 million in first-year construction funding. The VA-HUD Subcommittee, now under Republican control, omitted the item from its bill. But it was eventually included in the FY 1996 omnibus bill; $60 million was added in FY 1997, bringing the two-year total to $110 million.

From my involuntary exile, I made calls and wrote letters of support to the ranking Democrats on the House authorizing committee, now called Transportation and Infrastructure, and on Appropriations, noting that the project once again had bipartisan backing. But by now the 1996 campaign was heating up, and Heineman and his aides were publicly claiming that he had succeeded where I had failed and even that my Democratic allies and I were attempting to sabotage the project. To the extent that the competition between us motivated Heineman to pursue funding and Republican leaders to respond favorably, I suppose the cause was helped.[24] But in denigrating my longest-running and most difficult appropriations undertaking and accusing me of bad faith, the attacks hit close to home and provoked some of the sharpest exchanges of the 1996 campaign.

On returning to the House and the Appropriations Committee in 1997, I expected to seek the $122 million in construction funding not yet appropriated. This was one reason I was so pleased when I unexpectedly gained a seat on the VA-HUD Subcommittee. But it turned out that I needed that seat more than I had thought, for the bids on the project came in $40 million to $80 million higher than anticipated. EPA was faced with the unattractive alternatives of breaching the authorization figure that Heineman and Faircloth had made sacrosanct or cutting back on elements integral to the building's design. My staff and I examined the situation carefully, including the economies earlier achieved through the value engineering process, the reasons for the high bids, and what components should not be sacrificed. I concluded that a $40 million increase in the authorization to $272.7 million was fully justified and that we should seek to implement it through the appropriations process if possible, avoiding another visit to the authorizing committees.

Faircloth was now on the Senate Appropriations Committee, and I had no idea how he would react. I proceeded carefully, working closely with EPA, securing the support of VA-HUD chairman Jerry Lewis (R-California) and ranking Democrat Louis Stokes, making certain that VA-HUD chief clerk Frank Cushing, who knew the project well, was fully briefed on the situation we faced, and attempting to give the authorizers due notice without encouraging their intervention. I also pursued a sizable increment of funding. Chairman Lewis put the full $162.7 million needed to complete the project, $40 million above the president's request, in the House bill, and the conferees agreed on $90 million. But I placed even greater importance on getting the total $272.7 million authorization written into law. This we were able to do, passing the VA-HUD bill in the House on July 16, 1997, and, with Cushing's help, persuading Senate staff to retain the authorization provision in conference.[25] Faircloth did not object, and when the president signed the bill on October 27, I felt that the project had cleared its last major

Figure 5.3 Installing the flagpole and raising the flag at the EPA construction site in Research Triangle Park, with chief administrator William Laxton, April 7, 2000.

hurdle. All that remained was to appropriate the remaining $72.7 million, which we did in the fiscal 1999 and 2000 bills.

In the meantime, construction on the building proceeded (see Figure 5.3). On September 11, 2000, Administrator Browner came to RTP to dedicate the cornerstone, and on May 29, 2002, the completed facility was dedicated with President Bush's EPA administrator, Christine Todd Whitman, in attendance.

The twists and turns of the EPA story, I said to a reporter after one particularly narrow escape, were reminiscent of the silent movie saga *The Perils of Pauline*. There was never much doubt that the project was important to North Carolina: EPA employed some 1,300 in the state at the time and contracted with 900 more, injecting $220 million into the state economy annually. Constructing the lab made sense in terms of ultimate savings and EPA operating efficiency, to say nothing of our nation's ability to base environmental policy on sound science—an objective that now seems more important than ever. But the nine-year appropriations effort was shaped and almost overcome by partisan politics within and beyond Congress and by broader conflicts over environmental funding. The complexity of the process, with its requirements for authorizer-appropriator as well as House-Senate concurrence, often gave opponents an opening, but it also sometimes gave proponents a chance to recoup. The saga illustrates the potential for policy entrepreneurship from the Appropriations Committee, but it also reveals a complex process with many unique challenges.

The closest I have come to an encore is the funding of a headquarters building for the North Carolina National Guard (NCNG) through the American Recovery and Reinvestment Act (ARRA) of 2009. I had obtained several earmarks for Guard facilities over the years but always knew that the main event was yet to come: constructing a modern, serviceable state headquarters building. Under the energetic leadership of the state Adjutant General, Lt. General William Ingram (2001–2010; later director of the U.S. Army National Guard, 2011–2014), the NCNG developed detailed plans for such a facility and pressed for funding annually from the National Guard Bureau's construction account. North Carolina was turned down several times; we suspected that the opportunity to accommodate multiple states with smaller projects was leading to the deferral of North Carolina's more expensive proposal. But when the call came for "shovel-ready" projects for the economic stimulus bill, with which President Obama began his administration, General Ingram and I had just what the doctor ordered.

House Appropriations Chairman David Obey and the Democratic leadership had ambitious plans for the Recovery Act but decided not to permit earmarks. This was a good decision—to focus on larger programmatic funding items and to avoid the more scattershot and politically controversial approach that earmarks might entail. It did, however, define the approach I had to take to get the NCNG project funded. There had to be a specific line item for Army National Guard Construction in the bill. If there were, we had good reason to believe that North Carolina's project would be at the top of the national list; it had long been deferred and was truly shovel-ready. Fortunately, Chet Edwards (D-Texas), chairman of the Military Construction Subcommittee, was ready to help. A $50 million construction item was written into the bill, of which $44 million was allocated to the North Carolina project by the Bureau in fairly short order. By July, 2009, construction was underway. We estimated that the project supported some 3,400 jobs, true to the purposes of the Recovery Act.

In the meantime, the NCNG finalized an agreement with the administration of Governor Beverly Perdue to include a new headquarters for NC Emergency Management and additional Department of Transportation offices in the new facility. This brought in some $15 million in state funding, to which I added $2 million in subsequent Department of Homeland Security (DHS) earmarks.

The dedication of the facility on February 10, 2012, marked the culmination of a decade of effort and another major investment, via federal appropriations, in North Carolina. But the contrast with the EPA saga was also striking: both required years of preparation, but with the NCNG, the premium was on quickness and agility when a one-time opportunity arose, with few obstacles in our path once we found our way forward. It was a satisfying exercise in appropriations politics, and I was especially pleased to bring Chet Edwards, who by then had been defeated in the 2010 Republican sweep, to the ceremony to receive our thanks and to see the results of his hard work.

Appropriations and Policy

Appropriations members often champion programs and agencies we regard as especially deserving of support, requesting significant increases in funding beyond the president's request or the current year's level. During my entire time in Congress, I have requested robust funding for NIH and NSF research, HOME Investment Partnerships, Historically Black Colleges and Universities, Pell Grants for college scholarships, and other major programs, motivated by a sense of both district relevance and national significance.

Such items, of course, have many advocates. In areas of narrower scope, however, persistent advocacy by one or a small group of members can have more discernible effects. Early on, for example, I took up the cause of VA medical and prosthetic research, impressed by work being conducted at the Durham VA Medical Center and concerned by the Clinton administration's weak budget requests. We effected a turnaround in the late 1990s; today Congress routinely provides research funding commensurate with the rest of the VA budget. I also maintained special interest in the ATE program at NSF that I had initiated. I was able to take funding from the mid-twenties to $45 million by 2004 and $65 million today. I could also see the results at home; over the years 2011–2019, sixteen schools in North Carolina, led by Wake Technical Community College, received 22 ATE awards.

As I have moved into subcommittee leadership—Homeland Security and then Transportation-HUD—my policy focus has broadened: I have a greater ability to advocate increases (or decreases, or the attachment of conditions) for specific programs, but I and my staff also must pass judgment on every program and agency funded in the bill. Many factors influence the "mark" one drafts as chairman or the comprehensive list of recommendations one makes as ranking member—the administration's request and justifications; information gathered through hearings, exchanges with the agencies, and outside assessments; recommendations of advocates or critics; requests from colleagues; and one's own assessments and priorities.

While we pride ourselves on scrutinizing the entire budget line-by-line, we also give some items special attention and emphasis. As the new Homeland Security chairman in 2007, I was prepared to champion the rebuilding of FEMA in Hurricane Katrina's aftermath, DHS's research and health affairs functions, and the Coast Guard—national priorities that also had special relevance to North Carolina projects and facilities. Two additional issues required constant and careful attention because of underlying policy conflicts and my disagreement with the magnitude of the expenditures proposed by the Bush administration: the extensive construction of border fencing and the stepping up of immigration enforcement without prioritizing those who truly posed a risk to the community.

The administration's emphasis on border security was linked to its push for comprehensive immigration reform, which was killed by a Senate filibuster in 2007. Both this bill and the administration's annual budget request proposed some 650 miles of border fencing, dozens of camera and radar surveillance towers, and thousands of additional border patrol officers. Most Democrats, myself included, were skeptical of the size of the requests but aware that they might well be the price to pay if we were to provide a path to citizenship for undocumented immigrants living and working in the United States and to realize the other goals of comprehensive reform.

As chairman, I tried both to moderate the requests and to subject them to critical scrutiny. Border fencing was particularly challenging: we required the administration to break down its request into 20–40-mile segments and to justify each with a rough cost-benefit analysis. Was a fence the best means to achieve border security in this area, and how did the cost compare to other means? How could physical barriers, high-tech surveillance, and increased personnel most efficiently complement one another? Were there portions of the proposed fence that should be relocated to accommodate environmental or other public concerns? I would not claim too much for this process; we certainly threw more money at border security than I thought necessary. But we did prompt important fence modifications in certain areas—avoiding bisecting a community college campus in Brownsville, for example, and designing a creative levee-fence combination—and made the overall process more transparent and accountable. In the end, the border security push over fiscal years 2008–2009 produced increases from 154 to 337 miles of pedestrian fencing and 110 to 299 miles of vehicular fencing. Border Patrol funding was increased 54 percent, bringing the number of agents from 13,297 to 17,408. By the end of the Obama administration, with Republicans back in control of the appropriations process, border fencing totaled 654 miles and appropriations for Border Patrol operations stood at $4.4 billion.

None of these facts got in the way of candidate Donald Trump's claim that the U.S. had essentially "open borders" with Mexico. He proposed the construction of a fortified wall along most of the border, with initial cost estimates ranging upward of $40 billion (which he absurdly claimed he could force Mexico to pay). By this time, although I was still a member of the Homeland Security subcommittee, I was neither chairman nor ranking Democrat. This fact, in addition to my conviction that Trump's proposal was extraordinarily wasteful and based on demagogic premises, led me to concentrate less on funding questions than on the underlying policy question: the wall was and is a spectacularly bad idea. The subcommittee gave me a platform from which to resist funding as well as to provide a reality check as to the billions that had already been poured into border security and the impossibility of *any* fence or wall providing the degree of security promised.

Questions as to the wall's foolishness escalated into an intractable standoff between Congress and the president with serious constitutional implications (see Chapters 7 and 11). Homeland Security appropriations bills became impossible to pass, and a continuing impasse on wall funding prompted the longest shutdown in history in early 2019 as even stopgap appropriations bills languished. Trump never got more than a fraction of the wall funding he wanted from appropriations bills, even under extreme duress. His solution was to declare a national emergency—under conditions that obviously fell short of what historically had been regarded as emergencies—in order to divert to wall construction some $8 billion from 2019 and 2020 appropriations for military construction, counternarcotics, and other purposes. Not only did Senate Majority Leader Mitch McConnell acquiesce in this affront to the power of the purse; so did the top Republican on the House Appropriations Committee, meekly stating that the failure of Democrats "to work with us on border security" had "forced the president to redirect funds."[26]

My engagement on the question of immigration enforcement followed a similar trajectory. As I assumed the chairmanship, I had searching conversations with colleagues and staff as to how to discipline and target enforcement—both to rein in workplace raids and other indiscriminate approaches but also to demonstrate that Democrats could be tough when it came to truly dangerous people. In 2006, the DHS Inspector General had estimated that some 600,000 undocumented persons were serving prison sentences, were for the most part unknown to Immigration and Customs Enforcement (ICE), and therefore were likely to remain in the United States upon release. In the first bill we reported, for fiscal 2008, we provided $200 million for a comprehensive effort to identify these individuals and to remove those judged deportable.[27]

The Secure Communities program at ICE, begun in 2008 by the Bush administration and continued under President Obama, was in part a response to appropriations pressures to target immigration enforcement. But it was never focused as tightly on persons convicted of serious crimes as we intended. Serious controversies arose as to the circumstances under which ICE "detainers" might be placed on persons arrested for minor infractions and the degree to which local law enforcement—far beyond the penal system—might be drawn into immigration enforcement. ICE Director John Morton issued a "prosecutorial discretion" memo in 2012 ordering that enforcement be focused on those guilty of serious crimes, and in 2014 the administration replaced Secure Communities with the Priority Enforcement Program (PEP), designed to focus enforcement more tightly on dangerous individuals.

All this was reversed by the Trump administration, which restored Secure Communities and denounced local law enforcement officials who declined to be fully drawn into federal immigration enforcement. The number of people in ICE detention rose from 41,163 in 2016 to 49,396 in 2019, but the number of those individuals who had serious "level 1" criminal records declined from 7,475 to 6,048. The percentage of those detained with no criminal conviction at all rose from 57 to 64. In other words, ICE raids became both more frequent and less discriminating, assuming a certain random quality that greatly increased levels of anxiety and fear in my district and across the country.[28]

Throughout this history, I pushed ICE to exercise the prosecutorial discretion which any law enforcement agency must exercise—after all, ICE can deport at most four percent of those here illegally each year, so it clearly must set some priorities—with transparency and clarity of purpose. Trump administration officials, when criticized for the apparently indiscriminate nature of their arrests and deportations, typically claimed both to be targeting criminal elements *and* to be following "the law" in going after all undocumented people. As DHS Secretary John Kelly put it:

> If lawmakers do not like the laws they've passed and we are charged to enforce, then they should have the courage and skill to change the laws. Otherwise, they should shut up and support the men and women on the front lines.[29]

"Which is it?" I asked ICE Director Thomas Homan when he testified before our subcommittee in 2017. "You are saying, yes, we are prioritizing these dangerous folks, but by the way, we are going after everybody." Homan's answer was essentially to repeat the contradictory claims.[30]

The questions of detention and deportation hit closer to home in early 2019, when ICE conducted raids in and around my district, arresting some 200 individuals, most without any criminal record. The situation became even more ominous when the director of ICE's Atlanta field office publicly linked the raids to recent decisions by three newly elected sheriffs to terminate supposedly voluntary enforcement agreements with ICE. "Is the Department predicating raids as retaliation against local law enforcement agencies who are exercising their own discretion … and have reasonably decided that maintaining community access and trust is absolutely critical to their law enforcement mission?" I asked Acting DHS Secretary Kevin McAleenan in an April 30 hearing. McAleenan offered carefully worded assurances, but I nonetheless added language to the committee report on the fiscal 2020 bill "reminding" ICE that "immigration enforcement should not be used either to induce communities to enter or deter them from discontinuing [enforcement] agreements."[31]

My periodic encounters with John Kelly illustrate both the major changes in immigration policy under Trump and the ways, partly as a consequence, my own role changed. I first met General John Kelly on a visit to Guatemala City and Tegucigalpa with other appropriators in 2014. We were there to explore the conditions surrounding the surge in mothers with children and unaccompanied children making their way from the Triangle countries of Central America—Guatemala, Honduras, and El Salvador—to the U.S. border, usually turning themselves in to authorities and seeking asylum. Kelly flew from Southern Command headquarters in Miami to meet us, showing great interest in our mission and reiterating what he had written in a *Military Times* piece the week before: this was not mainly an issue of border security. It had to be addressed by dealing with the situations that were driving desperate people to flee their own countries. "The only viable approach," he wrote, "is to work as closely as we can with as many nations [as possible, toward] an economically integrated region that offers reasons for its people to build their futures at home." Kelly went on to invoke Colombia as an example of what "should be and could be," urging "a new approach to Central America that balances prosperity, governance, and security [with] funding that has to involve every agency of the US government."[32]

Kelly's advocacy reinforced the recommendation of Vice President Joe Biden, tasked by President Obama to formulate a response to the Triangle migration, for an all-of-government, non-incremental increase in aid. The result was a $754 million appropriation for Fiscal Year 2016, doubled from previous years.[33]

All of this was lost on the incoming Trump administration, whose proposed budget for individual-country aid cut El Salvador from $65 to $45 million, Guatemala from $112 to $77 million, and Honduras from $93 to $67 million. "Where is that coming from?" I asked General Kelly, now Secretary of Homeland Security, as he testified before our subcommittee in 2017. Reminding him of our discussions in 2014, I questioned the relevance of Trump's border wall to the situation and asked what Kelly's reaction had been to the proposed cuts in the foreign operations budget. He did not answer directly but acknowledged that the Obama administration's increases had been "very, very helpful," drawing a parallel to "where Colombia was at the beginning of Plan Colombia."[34] Obviously, there was a major disconnect between this assessment and the Trump budget, suggesting that Kelly had either been ignored or had chosen not to assert himself.

The final appropriations bill for 2018 rejected the president's most extreme proposed cuts but still reduced the overall Central American appropriation to $615 million. And when the migrant flow began to increase again in 2018, the Trump administration reacted with a draconian "zero tolerance" policy that dictated the criminal prosecution of all those crossing the border and the separation of minor children from parents while the latter awaited trial. John Kelly, now the president's chief of staff, was again at the center of the controversy, and his widely quoted comments bespoke how badly the situation had deteriorated and how far astray American policy had gone:

> A big name of the game is deterrence. The children will be taken care of —put into foster care or whatever—but the big point is they elected to come illegally into the United States, and this is a technique that no one hopes will be used extensively or for very long.[35]

These and other controversies prompted an unusual number of immigration-related amendments during the 2018 appropriations markup season.

Most were rejected on party-line votes, but Republican committee leaders accepted enough to signal misgivings if not a rebuke of the Trump administration's excesses. Two of the successful amendments were mine. The first tightened language in the Labor-Health and Human Services bill regarding the monitoring and reporting of child-family separations and reunifications. The second amendment, added to the Homeland Security bill, denied funding for Citizenship and Immigration Services (CIS) to implement a recent directive from Attorney General Jeff Sessions to remove a credible fear of domestic or gang violence as a basis for an asylum claim. Bipartisan agreement to this amendment inspired immediate, vociferous attacks on Subcommittee Chairman Kevin Yoder (R-Kansas) from right-wing commentators, after which he promised to remove my provision before the bill was finally enacted.[36]

In 2019, the president's approach to Central American aid became far more extreme, as it had for border wall funding, and with similar constitutional principles at stake. The president suspended or reallocated almost all aid, including $550 million from previous years, as well as the 2019 appropriation. I became involved in a number of attempts to protect or reverse the cutoff, including the placing of provisions in the Fiscal 2020 State Department and Foreign Operations (SFOPS) appropriations bill to deny flexibility to the president in releasing the Central American aid funds.

The policy leverage afforded by my leadership positions on Transportation-Housing and Urban Development (T-HUD) contrasts significantly with Homeland Security, or at least what Homeland Security has become. T-HUD has always been a challenging bill that elicited partisan differences on domestic spending and policy priorities. On the other hand, once a bipartisan agreement on top-line numbers has been attained, the subcommittee has generally been able to work cooperatively. My own priorities have remained consistent: to secure an adequate budget allocation for our bill relative to other bills, to push for a greater HUD share within the bill, and to obtain robust funding for programs that are particularly relevant to areas experiencing high growth and congestion and/or have been seriously underfunded in recent years.

For example, I have taken on the cause of intercity rail and the development of regional passenger service. President Obama directed $8 billion in Recovery Act funds to intercity rail, of which North Carolina utilized over $500 million to greatly improve Raleigh-Charlotte AMTRAK service. Developing a direct Raleigh-to-Richmond corridor is the next step toward efficient service to Washington. Funding has been hard to come by under Republican leadership, but I have pushed successfully to increase Consolidated Rail Infrastructure and Safety Improvements (CRISI) and other rail improvement funding, particularly since becoming chairman.

I have also been the main champion among the four bipartisan, bicameral subcommittee leaders (the "four corners") for Choice Neighborhoods (formerly HOPE VI), a unique program that takes a comprehensive approach to transforming high-poverty, distressed neighborhoods into viable mixed-income communities. The program is challenging to administer and requires special care to ensure adequate replacement housing for those who may be displaced. But I have witnessed its transformative potential in North Carolina, and there is nothing else with comparable impact in HUD's portfolio. Despite the Trump administration's proposal to eliminate the program, we maintained funding at the $150 million level in fiscal 2018 and 2019, while pressing HUD to implement the program effectively. After becoming chairman, I raised the level to $300 million in the House bill for fiscal 2020, which became $175 million in the final version.

I have also taken a distinctive position in support of "Section 202" rental housing for the elderly (named after the relevant section of the Housing Act of 1959) and "Section 811" supportive housing for people with disabilities (from the National Affordable Housing Act of 1990). These programs have been well utilized in my district; I got particularly involved with Section 202 as congregations in Raleigh, Durham, and Chapel Hill formed nonprofit arms and pursued applications successfully.

Both programs historically have provided for an expanded supply of housing through construction or rehabilitation and for subsidies after construction to help keep the projects affordable. After the budget cutbacks of 2011, however, the programs were appropriated sufficient funding only to maintain existing projects. Some of the slack was taken up with flexible HOME funding, but this too was limited and was proposed for elimination by the incoming Trump administration. I had been wanting to get sections 202 and 811 back into the housing production business for several years and got my chance when the fiscal 2018–2019 budget agreement gave our subcommittee an improved top-line number. Each of the "four corners" leaders had an opportunity to add a modest amount for programs of special interest. I used my allocation to add $102 million in section 202 and $83 million in section 811 for new construction in 2018 and have continued to add to these amounts, as our allocations permitted, in subsequent years. Today, more than $400 million has been appropriated, and HUD has begun making awards across the country.

My other policy priorities during my four years (2015–2018) as T-HUD ranking member had stronger support among other subcommittee leaders—HOME Investment Partnerships, public housing capital and operating funds, "Section 8" rental assistance, Community Development Block Grants (CDBG), TIGER (now BUILD) grants for innovative multi-modal transportation projects, AMTRAK capital and operating funds, and Capital Investment Grants ("New Starts") for mass transit. The list was made longer by our chronic underinvestment in most HUD programs and by ill-advised proposals from the Trump administration—for example, the elimination of HOME, CDBG, TIGER, and New Starts. Fortunately, very few members of Congress agreed with these cuts, rather viewing the T-HUD bill as a chance at least to get started on the long-overdue infrastructure investments Trump had promised but never delivered.

I had tangible evidence in my district of the worth of many of these investments—Union Station in Raleigh, built with the help of TIGER funds; four AMTRAK trains each way, each day between Raleigh and Charlotte; transit plans for the Triangle that will eventually qualify as New Starts; and numerous HOME and CDBG-assisted projects. But I was also certain of the national importance of the funding streams, as I determined to bring affordable housing to the fore as a front-burner issue and to make a down payment on longstanding infrastructure needs.

Moving into the T-HUD chairmanship enabled me to extend the sub-committee's policy reach beyond issues of funding. For example, we held oversight hearings on critical matters such as the Federal Aviation Administration's aircraft certification program in the wake of the fatal 2018 and 2019 Boeing 737 MAX crashes and HUD's delinquent administration of CDBG disaster recovery funds in Puerto Rico after Hurricane Maria. We often achieved our policy objectives by attaching conditions to funding items. When HUD refused to release disaster relief funds for Puerto Rico, likely because of political interference from the White House and the Office of Management and Budget (OMB), we withheld funds for a top priority of HUD's administrators. Within weeks, the Department reversed course.

Sometimes our requirements were simple and specific—forbidding the administration from reducing the federal share of local transit projects below 40 percent, for example. Or they could be broad and sweeping, as when we directed that resiliency in the face of natural disasters and climate change be a criterion for all future Department of Transportation (DOT) and HUD awards. I also sometimes attached policy riders, which might or might not survive in omnibus bills but nonetheless could give a nudge or deliver a rebuke to administration agencies. I placed particular importance, for example, on 2019 riders that codified an Obama-era rule for the non-discriminatory treatment of transgender individuals in emergency shelters and that forbad HUD from proceeding with a rule to expel mixed-status families (where at least one person had legal immigration status but others might not) from federally assisted housing. The policies being proposed by the Trump administration promised to do great harm, and I readily used our bill to serve notice that they would be met by strong congressional resistance.

Hearings on our Fiscal 2021 bill were rudely interrupted by the coronavirus, but work on assembling the chairman's mark—gathering member requests, securing ranking member Diaz-Balart's input, soliciting agency and stakeholder views—proceeded online. We had a live markup, masked and distanced, and took the bill to the floor as part of a six-bill "minibus" on July 30–31, 2020. I secured substantial increases in funding for intercity rail, HOME, public housing maintenance and safety, and homeless assistance. The heightened national concern for racial justice was reflected in adjustments we made in several accounts and in our messaging of the bill. In light of the pandemic and as a hedge against shortfalls in relief funding, we also included $75 billion in emergency funding, targeting all transportation modes, public housing capital funds, and HOME. I added an amendment in markup requiring that passengers and employees on airlines, AMTRAK, and public transit wear masks for the duration of the pandemic. I regarded it a badge of honor when President Trump included the requirement among the reasons for his veto threat.

House Republicans voted against all of the appropriations bills, because we did not yet have an agreement with the Senate on top-line numbers and because they objected to the emergency spending. But they found a lot to like in the bills, certainly in T-HUD, and we passed them with a sense of achievement, given the extraordinary circumstances, and confidence that they placed us in a strong position going forward.

Notes

1 David E. Price, "Professionals and 'Entrepreneurs': Staff Orientations and Policy Making on Three Senate Committees," *Journal of Politics*, 33 (May 1971), pp. 316–336, and *Who Makes the Laws?* (Cambridge, MA: Schenkman, 1972).

2 Robert A. Dahl, *Pluralist Democracy in the United States: Conflict and Consent* (Chicago, IL: Rand McNally, 1967), p. 136. Dahl qualified this view considerably in later editions. See, for example, *Democracy in the United States: Promise and Performance*, 4th ed. (Boston, MA: Houghton Mifflin, 1981), pp. 135–138.

3 For an account of how an unlikely Senate committee, Commerce, chaired by Senator Warren Magnuson (D-Washington), became an entrepreneurial prototype, see Michael Pertschuk, *When the Senate Worked for Us* (Nashville, TN: Vanderbilt University Press, 2017).

4 Despite difficulties in precise measurement—owing, for example, to changed rules of cosponsorship—Roger Davidson found overall "a sudden and striking contraction" in congressional workload indicators during the 1980s. "The New Centralization on Capitol Hill," *Review of Politics*, 50 (Summer 1988), pp. 352–355.

5 More detailed accounts of the ventures described in the next two sections may be found in earlier editions of this book.

6 On the incentives to policy entrepreneurship provided by "environmental factors," especially perceived levels of public salience and conflict, see David E. Price, *Policymaking in Congressional Committees: The Impact of "Environmental" Factors* (Tucson, AZ: University of Arizona Press, 1979). Abridged version in *American Political Science Review*, 72 (June, 1978), pp. 548–574.

7 Testimony of Chapel Hill Mayor Jonathan B. Howes, *Affordable Housing*, field hearing before the Subcommittee on Housing and Community Development, Committee on Banking, Finance and Urban Affairs, U.S. House of Representatives, 101st Congress, January 26, 1990, pp. 14, 153. Also see the exchanges on pp. 33–40.

8 Testimony of Floyd T. Carter, *Affordable Housing*, field hearing before the Subcommittee on Housing and Community Development, Committee on Banking, Finance and Urban Affairs, U.S. House of Representatives, 101st Congress, January 26, 1990, p. 124.

9 *Scientific and Technical Literacy in the Workforce*, field hearing before the Subcommittee on Science, Research, and Technology of the Committee on

Science, Space, and Technology, U.S. House of Representatives, 100th Congress, November 9, 1987.

10 Also on the list was Tom Sawyer (D-Ohio), sponsor of the Adult Literacy and Employability Act, a bill dealing mainly with the Adult Education Act and the Job Training Partnership Act, both under the jurisdiction of the Education and Labor Committee. To stress the continuity of our efforts, we cosponsored one another's bills and numbered them sequentially (H.R. 3122 for mine, H.R. 3123 for his). We then testified at each other's hearings.

11 When pressed, Bassam Shakhashiri, NSF's assistant director of science and engineering education, acknowledged that the distinction between science education and technical training had narrowed considerably, falling back on a plea that NSF not be "overloaded." See *Scientific, Technical, and Literacy Education and Training*, hearing before the Subcommittee on Science, Research, and Technology of the Committee on Science, Space, and Technology, U.S. House of Representatives, 101st Congress, October 31, 1989, pp. 65–66, 159–160.

12 *Precollege Science and Mathematics Education*, hearing before the Subcommittee on Science, Research, and Technology of the Committee on Science, Space, and Technology, U.S. House of Representatives, 101st Congress, February 28, 1990, pp. 66, 84.

13 Price, *Who Makes the Laws?* p. 229.

14 Committee on Science, Space and Technology, U.S. House of Representatives, 102nd Congress, *Report to Accompany H.R. 2936*, April 30, 1992, pp. 6–7.

15 *Challenges and Innovations in Elementary and Secondary Education*, field hearing before the Subcommittee on Early Childhood, Youth and Families, Committee on Education and the Workforce, U.S. House of Representatives, 106th Congress, September 8, 1999, pp. 4–5, 36–37, 51–54.

16 *Congressional Record*, daily ed., July 8, 2003, pp. H6366–67.

17 HR 3700, 114th Congress, passed by the House on February 2, 2016.

18 HR 2500, 116th Congress, passed by the House on July 12, 2019.

19 HR 2740, 110th Congress, passed by the House on October 4, 2007. See David E. Price, "Private Contractors, Public Consequences: The Need for an Effective Criminal Justice Framework," in Christopher Kinsey and Malcolm Patterson, eds., *Contractors and War: The Transformation of US Expeditionary Operations* (Palo Alto, CA: Stanford University Press, 2012). Asher Hildebrand, my defense and foreign policy aide at the time, did major work on this article.

20 For example, I helped organize support for a bill (H.R. 2050)—introduced by the Energy and Commerce Committee's ranking Democrat, John Dinged (D-Michigan) and, in the Senate, by Richard Burr (R-North Carolina), whom Goodmon had recruited to the cause—to retain the cap of 35 percent on the share of the national audience television stations owned by any one company would be allowed to reach. But such authorization proposals were sure to be blocked by Republican committee and party leaders.

21 Frank Ahrens, "Democrats Decry 'Compromise' on FCC Rule," *Washington Post*, November 26, 2003, p. E1.

22 Jonathan Rausch, "Earmarks Are a Model, Not a Menace," *National Journal*, March 14, 2009.

23 See, for example, James T. Walsh, Melanie Sloan, Rich Gold, and Craig Holman, "The Case for Restoring Earmarks," *Washington Post*, January 23, 2018.

24 See David Rogers, "House Republicans Offer Concessions on Domestic Spending as Elections Near," *Wall Street Journal*, May 31, 1996, p. A12. Rogers cited the EPA building as one of several examples. Democrats, he noted, "seemed torn between declaring victory and crying foul."

25 See the justification provided in the House report on the bill: Committee on Appropriations, *Report to Accompany H.R. 2158*, 105th Congress, July 11, 1997, p. 64.

26 Rep. Kay Granger (R-Texas), quoted in "Trump Administration Diverts $3.8 Billion in Pentagon Funding to Border Wall," *National Public Radio*, February 13, 2020.

27 In early 2008, ICE director Julie Myers reported that the agency was on track to issue some 200,000 "charging documents," up from 57,000 in 2006, covering all federal and an increasing percentage of state and local institutions. *Department of Homeland Security Appropriations for 2009*, hearing before the Subcommittee on Homeland Security, Committee on Appropriations, US House of Representatives, 110th Congress, February 26, 2008, p. 61.

28 "Growth in ICE Detention Fueled by Immigrants with No Criminal Conviction" and "ICE Detains Fewer Immigrants with Serious Criminal Convictions under Trump Administration," *TRAC Reports*, University of Syracuse, November 26 and December 6, 2019. The most common "Level 1" offenses were assault, burglary, and drug trafficking.

29 Devlin Barrett, "DHS Secretary Kelly Says Congressional Critics Should 'Shut Up' or Change Laws," *Washington Post*, April 18, 2017.

30 *Department of Homeland Security Appropriations for 2018*, hearing before the Subcommittee on Homeland Security, Committee on Appropriations, US House of Representatives, 115th Congress, June 18, 2017, p. 280.

31 Ibid., 116th Congress, April 30, 2019; and *Report to Accompany H.R. 3931*, June 11, 2019, p. 30.

32 John Kelly, "Central America Drug War a Dire Threat to US National Security," *Military Times*, July 8, 2014.

33 Joseph Biden, "The Border Won't Be Secure Until Central America Is," *Washington Post*, June 25, 2018.

34 *Homeland Security Appropriations for 2018*, May 24, 2017, p. 106.

35 Juliet Hirschfeld Davis and Michael D. Shear, "How Trump Came to Enforce a Practice of Separating Migrant Families," *New York Times*, June 16, 2018.

36 John Hann, "Immigration Tricky Issue in Tight Kansas Congressional Race," *The Kansas City Star*, September 9, 2018.

6   The Party Connection

Political parties loom large in today's Congress. Increasingly, candidates in competitive districts are recruited, financed, and coached by the Democratic Congressional Campaign Committee (DCCC) and the National Republican Congressional Committee (NRCC), the political arms of the congressional parties. But even candidates who run their campaigns relatively independently quickly confront the realities of party leadership and control and the pervasiveness of partisan divisions. Parties may have a tenuous hold on much of the electorate, with the ranks of independents and "unaffiliateds" increasing, but in most districts the party bases have become more distinctive ideologically and more demanding. Party solidarity in roll-call voting still falls short of what is found in most parliamentary systems, but it is coming close, reaching its highest levels since the early twentieth century and increasing markedly from its low point in the 90th–92nd Congresses (1967–1972).

Partisan polarization—increases in homogeneity within the parties and in the ideological distance between them—has accelerated both in the congressional parties and in their electoral bases. The effects go far beyond sharpened divisions in roll-call voting and partisan gridlock. In the next two chapters, I will explore a range of impacts—from increasingly centralized leadership, a diminished role for committees, and altered patterns of lawmaking to changes in appropriations and budgeting—for which polarization bears a heavy, if not exclusive responsibility. Not all of these developments are negative, but overall, I will argue, they have resulted in a diminished capacity for the institution.

Initially, I will elucidate congressional party and presidential relations by describing my own interactions with the Democratic Party while running for office and serving in the House—in the majority and the minority, under Democratic and Republican presidents. Not every member's story would be the same. Party organizations outside the Congress vary in their hold on voter loyalties and their control of campaign resources, and candidates depend on them to varying degrees. Although parties perform crucial institutional functions and every representative must come to terms with them in some fashion, personal and political considerations, as well as constituency-based incentives, often limit or condition party regularity in the House. Members differ in how they relate to party efforts to engage or cajole them, and hence in the alliances they form and the voting patterns they display.

Despite these variations, members of both parties have generally supported, or at least acquiesced in, strong leadership prerogatives. What are the limits of party leadership and control, and how do they differ for Democrats and Republicans? How does strong, disciplined leadership by the majority party compare with bipartisan accommodation and cooperation as a way of governing? I will explore, if not definitively answer, such questions by describing the leadership structures and practices developed by Democrats and then Republicans, and some of the incentives to participation and support experienced by members like myself. I will describe the difference it made for Democrats—for two, all-too-brief two-year periods—to gain unified control of government. Finally, I will consider what might be learned from several recent exercises in partisanship: from the "responsible party" triumph on the 1993 budget to the tactics adopted by Republicans and Democrats as they alternated leadership control and the contrasting impeachment battles of 1998 and 2019.

Parties and Elections

As a candidate for Congress, I had unusually strong party credentials. I had paid my dues through local party service and as a foot soldier in other Democrats' campaigns, and my background as executive director and chairman of the North Carolina Democratic Party gave me major advantages as a congressional candidate. The party chairmanship has changed in this regard; I remember being told when I accepted the job that the infighting would inevitably leave me with more enemies than friends and finish me politically. But the chairmanship had become a more visible public role, particularly in a marquee race like Hunt-Helms. What gave me credibility as a potential candidate in 1986 was receiving media exposure and being identified as a spokesman on key issues during the Senate race and the other campaigns of 1984, much more than my behind-the-scenes organizational activity.[1]

I chose the county Democratic conventions in my district (held simultaneously on April 13, 1985) to announce my candidacy, believing (as I still do) that party activists were an essential core of my political base. After surviving the primary, I received substantial support from the DCCC and integrated my grassroots campaign with that of county party organizations. My campaigns thus illustrate the role that party can play. They also demonstrate the limits of that role, even when a candidate has an inclination (which many candidates do not) to run as part of the party team.

As recounted in Chapter 2, neither my familiarity among party activists nor my wider exposure as a party spokesman made me the favorite or gave me substantial name recognition in a Democratic primary. That came only as we formulated a television message and scraped together enough money to put it on the air. Relatively little of that money came from party sources; Democratic Party activists are generally able to contribute only modestly. North Carolina party organizations (like others in states with a one-party past where nomination was once tantamount to election) have a tradition of remaining neutral, financially and otherwise, in primary contests. The same was true in my case for the DCCC. Nonetheless, I called on its leaders during the primary season. I knew that a direct contribution was out of the question but hoped to convince them that I would be the best candidate against the GOP incumbent, thinking that they might informally pass the word to potential contributors. This happened only to a very limited degree. It was not within the power of local, state, or national party organizations to deliver the Democratic nomination. My fledgling campaign team and I were largely on our own in pursuing that goal.

That changed somewhat but not entirely after the primary. I was one of four Democratic challengers from North Carolina whom the DCCC was targeting for assistance in 1986. The committee expended $39,848 on my behalf, which, when added to the state tax checkoff money funneled through the state Democratic Party, came close to the legal maximum. This, of course, was a pittance compared to what the national committees now do, mainly through independent expenditures, but we welcomed it as an indication of the significance of our race. The state party, having lost the organizational resources of the governorship in 1984 and having nothing like the Hunt-Helms Senate race to attract contributions and participation in 1986, was not in a position to replicate the state-level voter-contact operations undertaken two years before. I was fortunate, however, in having relatively active Democratic organizations in most of my counties and a tradition of extensive phone bank and get-out-the-vote (GOTV) activity in Raleigh and Chapel Hill. We therefore decided after the primary to run our voter-contact operations as part of a Democratic "unity campaign," and our Senate candidate, Terry Sanford, did the same.

Although my campaign thus evinced relatively strong participation from the national campaign committee and local party organizations, it could not, when compared to parliamentary elections in other Western democracies or earlier American practice, be judged a party-centered effort. We gained numerous foot soldiers and saved scarce campaign dollars by combining forces with other Democratic candidates in our canvassing and turnout operations, but even here we gave as much as we got. Party precinct structures were spotty at best, and the cadres of volunteers often needed shoring up. So, activists from the Price campaign helped make the party efforts work, as well as the reverse.

In other facets of the campaign, the party role was far less prominent. The state party organized a rally in each congressional district for all the Democratic candidates, and most county parties did the same thing locally.

But most of my campaign appearances and fundraising events were organized by our campaign alone. We drew on the state party's research and press resources, but we were largely on our own in devising a press strategy, formulating a message, putting together an advertising campaign, and raising the money to pay for it.

In the campaigns I waged after 1986, often against aggressive, well-financed opponents, the party role slipped even further. Only in my comeback race of 1996 did the DCCC come close to matching its 1986 financial support; I have not generally been in the top tier of most vulnerable candidates or most financially strapped campaigns. We often drew on the expertise of the DCCC-affiliated National Committee for an Effective Congress (NCEC) in targeting precincts for door-to-door walking and GOTV activity and in calculating the likely effects of various redistricting proposals. We continued to cooperate with our state and county party organizations, particularly in implementing voter-contact operations, and to develop synergetic relationships with other Democratic campaigns.

Besides trying to make the most of the party potential in my own campaigns, I have attempted to keep my local and campus party ties in good repair between elections—attending and speaking at meetings, helping organize and promote events, consulting with party leaders. I value these organizations and believe elected officials can do much to enhance their role. Politicians who complain of the party's weakness and irrelevance and treat the organization accordingly often are engaged in a self-fulfilling prophecy; we do have significant choices as to how we relate to party organizations, and the choices we make have a considerable potential to harm or help. Candidates or officeholders should not be expected to sacrifice their basic interests to those of the party, but they normally have a range of viable strategies of campaigning and governance available, of which some reinforce and others undermine party strength.

The parties, however, must also help themselves. The six national committees (the House and Senate campaign committees, and the Democratic and Republican National Committees) and some state parties have done a great deal to remodel themselves—increasing their financial base and their capacity to recruit candidates and offer a range of supportive services—and these efforts have paid off handsomely. Much depends on the quality of party leadership at all levels. Local parties are not tidy organizations, and they would lose much of their vitality if they were. Gone forever is the patronage system that bound loyalists to "the organization" and assured tight leadership control. Today's party activists are motivated mainly by issue and candidate enthusiasms, and they often give organizational maintenance a decidedly lower priority. Candidates and officeholders who would work with the party must recognize this and adapt to it. At the same time, partisans and their leaders need to understand that if they allow the party to degenerate into contending factions—each pushing for its own "pure" policy position or preferred candidate, unable or unwilling to work together after the nomination and platform battles are over—candidates and office-holders will be tempted to distance themselves, seeing the party tie as more hassle than help.

The 1994 Republican campaign to take control of the House represented a high point of party effort and impact and set a standard for the future. Republican leaders recruited and coached candidates vigorously, and the Contract with America provided a common party message. Newt Gingrich and his colleagues effectively directed resources to Republican challengers and open-seat contenders, not so much through the NRCC as through generous giving by GOP incumbent members and political action committees (PACs) under their influence. Given the party role in their election, it is hardly surprising that the Republican class of 1994 demonstrated exceptional partisan solidarity once in office. Still, traditional factors such as incumbency, candidate experience, and the political makeup of the district shaped electoral outcomes, often determining the reception given the GOP national effort.[2]

A heightened role for the national parties in House campaigns has now become institutionalized. It is most obvious in "wave" election years, such as 2006 for Democrats, where the slogan "Six [key issues] for '06" became the functional equivalent of the Contract with America in 1994. But the two congressional parties, each hungry to be in the majority, now mount far-reaching efforts every cycle. In the midterm elections of 2018, for example, the six national party committees spent over $1.1 billion; the DCCC disbursed $298 million, and the NRCC $201 million. The campaign committees contributed to candidates on one or both sides of some 150 races, but the bulk of their funds went to "independent" media expenditures for candidates (or against their opponents) in a much smaller number of targeted contests.[3]

The fact that most districts are not targeted in this fashion does not free other members from increased party involvement. We may or may not pick up on the recommended campaign slogans and themes, but all are expected to contribute to the common effort; in 2018 House Democrats transferred $33.2 million from our own campaign treasuries to the DCCC, while Republican members transferred $31.8 million to the NRCC.

Some have heralded the more prominent role of the national committees in political finance as both a sign of and a key to party renewal. Certainly, Senate leader Mitch McConnell seems to think that way, as he presses on every front to eliminate limits on giving to and by the parties. I am not so sure. The enhanced financial role clearly has implications for the capacity of leaders to discipline members and to manage and message congressional operations more generally, as we shall explore in this and the following chapters. But as I argued in my 2002 amicus brief regarding unlimited "soft money" for the party committees (Chapter 3), utilizing parties mainly as conduits for large contributions may in fact "hollow out" and marginalize their traditional organizational functions.

Political scientists Daniel Schlozman and Sam Rosenfeld make the case that "strong parties are not simply weak parties with strong bank accounts, but formal institutions that effectively and continually engage with voters, activists, and politicians to formulate and then implement party programs that clarify citizens' choices." It is not clear that American parties currently measure up, particularly when it comes to providing a center of gravity for disparate ideologies and movements and a coherent agenda for governing. Instead, we often witness the "paradox of ineffectual parties in an age of hyperpartisanship."[4]

In any event, as party spending has gone up, so too has the cost of campaigns and the role of non-party groups. This has left candidates still raising the bulk of their funds from non-party sources. Independent expenditures by the DCCC on behalf of a candidate seldom exceed $1 million. Moreover, electorates rarely vote on partisan grounds alone, and incumbents rightly believe that their various ways of serving and communicating with their districts—mostly unmediated by party—can have a powerful electoral impact (see Chapter 9).[5] When the time comes to cast controversial roll-call votes, thoughts of the use an opponent might make of an issue in fire-breathing thirty-second televisions ads—particularly if one's district is closely contested—can make the blandishments of party leaders pale by comparison.

Still, the overall trend is unmistakable. Not only has the party role in elections increased; as politics has become more ideological and polarized, elections have been driven by national forces and trends. As I noted in Chapter 2, national partisan swings in 1994, 2006, 2010, and 2018 swamped many incumbents and left friends-and-neighbors politics at the mercy of national forces. As a result, most members have come to recognize a heightened stake in the success of their party, electorally and in producing policy outcomes. Moreover, fewer members are under severe cross-pressures, as geographical and cultural "sorting," abetted by gerrymandering, have given them more homogeneous districts. Nationalized elections have reduced split-ticket voting and produced fewer members of Congress who are at odds with their districts' partisan alignment. There remains some slack to be filled by members' own policy preferences and distinctive constituency interests. Both parties experience centrifugal pressures from their various ethnically based and ideological caucuses. But overall, the incentives to party regularity have become stronger during my time in office, and the House has become a more regimented and centralized institution.

Organizing the House

The modern march toward House centralization began with the strengthening of party operations in the Democratic-led House in the 1970s. The elections of 1958, 1964, and 1974 had brought large numbers of liberal activist Democrats into the House, while Black enfranchisement and party realignment in the South had gradually produced a new breed of Democratic

House member from that region, much closer to the party's mainstream. Members of this more homogeneous majority came to see the strengthening of party organs as a way of realizing their personal and policy goals within the chamber.[6]

That is not to say that strengthening parties was the dominant goal of congressional reform. In fact, its initial and main thrust was decentralization—the *dispersal* of authority, resources, and visibility throughout the chamber. From 1965 to 1978, this produced what Roger Davidson termed the "rise of subcommittee government."[7] Reform, however, had a centralizing component from the first. The reformers' main targets were the senior committee chairmen, many of them conservative southerners, who stood in the way of the progressive policies and greater visibility and power that junior members desired. Revitalizing the House Democratic Caucus proved necessary in order to rewrite the rules, depose recalcitrant chairmen, and otherwise effect the desired transfer of power.

The leadership, moreover, was the only available counterweight to conservative bastions like the House Rules and Ways and Means Committees. Therefore, two key early reforms removed the committee-assignment function from Ways and Means Democrats and placed it in a leadership-dominated Steering and Policy Committee and gave the Speaker the power to nominate the chair and the Democratic members of the Rules Committee. For some reformers, such as Rep. Richard Bolling (D-Missouri), the strengthening of party organs was quite deliberate, aimed at giving a true "majority of House Democrats ... effective control of the House" and enabling them to enact their legislative program.[8] For others, it was mainly a means to the end of reducing the oligarchic power of the committee barons. The effect was to strengthen the party involvement of younger members and enhance the role of the leadership, even as rules changes by the Caucus were dispersing congressional power.

This decentralization, as it proceeded through the 1970s, gave more and more members a stake in the new order. But it also created new problems for the institution that only strengthened parties could solve. The proliferating bases from which issues could be publicized and initiatives generated could also encourage conflict and obstruction when the time came to mobilize the chamber. Consequently, there was widespread support for leadership efforts to overcome organizational fragmentation, including the use of intercommittee task forces, enhanced bill referral powers for the Speaker, the development of leadership agendas, and the strengthening of whip operations.

The decline in the deference paid to committees, the desire of members for visibility, and various rules changes resulted in increased amending activity on the House floor. In time, many members came to see this as more of a threat than an opportunity, as measures they favored were damaged or delayed and as members of the opposition party used the amendment process to force politically charged record votes. Thus the leadership began, with widespread member support, to pass more bills under "suspension of the rules" procedures that forbad amendments, to employ more special rules that restricted amending activity, and to otherwise rein in floor activity.

The budget process instituted in 1974 and the politics surrounding it also strengthened the role of the congressional leadership. Party leaders assumed control over appointments to the new budget committees and, of necessity, brokered negotiations among committees and between Congress and the White House. Budget measures became more complicated, comprehensive, and conflicted, spilling over established timetables and processes and committee jurisdictions. Working out budget deals year to year with Republican administrations increasingly became a critical function of the Democratic leadership.

Many Democratic members of the House therefore became willing to support an enhanced party role. As the party organization developed, it reinforced these tendencies with a reward structure of its own. Meanwhile, the costs of cooperation were decreasing for many members as well. The political and budgetary climate of the 1980s made for less freewheeling policy entrepreneurship. Members had less to lose by being reined in and more to gain as the leadership sought to overcome some of the adverse conditions making legislative action difficult. Nor did House Democrats have as much trouble uniting under the party banner as they had in the recent past. Plenty of diversity remained, but the north–south gap that had bedeviled the party and had fueled much of the early reform effort continued to narrow. Thus, the potential costs of assertive Democratic leadership in terms of disaffection and division were greatly reduced.

These trends toward strengthened leadership were evident during my first term in the House, the 100th Congress of 1987–1988, as an assertive new Speaker, Jim Wright (D-Texas), came to power. Wright saw to it that the first five bills introduced, numbered H.R. 1 to H.R. 5, were those he regarded as lead items on the Democratic agenda. Two of these, the Clean Water Act and an ambitious highway bill, were passed shortly after Congress convened in January 1987; by April 2, both had been whipped through over President Reagan's vetoes. The remaining three bills, an omnibus trade measure and reauthorizations of elementary and secondary education and housing programs, were all passed in the next two years, as were significant welfare reform, Medicare expansion, fair housing, farm credit reform, plant closing notification, and homeless assistance measures. The 100th Congress could fairly be regarded as the most productive since the Great Society congresses of the mid-1960s, and strong leadership in the House was a critical part of the equation. Observing this as he plotted his rise to power was a Republican backbencher named Newt Gingrich, whose Contract with America eight years later owed more to Wright's precedent than he ever cared to acknowledge.

The 101st and 102nd Congresses found it difficult to maintain the same level of productivity, and House operations assumed a sharper partisan edge.

Gingrich, who in 1988 had begun pressing the ethics charges against Wright that would lead to the Speaker's downfall, was elected Minority Whip in early 1989. Replacing Dick Cheney, whom President Bush appointed Secretary of Defense, Gingrich's two-vote victory was a clear rebuke to Minority Leader Robert Michel (R-Illinois) and his more collegial style of leadership. By mid-1989, both Wright and hard-charging Democratic Whip Tony Coehlo (D-California) had departed. Democrats lost momentum as we adjusted both to leadership upheavals and the disappearance of the policy vacuum we had moved to fill in the last years of the Reagan administration.

Still, there was no major reversal of the trend toward expanded leadership operations. Majority Leader Tom Foley (D-Washington) was elected Speaker. Less aggressive in style than Wright, Foley nonetheless became increasingly assertive in using the tools of leadership, while majority leader Dick Gephardt (D-Missouri) emerged as a forceful party spokesman. President George Bush sometimes proved a strong adversary, stymieing congressional action in areas ranging from civil rights to the minimum wage, campaign finance reform, and family and medical leave. But in other areas, he proved more flexible than President Reagan, cooperating with the Congress to produce major clean air, rights for people with disabilities, energy deregulation, and housing legislation, as well as a major bipartisan budget agreement. Under conditions of either confrontation or cooperation, the need for strong party leadership was generally supported by most Democratic members.[9]

The election of Bill Clinton in 1992, ending twelve years of divided party control of the executive and legislative branches, both empowered the House Democratic leadership and reduced its autonomy in defining the party's agenda. Congress passed and the president signed a number of bills that had been vetoed or otherwise held up during the Bush administration, including a National Institutes of Health reauthorization that permitted research utilizing fetal tissue, the Family and Medical Leave Act, the Motor Voter law linking voter registration to the driver's license process, and the Brady Law requiring background checks before handgun purchases. Also approved were the bill instituting National Service, the Goals 2000 education reform initiative, legislation implementing the North American Free Trade Agreement (NAFTA) and the General Agreement on Tariffs and Trade (GATT), the 1994 Crime Bill, and the five-year budget plan of 1993. With the exception of the trade agreements, these were partisan measures that the House Democratic organization was largely responsible for passing. Yet the budget and crime victories came after long struggles that revealed deep divisions among Democrats, and the president's initiatives in health care and welfare reform died conspicuous deaths. The House Democratic leadership ended the 103rd Congress looking ineffectual and beleaguered—an impression that did not do justice to its substantial accomplishments but nonetheless contributed to the party's negative image going into the 1994 elections.

Those elections produced a new majority, a new Speaker, Newt Gingrich, and a major consolidation of leadership power. Republicans in earlier years had tracked Democratic rules changes that shifted power from committee to party leaders, but in both parties, leaders of major committees retained considerable autonomy and power. Gingrich changed that radically. Party rules were altered to give the leadership a stronger hand in making committee assignments, and Gingrich saw to it that numerous freshmen indebted to him were given coveted slots on the Appropriations, Ways and Means, Rules, and Commerce Committees. Gingrich ignored seniority in engineering the selection of several key committee chairs, including fifth-ranking Bob Livingston (R-Louisiana) on Appropriations, second-ranking Tom Bliley (R-Virginia) on Commerce, and second-ranking Henry Hyde (R-Illinois) on Judiciary. Committee chairs were weakened by the imposition of six-year term limits, staff reductions, and the abolition of proxy voting. In turn, committee chairs were given the power to appoint subcommittee chairs and hire all staff, reversing Democratic practice. But here too Gingrich did not hesitate to intervene. For example, he directed that two freshmen be given Government Reform subcommittee chairmanships, dismissing the claims of more senior members.

Gingrich also took control of the House agenda to an extraordinary degree, forcing consideration of the Contract with America in the first one hundred days of the 104th Congress and imposing a master schedule on committees and subcommittees. He made extensive use of intercommittee legislative task forces and did not hesitate to bypass committees, issue directives to their chairmen, or alter their handiwork in order to accomplish the party's objectives. The objections of Republican members to these changes were minimal. Gingrich had a special relationship with the enormous freshman class, and initially he took pains to maintain active involvement from all elements of the party. This greatly facilitated his consolidation of power, aimed at achieving Republican policy goals and maintaining majority control.

Member support came under increasing strains as the 104th Congress wore on and Gingrich and the Republican revolution lost popular approval. GOP leaders shifted tactics as they looked toward the 1996 elections, turning from provoking shutdowns to striking bipartisan deals on health insurance portability, welfare reform, drinking water protection, and the minimum wage. In the process, they delegated more responsibility to committees. Gingrich was further weakened by an ethics investigation that culminated in his admission of serious lapses and House approval of a reprimand and a $300,000 penalty.

Gingrich was narrowly reelected as Speaker for the 105th Congress, but his troubles subsequently deepened. His resignation was finally forced when the GOP nearly lost the House majority in the 1998 elections. Ironically, the solidarity the GOP then displayed in impeaching President Clinton and blocking any path to compromise was less an indication of strong leadership than of weakness at the top that allowed Republican whip Tom DeLay (R-Texas) and other impeachment hard-liners to seize control and set a politically disastrous course.

Part of the appeal of Bob Livingston (R-Louisiana) as Gingrich's prospective successor was that, as a generally respected Appropriations chairman, he balanced an assertive leadership style with an appreciation of the strengths of the committee system. But Livingston withdrew his name when news of his marital infidelities became public, and Republicans settled on Dennis Hastert (R-Illinois), a colleague of mine from the class of 1986. Hastert was a behind-the-scenes operator who displayed little of Gingrich's bombast and charisma. He was often beholden to the conservative activists in the Republican Conference, organized as the Conservative Action Team (called the Republican Study Committee after 2001). The conservatives held the party hostage by virtue of its narrow margin of control, and they had in DeLay (who became majority leader in 2003) a leader who was willing and able to press their advantage.

Hastert's speakership began with another round of assurances that leaders would consult widely and work cooperatively with committee and subcommittee chairs, and indeed there was a partial return to the "regular order" whereby most legislation proceeded through committee channels. But leadership and the capacity for deliberation had atrophied on a number of committees, and incentives and member support remained strong for party leaders' continued control over committee appointment, leadership, and policy decisions. With the election of a Republican president in 2000, the trend toward consolidation fully resumed.

As long as Clinton was in the White House, Hastert was at pains to avoid a replay of the 1995–1996 government shutdowns that had been so damaging to Republicans. This encouraged a degree of accommodation, especially on funding issues, and gave leverage to moderates and appropriators in the Republican Conference. Some predicted that the advent of George W. Bush, who had campaigned as a "compassionate conservative" and touted his ability to work with Democrats, would have a similar effect. But this turned out to be a misreading of Bush and of the role the House would assume as a counterbalance to the more moderate and less regimented Senate. In most instances, Bush chose to govern from the "right in" rather than the "center out," and House Republican leaders put together their winning majorities in the same way. The 2001 reauthorization of the Elementary and Secondary Education Act (a.k.a. No Child Left Behind) was a significant exception, but the pattern held on budget resolutions, tax cuts, energy, Medicare prescription drugs, family planning and abortion, trade, and most other major bills. Democrats were largely left out of the equation as what came to be known as the "Hastert rule" dictated Republican practice: only matters that commanded the support of a "majority of the majority" would be permitted a floor vote.[10]

The right-in approach exacted a high price in partisan alienation and conflict. Power-concentrating leadership tactics also had to be ratcheted up to keep the narrow Republican majority in line and safeguard against deviant outcomes. Most obvious was the tactic of going to the floor with a narrow whip count and holding the vote open, if necessary, to cajole the last few members to vote yes. This tactic reached its apogee on November 22, 2003, as the vote on the Republicans' privatized Medicare drug benefit was held open for almost three hours. This was not totally without precedent. Then-Republican Whip Dick Cheney had castigated Speaker Jim Wright for "the most arrogant, heavy-handed abuse of power I've seen in the two years I've been here" when he held a budget vote open for *fifteen minutes* in 1987.[11] Republican leaders also brought bills to the floor under increasingly restrictive rules, excluded Democrats from participation in key House–Senate conferences, and intervened in committee work in ways that damaged and devalued long-standing processes of deliberation and bipartisan accommodation.

In late 2005, I joined with a group of four members led by Dave Obey (D-Wisconsin) in putting forward H. Res. 659, a resolution that proposed, in addition to lobbying and earmark reforms, the elimination of abusive practices that had been used by Republican leaders to enhance their control.[12] It forbad protracted roll calls, for example, the addition by leadership of provisions to House–Senate conference reports that had not been approved by the conference, and "self-executing" rules whereby leadership inserted substantive provisions into procedural motions.

As Nancy Pelosi became Speaker in 2007, it is safe to assume that she never entertained the thought of returning to the pre-Gingrich model of House leadership—nor did most Democrats, with the possible exception of a few senior committee chairmen, want her to do so.[13] We understood the need for decisive leadership in an increasingly polarized and contentious environment. We also, however, wished to avoid the Gingrich-Hastert excesses, revitalize committee operations, and move toward the "regular order" in conducting House business. In this we only partially succeeded. We avoided three-hour roll-call votes but did not ease up appreciably on the restrictive rules governing floor debate. We adopted several of the reforms from H.Res. 659, including protections of the conference process, but serious conference deliberations were still frequently displaced by behind-the-scenes agreements among party leaders. We restored the presumption that the most senior member of a committee would get the first shot at the chairmanship (subject to caucus confirmation by secret ballot), but the most venerable chairman in the House, Energy and Commerce's John Dingell (D-Michigan), was successfully challenged by Henry Waxman (D-California) with Pelosi's support. Financial Services Chairman Barney Frank (D-Massachusetts), in steering the Wall Street Reform and Consumer Protection Act to passage in 2010, restored robust committee deliberations, with ample opportunities for amendment and debate, but the partisan polarization had become so severe that Republicans largely failed to engage, settling into a purely oppositional stance.[14]

The legislative agenda, starting with "Six for '06," was articulated and pushed forward by Democratic leadership. The pledge to go Gingrich one better and complete these items within the first 100 *hours* of the new Congress obviously ruled out serious committee deliberation. The longer-term agenda was also ambitious, and many items, including offshore drilling, war funding, and children's health insurance, required major efforts to achieve Democratic unity in the face of unified Republican opposition or hard bargaining by the Bush administration. The demands were even greater as Barack Obama assumed office in 2009 with a program that included economic recovery, the "cap-and-trade" plan to promote clean energy and reduce greenhouse gas emissions, health care reform, and what became the Dodd-Frank financial services reform bill.

These daunting challenges argued for energetic and well-coordinated leadership, an approach to which Speaker Pelosi was naturally inclined. She had considerable talent for detailed management and many-sided negotiations, and her position as the first female Speaker and a committed progressive gave her credibility in seeking compromises across the party spectrum—not merely from those moderate or marginal members on whom the pressures were usually greatest. It was not easy, nor did it usually look easy: these were the years when Republican politics turned in the "tea party" direction and opposition tactics became even more confrontational. But the legislative achievements of the 110th Congress (2007–2008) were considerable—major higher education, agriculture, and AMTRAK reauthorizations; HIV/AIDS and other global health initiatives; and legislation leveling the playing field between Medicare and privatized Medicare Advantage—and the House then became the tip of the spear for the Obama agenda, particularly the Clean Energy and Security Act and the Affordable Care Act.

The electoral upheaval of 2010 brought back to power Republicans no less committed to centralized leadership but beset by ideological divisions that made it increasingly difficult to govern.[15] The new Speaker, John Boehner (R-Ohio), often regarded as a "politician's politician," was determined to repeal Obama's heath care law, cut taxes, and slash spending, but he consciously eschewed the Gingrich model, valuing managerial efficiency over ideological bombast.[16] While this pleased many Republican veterans, it did not necessarily bode well for Boehner's relationship with the party's 87 new arrivals.

Again, there were promises of a return to the regular order. But the most-touted example—H.R. 1, the tea-party inspired continuing resolution to fund (and drastically cut) government operations for the balance of fiscal 2011—displayed the limits of the commitment. Debate continued for four days, February 15–18, 2011, with numerous amendments permitted from both sides. But the procedure was largely leadership-driven, avoiding formal

Appropriations Committee consideration, and the rules governing debate forbad any amendments that would have seriously altered the spending provisions in the leadership's bill.

The Budget Control Act of 2011, which imposed stringent caps on appropriated spending for the next ten years as the price for agreeing to raise the debt ceiling, reflected the ascendance of the Republican House—and the marked shift toward libertarian "tea-party" ideology *within* the House majority (see Chapter 7). It also set the Republicans up for repeated budget showdowns: the caps were too low to accommodate workable appropriations bills, but the majority, by virtue of pressures within their conference, were bound to try. Typically, as the new fiscal year and the prospect of a shutdown loomed, it became necessary to raise the caps through a bipartisan budget deal so that appropriations bills could finally be passed. Four such two-year agreements were passed beginning in 2013, but rarely with the assent of Republican tea-partiers (organized as the Freedom Caucus in 2015), which meant that Democratic votes were needed and the Hastert rule was in constant jeopardy.

Boehner did not loosen the reins of leadership, but he increasingly faced far-right rebellions he could not control. Early on, he had exerted decisive influence in key leadership races and had removed four recalcitrant members from plum committee assignments.[17] But this hardly blunted conservative resistance to the accommodations he had to make—the resolution of the "fiscal cliff" issue posed by the expiration on December 31, 2012, of the George W. Bush tax cuts went down especially hard—and he faced internal opposition in his race for speaker in both 2013 and 2015. The Freedom Caucus was formed partially in reaction to Boehner's removal of his main 2015 challenger, Daniel Webster (R-Florida), from the Rules Committee.

The rebellion reached its culmination amid escalating disagreements in 2015, when right-wing dissidents presented Boehner with an impossible choice: if he did what he had to do to pass a short-term continuing resolution (CR) to avoid a government shutdown—namely, seek Democratic votes to compensate for Republicans sure to vote "no"—then he would immediately face a vote to remove him from the speakership. Boehner would have survived such a vote, but he chose not to put colleagues through the ordeal and announced his resignation, effective October 29, 2015. He bought the House and his successor as Speaker, Rep. Paul Ryan (R-Wisconsin), a six-week respite by passing, in addition to the CR, an increase in the debt ceiling and revised two-year budget numbers capacious enough to permit significant revisions in the stalled 2016 appropriations bills. Every Democrat voted for the revised budget, but only 29 of 247 Republicans did so—a further blow to the Hastert rule.

The coming weeks saw some degree of bipartisan progress, but hardly enough to declare the gridlock broken. Reauthorization of the Export-Import Bank, long-blocked by far-right Republicans, was brought directly to the floor and passed under a Discharge Petition, the first successful use of this device since the Shays-Meehan campaign reform bill of 2002 (see Chapter 3), and one of only four in the rule's history. The Elementary and Secondary Education Act, which had expired in 2007, was finally reauthorized. A five-year highway and transit authorization was also approved—seven years overdue, after 15 short-term extensions, and still underfunded because of the failure to raise fuel taxes or otherwise provide a long-term revenue source. And finally, the omnibus appropriations bill for fiscal 2016 was approved on December 18, albeit with 95 Republicans in opposition.

"We want him to be successful," Freedom Caucus member Raul Labrador (R-Idaho) said of Ryan, "but we also want to make sure he understands this is not about crowning a king."[18] Ryan made a point of expanding the party's Steering Committee and conferring with all factions, and in 2017 he avoided a direct challenge to his re-election as speaker. But he was not able to overcome the divisions that had felled Boehner, and the election of Donald Trump posed major additional challenges. Ryan caught continuing grief from conservatives, particularly for maintaining the budget agreement he inherited from Boehner and for acceding to a new two-year agreement for 2018–2019. Nor was his relationship with Trump ever secure: the President blamed him for specific failures, such as not funding his border wall, and was quick to react to anything less than a total display of loyalty. In mid-2018, for example, Trump tweeted in reaction to a report of Ryan's earlier critical comments: "Weak, ineffective, and stupid are not exactly the qualities that Republicans, or the CITIZENS of our Country, were looking for."[19]

On April 1, 2018, as the turbulence continued and the possible loss of the Republican House majority loomed, Ryan announced that he would not stand for re-election. "I think he's tired," former Speaker Gingrich commented knowingly. "It's a combination of dealing with 240 House Republicans, the United States Senate, and President Trump. That trio was about enough."[20] The major legislative achievement of Ryan's speakership was a massive tax cut in 2017 that was skewed toward corporations and wealthy individuals and added more than $2 trillion to the debt over ten years. Beyond that, Obama's Affordable Care Act remained intact, despite repeated repeal attempts; deficits were ballooning; and Medicare and Social Security, which Ryan had long wanted to cut and/or privatize, were largely untouched. Moreover, under Trump's influence, House Republicans were fast abandoning the positions on immigration and free trade that Ryan had long advocated.

Nancy Pelosi resumed the speakership in 2019 with support from all segments of the Democratic Caucus. She had maintained a strong leadership position during our years in the minority. I did not always agree with the legislative accommodations she made—for example, in acceding to Sen. Elizabeth Warren (D-Massachusetts) and other vocal detractors in almost bringing down the "Cromnibus" appropriations bill for fiscal 2015 favored by the Obama administration.[21] But I greatly respected her commitment to a strong agenda and her ability to exert herself effectively and rally the Caucus when the chips were down, as exemplified in our efforts to protect the Iran nuclear agreement (see Chapter 8) and, on numerous occasions, the Affordable Care Act.

Democratic restlessness at being in the minority and at the lack of mobility into leadership ranks encouraged Tim Ryan (D-Ohio) to challenge Pelosi for the minority leadership after the 2016 elections. Pelosi prevailed easily, but subsequently created three new leadership positions in the area of message development to accommodate junior members. A scattering of members announced their opposition to Pelosi in 2018; this created some uncertainty because, while Ryan had received only 63 Caucus votes in 2016, a far smaller number of Democratic defectors, 19, could deny her a majority in the House in 2018. But Pelosi had just led Democrats to victory, largely refuting the notion that she, despite being demonized in countless Republican ads, was an electoral liability. No challenger emerged, and the opposition folded. Pelosi then took the gavel with a sure hand and proved herself an able match for Donald Trump, resulting in a marked and rapid increase in her stature among Democrats in Congress and beyond.

With the election of Steny Hoyer (D-Maryland) as majority leader and Jim Clyburn (D-South Carolina) as whip—both, like Pelosi, in their late 70s—the top Democratic leadership remained unchanged from 2007–2010. The most obvious heirs apparent were no longer in the House: Chris Van Hollen (D-Maryland), former DCCC chair, had been elected to the Senate; Xavier Becerra (D-California), former Caucus chair, had become his state's attorney general; and sitting Caucus chair Joe Crowley (D-New York) had lost his primary. Amid the turbulence of Trump's presidency, there was a strong case to be made for stable and experienced leadership. In the meantime, there was no shortage of members vying for lower-ranking party positions. It is difficult to predict who might emerge from the pack, but a major changing of the guard is in prospect, probably after the 2022 elections.

Democrats reserved the numbers H.R. 1–10 for the lead items in the party's agenda. The first, as described in Chapter 3, was a broad political reform measure, passed on March 8, 2019. Bills on LGBTQ equality, pay equity for women and men, the DREAM Act (providing a path to citizenship for undocumented young people who were brought to the U.S. as children), comprehensive background checks for gun purchases, and reentering the Paris Climate Agreement followed in rapid succession, while more complex measures on voting rights and prescription drug prices made their way through the committee process and were passed later in the year.

Pelosi did not totally bypass the committees on any of the bills and took other steps toward restoring the regular order. For example, she (along with Senate Majority Leader McConnell) partially restored the traditional House–Senate conference process after ending the five-week partial government shutdown Trump precipitated in a fit of pique over his border wall. The conferees, of which I was one, had three weeks to finalize an omnibus appropriations bill to keep the government running for the rest of Fiscal 2019. This we did, led by the two appropriations chairs, Rep. Nita Lowey (D-New York) and Sen. Richard Shelby (R-Alabama), albeit under the leadership's watchful eye. Democratic House members were glad to see both committees and the floor more open to participation and deliberation. But we were aware as well of our collective stake in strong and unifying party leadership, particularly as impeachment investigations heated up in the fall.

"… To the Aid of the Party"

Newly elected members of Congress quickly confront the fact that the House is a party-led chamber—from orientation sessions organized by leadership, to early votes to choose party leaders and adopt caucus rules, to jockeying for committee assignments in a process that necessitates serious conversations with party leaders (see Chapter 4). Members learn of opportunities to become active participants in the party network, at least at its outer reaches, and of expectations that they will give due consideration to arguments and entreaties coming from leadership sources. At least for members of my generation, our high school typing test was likely to come to mind: "Now is the time for all good men [and women] to come to the aid of the party!"

Party participation offers a way to place oneself in the crosscurrents of information and influence, and for some but not all, it is a pathway to power within the institution. The leadership ladder is crowded, with numerous members competing for every appointive and elective leadership post. But all members can become involved in the work of their caucus or whip organization. This is a legacy of the 1970s, when these organizations were revitalized and expanded. It represented a deliberate strategy of inclusion by leaders of both parties, who recognized that members were more likely to be cooperative and helpful when they felt they were being informed and consulted and had a role to play in party affairs.

The fact that I came to the House with a strong party background—as state Democratic chairman and staff director of the Democratic National Committee (DNC)'s Commission on Presidential Nomination (Hunt Commission)—meant that I already knew several of my new colleagues and was relatively knowledgeable about national party affairs. I said after the Hunt Commission that I had had my fill of party rules-writing, but I nonetheless agreed to "come to the aid of the party" in 2005 as co-chair (with former Secretary of Labor Alexis Herman) of the DNC Commission on Presidential Nomination Timing and Scheduling. The commission included forty local, state, and national party leaders and elected officials from across the country. More narrowly focused than the Hunt Commission, we addressed widespread concerns about the disproportionate role of the "first in the nation" contests in New Hampshire and Iowa in shaping the nomination outcome, as well as the "front-loading" of contests early in the official primary season.[22] Our recommendations resulted in a greater geographic and ethnic/racial diversity as Nevada and South Carolina were added to the pre-season contests, but had limited effect on the distribution of primaries and caucuses otherwise. Any doubts as to the significance of our work were belatedly dispelled, however, by South Carolina's dramatic role in reversing Joe Biden's fortunes and putting him on the path to nomination in revers in the presidential contest of 2020.

I largely stayed clear of the controversies surrounding the work of the Hunt Commission as candidates Barack Obama in 2008 and, to a much greater degree, Bernie Sanders in 2016, objected to the role the Commission had given unpledged party leader/elected official (PL/EO) delegates in the nomination process. Often misleadingly termed "superdelegates" by their detractors, these unpledged "add-on" delegate slots for each state were designed to correct an unintended consequence of earlier reforms: the virtual elimination of elected officials and even some top party officials from convention delegations. Such leaders were not likely to become delegates if that meant running against their own constituents, and often they were not willing to make an early pledge to a presidential candidate or not able to get on a candidate's approved slate. So, we created a limited number of unpledged Party Leader/Elected Official slots, to which Democratic National Committee members added a larger number to accommodate themselves.

There was some discussion on the Hunt Commission of the rare circumstances—a deadlocked contest, closely divided platform questions, a situation when a candidate became disabled or disgraced—when the decision-making capacity the PL/EOs would bring to the convention might prove valuable. But we certainly did not see them as king- or queen-makers, much less as some sort of rump convention. Today, it is even harder to imagine PL/EO delegates reversing a primary outcome that gave a candidate a majority or even a large plurality of pledged delegates. Such a reversal would be widely portrayed as undemocratic and illegitimate. PL/EO delegates would be far more likely to resolve than to create uncertainty, to consolidate behind the winner among the pledged delegates and to ratify that choice.

As it became clear after the 2016 elections that the "superdelegate" controversy was not going away and that the DNC leadership was in fact likely to make major rules changes, I and several other members of Congress reluctantly got involved. DNC chair Tom Perez got an outraged reception on June 5, 2018, when he presented to the House Democratic Caucus—as a *fait accompli*, we suspected—a plan to deny unpledged delegates a convention vote for president. I subsequently drew up a plan that demonstrated how to reduce the number of unpledged convention delegates from 750 to fewer than 500, still giving the states ample opportunity to accommodate top PL/EOs and not denying any delegate a vote. But that was not good enough for the Sanders faction or the DNC leadership, who insisted on denying the first-ballot vote to unpledged delegates. This is a worrisome outcome, not mainly for the members of Congress, governors, and mayors who justifiably feel aggrieved, but for the party itself, which seems to be once again inviting the disengagement of its elected officials from the convention and party affairs.

Within the House, I have not been tempted to get on the party leadership ladder. But I did take on assignments which drew on my earlier experience with party rules-writing—the Caucus's Organization, Study and Review (OSR) Committee—and in assembling Democratic platforms—the issues task forces of the caucus, which I coordinated in the 101st and 102nd Congresses (1989–1992). I also learned quickly that the most informative meeting of the week was the Thursday morning whip's meeting, where plans for the coming week were discussed and strategy was debated in a relatively open fashion. These meetings were open to interested members but, unlike today, did not involve the entire caucus. I began attending regularly, volunteered for ad hoc groups to count votes and mobilize support on specific bills, and in 1991 formally became part of the organization as one of 48 at-large whips.

I served on OSR (renamed the Committee on Caucus Procedures in 2017) intermittently until I became busier with my committee leadership responsibilities. It is the housekeeping committee of the caucus, highly responsive to the Speaker (or minority leader), which screens proposed changes in caucus or House rules and renders judgment on requests for waivers of the rules or adjudication of rules disputes. The Committee's role steps up greatly in periods of transition to Democratic leadership. Most of the time it operates behind the scenes—a good place for a member to learn the organizational ropes and work with party leaders on internal House matters.

The task force projects I coordinated in 1990 and 1992 were the latest in a series of election-year efforts begun when Democratic Caucus chairman Gillis Long formed the Committee on Party Effectiveness (CPE) in 1981–1982. The CPE was an ambitious effort to fill the agenda-formation gap that had come with the loss of the White House. It was intended to develop issues and formulate positions that could inspire agreement among Democrats; involve caucus members, many of them quite junior and from outside the relevant committees, in broad policy discussions; and nudge reluctant committee leaders along.[23] It fed directly into the formation of the Democratic Leadership Council in 1985, but by the time I came to the House, the CPE had devolved into a series of caucus-sponsored "party effectiveness" luncheons on important national issues. Caucus Chairman Steny Hoyer saw a need for more focused discussions and documents, aimed at trumpeting Democratic achievements and aspirations in advance of the 1990 elections. As a second-term member, I was pleased to be asked to coordinate the task force project.

Our nine task forces contained members from the relevant committees and interested additional members as well. Although they had no legislative function, some committee chairmen still found them threatening and declined to help; others cooperated fully. After a February 1990 kickoff at the annual caucus retreat, several task forces met repeatedly and hammered out consensus positions, while others did little more than order staff-produced drafts. After much cajoling and editing, we produced an issues handbook, *Investing in America's Future*, stressing that it represented neither an official party position nor a short-term legislative program but rather "a set of goals and aspirations that Democrats seek to accomplish." Along with the similar handbook produced by the 1992 task forces, these efforts provided useful resources for the ensuing campaigns and laid groundwork for the 1992 national platform.[24] Compared to more recent Caucus messaging projects, ours was more focused on hammering out policy ideas and less on poll-driven message formulation. Still, issue and message development under Caucus auspices remains a promising area of involvement for many members and of advancement to party leadership for some.

My third area of early party involvement, working with the whip organization, was useful to me in at least three ways. First, it let me help mobilize support for measures that I thought were important, such as the 1990 housing bill, on which I had worked extensively in the Banking Committee, and the Clinton administration's 1993 budget legislation. Second, it made me a partner, albeit a junior one, in leadership undertakings. This was intrinsically satisfying and could bring other rewards. Throughout 1990 those of us who were trying to position ourselves to gain the next Appropriations Committee seats joked about the amazing coincidence that we so often found ourselves on the whip's task forces. Finally, it brought me into discussions of floor strategy and the last-minute alterations needed to maximize votes on various bills. Certain committees, most notably Judiciary and Education and Labor, tended to bring bills to the floor that were acceptable to the liberal majorities on those committees but needed further work to gain the assent of a healthy majority of Democratic members. This happened too often, and whip task forces were hardly the ideal place to work out accommodations. But on bills like child care in 1990 and striker replacement in 1991, the vote counts and feedback garnered by the whip organization served as a reality check for committee leaders and gave members like me a means of pushing for needed refinements in advance of floor consideration.

On returning to the Congress as a minority member in 1997, I again worked with the whip organization. David Bonior (D-Michigan) was still Democratic whip, task forces were still organized to whip specific bills (with participation essentially open to all comers), and the Thursday morning whip meeting was still a fixture on the weekly schedule. Nowhere, however, was it more evident what a difference it made to be in the minority. Those Thursday meetings were painful reminders that Democrats were not in charge. We often faced uncertainty about the week's schedule and frustration that our amendments or alternative proposals were being denied floor consideration or were being placed at a disadvantage by virtue of the rules governing floor debate. We were more often trying to defeat rather than pass major bills, as well as to mobilize votes for Democratic amendments or alternatives and against the majority's restrictive rules.

Leadership changes came in 2002, as Bonior left the whip position to run for the Michigan governorship, and in 2003, as Gephardt left the leadership to run for president. I worked closely with Hoyer in the hotly contested race to succeed Bonior. He lost the race to Nancy Pelosi, who thereafter was on a path to the speakership. When she assumed the minority leadership a year later, Hoyer was the Caucus's unanimous choice for whip. He expanded the whip organization, relying less on ad hoc task forces and more on appointed groups of twenty-eight senior whips and thirty-eight assistant whips to follow up with members after the initial contact made by the regional whips (24 members, still elected by the 12 regional caucuses).

As an assistant whip, I had a list of five members with whom it was my responsibility to check on every major bill. Hoyer's successor in periods of Democratic leadership, Jim Clyburn, maintained a similar operation, and my role as a whip remained basically unchanged. What changed more dramatically, however, were mobilization efforts above and beyond those of the whip organization. The efforts to line up votes, sponsors for resolutions, and signers for letters with regard to the Iran nuclear agreement, described in Chapter 8, illustrate the phenomenon. Such efforts, in which Speaker (or Minority Leader) Pelosi has not hesitated to get directly involved, have sometimes involved issues on which the party did not officially take a position, but more often have reflected a need for persuasion and pressure beyond the normal capacities of the whip organization.

More extensive and intensive whipping operations in both parties are an essential component of the strengthened leadership role I have described. They function in a context of growing divergence between and convergence within the congressional parties and have helped reinforce those trends. As Figure 6.1 shows, members have become more and more inclined to stick with their party on divided votes. Party voting since the 1990s has exceeded the levels established during Harry Truman's presidency, a time when party divisions were sharp and party loyalties were well defined in the electorate.

Figure 6.1 reflects growing Republican solidarity under more militant leadership. This began in the 102nd Congress, was reinforced by the galvanizing effects of Bill Clinton's presidency, and reached a new high under George W. Bush. The crossing of the Democratic and Republican trend lines after one party or the other gained control suggests some of the advantages that come to the majority party from the control it wields over the agenda and the rules governing floor debate. While it is sometimes easier to maintain party solidarity as a beleaguered minority, leaders of the majority can make life difficult, especially for members in swing districts. They can frame legislation and floor amendments to attract votes from the other side and/ or make a no vote politically difficult. By the same token, they can refuse to permit the consideration of amendments or alternatives that might divide their own majority vote.

Vote gathering in both parties frequently runs up against the electoral and constituency pressures experienced by individual members, and leaders frequently have to decide how vigorously to use the carrots and sticks at their disposal. During the early 1980s, for example, the Democratic

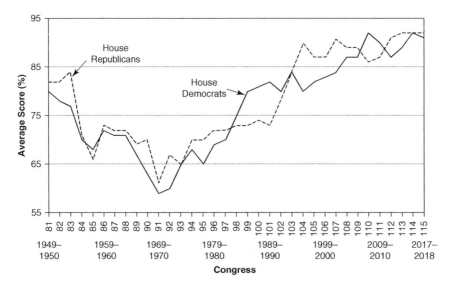

Figure 6.1 "Party unity" voting for House Democrats and Republicans. Average individual support for party on votes dividing party majorities, 81st–115th Congresses (1949–2018).

Source: Data from Congressional Quarterly Almanacs and CQ *Weekly*, February 24, 2020, p. 42.

leadership fluctuated in its treatment of the so-called boll weevils—conservative Democrats who were prone to vote with the Reagan administration—sometimes attempting to win their loyalty through generous treatment and choice committee assignments, but other times passing over them in favor of their loyalist rivals.[25] The approach taken was dictated by the political situation the Democrats faced. They were more accommodating to the conservatives when their House majority was shaky and Reagan was riding high, less accommodating when they had regained the initiative.

I noted in Chapter 4 how Speakers Wright and Foley differed in utilizing their influence over committee assignments. Wright once floated the unheard-of idea of putting members on probation for their first term in a new assignment.[26] Foley at first kept hands off, with the result that two choice committee slots that became available midterm—including the Appropriations position for which I was vying—went to members who had voted against the leadership on high-profile party tests. The Speaker's thumb on the scale became far more evident in the committee assignments made by Steering and Policy at the beginning of the 102nd Congress, and I was elected at that point to Appropriations as part of a slate he endorsed.

Foley's successors, Gephardt and Pelosi, have kept an increasingly strong grip on Steering and Policy decisions, including committee assignments. The Speaker (or Minority Leader) presides over the committee, appoints its co-chairs, directly names 14 of the 53 members, and usually is in a position to carry the day. Party voting and support of the leadership are often rewarded, but other criteria also come into play—the need for regional, ideological, and demographic diversity; fundraising prowess and help with recruitment and other DCCC activities; relevant policy backgrounds and re-election needs; and, in the case of committee chairmanships, seniority and levels of political support in the Caucus.

House Republicans have generally surpassed Democrats, at least in the post-1991 years of conservative ascendancy, in their ability and willingness to use leadership tools to encourage partisan solidarity. This includes expectations that accompany campaign assistance; the use of committee assignments, leadership positions, and other perquisites to cement and reward loyalty to the Speaker (or minority leader) and the party; and whip operations that display a harder edge than their Democratic counterpart. The Republican leader's control over the decisions of the Steering Committee's 29 members (the Policy Committee is organized separately) is facilitated by a scheme of weighted voting and by relatively weak constraints compared to what Democratic leaders face. Less deference is given to seniority, for example, and term limits on committee chairs offer more opportunities to sideline ideological outliers and reward strong political and financial performers. Republicans also are less constrained to consider demographic diversity, of which their conference displays relatively little.

Republicans have therefore been more likely than Democrats to exercise the sterner forms of party discipline, such as removing deviant members from committees. This has sometimes produced a backlash, but less than what one would anticipate if the same were attempted on the Democratic side. Levels of partisan voting have remained high, but, as we have seen, this has not always applied to major votes on government funding or other make-or-break issues when ideological diversions come into play. Republicans have often needed Democratic votes in such instances, even when Republicans commanded a healthy majority in the House, and the much-touted Hastert rule has been set aside with some regularity.

Figure 6.2 sheds further light on these partisan voting trends. In 1969–1970, the parties were clearly distinguished ideologically but with considerable overlap; a number of members were situated near the middle, with substantial numbers of conservative Democrats to the right of moderate Republicans and vice versa. Significant change was underway by 1987–1988, the first years I was in the House. Both parties were becoming more homogeneous, and Republican moderates were fewer in number, establishing the preconditions of the Gingrich rebellion. By 2019–2020, the changes are far more dramatic. Most Democratic members are situated slightly farther to the left and most Republicans considerably farther to the right, with no overlap—not a single Democrat to the right of any Republican or vice versa.

The movement, moreover, has been asymmetrical. The Republican mode has moved much farther to the right than the Democratic mode has to the

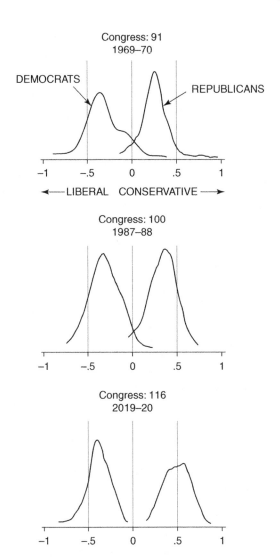

Figure 6.2 Changing ideological distributions of House Democrats and Republicans.
Source: DW-Nominate Scores First Dimension, voteview.com.

left. And while the ideological distribution among Democrats around the mode remains relatively concentrated, that among Republicans has become less so, despite the virtual disappearance of Republican moderates. A much greater number of Republicans now occupy the far right of the spectrum than Democrats occupy the far left. The trend has accelerated over numerous elections, with newly elected Republicans scoring, on average, to the right of returning Republicans and those they replaced.

The high point was reached in the wave election of 2010: "An amazing 77% of the newly arriving Republicans included dozens of Tea Party-backed Republicans," noted political scientists Theda Skocpol and Vanessa Williamson,

> are to the right of the typical Republican in the previous Congress—and many are to the right of *almost all* continuing Republicans.... Ideological sorting out between the two parties in Congress has been going on for decades, but in recent years virtually all of the incremental polarization comes from Republicans moving ever further rightward while the Democrats mostly stay put.[27]

Thus does a picture emerge of the configuration of the parties in the contemporary House:

- increased *polarization* of both the congressional parties and their electoral bases, entailing greater ideological homogeneity within the parties and a widened distance between them;
- the persistent *competitiveness* of the parties in Congress, "the continuous prospects for change, in party control," with each party aspiring to majority status and seeking to take full advantage of any opening provided by the other;[28] and
- the *asymmetrical movement* of one party toward an ideological extreme, that is, the emergence of the Republican party as what Thomas Mann and Norman Ornstein term an "insurgent outlier."[29]

Polarization plus: we have already begun to see some of the patterns of party leadership, organization, and voting that have accompanied these trends. In the next chapter, I will explore more fully their impact on performance—on how, and how effectively, the House functions.

Notes

1 Four of the Democratic state chairs with whom I served—Nancy Pelosi of California, Bart Gordon of Tennessee, Dave Nagle of Iowa, and Chester Atkins of Massachusetts—later became House colleagues.
2 Gary C. Jacobson, "The 1994 House Elections in Perspective," in Philip A. Klinker, ed., *Midterm: The Elections of 1994 in Context* (Boulder, CO: Westview, 1996), chap. 1.
3 Source: Federal Election Commission. Direct DCCC contributions to candidates and expenditures coordinated with their campaigns are limited to $5000 and $50,900 ($101,900 in states with one U.S. representative), respectively (as adjusted in 2019). By contrast, party expenditures on behalf of candidates but not coordinated with them cannot be limited, as the Supreme Court ruled in 1996. *Colorado Republican Federal Campaign Committee v. Federal Election Commission*, 518 U.S. 604. The Court later affirmed that *coordinated* expenditures, made in consultation with a candidate, *could* be constitutionally limited. *Federal Election Commission v. Colorado Republican Federal Campaign*

Committee, 533 U.S. 431 (2001). With some logic, the Bipartisan Campaign Reform Act (BCRA) of 2002 determined that a single party committee could not make both sorts of expenditures (sec. 213). But *McConnell v. FEC*, while generally upholding the Act (see Chapter 3), ruled this restriction unconstitutional. 540 US 93 (2003).

4 Daniel Scholzman and Sam Rosenfeld, "The Hollow Parties," in Francis E. Lee and Nolan McCarty, eds., *Can America Govern Itself?* (New York: Cambridge University Press, 2019), pp. 125–126, 137.

5 See Michelle Ye Hee Lee and Ann Narayanswamy, "Despite Record Spending, 2018 Midterms Highlighted the Limits of Campaign Cash," *Washington Post*, November 7, 2018.

6 For useful accounts that base strengthened party operations in the profit-and-loss calculations of individual members, see Barbara Sinclair, *Legislators, Leaders, and Lawmaking: The U.S. House of Representatives in the Postreform Era* (Baltimore, MD: Johns Hopkins University Press, 1995), chaps. 1–2, 4–5; and David W. Rohde, *Parties and Leaders in the Postreform House* (Chicago, IL: University of Chicago Press, 1991).

7 Roger Davidson, "The New Centralization on Capitol Hill," *Review of Politics*, 50 (Summer 1988), pp. 350–351.

8 "Three important goals for the Democrats are to enhance the authority of the Speaker; make sure that Democratic membership on legislative committees is representative; and to increase the individual responsibility of each Democrat toward his leaders." Richard Bolling, *House Out of Order* (New York: Dutton, 1965), pp. 236–238.

9 Foley continued to experience and express some discomfort with demands for tightened discipline in the Democratic Caucus. Revealingly, after he and House Democrats were defeated in 1994, he acknowledged the attraction of the parliamentary model of the "honorific and politically impotent" speaker. But he then emphasized, as if correcting himself, "that there is need for a centralizing, organizing principle in the House of Representatives that is best expressed by the Speakership." See Jeffrey R. Biggs and Thomas S. Foley, *Honor in the House: Speaker Tom Foley* (Pullman, WA: Washington State University Press, 1999), pp. 135–137, 272.

10 Hastert listed as one of the principles guiding his speakership "to please the majority of your majority." Remarks at a conference on "The Changing Nature of the House Speakership," sponsored by the Congressional Research Service and the Carl Albert Center, November 12, 2003, p. 4. "Time and Again," Juliet Eilperin observed, "Hastert and his lieutenants have calibrated the likely yeas and nays to the thinnest margin possible, enabling them to push legislation as much to their liking as they can in a narrowly divided and bitterly partisan House. More often than not, that direction is to the political right, and generally in line with President Bush's priorities." "Practicing the Art of One-Vote Victories," *Washington Post*, weekly ed., October 20–26, 2003, p. 13.

11 Quoted in "Government by Juggernaut," *Washington Post*, November 26, 2003, p. A24.

12 See Dave Obey, *Raising Hell for Justice* (Madison, WI: University of Wisconsin Press, 2007), pp. 378, 407.

13 This account draws on David E. Price, "After the 'Housequake': Leadership and Partisanship in the Post-2006 House," *The Forum*, 8 (2010).

14 See Barney Frank, *Frank: A Life in Politics from the Great Society to Same-Sex Marriage* (New York: Farrar, Strauss and Giroux, 2015), chap. 10; and Robert Kaiser, *Act of Congress* (New York: Alfred A. Knopf, 2013), chaps. 14–19.

15 The account below draws on David E. Price, "Congressional-Executive Balance in an Era of Congressional Dysfunction," *PS: Political Science and Politics*, 49

(July 2016), pp. 485–487; and John H. Aldrich and David W. Rohde, "Lending and Reclaiming Power: Majority Leadership in the House since the 1950s," and Steven Smith and Gerald Gamm, "The Dynamics of Party Government in Congress," both in Lawrence C. Dodd and Bruce Oppenheimer, eds., *Congress Reconsidered*, 11th ed. (Washington, DC: Congressional Quarterly Press, 2017), chaps. 2 and 7.

16 Major Garrett, "A Politician's Politician," *National Journal*, January 8, 2011.

17 Jonathan Strong, "Speak Softly or Carry a Big Stick," *CQ Weekly*, January 14, 2013, pp. 62–64.

18 Shawn Zeller, "Crash Course," *CQ Weekly*, October 26, 2015, p. 18.

19 Quoted in Jonah Goldberg, "Why Is Trump So Down on Paul Ryan?" *Los Angeles Times*, July 16, 2018.

20 Sheryl Gay Stolberg and Thomas Kaplan, "Ryan Found Himself on the Margins as GOP Embraces Trump," *New York Times*, April 11, 2018.

21 See Ed O'Keefe, "House Passes $1.1 Trillion Spending Bill," and Paul Kane, "Democrats' Warren Wing Sends Message," both in *Washington Post*, December 12, 2014, p. A1. "Cromnibus" refers to the combined CR (for Homeland Security) and omnibus appropriations bill (for the rest of government) for the balance of the year.

22 Democratic National Committee, *Report of the Commission on Presidential Nomination Timing and Scheduling*, December 10, 2005. See also David Price, "The Way We Choose Presidential Nominees: Problems and Prospects," in Jack Citrin and David Karol, eds., *Nominating the President* (New York: Rowman and Littlefield, 2009), chap. 7.

23 See David Price, *Bringing Back the Parties* (Washington, DC: Congressional Quarterly Press, 1984), pp. 280–282; and Al From, *The New Democrats and the Return to Power* (New York: Palgrave Macmillan, 2013), chap. 4.

24 For an analysis by two political scientists who, as Congressional Fellows, helped execute the projects, see Paul S. Herrnson and Kelly D. Patterson, "Crafting a Partisan Agenda in the House," in Colton C. Campbell and Herrnson, eds., *War Stories from Capitol Hill* (Upper Saddle River, NJ: Prentice-Hall, 2004), pp. 51–65.

25 See Rohde, *Parties and Leaders*, pp. 47, 78–81. On the particularly instructive case of Rep. (later Sen.) Phil Gramm, who convinced his constituents that his richly deserved discipline by Democrats was a badge of honor and used it to gain reelection as a Republican, see Price, *Bringing Back the Parties*, p. 67.

26 See the episodes recounted in John M. Barry, *The Ambition and the Power* (New York: Viking, 1989), pp. 393, 542–543.

27 Theda Skocpol and Vanessa Williamson, *The Tea Party and the Remaking of Republican Conservatism* (New York: Oxford University Press, 2012), p. 170; cf. Aldrich and Rohde, "Lending and Reclaiming Power," p. 41.

28 Frances E. Lee, "Legislative Parties in an Era of Alternating Majorities," in Alan S. Gerber and Eric Schickter, eds., *Governing in a Polarized Age* (New York: Cambridge University Press, 2017), p. 116. The fact that party control of Congress has remained a persistent and open question since the 1980s, Lee concludes, has given members "strong reasons to create and empower party organizations in hopes of affecting their party's overall fate."

29 Thomas Mann and Norman Ornstein, *It's Even Worse Than It Looks* (New York: Basic Books, 2012), pp. xiv, 184–197.

7 Polarization and Performance

I will not pretend to separate my assessment of partisanship from the substance of what the parties stand for and are trying to accomplish. I give Democratic party solidarity in enacting the Affordable Care Act a far different evaluation from Republican solidarity in attempting to repeal it. Still, the trends toward more centralized and polarized congressional parties identified in the last chapter can be linked to congressional performance, and to functionality in carrying out the basic tasks of governance, independently of which party is ascendant or which politics are being pursued. I will explore some of the consequences for the House as an institution in the present chapter, and in the process will provide a fuller picture of how the contemporary parties perform.

The Budget Process: From Grand Bargains to Sequestration[1]

The congressional budget process has always been characterized by sharp partisan differences but has declined significantly as polarization has become more intense. The process was established by the Congressional Budget and Impoundment Control Act of 1974, partly in response to President Richard Nixon's extensive impoundment of duly appropriated funds—a situation reminiscent of President Donald Trump's 2019 diversion of military construction and other appropriated funds (under the guise of his emergency powers) to build a border wall. But the 1974 legislation also reflected longer-term congressional concerns about failures of budgetary coordination and control and the president's domination of the budget process.

New House and Senate Budget Committees were authorized to bring to the floor, early in each congressional session, a budget resolution that would set overall spending limits and guide other committees as they passed individual authorization, appropriations, and tax bills. The Congressional Budget Office (CBO) was established as a nonpartisan, independent source of budgetary expertise. The idea was to empower Congress without creating major new power centers within Congress. In the House especially, with term limits for members and the chairman and required representation from the Appropriations and Ways and Means Committees, the Budget

Committee's independence and continuity of membership were limited. I am now in my third period of service on the committee as an Appropriations representative.

During the first year of Ronald Reagan's presidency, the concentration of budgetary power reached new heights, albeit under conditions that enhanced presidential, rather than congressional, control and with results that mocked the ideal of fiscal responsibility. The administration made novel use of the budget law's "reconciliation" process, which exempted from the Senate fili-buster legislation that brought tax and other authorizations in line with the parameters of a budget resolution. They pushed through a series of bills that reduced tax revenues over the next five years by nearly $700 billion, reduced domestic spending by more than $100 billion over three years, and paved the way for a doubling of defense spending. The numbers added up to massive annual deficits and eventually to a tripling of the national debt. As Reagan's budget director David Stockman later acknowledged, "The White House proclaimed a roaring economic success . . . when, in fact, [its policies] had produced fiscal excesses that had never before been imagined."[2]

I arrived in the House in 1987 amid ongoing budget struggles, which the stock market crash ten months later imbued with a great sense of urgency and political peril. The term "sequestration" had been added to the political lexicon by the 1985 Gramm-Rudman-Hollings (G-R-H) law, named after its Senate protagonists. The idea was to impose increasingly strict deficit targets on the budget process year by year until balance was reached. If the target was not met in a given year, percentage cuts would be imposed across all accounts (except Social Security and some other mandatory programs) to bring the budget into line. Presumably, the threat of this indiscriminate sequestration would give all parties the incentive to reach a settlement.

The G-R-H process looked far more viable on paper than it proved to be in practice. Even with optimistic projections (the infamous "rosy sce-narios") and various budgetary gimmicks, the increasingly stringent goals promised protracted political jockeying with no assurance of success. Many had expected George Bush, who earlier had derided as "voodoo economics" Ronald Reagan's supply-side dogmas that tax cuts pay for themselves, to take a more flexible and cooperative approach to budget matters than had his predecessor. But such hopes were dashed as he assumed a rigid campaign stance on taxes. "Read my lips: no new taxes," he declared in his accept-ance speech at the 1988 Republican National Convention, and he essen-tially threw the budget problem in the lap of the 101st Congress as his term began. It was not until after two years of exhaustive effort had produced an underwhelming deal that both congressional and administration leaders began to talk about a different sort of multiyear budget plan.

The constant budget wrangling was bringing both branches into disre-pute, yet we had remarkably little to show for our efforts. More ambitious G-R-H targets loomed, sequestration was unthinkable, and band-aid agree-ments like those of 1987 and 1989 would not suffice. The White House was locked into a rigid position on taxes and displayed only minimal flexibility on defense; neither party felt it could afford to tamper with Social Security; and congressional Democrats were unwilling to sacrifice domestic programs, which already had borne the brunt of Reagan era cutbacks. No one, therefore, could imagine where savings of the magnitude required were going to come from, unless a new kind of agreement (Budget Director Richard Darman liked to speak of the "deal of the century") could be reached. When talk turned to an unprecedented five-year plan aimed at $500 billion in deficit reduction, those of us who had long advocated a major effort to break the budget impasse imagined that our day finally had come. After several months of posturing and positioning, a serious agreement finally began to emerge, the first of what would come to be called the three "grand bargains" of the 1990s.

"So far it's been like a bunch of strange dogs sniffing at each other," Budget Committee Ranking Member Bill Frenzel (R-Minnesota) reported to our Democratic Budget Group. "If you are a defense hawk, or welfare bleeding heart, or antitax zealot, there's no comfort in this for you." Budget Chairman Leon Panetta (D-California) reported a lack of a real sense of urgency despite the magnitude of the problem, and he reminded us that it had taken a stock market crash to produce the modest 1987 agreement. Most of us agreed that the threat of sequestration was unreal for our constituents, while anti-tax sentiment was high. This meant that the pressures the negotiators felt to push toward agreement were matched by a desire to avoid blame for unpopular moves on taxes or entitlements.

Finally, on September 30, 1990, after weeks of talks in semi-seclusion at Andrews Air Force Base, the breakthrough occurred. President Bush appeared with the summit participants to announce that a five-year agreement had been reached. The negotiators had dropped both capital gains tax reductions (which Republicans advocated) and top-rate increases (pushed by Democrats) from the package and had backed away from any alterations in Social Security. But the plan still projected $500 billion in savings from the current-services baseline (i.e., from the levels required to maintain current activity, adjusted for inflation and, in the case of entitlements, for the size and circumstances of eligible populations) over the next five years, with $134 billion of this coming from tax increases, $65 billion from debt-service savings, and $301 billion from spending cuts. Almost two-thirds of these cuts would come from defense and the rest mainly from entitlement programs like Medicare, agricultural price supports, and civil service retirement. Domestic and international discretionary spending would increase only for inflation.

Substantial budget process and enforcement reforms were also proposed. The G-R-H deficit targets, susceptible to evasion and manipulation, would be replaced by statutory caps on discretionary spending to be enforced by sequestration. For the first three years there would be separate caps for domestic, international, and defense spending, with "firewalls" between them. Reductions in one category could not raise the caps for another, nor could excesses in one area trigger sequesters in another. For mandatory (non-appropriated) spending and revenues, new pay-as-you-go (PAYGO) rules would require tax reductions or entitlement increases to be accompanied by whatever revenue increases or entitlement cuts were required to offset their budget impact.

This moment also marked the birth of the anti-tax absolutism that has defined the Republican party to this day. Minority whip Newt Gingrich pointedly skipped the White House announcement and began to organize Republican opposition to the plan in defiance of President Bush and his own minority leader. Gingrich's point of departure was not any alternative plan for reducing the deficit—he had none—but rather a dogmatic insistence that taxes not be raised and a conviction that the GOP politically could not afford to abandon that position. As the *Washington Post* editorialized:

> The balking Republicans say they are against all tax increases. But they are of course against the deficit as well—and no more willing or able than Ronald Reagan or George Bush has been to name the spending cuts that by themselves might bring the deficit out of the red zone. Instead they continue to parrot that what the country needs is more tax cuts to grow its way out of the deficit. You last heard that sort of happy talk about $2 trillion in debt ago.[3]

Speaker Foley and other House Democratic leaders presented the package as the best that could be attained after five months of negotiations and warned that we would reject it at our political peril. "We're about to hand the president a pardon and a machine gun," Foley told a Democratic Caucus meeting as the negative whip counts came in. Democratic rejection would take the spotlight off GOP disarray and Gingrich's rebellion and would give the president an excuse to "do anything he wants," perhaps to assume extraordinary powers to avert governmental breakdown.

Such pleas were to no avail. The problem with the package, commented Rep. Charles Schumer (D-New York), was that "Democrats think it's a Republican budget and Republicans think it's a Democratic budget."[4] Despite the importuning on both sides, including a national television address by the president, the budget agreement was rejected by a vote of 179–254, with a majority voting no among both Democrats (108–149) and Republicans (71–105).

One reason for the skittishness in both parties was the tendency of the media, especially television, to cover the budget agreement by focusing on its supposed victims. I knew we were in trouble when I saw the network news coverage immediately after the agreement was announced: motorists at the gas pump, frail nursing home residents (who probably would not have been affected by the proposed Medicare premium increases), and others bewailing their victimization. Not much was made, however, of the potential victims of sequestration, a much larger list, or of the effects of the economic downturn to which the deficit was contributing. The media provided almost no context for understanding the agreement—why it was necessary, why it was difficult to conclude, why it could not be painless. They instead focused on alleged victimization and governmental ineptitude, which greatly reinforced the tendency of members of Congress, especially in an election year, to distance themselves as far as possible from budgetary unpleasantness, to simply vote no.

I voted for the agreement, although I had my own list of objections and could only imagine what my Republican opponent would make of my vote in his campaign ads. I did not see how I, after having stressed the urgency of putting our fiscal house in order, could credibly vote against a plan that represented the largest deficit-reduction package in our nation's history. I felt that we Democrats would be in a stronger position to shape the final implementing legislation to our liking if we produced our quota of votes for the agreement. This reasoning was reflected in notes I made the day after the vote:

> What a different situation it would be today if the budget agreement had gone down for a lack of Republican votes alone, with some 130 [instead of 108] Democrats recorded "yes." The news stories would be of Republican division and default, and we would have the upper hand in rewriting a budget that more faithfully reflects Democratic priorities. As it is, we share in the public blame for the failure to act, and we seek partisan accommodation with a weaker hand.... If, on the other hand, the agreement had gone down for a lack of Democratic votes alone, there would be hell to pay. The fact that both parties defaulted forces the president to moderate the blame game and in fact helps turn the spotlight back on him and his failure to lead.

The budget vote produced the spectacle of a weekend government shutdown, and public estimation of both Congress and the president plummeted.[5] House and Senate leaders (minus the divided House Republicans) frantically sought to get a slightly altered budget resolution approved to replace the failed agreement. This was accomplished by a 250–164 vote (including only thirty-two Republican yeas) in the House and a bipartisan 66–33 vote in the Senate. More than one hundred House Democrats switched to a yes vote, moved by a relaxation of Medicare and other reconciliation requirements and shaken by growing public outage.

The normal budget process, without summitry, could not have produced anything approximating the final 1990 outcome, given the shakiness of the Democratic majority in the Senate and the realities of divided government. The president's resources included not only a veto pen but also the rhetorical high ground. Unless he could be brought into the fray and compelled to offer genuine solutions, Democrats faced the prospect of becoming the party of sacrifice and pain and inviting their own political demise. The summit process, although it blurred the lines of institutional and party responsibility, forced a measure of seriousness and realism on the leaders of both branches (with the notable exception of House Republicans) and heightened their incentives to formulate a constructive solution to an intractable national problem.

Might the process have worked better under unified party control of Congress and the White House? Those who raised that question soon had a chance to answer it, as deficits and pressures for renewed action continued to mount. Whoever won the 1992 election was certain to face the necessity of negotiating another multiyear agreement. That turned out to be a Democratic president paired with a Democratic congressional majority, a situation that had not existed since the early, tentative years of the budget process. This set up a political dynamic for 1993 that contrasted sharply with that of 1990 while producing a remarkably similar substantive outcome.

Congress adhered to the 1990 budget agreement for the remaining two years of the Bush presidency. The discretionary spending caps and pay-as-you-go rules proved less susceptible to gamesmanship than the former G-R-H procedures. But deficit-reduction hopes were frustrated as the economy slid into a recession and health care inflation produced higher than anticipated entitlement costs. In early 1991, when the Congressional Budget Office predicted that the deficit for the current fiscal year would exceed $300 billion, Budget chairman Leon Panetta spoke for many of us in exclaiming, "We went through an awful lot of hell to get to $300 billion deficits. I never see the light at the end of the tunnel. Everybody predicts it, but we never get there."[6] Although the CBO explained that without the 1990 agreement the projected deficits would have been far worse, it soon concluded "that the main accomplishment of [the agreement] was not to reduce the size of the structural deficit, but rather to prevent it from becoming substantially larger."[7]

As Bill Clinton prepared to take office, there was little question that budget issues would be his first major test. The deficit had reached a record high of $290 billion in 1992 and showed no signs of abating. Interest payments on the national debt had topped $200 billion, more than any other budget items except defense and Social Security. Medicare and Medicaid costs were growing at double-digit rates, nullifying the effects of discretionary spending restraint. The 1990 firewalls were coming down, and the agenda of both congressional Democrats and the new president required securing a better deal for their domestic priorities. The president announced his goals in an address to a joint session of Congress on February 17, 1993: "jump-starting the economy in the short term and investing in our people, their jobs, and their incomes over the long run" while "substantially reducing the federal deficit, honestly and credibly."[8]

Clinton proposed savings of $704 billion from projected five-year spending, $375 billion from spending cuts and $328 billion from tax increases, with a third of the savings applied to a "stimulus package" to get the economy moving and to longer-term domestic investments in infrastructure, education, health care, and other areas. His tax increases were primarily aimed at upper-income taxpayers, proposing a new top rate of 36 percent for joint filers making more than $140,000 and a surtax that would give those making more than $250,000 a marginal rate of 39.6 percent. He also proposed a more broadly based "BTU" excise tax based on the heat output of various energy sources. For the 17 percent of taxpayers at the low end of the income scale, he proposed a tax reduction through an expanded earned income tax credit (EITC).

No Republican ever voted for the proposal in either chamber. Most adopted the no-new-taxes stance Newt Gingrich had enunciated in walking away from the 1990 bipartisan agreement. Many thought George Bush had erred fatally in abandoning his "read my lips" pledge and regarded reinstating it as the key to Republican electoral success. The BTU tax gave them a pretext for portraying the entire package as a hit on middle-class taxpayers. House leaders kept the BTU provision in the bill by a narrow vote only to see the Senate drop it later, with the administration's acquiescence. Many House members concluded we had taken a tough vote for naught. Thus did a new term enter the congressional lexicon: "being BTU'd," i.e., walking the plank for something likely to be rejected by the Senate or abandoned by the White House.

I admired the president's willingness to take on the fiscal issue seriously and got involved in the fight as a new member of the Budget Committee and part of the whip's task force on the reconciliation bills that implemented the specifics of the plan. I worked with Martin Sabo (D-Minnesota), the new Budget chairman (Leon Panetta left the House to become Clinton's Office of Management and Budget Director), to tweak the bill so as to cut spending and reduce the deficit slightly more.

The final vote of August 5, 1993, on the conference report on the reconciliation bill was 218–216—only one vote to spare. The politicking surrounding the vote was the most intense I had experienced. Ironically, many of the defecting Democrats were conservatives and moderates who had argued strongly for deficit reduction in the past. But they frequently came from marginal districts and felt particularly vulnerable to the drumbeat of Republican criticism, picked up in the talk shows and in the media, that this was a tax-and-spend plan that would hurt ordinary Americans. Too many of our members were cowed by such tactics, including some from relatively safe districts, some of them committee or subcommittee chairs. I have an indelible memory of such members voting no and standing by to let vulnerable freshmen provide the margin of victory. But the showdown also produced numerous profiles in courage, some of whom paid dearly in the next election.

Republican predictions, which became more and more frantic, read strangely within a few months as the markets responded favorably to the plan and it began to have its desired effects. Conference Chairman Dick

Armey (R-Texas) spoke scornfully of "the hollow promises of deficit reduction and magical theories of lower interest rates" and predicted that the plan would "grow the government and shrink the economy," precisely the reverse of what occurred. Republican whip Newt Gingrich said the plan would "lead to a recession and ... actually increase the deficit."[9] "Right, guys," the Raleigh *News and Observer* declared six months later in an editorial that delighted me but provided only limited political benefit:

> That must be why all of us got up this morning to endure still another day of low interest rates, booming housing markets, rising business investment, job creation roaring along faster than the Bush years ever saw, and—in the Triangle—a business climate rated second to none in the land.[10]

Some persisted in the view that a bipartisan approach to the budget might have been crafted, had President Clinton extended his hand.[11] But that was never a realistic possibility. The Republican attitude after 1992 was, "You won the election; be our guest." GOP members had no interest in putting their fingerprints on any budget deal, and many even argued against formulating a Republican alternative. Their opposition was monolithic, and it clearly served a partisan purpose—creating maximum pressure on Democrats, setting off a scramble to win the votes of wavering members, and exposing the limits of party discipline. The final outcome—getting 84 percent of the Democratic votes in the House and all but six Democratic votes in the Senate—represented a (narrow) victory for party responsibility. (Under Senate rules, reconciliation bills were not subject to filibuster, requiring only a majority vote.) Press coverage and public perceptions, which focused on the struggle for marginal votes under unrelenting opposition attack, suggested desperation and disarray. The president and the Democratic Party in Congress won a fight that was unthinkable to lose, but the battle exposed dangerous weaknesses and left us largely unfortified for the escalating struggles of 1994.

Republicans continued to speak (inaccurately) of "the greatest tax increase in history," and made it a major theme of the 1994 election. Their success in winning control of the House presented a dilemma, however: they had to come up with a plan of their own. Having promised massive tax cuts and increased defense spending, they turned to the only places left, proposing unprecedented cuts in domestic appropriations bills and in Medicare and Medicaid as well. Democrats were able to convey a message of GOP extremism, noting, for example, the comparability of the Medicare reductions to the tax cuts mainly benefiting the wealthy ($270 billion and $245 billion, respectively, in the final budget resolution for 1996) and the trade-off between them. Republicans achieved more discipline than Democrats had in 1993 in passing their budget measures. But they ran into firm resistance from President Clinton, provoking repeated vetoes and two highly unpopular government shutdowns, which the public mainly blamed on the Republicans.[12]

The GOP thus learned in the 104th Congress what Democrats had learned in 1993: it is extremely difficult and often politically damaging to attempt major budgetary change from one side of the aisle alone. By 1997 it was clear that another five-year budget plan was due. But neither party was disposed to go it alone, and the 1996 election's mixed verdict both necessitated and offered positive incentives for cooperation.

The Republican margin in the House was reduced (including the Fourth District of North Carolina!) but not by enough to put Democrats in charge. That is not to say the election was inconclusive, however. What I had heard during my comeback campaign was unmistakable: a disgust with political posturing and excessive partisanship and a desire to see the country's problems, including the budget deficit, addressed. As the 105th Congress convened, many members had come to a similar conclusion: neither party was going to be totally in control, and both would look better if they found a basis for cooperation.

Therefore, the president, looking for a positive start for his second term, and congressional Republicans, seeking to shed the image of revolutionary excess and government shutdowns, found a common interest in negotiating a new five-year budget deal. Fortunately, the economic conditions also were auspicious, posing win-win possibilities that contrasted with the zero-sum conflicts of years past. The deficit had come down more rapidly than anticipated, and the strong economy made it feasible to balance the budget in five years while providing a sizable tax cut and increased spending for domestic needs in the bargain. That is precisely the deal administration and congressional negotiators put together over a two-month period, announcing on May 2, 1997, what Clinton called "a balanced budget with balanced values."[13]

The agreement was translated into a budget resolution that called for five-year reductions from the current-services baseline of $139 billion in discretionary spending ($77 billion in defense, $62 billion in nondefense) and $170 billion in entitlements, tax cuts netting $85 billion, and new spending of $38 billion, mainly to extend health insurance to 5 million uninsured children and restore some benefits to documented immigrants denied them by the 1996 welfare reform law. The resolution called for two reconciliation bills, one to implement Medicare as well as other entitlement reductions and the second—the Taxpayer Relief Act—to implement tax cuts, including my student loan provisions (see Chapter 5). The pay-as-you-go rules and caps on discretionary spending instituted in 1990 would be extended through 2002. The result was $204 billion in deficit reduction and a balanced budget projected within five years—not as large as the 1990 and 1993 deals, but enough to finish the job.

The budget actually registered a surplus much sooner, in fiscal 1998. By fiscal 2000, the Treasury was able to discontinue its longtime practice of borrowing from the Social Security trust fund to meet current obligations; the general fund was itself in surplus. Both parties proceeded to pledge "hands off" the Social Security surplus. It would still be invested in Treasury bonds, but the proceeds would only be used to buy down publicly held debt, thus reducing the annual burden of debt service and putting the Treasury in a stronger position to meet its eventual obligation to the trust fund when and if the surplus in Social Security receipts went away.[14]

All told, the publicly held debt was reduced by $485 billion over fiscal years 1998–2001. This did not produce tranquility in budget politics: Democrats strained against spending limits and Republicans clamored for massive tax cuts. But both sides were constrained by their promises to keep Social Security sacrosanct; the "Social Security surplus is more of a restraint on spending than the budget caps ever were," one budget expert noted.[15] After a presidential campaign in which both candidates pledged to keep Social Security revenues in a "lock box" forever, many assumed that both parties had drawn an inviolable line in the sand. As it turned out, those sands were about to shift, and our four-year winning streak of balanced budgets was about to end.

With the advent of the George W. Bush administration in 2001, the political standoff and budgetary inhibitions that had protected the surplus in the late 1990s fell away. Large tax cuts trumped everything else, becoming the predominant factor in a precipitous national fiscal reversal that was then exacerbated by the terrorist attacks of September 11.

The year began with the most optimistic surplus projections ever—$5.6 trillion over ten years—and a debate (quaint in retrospect) about how quickly and how completely the publicly held debt should be retired. The president proposed tax cuts that would absorb almost all of the ten-year non–Social Security, non-Medicare surplus. He also held out the promise of a significant long-term defense buildup and the addition of a prescription drug benefit to Medicare, while ignoring or greatly underestimating their costs. This raised the prospect—which became a certainty as budget projections worsened—that the Bush budget would not only require spending the Social Security revenues that had been declared forever off limits but would also take the overall budget back into deficit.

Utilizing reconciliation procedures as protection against a Senate filibuster, the president and the Republican congressional leadership made the tax cut their first order of business, far in advance of congressional spending decisions for fiscal 2002. The true cost of their measure, including interest savings foregone, was close to $2.6 trillion over ten years.[16] They stayed within a $1.35 trillion ten-year ceiling only with complicated phase-ins and an unlikely provision that most of the cuts would "sunset" after nine years, thus setting up the "fiscal cliff" showdown of 2012. Budget estimates released by the CBO in August confirmed that because of the tax cuts and the deteriorating economy, the Bush administration was on track to invade the Social Security surplus for each of the next six years and the Medicare surplus for the next eight. These "baseline" estimates, moreover, omitted any additional spending planned for defense and Medicare prescription drugs, as well as likely disaster relief, the pending farm bill, alternative minimum tax adjustments, and the continuation of expiring tax provisions.[17]

Then came the terrorist attacks of September 11, which dealt the economy a further blow and immediately necessitated another $40 billion in emergency spending. This made for a temporary reduction in budgetary conflict, but the parties continued to push sharply differing economic stimulus proposals, finally settling in early 2002 on a scaled-back package of unemployment benefits and business tax breaks. Most members agreed that both the state of the economy and the challenge of terrorism required a substantial commitment of budgetary resources. We disagreed strongly, however, on both taxing and spending priorities and, above all, on whether we could have it all—hundreds of billions of dollars in tax cuts disproportionately targeted to the wealthiest Americans, with limited stimulative impact—in disregard of deteriorating budget projections and mounting debt. These questions dominated our 2002 budget debates and continued to divide the parties and polarize the Congress.

Republicans, regaining the Senate majority and thus unified control of government in the 2002 elections, proceeded to double down on budget policy. Having waived PAYGO rules to make way for their 2001 tax cut, they allowed them to expire entirely in 2002, thus making way for another round of tax cuts and a Medicare prescription drug benefit without budget offsets. The 2003 tax bill provided rate reductions to 15 percent for dividends and capital gains and moved up the implementation date for the 2001 income tax rate reductions. Democrats, led by our new minority leader, Nancy Pelosi, developed an alliterative formula to highlight our alternative plan's virtues: *fast acting* (tax cuts for 2003, mainly one-time rebates, exceeding those proposed by the Republicans; immediate aid to the states; and unemployment insurance extensions); *fair* (targeting all taxpayers); and *fiscally responsible* (mostly short-term measures with a minimal out-year budget impact).

It was not difficult to demonstrate that the Bush plan failed this three-way test, but the president, unlike Reagan in 1982 and George H.W. Bush in 1990, refused to moderate his budgetary policy in the face of worsening economic reality. Meanwhile, the institutional constraints imposed by the 1990 budget rules and divided party control of government had fallen away. The unified budget deficit for fiscal 2003 thus ended at $374 billion—$531 billion without the cushion of the Social Security surplus—with a further plunge predicted for 2004, all for a relatively small economic impact.[18]

The Bush administration's reversal of budget policy marked not only a return to deepening deficits but also the end of the era of comprehensive, sometimes bipartisan, budget agreements. The Bush tax cuts—extended to counter the Great Recession as his term ended and then only partially terminated by the "fiscal cliff" deal of 2012—added some $5.6 trillion to federal deficits from 2001 to 2018.[19] The economic downturn resulted in precipitous further declines in revenue and necessitated countercyclical spending as well, taking the Fiscal 2009 deficit to 9.8 percent of GDP (see Figure 7.1), the highest level since the World War II.

President Obama, coming to office in 2009, regarded economic recovery as his first order of business. But like Clinton in 1993, he also saw the necessity of addressing the long-term fiscal situation in a comprehensive way. In early 2010, he named a bipartisan, bicameral National Commission on Fiscal Responsibility and Reform and charged it with identifying "policies to improve the fiscal situation in the medium term and to achieve fiscal sustainability over the long run."[20] The commission consisted of six senators, six House members, and six public members and was chaired by former Senator Alan Simpson (R-Wyoming) and former White House chief of staff (and Democratic Senate candidate in North Carolina) Erskine Bowles.

The Simpson-Bowles Commission made its report within ten months, modeling its approach on the 1990 and 1993 agreements, but going beyond them significantly. The Commission proposed to leave countercyclical tax and spending measures in place for two years until the recession abated, but then to lower the deficit to 2.3 percent of GDP by 2015. The eventual goal was to peg both annual government spending and revenues at 21 percent of GDP.

The Commission proposed approximately $2 in spending cuts for every $1 in tax increases but provided multiple challenges to Republican anti-tax orthodoxy. The cuts to entitlement spending were especially controversial, and gave me considerable pause, e.g., increases in the retirement age that would be especially problematic for manual laborers, and adoption of the "chained" Consumer Price Index (CPI) as a way of calculating inflation adjustments for all indexed programs (thus reducing payments for lower- and upper-income beneficiaries alike). I would have preferred less regressive approaches such as raising the wage base on which Social Security taxes were levied, subjecting the full benefits of wealthy individuals to income taxation, and revisiting the Bush tax cuts on capital gains and dividends.

The final vote on the Simpson-Bowles report was a clear signal of the increasing difficulty of reaching partisan compromise, especially in the House. The vote was 11–7, which fell short of the 14–4 supermajority required. Five of the six House members (two Democrats and all three Republicans, including future speaker Paul Ryan) voted "no," albeit for diametrically opposed reasons.

In the meantime, the 2010 elections brought a Republican majority heavily influenced by libertarian "tea party" ideology to power. Their first major legislative effort—the infamous H.R. 1—was an attempt to cut fiscal 2011 appropriations, which had not yet been finalized, by an additional $100 billion, almost entirely from domestic programs. Fortunately for the still-fragile recovery, the Democratic Senate resisted this move. But the looming imposition of the debt ceiling, on which Congress was required to vote, gave the Republicans a strong hand in dealing with the Obama administration.

In mid-2011, President Obama and Speaker John Boehner began talks aimed at a comprehensive budget agreement, with the Simpson-Bowles recommendations as a major point of reference. These talks intersected, not always helpfully, with the ongoing discussions of a self-designated "Gang of Six" senators that ranged ideologically from Dick Durbin (D-Illinois) to Tom Coburn (R-Oklahoma). None of these talks succeeded. In retrospect, it is striking how close they came and what both sides were willing to consider. But the talks nonetheless dissolved amid charges that each side had "moved the goalposts" and other recriminations, demonstrating that deepening political polarization—especially anti-tax absolutism among Republicans—had placed grand bargains on the 1990s model out of reach.[21]

What we got instead was the Budget Control Act (BCA), signed on August 2, 2011, as the debt ceiling reached its limit (but not in time to avoid a much-disputed downgrading by Standard and Poor's of the nation's credit rating). The bill put stringent caps on appropriated spending, designed to offset the debit ceiling increase, for the next ten years. It then set the stage for another try at a comprehensive budget agreement, setting up a Joint Select Committee on Deficit Reduction (later dubbed the "Supercommittee") and charging it with formulating a grand bargain by the end of the year. If agreement could not be reached, a retooled version of sequestration would impose automatic cuts totaling $1.1 trillion over fiscal 2013–2021 on military and domestic accounts alike (with exceptions for Social Security, Medicaid, federal pensions and veterans' benefits and a partial exemption for Medicare). This at first would result in deep, indiscriminate cuts across all accounts and in the out-years would bake lower limits into the already-stringent statutory spending caps.

The Obama administration urged adoption of the BCA, albeit under extreme duress, and Democrats in the House split their vote, 95–95 (I adamantly voted "no"). Republicans approved the bill by 174–66, with Boehner boasting he got "98 percent of what [he] wanted" in the deal.[22] I never thought it would work, and said so at the time. The political calculation was that sequestration would never be allowed to happen because Democrats would be deeply concerned to protect domestic spending and Republicans equally concerned about military spending. I thought that the only sequestration device that might compel Republicans to act would be the threat of a tax surcharge. That was never tested, but it soon became clear that Republicans were willing to let the sequester ax fall on defense before they would acquiesce in the tax increases that a grand bargain would require.

And fall it did. The Supercommittee announced its failure on November 21, 2011, setting off a scramble over the next year to avoid or deflect the automatic cuts that were scheduled to occur on January 2, 2013—the same date that the 2001 and 2003 Bush tax cuts were set to expire. The legislation which addressed this "fiscal cliff"—the American Taxpayer Relief Act of 2012—restored the 39.6 percent top tax rate on individuals but otherwise made 82 percent of the tax cuts permanent. It also delayed sequestration by two months. But on March 1, as required, President Obama ordered the cuts, warning that they would damage the economy—as indeed they did, cutting functions ranging from medical research to military readiness as well as the recovering economy's growth rate, reducing it by some 0.5 percent of GDP. Sequestration was an especially mindless and ineffective way of addressing fiscal challenges, a monument to political polarization and ideological rigidity.[23]

The damage inflicted by sequestration was compounded in October as fiscal year 2014 began. Efforts to enact a continuing resolution floundered, mainly on Republican efforts to defund Obama's Affordable Care Act, resulting in a 17-day government shutdown. But the larger problem was sequestration itself, locked into place by the Republican majority's 2014 budget resolution. This left Republican appropriators with impossibly low allocations for their bills. Our T-HUD bill was pulled from the House floor in July when it became apparent to Republican leaders that many of their own members, as well as most Democrats, would very likely vote against such drastic cuts. Meanwhile, the Interior and Environment bill was suspended indefinitely amid a contentious committee markup. All of this, I editorialized at the time, threatened a total breakdown of appropriations. "By institutionalizing anti-tax ideology and an almost exclusive focus on domestic discretionary spending"—that is, locking sequestration of non-military accounts into their budget resolution—"the House Republican leadership not only makes bipartisanship impossible; it also makes appropriations as we know it impossible."[24]

The crisis was eased if not resolved by the enactment of the Bipartisan Budget Act in December. In what became the model for the successive two-year budget deals that got us through the decade, the top-line caps were increased by $45 billion for fiscal 2014 and another $15 billion for 2015, providing additional headroom for domestic and defense spending bills alike. The large bipartisan vote in the House, 332–94, was an indicator of alarm and exhaustion in equal measure. House leaders made only limited claims for the deal, acknowledging that the grand bargains of years past were now impossible to obtain.[25]

In the meantime, the budget process itself was functioning more and more erratically. Republicans made some process changes that fit their supply-side ideology—replacing PAYGO with Cut-as-You-Go (CUTGO) in 2011, for example, dictating that tax cuts would not have to be paid for and that increases in mandatory spending would not require increases in revenues. In 2015, Republicans wrote into House rules a requirement that the Congressional Budget Office employ "dynamic" as opposed to "static" scoring in assessing the macroeconomic effects of policy changes. The idea was to take fuller account of the positive economic effects of tax cuts and thus to minimize estimated negative effects on the deficit. They displayed much less interest in applying the concept to the stimulative effects of government spending.[26] In any event, the requirement was dropped, and PAYGO restored, when Democrats reclaimed House leadership in 2019.

Both parties have continued to use reconciliation to bypass Senate filibusters and muscle through controversial measures. Republicans used reconciliation to ease passage of the Bush tax cuts of 2001 and 2003 and the Trump tax cut of 2017; Democrats used the process to amend the Affordable Care Act and reform student aid in 2010. Republicans tried twice to use reconciliation to repeal the health care law. The first bill was vetoed by President Obama in 2016, and the second, proposed in 2017 under united Republican control, failed to gain a Senate majority.

Reconciliation requires a bicameral budget resolution, however, and budget resolutions have become increasingly difficult to pass. The House and Senate have failed to agree on a resolution eleven times since the inception of the budget process, all since Fiscal 1999. Failure has most often been linked to divided party control of the two chambers, but in recent years both parties in both houses have had increasing difficulty in formulating a budget resolution in the first place. This too is related to polarization and intense partisan competition: the grim realities of budget tradeoffs offer ample material for campaign attacks against vulnerable members—attacks party leaders would prefer to avoid.

I was on the Budget Committee in 2002 when Democrats, then in the minority, first failed to put forward an alternative budget resolution. I backed our ranking member, John Spratt (D-South Carolina) as he attempted to convince the party leadership that our credibility in debate would be weakened without an alternative. But the economy was languishing, and our leaders were reluctant to open front-line members to charges that they might rescind the Bush tax cuts or resume borrowing Social Security revenues.

Such difficulties have not lessened in the intervening years. In fact, Democrats in 2019, newly returned in the majority, declined to pass a conventional budget resolution for fiscal 2020. Once again, our Budget Committee chairman, John Yarmuth (D-Kentucky), tried to put a proposal together. But the prospect of putting marginal members on the spot on taxes and entitlements, plus the possibility of losing members on our far left who were opposed to most military and security spending, led our leadership to settle for a "deeming" resolution instead.

Such deeming resolutions have been increasingly utilized by both parties.[27] They provide a tentative framework for allocating top-line numbers to the appropriations committees, allowing their markups to proceed. But they add to the challenge of reaching agreement between House and Senate, since the allocations as well as the details of the bills will eventually have to be reconciled. During the past decade, the process has been especially difficult in the absence of two-year budget agreements. Republican budget resolutions have initially been written to BCA (sequestration) levels, which has made it impossible to pass appropriations bills on a bipartisan basis in the House and often to pass them at all in the Senate. All of this, of course, could be anticipated, and budget agreements would ideally be concluded early in the year. Typically, however, resolution has come late, as the new fiscal year and the threat of a shutdown has loomed. Usually, only a few of the appropriations bills have been passed in either chamber by this time. Therefore, continuing resolutions (CRs) have been required to keep the government open until appropriations bills, typically in the form of omnibus or "minibus" clusters of bills, could be rewritten in accordance with the budget agreement numbers.

Such delays and reliance on continuing resolutions—not as dramatic or damaging as a shutdown, but still disruptive in terms of uncertainty, scrambled award and funding schedules, and delays in implementing the adjustments provided in the regular bills—have become endemic. Congress has passed all twelve appropriations bills on time only four times since 1977 and never since 1997, relying on at least one and often multiple CRs for some or all of the bills for thirty-nine of the forty-three years. In instances of especially serious breakdown, such as the failure of the Tea Party House and the Democratic Senate to bridge their differences in 2011, or after sequestration in 2013, CRs may extend for the entire fiscal year.

The system is prone to breakdown even when it seems to be going relatively well. In 2018, for example, appropriators took some bipartisan satisfaction in getting five bills—Energy, Military Construction-VA, Legislative Branch, and, most significantly, the large Defense and Labor-Health and Human Services bills—to the president before the October 1 start of the 2019 fiscal year. We had the benefit of workable allocations, thanks to the 2018–2019 budget agreement, although not a bicameral budget resolution. Another "minibus" of four bills, including T-HUD, was almost ready to go when we adjourned for the election season; these and the other remaining bills were deferred through a CR, with the expectation that they would be enacted soon after the election. But the cycle that began so auspiciously ended with the longest shutdown in history. President Trump refused to agree to a third CR, required to continue funding past December 21, when he failed to get agreement on $5.8 billion for his border wall, and Senate Leader McConnell refused to consider any measure that did not have Trump's advance approval. The matter was finally resolved after five weeks, when a fourth CR reopened the government and an omnibus bill, devised by House-Senate conferees over the next three weeks, was finally accepted by all parties in mid-February—almost five months into the fiscal year.

Having confronted this five-week shutdown immediately upon coming to power, House Democrats were determined to do better in the 2020 budget cycle. Knowing that a fourth budget agreement would be necessary to escape the strictures of the BCA, we pushed for a spring agreement. Failing that, and deciding to forego the challenge of pressing a conventional budget resolution, we approved a deeming resolution on April 9, 2019, and proceeded to mark up our appropriations bills and to pass ten of them before the August recess.

The Republican Senate passed neither a budget resolution nor any individual bills, but we did agree just before the August recess on a two-year deal that lifted the sequestration-level caps. The Senate finally passed four appropriations bills in October, but by then the fiscal year had begun and the government was operating under a CR. It was clear that reaching agreement between the appropriations levels passed in the House and those permitted by the less generous budget agreement would be difficult. But the difficulty was compounded when the Senate adopted allocations that were distorted for almost all subcommittees by the determination of Republican leaders to make room, once again, for Trump's border wall.

As impeachment loomed in December, we seemed to have the makings of a prolonged crisis, perhaps including another wall-induced shutdown. On our T-HUD bill and most others, an unusual number of disputed policy riders had to be kicked upstairs for leadership approval by virtue of Republicans' insistence that even the smallest items be cleared with the White House. In the end, however, the appetite for confrontation in both chambers and at the White House proved to be limited, and we secured passage of two complementary minibuses on December 17, 2019, one day before impeachment. It was a win of sorts for Appropriations, but as I told constituents, it was indicative of how far we had fallen that avoiding a shutdown and passing appropriations bills *only* three months into the fiscal year was considered a victory for "regular order"!

Figure 7.1 depicts the trajectory of the federal deficit (and fleeting surpluses) since the onset of the Reagan administration—in the wake of the grand bargains of the 1990s, the great recession, and the Bush and Trump

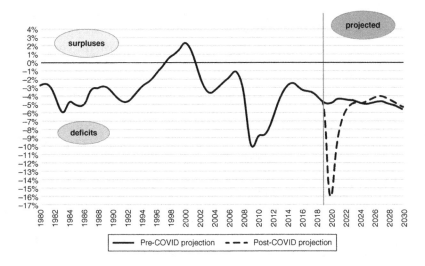

Figure 7.1 Budget deficits/surpluses as percentages of GDP since 1980.

Source: Congressional Budget Office; Center for Budget and Policy Priorities.

tax cuts. The deficit reached $984 billion in fiscal 2019, 4.6 percent of GDP, up almost a point from the year before. This was the highest deficit as a share of GDP since 2012, when the unemployment rate had been more than twice as high. Deficits normally go down in times of economic growth, but they instead increased for four years running. This was partly attributable to the suppression of revenues by the Trump tax cut, which accounted for an estimated one-quarter of the fiscal 2019 deficit.[28]

Before the coronavirus struck in early 2020, deficits averaging 4.7 percent of GDP were projected to continue growing over the next decade, with the debt reaching 79 percent of GDP in 2019 and 95 percent by 2029. With the onset of the pandemic, deficit projections for 2020 soared to $3.3 trillion, 16.0 percent of GDP, with the debt predicted to equal 98.2 percent of GDP by the end of the year.[29] This underscored the folly of the $2 trillion Trump tax cut, which had given the economy a "sugar high" in 2018–2019 when no stimulus was needed, but now deprived the country of resources needed to counter the pandemic and fuel an economic recovery.

The first coronavirus relief bills exceeded $2 trillion and promised to go much higher. The immediate danger was to do not too much but too little to see individuals, businesses, and communities through the severe downturn and to provide a stimulus sufficient to bring the economy back to health. The lesson of the 2009 Recovery Act should be to beware of falling short.

Still, as the economy recovers, the question of fiscal sustainability will recur. The tax code, grossly inequitable and insufficient to pay the nation's bills before the crisis, will have to be revisited. The Social Security and Medicare trust funds, while not in immediate crisis, will face increasing strains. The question of what, if any, ratio of debt to the size of the economy might represent a "tipping point" will again be debated.

Given the track record of the budget process, recounted in this chapter, it is hard to believe that it—or the politics surrounding it—is up to these challenges. The architects of the process aspired to improve the coordination and accountability of congressional policymaking, making certain the fiscal impact of disparate decisions was taken fully into account. At best, the historical verdict is mixed, representing as much a commentary on the quality of political leadership as on budgetary architecture.

The budget leaders of the 1980s sometimes struggled valiantly, but the solutions to the problems they faced exceeded what any achievable political consensus would support. The result, all too often, was budget deliberations and decisions that became exercises in smoke-and-mirrors accounting and political evasion and only patched things up from year to year. The comprehensive plans of 1990 and 1993—and to a lesser extent 1997—broke with this pattern at considerable political cost to those supporting them but with eventual budgetary gain. This gain came not only through year-to-year cuts in spending and increases in revenue but through improved budget machinery, which replaced the easily manipulated G-R-H procedures. The results included lower interest rates and more confidence in the economy, which in turn led to increased investment, job creation, and productivity.[30] In the meantime, overly simplistic fixes like the balanced budget amendment to the Constitution and the line-item veto (see Chapter 12) fell by the wayside.

While the budget process and its responsible use helped produce a brief era of balanced budgets, it has now fallen to the lowest point in its forty-five-year history in terms of influence and effectiveness. The George W. Bush administration learned the wrong lessons from the 1990s, at first declaring budget discipline irrelevant in a time of surpluses and then abandoning it entirely as economic and budgetary storm signals worsened in 2001. By the time of the Obama administration, bipartisan agreement was impossible to come by, either on basic recovery measures or on comprehensive budget reform. Meanwhile, the budget process itself deviated increasingly from its prescribed schedules and functions, complicating rather than channeling the appropriations process.

The budget process has always been highly partisan. But it has gone from placing necessary parameters around taxing and spending to being a distraction from those basic decisions and/or making them more divisive and difficult. As such, it has both reflected and contributed to the increasing partisan polarization that has divided and disabled the House.

The distinctive aspects of polarization outlined in Chapter 6 are reflected in contemporary budget politics. The sharp right turn of Republicans, for example, especially the hardening of anti-tax ideology, was the most important reason for the failure of renewed efforts at comprehensive reform that began in 2010 and culminated in sequestration. The close and constant competition between the parties—and the fear of exposing vulnerable members to attack—powerfully explains not only the difficulty of achieving grand bargains but also the increasing reluctance *within* the congressional parties to formulate and debate budget resolutions.

Budget politics has also contributed importantly to the concentration of power in party leadership. The process from the first was aimed at establishing coordination and discipline under the aegis of the majority party. Such measures as requiring Appropriations and Ways and Means representation on the Budget Committee were designed to limit any resulting concentration of power. But as budgetary standoffs came to require grand bargains, and then as the process fell into serious disarray, power shifted decisively from the committees, including the Budget Committee, to party leadership (and the White House). It has become increasingly rare for an appropriations subcommittee chair, working with the ranking member and their Senate counterparts, to steer an individual bill to passage. And even when it occurs in one or both chambers, it almost always then becomes part of a complicated and contentious end-game—successive continuing resolutions, combination with other measures into an omnibus bill, negotiation of multifaceted packages with the president, often of the opposite party, and so forth. All of this takes matters, as we appropriations chairs often say to each other, "above our pay grade." These days, however, the culprit is less the budget process itself than the breakdown of that process, which then requires resolution at higher levels.

Partisan and Bipartisan Capacity

The late congressional scholar Barbara Sinclair was an insightful observer of the House who based much of her work on intensive interviews with members and staff; I still miss our annual debriefs. Not long after I saw my home equity loan disclosure and Advanced Technological Education bills to passage, largely in classic a-bill-becomes-a-law fashion (see Chapter 5), Sinclair was noting the increasing prevalence of "unorthodox lawmaking" that departed from the textbook process in major ways. "The gap between the legislative process that I observe and the process described in U.S. government textbooks," she declared, "has become a chasm."[31]

Bills were increasingly being referred to multiple committees in ways that increased member participation but also required leadership mediation. Omnibus bills were becoming more common, especially for appropriations. Leadership was taking a more decisive hand in drafting and scheduling legislation, as well as in negotiating House-Senate differences formerly left to conference committees. Attempts to amend bills on the floor proliferated, as did special rules designed to control the amending process. While these changes often promised inclusion, transparency, and efficiency, their overall effect was to make the legislative process more complicated, cumbersome, and difficult to navigate.

The explanations for these changes range widely—from the increasing desire of members to make an individual mark, to institutional reforms and changes (especially by Democrats in the mid-1970s and after the Republican takeover in 1995), the establishment of the budget process, and technological changes such as electronic roll-call voting and televised proceedings. But Sinclair increasingly came to focus on "the increase in partisan polarization .... both as a root cause and as a shaper of the forms that changes with other origins have taken."[32] The institutional results included weakened committees and more centralized party leadership, exerting itself at every stage of the legislative process.

The polarization that led to a more convoluted and contentious legislative process and pervasive leadership intervention also shifted power and responsibility to the executive, giving the president a more prominent, if not necessarily more efficacious, policy role. The prevalence of end-game politics pulls the president into negotiations and mediations among congressional leaders. And as presidents see their legislative priorities run afoul of gridlock, they are more likely to utilize executive orders, presidential memoranda, Statements of Administration Policy (SAPs), and other such tools to bypass the congressional process. President Obama's 2012 order shielding "Dreamers" from deportation was a perfect example—although he readily acknowledged that legislation would have been preferable and saw his order reversed soon after Donald Trump took office.

What do we conclude as to the overall legislative capacity of Congress and of the House in particular? We are not the first, of course, to raise the question of capacity or to relate it to how the parties function. I received my training as a political scientist while there was still a lively debate in academic circles—which found resonance among Richard Bolling and other House reformers in the 1970s—about the need for more coherent, programmatic, "responsible" parties in American politics. In retrospect, we are reminded to "be careful what you wish for." Mann and Ornstein in fact treat current dysfunction as a vindication of the critics of "Toward a More Responsible Two-Party System," the American Political Science Association's (APSA's) seminal 1950 report. "Parliamentary-style parties," they argue, are ill-suited to "separation-of-powers government," and efforts to combine them invite "willful obstruction and policy irresolution."[33]

I would modify that conclusion in two respects. First, while party development in the House has in some ways tracked the APSA recommendations—most obviously in curtailing the power of committee chairs out of step with their party's majority—it is by no means an inevitable outgrowth of those ideas. Greater ideological cohesion and distinctiveness were called for, but there was no expectation one party would move so "far from the center of American politics ... ideologically extreme; contemptuous of the inherited social and economic policy regime; scornful of compromise; unpersuaded by conventional understanding of facts, evidence, and science; and dismissive of the legitimacy of its political opposition."[34] This movement *within* the Republican party has more to do with our current dysfunction than do "responsible party" developments per se.

Secondly, there have been periods when strengthened party organs and more coherent programs have produced not "policy irresolution" but something closer to what the APSA advocates had in mind. Naturally, I am thinking particularly of the first two years of the Clinton (1993–1994) and Obama (2009–2010) administrations and of the team efforts that produced significant legislative successes. Most Democrats in the House felt we were doing what we were elected to do as we pushed long-stalled measures to passage.

Even relatively productive periods of unified party control offer ample reminders that the U.S. Congress is not a parliamentary system. Many failures occur as the opposition takes advantage of the multiple checkpoints the system provides (particularly the Senate filibuster), but also as a result of divisions and failures within the majority itself. The first two Clinton years saw health care and welfare reform remain on the table; the same was true of "cap and trade" emission controls, immigration reform, and infrastructure reauthorization in the first two Obama years.

In the post-World War II era, in fact, David Mayhew found that the legislative success rates for presidents of both parties during the first two years after their election or reelection hovered around 60 percent and improved only marginally when Congress was under control of the president's own party.[35] This is consistent with Mayhew's broader argument that the volume, and to a significant degree the content, of important laws enacted by Congress does not vary greatly under conditions of divided and unified party control. From this he draws reassurance as to the resiliency and ultimate responsiveness of the American constitutional system. Others draw more ominous conclusions, particularly from the deepening divisions and more severe gridlock of recent years. And of course, what one analyst regards a success rate may be seen as a failure rate by another. Overall, political scientist Sarah Binder's conclusion seems justified:

> We are left in the meantime with a national legislature plagued by low legislative capacity. Half-measures, second bests, and just-in-time legislating are the new norm, as electoral, partisan, and institutional barriers limit Congress' capacity for more than lowest common-denominator deals.[36]

As we have noted, polarization and its attendant centralization have not been kind to the committee system. Both as a student of Congress and as a member, I have been disinclined to regard leadership strength and committee vitality in zero-sum terms. Effective party and committee leadership can reinforce each other, producing both a better legislative product and a smoother route to passage, especially under conditions of polarization and conflict.[37] This seems to be Speaker Pelosi's assumption as well, particularly during her second term of service. She consults with key committee leaders on important decisions and publicly highlights that consultation. But there is little doubt who is, and in tough fights often needs to be, ultimately in charge. There is also considerable evidence of reduced committee autonomy and productivity, particularly over the last 25 years.

This is not simply a matter of leadership preemption of committee authority and functions. For a number of committees which have traditionally drawn strength and legitimacy from their bipartisanship, the problem has been the growth of partisan divisions *within*, making a united front more difficult to attain or to present to the full chamber, as well as less bipartisan receptivity in the House itself. Prominent examples are Armed Services, Agriculture, and Transportation and Infrastructure. But the most consequential case is Appropriations, where the polarization may not be as far advanced internally but has greater institutional effects because of the committee's centrality to the House's fundamental constitutional prerogative, the power of the purse.

Historically, Appropriations has attempted to minimize partisanship, both in its internal operations and in maintaining a united front on the floor.[38] This has enabled the committee to play an institutional, as opposed to purely partisan, role vis-a-vis the executive, whatever the configuration of party control might be, in scrutinizing and modifying proposed budgets and exercising oversight.

I and other Appropriations leaders received rude notice of how much this had changed as we assumed House control in 2007 and attempted to steer our bills to passage.[39] My bill, Homeland Security, was one of nine overdue appropriations measures Republicans had dumped in our laps as they exited leadership. Subcommittee and full committee markups had gone fairly smoothly, and our Democratic leaders hoped that by putting the relatively bipartisan Homeland bill on the floor first, they might mitigate the partisan conflict they knew was brewing.

These hopes proved illusory, however, and I received a baptism of fire in my first experience as a floor manager. A band of some three dozen members—mostly younger, mostly from the right-leaning Republican Study Committee—took full advantage (and then some) of the open rule under which appropriations bills were traditionally debated, offering trivial and pro forma amendments in succession, each providing the opportunity for a repetitive string of five-minute speeches. The most prominent theme of the protests, to the extent there was one, was earmarks, but the main intent seemed to be merely to throw the House into disarray. Republican party leaders, including senior appropriators, stood by, some approving, some acquiescing, but none seriously defending the bill they had had an active hand in shaping only a few weeks before.

We kept the House in session, slogged our way through the bill, and finally got a consent agreement to bring the debate to a conclusion—but not before the Homeland Security bill had been debated for twenty-seven hours (compared to nine the year before) and roll calls had been held on thirty-nine amendments and eight desultory "motions to rise" from the Committee of the Whole. None of the subsequent bills received quite the same treatment, but several came close: overall, it took 169 hours of floor time to debate the appropriations bills, compared to 101 hours the year before.

Appropriations Committee Chairman David Obey, working with the Democratic leadership, resolved in 2008 to avoid a replay of 2007; he would take bills through the process, but if the Bush administration continued to reject bipartisan accommodation, we would simply pass a continuing resolution and wait out the election. As it happened, pre-election sparring between the parties, focusing on $4-per-gallon gasoline and offshore oil-drilling, brought a halt to the process far earlier than anticipated, after only five bills had been marked up in full committee and before any were considered on the floor.

The intrusion of partisan warfare into the formerly collegial full-committee markup process was total. The turning point came in late June when Republicans sought to replace the Labor-HHS-Education bill being marked up with another bill entirely, Interior, so as to offer an amendment opening up offshore drilling that would put at-risk Democrats on the spot. Obey indignantly adjourned the meeting and suspended further markups.

Attempting to return to the "regular order" in the non-election year of 2009, we were still mindful of 2007 and alert to signs of obstruction from across the aisle. They were not long in coming—one hour, in fact, into the debate on the first (this time, Commerce-Justice-Science) bill. Obey then moved to stop debate and announced his intention to do what he had refrained from doing earlier despite great provocation: ask the Rules Committee for a rule designating which amendments would be in order and limiting debate. This was done for all subsequent bills: my Homeland bill had 14 amendments allowed, and we wrapped up debate in less than seven hours—still an expansive process, but a far cry from 2007. The decision to constrain debate was in fact necessitated by the heightened partisanship of floor proceedings, and it has not since been reversed by either party.

I had some regrets about the constraining of appropriations debates, but it was hard to argue that completely open rules were integral to appropriations *per se*. The other key "control committee," Ways and Means, had long protected its bills on the floor.[40] I was more critical of our leaders' risk-aversion in 2008 and again in 2010 in pulling back bills from committee and/or floor consideration. But they reckoned that even if the bills made it through the House—at the price of numerous "gotcha" votes for vulnerable Democrats—they would likely face Senate filibusters or, in 2008, a presidential veto. They then attempted to stitch together omnibus bills after the elections which, given the outcomes, succeeded in 2008 and failed in 2010.

In 2011, I became Homeland Security's ranking minority member and once again saw the relatively bipartisan subcommittee process overcome by partisan warfare. For two years running, 2012 and 2013, the bills I had helped assemble were blown up on the floor by incendiary amendments on immigration offered by Rep. Steve King (R-Iowa). Republican leaders made some effort to fend off the amendments, but once they were offered, almost all Republicans supported them—a striking indication of the party's move to the right and of immigration as a defining issue that eventually would transform Homeland Security from the least to the most controversial appropriations bill. It hardly mattered that adoption of the amendments would spell the end of my support and that of most Democrats. In the face of an amendment from the Republican fringe, appropriations bipartisanship did not stand a chance.[41]

As noted earlier in this chapter, the passage of the BCA in 2011 and reduction of appropriations allocations to sequestration levels posed an even more fundamental threat to appropriations, making impossible not only bipartisanship but "appropriations as we know it."[42] Continuing resolutions became routine; appropriations bills were rarely passed singly or on time. The new normal became the just-in-time adoption of budget deals to lift the sequestration caps and the belated stitching together of omnibus appropriations bills well into the fiscal year. There is currently a glimmer of hope by virtue of the expiration of the BCA and the determination of members, or at least appropriators, of both parties not to repeat the 2011–2019 experience. Certainly, the future of Appropriations as a productive place to work and a bastion of institutional strength will depend on what comes next.

Finally, polarization has had a devastating effect on Congress's bipartisan capacity to address fiscal policy. The 1990 bipartisan budget agreement and the comparable 1993 measure, enacted unilaterally by Democrats, have not been replicated since. Each in its own way confirmed the maxim that bipartisan cover is generally required for such politically perilous endeavors to be viable. But as documented earlier, bipartisan cooperation has become increasingly difficult to come by, even as the economic and fiscal conditions calling for agreement have become more dire.

In his study of the 1983 rescue of Social Security, Paul Light coined the term "dedistributive" to denote policies such as budget agreements—not concerned mainly with distributing or redistributing desirable goods but instead, under pressure of necessity, cutting back by raising taxes and/or reducing benefits, imposing costs, and lowering expectations.[43] The 1983 plan certainly fit the description, raising payroll taxes and cutting back benefits as the Social Security trust fund was about to run dry. It required the strong support of both President Reagan and the Democratic congressional leadership. This was not merely because partisan control of government was divided, but because for either party to take up the cause unilaterally would have meant political suicide. Even with both parties knowing they must act, success came only with moving the decision from Congress to a bipartisan commission that operated outside the glare of daily publicity and permitted a sharing and blurring of the lines of personal and partisan responsibility.

The resemblance of the Social Security rescue to the 1990 bipartisan budget agreement—both the dedistributive character of the decisions and some of the expedients used to achieve resolution—is striking. It renders all the more remarkable what was done by Democrats alone in 1993 but leaves little doubt as to which is the more promising model for dedistributive decisions of the future, the formalities of united or divided party control notwithstanding. To be sure, single-party plans might have balanced the budget sooner, particularly compared to the 1997 bipartisan agreement. Democrats acting alone would have included fewer upper-bracket tax cuts, while Republicans would have been willing to cut Medicare and domestic discretionary spending more deeply. But if the cross-partisan accommodations rendered the agreement less heroic, they also mitigated its dedistributive character and increased both its legitimacy in the eyes of the public and its political viability.

Subsequent polarization has rendered such a comprehensive agreement, even on the 1997 model, far more difficult, perhaps impossible, to achieve. It has also heightened the costs of cross-party accommodation, and not only for budget agreements. Consider, for example, the price of accommodating three Republican senators—"moderates," supposedly, whose votes were essential to overcome a filibuster—on the American Recovery and Reinvestment Act (ARRA) in 2009. The result was far less money for constructing and upfitting schools, major cutbacks in infrastructure investment, and billions squandered on an Alternative Minimum Tax cut of minimal stimulus value. This moved me and many other Democrats to ask whether the price of achieving bipartisanship was unacceptably high. Must it take precedence over creating or saving tens of thousands of jobs? While there was little escaping what we had to do in 2009, the answer in other circumstances might not have been the same.

I take considerable pride in the *partisan* capacity Democrats have developed and deployed and have no doubt as to its continuing importance. But given our checks-and-balances system of government and the frequency of divided electoral outcomes, broader capacities are also needed and must be cultivated. Left unchecked, hyper partisanship can be corrosive of the norms of fairness and inclusion that enable the House to perform its most basic functions, give it legitimacy in the eyes of its members and the broader public, and ultimately will produce a more balanced and durable policy product. Congress needs both partisan and bipartisan capacities, but the challenge of keeping them in proper balance and in good repair has seldom been greater.

Two Impeachments

The attempt to impeach a president is bound to stir partisan passions. One of the most frequently quoted passages in the impeachment debates of both 1998 and 2019 was Alexander Hamilton's warning of the danger "that the decision will be regulated more by the comparative strength of the parties than by the real demonstrations of innocence or guilt."[44] Questions of motivation aside, the votes on both the Clinton and Trump impeachments closely followed party lines. In that sense, both were "partisan" impeachments that deserve, indeed demand, a place in a chapter on polarization and its effects.

The impeachments were not, however, partisan in the same way. The Clinton impeachment involved an offense for which impeachment was not the appropriate remedy, and it took place in a context of "constitutional hardball" among House Republicans.[45] Democrats were united in opposition but many were willing to support an alternative sanction for the offense. The Trump impeachment involved an offense much closer to what the framers anticipated and was pursued by Democrats only when the facts and our own perceived constitutional duty required us to set aside questions of partisan advantage. Republicans were not only united in opposition but indicated almost no willingness to acknowledge any offense whatsoever, much less to support an alternative sanction.

I realize that as a partisan and a participant, my views will be questioned, but I believe it is important to make the argument: what is at stake is not only the merits of the two cases, but questions about the use and abuse of partisanship. Hamilton was correct to condemn partisanship as the prime basis for judgment, but the presence of partisan voting patterns is not prima facie grounds for dismissing or delegitimizing a given impeachment.

The Clinton case reached a critical point on August 17, 1998, when the president, compelled to testify before Independent Counsel Kenneth Starr's grand jury, first acknowledged publicly a relationship with Monica Lewinsky that was "not appropriate" and "wrong" and about which he had "misled people, including even my wife."[46] Within a month, Starr had delivered his report, specifying eleven possible grounds for impeachment. The House vote to release the contents of the report was bipartisan (363–63), but every major decision after that displayed a sharp partisan cleavage. Speaker Gingrich sometimes paid lip service to the need for deliberation and objectivity, but his words and actions betrayed an assumption of the president's guilt and a determination to exploit the situation politically.[47] Judiciary Committee chairman Henry Hyde initially recognized that impeachment procedures needed to be bipartisan if they were to be seen as legitimate and fair and announced his intention to follow the "Watergate model." But the Judiciary Committee was among the most ideologically polarized in the House. From the beginning, its members voted overwhelmingly along party lines, and Hyde did very little to challenge or change that pattern.

The partisan divide was starkly evident in the House vote of October 8 to move forward with the impeachment inquiry. Unlike the actual impeachment votes to follow, this was not a matter of high principle. But it nonetheless became a partisan showdown. Republicans proposed an open-ended inquiry in terms of subject matter and duration; Democrats proposed to limit the inquiry to the Starr referral and set a termination date of December 31. As I recounted in Chapter 2, this vote caused me great anxiety, for I seemed bound to alienate voters no matter how I voted. Democratic leaders in the House helpfully modified the resolution formulated by Judiciary Committee Democrats to make it less restrictive, and some of them urged the White House to accept the Republic resolution once the Democratic resolution failed, thus sparing marginal Democrats a politically perilous vote. I argued that "defusing" the vote in this way would not only help members like myself but would also let the president (who was not going to win the vote in any case) appear confident and cooperative and would put the onus on the Republicans to proceed with fairness and restraint. But the president and his advisors did not see it that way, and the plight of imperiled congressional Democrats seemed low on their list of concerns.

As it turned out, Gingrich and the Republicans would have had more to gain than Clinton and the Democrats from defusing the vote. The GOP inquiry ended up adhering, for the most part, to the terms of the Democratic resolution. Had they simply accepted these terms at the outset, they would have given the process a bipartisan cast and could have put eighty or ninety liberal Democrats, who were skeptical of any inquiry whatsoever and had united behind the Democratic resolution only in the sure knowledge it would fail, in a tight spot. But Gingrich, like Clinton, conceived of his advantage narrowly and was loath to give it up. So, both sides charged ahead: Republicans voted 1–226 against the limited inquiry and 227–0 for the open-ended inquiry. All but ten Democrats (five of whom voted against both resolutions) voted for the limited inquiry, and when that resolution failed, only thirty-one then voted for the GOP resolution. I joined the 175 who did not—a decision I soon came to see as not only right on the merits but also politically advantageous. I continued to believe that the partisan showdown was unnecessary; had the vote been defused by one or both sides, the subsequent course of impeachment might have been quite different.

The kind of ads Tom Roberg had run against me in September became more common across the country in October as Gingrich and other Republican strategists urged candidates to exploit the scandal and staged a national media blitz toward the end of the campaign. The election results discredited the strategy and prompted Gingrich to resign. Members and pundits alike predicted that at least two dozen Republicans would vote against impeachment. But as it turned out, they underestimated both the intensity of Republican base voters on the issue and the determination of GOP leaders to see the process through.

Hyde and Judiciary Republicans pressed on inexorably. On November 19, they called Starr before the committee to give a lawyer's brief for impeachment and gave him a standing ovation at the end of his testimony. On December 8–9, they heard from Clinton's lawyers but drafted articles of impeachment and released them to the public before the lawyers had finished testifying.[48] In the meantime, Republican whip Tom DeLay, a longtime impeachment advocate, filled the vacuum left by Gingrich's resignation and by prospective Speaker Bob Livingston's aversion to controversy, devising a strategy to impeach the president with Republican votes alone.

That strategy had two major elements: denying members an opportunity to vote on censure as an alternative to impeachment and "defining down" impeachment itself, portraying it as the equivalent of an indictment (with definitive judgment to be rendered by the Senate) and/or a rebuke that the House could administer without further consequences (since the Senate was unlikely to convict). Impeachment proponents downplayed the historical and constitutional gravity of the step they were advocating and, in the process, misrepresented the threshold question facing the House. Most Democratic members, Republican rhetoric to the contrary notwithstanding, were appalled at the president's behavior and were prepared to hold him accountable. The threshold question was not whether the president had engaged in the behavior of which he was accused (which turned only partially on the legalistic definitions on which he and his lawyers insisted) or whether that behavior deserved condemnation. Rather, the question was whether impeachment, reserved by the framers of the Constitution for "treason, bribery, or other high crimes and misdemeanors [against the state]," was the appropriate remedy.[49] That decision was for the House to face, hardly a matter to be blithely bucked to the Senate.

The appropriate sanction, I and many others thought, was a resolution of censure. Even allowing for disagreement on the merits, there were no legitimate grounds for denying members the ability to offer and vote on this alternative. If there is any instance where this kind of high-handed manipulation of the rules is out of line, it is in carrying out the solemn constitutional duty of impeachment. As one editorial noted after the DeLay strategy became clear:

> Mr. DeLay and the Republican hard-liners on impeachment know that both the public and a majority of House members favor a condemnation of Mr. Clinton instead of impeachment, unless new evidence emerges. But Mr. DeLay calculates that if he can prevent a censure vote, the House may vote to impeach rather than to let Mr. Clinton go unpunished. But it is an insult to duty for any Congressional leader to ram through an impeachment vote by using parliamentary trickery of the kind more suitable to votes on highway bills.[50]

The closing off of the censure alternative, along with the intense pressures Republican members felt from their leaders and their core electorate, had the desired effect on December 19. All but five Republicans voted for the first article of impeachment (perjury before the grand jury) and all but twelve voted for the third (obstruction of justice). These were the two articles that passed, each with only five Democratic votes. I remember sitting in the chamber as debate began, wondering if anyone found the pleas to pull back from the brink persuasive and then rebuking myself for my naïveté. Republican leaders had proclaimed a "vote of conscience" to the end, but party lines in the House had never been more harshly drawn, nor partisan power exercised with a harder edge.[51]

I wrote a lengthy statement to insert in the *Congressional Record* and circulate among my constituents citing the constitutional arguments and historical precedents for censure as opposed to impeachment. I particularly noted Hamilton's warning against allowing partisanship to carry the day. But the time permitted for debate did not allow for lengthy floor statements by every member. In the one minute I was given to distill my argument, I linked the House's failure to live up to its historic responsibility to the abuse of partisan leadership:

> Where there should be an extraordinary effort to work across party lines and find a consensual basis for action, I see a hardy-charging majority bringing articles of impeachment to the floor on a strictly partisan basis.
>
> Where there should be scrupulous attention to the constitutional and historical basis for impeachment, I see a cavalier willingness to "define

impeachment down" to get a favorable vote, in disregard of what the farmers [of the Constitution] intended.

And where there should be assurances that this is a vote of conscience, I see a cynical and unfair manipulation of the rules [in order] to deny members the right to vote on a motion of censure and to tilt the outcome in favor of impeachment.

This shuts off consideration of the most appropriate sanction under the Constitution for the behavior we are considering. It denies many of us the right to vote out consciences on the most serious question we are ever likely to face as members of this body. It is manipulative, it is cynical, it is unfair. It is as though the Republican leaders of this House have set out to confirm all of the worst suspicions Americans have about politics and politicians.

Mr. Speaker, this House is on the brink of an historic and tragic failure. I beg my colleagues to take heed.[52]

The Clinton impeachment shaped House politics for years to come. I and many other Democrats warned that the 1998 exercise might dangerously lower the barriers to politically motivated impeachments. But we also observed the adverse public reaction to the House's action, and those recollections, far from encouraging us to forge ahead as Trump's offenses mounted in 2019, rather gave us pause.

The experience had few of the cathartic or sobering effects within the House that some predicted. On the contrary: the high-handedness of the Republican leadership and sharp polarization of the chamber continued to advance. Not even the September 11, 2001, terrorist attacks could induce more than a temporary and partial deescalation.[53] House Republicans under the second Bush presidency—with a presidential agenda anchored on the right, a narrow Republican House majority and conservative-dominated Republican Conference, and a desire to counter the Senate (even after Republicans regained the majority there)—took the tactics of partisan control to a level unprecedented in the modern history of the institution (see Chapter 6). "The Republicans had better hope," Senator John McCain (R-Arizona) commented in 2003, "that the Democrats never regain the majority."[54]

Democrats did indeed return to power, in 2007 and again in 2019, and it was that change in leadership that set the stage for the Trump impeachment. Contrary to what Trump and his defenders constantly charged, however, we did not begin the 116th Congress hellbent on his impeachment. Special Counsel Robert Mueller's report in March 2019 left no doubt that the Trump campaign had welcomed Russian help in 2016 and convincingly documented the president's efforts to curtail, discredit, and obstruct the Russia investigation. Mueller demurred from making a "traditional prosecutorial judgment" with respect to a sitting president but pointedly noted that the report did not "exonerate" him of multiple instances of obstruction.[55]

Unlike Kenneth Starr, he made no presumption about impeachment, much less proffer a list of charges for the House to consider.

Donald Trump was shadowed by questions of character, conduct, and competence from his first day in office, and calls for impeachment and impeachment inquiries steadily increased. Not every offense or flaw is impeachable, of course, no matter how appalling, but I publicly focused on three areas where I suspected Trump was on "thin ice": the encouragement of Russian interference in the 2016 elections, attempts to discredit and obstruct legitimate investigations of his conduct, and possible violations of the Constitution's Emoluments Clause (art. 1, sec. 9, par. 8) by virtue of his failure to completely divest from his businesses, which foreign governments were eagerly patronizing. The first two of these matters were under investigation by Mueller, and I urged through 2018 that we await his report while working to elect a Democratic House that would be willing and able to hold the president accountable on multiple fronts.

Democrats assumed House leadership in January of 2019, the Mueller report was released two months later, and House committees began multiple hearings concerning matters dealt with in the report and beyond. I was particularly struck by the report's recounting of the president's blatant and direct personal involvement in some ten efforts to obstruct Mueller's work and other investigations of his and his associates' conduct.[56] But Mueller pulled his punches on the questions of criminal prosecution and impeachment. His halting testimony before the Intelligence and Judiciary committees on July 24 dismissed Trump's characterization of the investigation as a "witch hunt" and refuted his claim of "total exoneration" but did not define a clear path forward.

In the meantime, committee investigations were turning up additional areas of misconduct, and the president's refusal to cooperate in providing witnesses and documents was causing mounting frustration. In mid-August, I added my name to the list of those calling for an impeachment inquiry. Acknowledging that multiple inquiries were already underway, I suggested that designating them as a possible prelude to impeachment could give them "focus" and possibly could give the House additional leverage, in the courts and otherwise, to compel the provision of information "in the face of the president's stonewalling and resistance."[57]

Speaker Nancy Pelosi was resisting such calls, concerned that pursuing impeachment without more broadly based public support, particularly in the newly won swing districts, might end up fueling Trump's reelection. But that changed abruptly in late September as a whistleblower report came to light, revealing a July 25 call on which Trump had pressed Ukraine's new president, Volodymyr Zelensky, to announce investigations of the business activities in Ukraine of Hunter Biden, the son of his prospective 2020 opponent, and of a discredited theory that Ukraine, rather than Russia, had interfered in the 2016 U.S. presidential election. Days before the call, it was later confirmed, the administration had withheld $391 million in military aid appropriated for Ukraine; on the call itself Trump insinuated that a coveted White House visit for the new president was also contingent on Zelensky's cooperation.

Immediately, we were in impeachment territory, with offenses that, if corroborated, compromised U.S. security interests and corrupted a key diplomatic relationship for the president's personal and political benefit. In a bold move, seven freshman Democrats—all of whom had flipped Republican seats and came from national security backgrounds—wrote an op-ed calling for an inquiry into Trump's conduct, stating that "if these allegations are true, we believe these actions represent an impeachable offense."[58] The next day, many more members called for an impeachment investigation, and Pelosi announced that a formal inquiry would begin. "The time has found us," she declared, quoting Thomas Paine's declaration at the end of the American revolution.[59] I and many others also found the phrase apt. The gravity and credibility of the charges left us no alternative but to undertake an inquiry focused on grounds for impeachment.[60]

Republican members were not similarly moved. They were disinclined to dispute the substance of the charges, but criticized the process relentlessly, objecting even to closing the early sessions to the public—routine practice in such investigations, to prevent key witnesses from coordinating their testimony. At one point two dozen Republican members—mostly junior but including Minority Whip Steve Scalise (R-Louisiana)—stormed the secure facility where depositions were being taken, delaying proceedings for some five hours. "Do Nothing Democrats allow Republicans Zero Representation, Zero due process, and Zero Transparency," Trump tweeted in encouragement.[61]

In launching the impeachment inquiry, Pelosi made two critical decisions: to focus on the Ukraine matter rather than Trump's other transgressions, and to put the Intelligence Committee in charge, headed by Adam Schiff (D-California), a knowledgeable and judicious former prosecutor. The committee deposed 17 current or former administration officials—some of them defying the administration's stance of non-cooperation—and 12 of them then testified publicly during two weeks of open hearings in mid-November. It would have been desirable, Schiff acknowledged, to hear from additional witnesses such as former national security advisor John Bolton and White House Chief of Staff Mick Mulvaney. But the evidence was already "overwhelming," he said, and the matter was urgent: "We are not willing to go the months and months of rope-a-dope in the courts, which the administration would love to do."[62]

The House Judiciary Committee, chaired by Jerry Nadler (D-New York), reviewed the results of the inquiry, and after additional hearings on the constitutional bases of impeachment proceeded to mark up two articles. They were approved on December 13 on a 23–17 party-line vote. The first article, charging abuse of power, spelled out Trump's efforts to "solicit" and "pressure" the government of Ukraine to "announce investigations that would benefit his reelection [and] harm the election prospects of a political opponent." The second article, charging obstruction of Congress, detailed Trump's "unprecedented, categorical, and indiscriminate defiance of subpoenas issued by the House of Representative pursuant to its 'sole power of impeachment.' ... This abuse of office served to cover up the President's own repeated misconduct and to nullify a vital constitutional safeguard vested solely in the House of Representatives." As a gesture to those who had argued that the articles should include offenses revealed by the Mueller inquiry, the resolution stated that Trump's alleged actions "were consistent with" his "previous invitations of foreign interference in United States elections" and his "previous efforts to undermine ... investigations" of such interference.[63]

The House debated the resolution on December 18. As in 1998, I had one minute to distill my thoughts. After describing the president's offenses, I stated that they "threaten the integrity of our elections, corrupt our diplomacy, and undermine national security."

> We sometimes regard constitutional checks and balances as the indestructible underpinnings of our democracy. In fact, they're not fixed. They're not indestructible. The president has demonstrated this beyond all doubt.
>
> It's up to the Congress, the first branch of government, to apply the remedy that the constitution prescribes, because the threats to our democracy are real and present.
>
> With this vote we affirm that no one, including the president, is above the law.[64]

The votes on the articles were 230–197 on the first and 229–198 on the second, with two (or three) Democrats and no Republicans breaking ranks. In debate, Democrats stuck fairly closely to the articles of impeachment, while batting down accusations about the fairness of the process. The few Republicans who addressed the president's alleged offenses did not deny that he had committed them but tended to dismiss them as mere "bungling."[65] None of them proposed censure or any lesser sanction, leaving Trump's declaration—in sharp contrast to Clinton in 1998—that he had done "nothing wrong" essentially unchallenged. ("You don't censure somebody when they did nothing wrong," Trump said.)[66]

The remarks of Chief Deputy Whip Patrick McHenry (R-North Carolina) were typical:

> In 2016, 63 million Americans went to the polls and elected Donald Trump President of the United States. House Democrats have been trying to overturn the election ever since....
>
> In January, House Democrats took control of this chamber.... They could use the tools of the majority to pursue legitimate priorities of the

American people ... or they could use the tools to undo the 2016 election. They made their choice....

Rather than launch a legitimate investigation, Democrats [turned] to focus groups to workshop their language, to see if they could sell this to the American people....

So here we are [after only] 12 weeks, voting [on] whether to impeach the President based on the thinnest record in modern history.[67]

Neither the outcome of the Senate impeachment trial, nor Majority Leader Mitch McConnell's determination to acquit with as little political damage to the president and his Senate majority as possible, were ever in doubt. "There will be no difference between the president's position and our position as to how to handle this," McConnell declared on Fox News on December 12.[68] The only serious challenge he faced was to keep fifty-one votes together against prolonging or complicating the trial by calling witnesses. The problem became acute when press reports indicated that, in a forthcoming book, former National Security Advisor John Bolton would reveal that the president told him personally of his intent to withhold military aid to Ukraine until its government announced the Biden investigation. This would corroborate the House's impeachment charges with a compelling firsthand account.

Bolton, who had refused to testify before the House inquiry, now made it clear that he would respond to a Senate subpoena. But in the end McConnell held his fifty-one votes, with only Senators Susan Collins (R-Maine) and Mitt Romney (R-Utah) voting with the forty-seven Democrats to call witnesses. From there, the only impeachment trial in American history not to call witnesses hurtled to its conclusion. The acquittal votes of 48–52 on the first article and 47–53 on the second came on February 5, with Romney's vote on Article I being the only instance of a member of either party breaking ranks.

Thus did the impeachment votes of 2019, like those of 1998, closely adhere to party lines. "The story of this impeachment," wrote one respected commentator, "is the story of American politics today: polarization."[69] The trends toward polarized and intensified partisanship traced in this and the preceding chapter did in fact shape both impeachments. But they did this in contrasting ways.

I recognize, as one who judged that the 2019 impeachment was warranted on the constitutional merits and that of 1998 was not, I might be expected to attribute stronger partisan motivations to the opponents in 2019 and the protagonists in 1998. Still, that is what I would argue: such motivations go farther in explaining Republican behavior than they do for Democrats. Democrats, of course, often thought in partisan terms as well, certainly about the implications for the next election. The result, however, was more to counsel caution and restraint than to motivate and inspire. Republicans likewise looked to placate their base, and many feared the wrath of Donald Trump, but they required less persuading. They were more inclined to make of the impeachments—pursuing one and digging in against the other—a rallying cry, a partisan cause.

Thus did Republicans outdo Democrats in their partisan fervor and discipline. The problem, however, is that impeachment is not a question best decided on the basis of party identity and loyalty.

Notes

1 For a more detailed account of this history through 2004, see the third edition of this book, Chap. 7.
2 David A. Stockman, *The Triumph of Politics* (New York: Avon, 1987), p. 409.
3 "Now for the House Republicans," *Washington Post*, Meg Greenfield, Editorial Page editor, October 3, 1990, p. A22.
4 Quoted in Helen Dewar and Tom Kenworthy, "Conservative Republicans Assail Budget Pact; Democrats Skeptical," *Washington Post*, October 1, 1990, p. A8.
5 Robin Toner, "Sour View of Congress Emerges from Survey," *New York Times*, October 12, 1990, p. A21.
6 Quoted in John Yang, "The One-for-You, Two-for-Me School of Budgeting," *Washington Post*, national weekly ed., February 11, 1991, p. 8.
7 Projections of the underlying standardized employment deficit, with the effects of the business cycle on federal revenues and outlays removed and with Iraq war contributions and savings and loan insurance expenditures and receipts excluded, were relatively constant, in the range of $164 to $188 billion from 1991 to 1996. "In relation to the size of the economy, such deficits are no better than those of the late 1980s and considerably worse than the average of the 1960s and 1970s." Congressional Budget Office, *The Economic and Budget Outlook: An Update: A Report to the Senate and House Committees on the Budget*, August 1991, pp. xi, xiii, 16.
8 *Congressional Quarterly Almanac* 49 (1993), p. 7-D; on the 1993 episode generally, see pp. 81–145, and Robert Rubin (with Jacob Weisberg), *In an Uncertain World* (New York: Random House, 2003), pp. 118–131.
9 *Congressional Record*, daily ed., August 5, 1993, pp. H6267–68.
10 "Disappearing Doom," *Raleigh News and Observer*, Editorial Board, February 20, 1994, p. 26A.
11 See, for example, David Broder, "Some Victory," *Washington Post*, August 10, 1993, p. A15.
12 For accounts of the events culminating in the government shutdowns of late 1995, see David Maraniss and Michael Weisskopf, *Tell Newt to Shut Up!* (New York: Simon & Schuster, 1996), chaps. 11–12; Sherrod Brown, *Congress from the Inside* (Kent, OH: Kent State University Press, 1999), chaps. 13–14; and Barbara Sinclair, *Unorthodox Lawmaking: New Legislative Processes in the U.S. Congress* (Washington, DC: CQ Press, 1997), chap. 11.
13 *Congressional Quarterly Almanac* 53 (1997), pp. 2–18. For an account of the 1997 negotiations and agreement, see Daniel J. Palazzolo, *Done Deal? The Politics of the 1997 Budget Agreement* (New York: Chatham House, 1999).
14 "Paradoxically," noted Henry Aaron, "the one line in this seemingly endless [budget] drama that is comprehensible, 'We must not raid the Social Security trust fund,' is nonsense.... Trust fund bond holdings will increase [by the amount of the Social Security] surplus, whatever budget decisions Congress and the White House may make." "Great Pretenders," *Washington Post*, weekly ed., November 15, 1999, p. 26.

15 Former CBO Director Robert Reischauer, quoted in Charles Babington and Eric Pianin, "Clinton Plan Ignores '97 Budget Pact," *Washington Post*, January 14, 2000, p. A1. Debt reduction calculation by Richard Kogan of the Center on Budget and Policy Priorities.

16 Joel Friedman, Robert Greenstein, and Richard Kogan, "The Administration's Proposal to Make the Tax Cut Permanent," Center on Budget and Policy Priorities (CBPP), April 16, 2002, p. 2. On this result and the complicity of "moderate" Democratic senators in producing it, see E.J. Dionne Jr., "Gutless Moderates," *Washington Post*, May 4, 2001, p. A25; Dionne, "Tax Cuts: The Fight Is Just Beginning," *Washington Post*, June 1, 2001, p. A31; Paul Krugman, "The Big Lie," *New York Times*, May 27, 2001, pp. 4–9; and Krugman, "Bad Heir Day," *New York Times*, May 30, 2001, p. A23.

17 Democratic Caucus, House Budget Committee, *CBO Confirms Bush Budget Taps Social Security and Medicare Surpluses*, August 27, 2001.

18 A widely cited study found most of the president's proposals to provide a relatively low stimulative impact per dollar of revenue loss or spending increase: 0.59 for the acceleration of personal rate reductions and a mere 0.09 for dividend taxation reduction. Leading Democratic proposals fared much better: 1.73 for the extension of unemployment benefits, for example, and 1.24 for state assistance. "The Economic Impact of the Bush and Congressional Democratic Economic Stimulus Plans," *economy.com*, February 2003. On the "mediocre" effects overall of the Bush tax cuts on growth, see William Gale and Andrew Samwick, "Effects of Income Tax Changes on Economic Growth," Brookings Institution, March 24, 2017.

19 Emily Horton, "The Legacy of the 2001 and 2003 'Bush' Tax Cuts," *CBPP*, October 23, 2017.

20 Executive Order 13531, February 18, 2010.

21 See Peter Wallsten, Lori Montgomery, and Scott Wilson, "Obama's Evolution: Behind the Failed 'Grand Bargain' on the Debt," *Washington Post*, March 17, 2012; and Matt Bai, "Obama vs. Boehner: Who Killed the Debt Deal?" *New York Times Magazine*, March 28, 2012.

22 Roll Call no. 690, August 1, 2011; Daniel Strauss, "Boehner: 'I Got '98 Percent' of What I Wanted in the Debt Deal," *The Hill*, August 2, 2011.

23 "The president got his tax hikes on January 1," said Speaker Boehner, referring to the fiscal cliff. "The discussion on revenues, in my view, is over." Paul M. Krawzak and Steven Dennis, "On the Cutting Room Floor," *CQ Weekly*, March 4, 2013, p. 414.

24 Price, "The Twilight of Appropriations?" *Politico*, September 22, 2013.

25 Lori Montgomery, "Budget Deal Expected This Week Amounts to a Cease-Fire," *Washington Post*, December 8, 2013.

26 See Paul Krugman, "Selective Voodoo," *New York Times*, January 23, 2015.

27 Megan S. Lynch, "Deeming Resolutions: Budget Enforcement in the Absence of a Budget Resolution," Congressional Research Service, Library of Congress, April 29, 2019.

28 Source: House Budget Committee, November, 2019.

29 Source: Congressional Budget Office, April, 2020. See Jim Tankersley, "A Giant Deficit, Once Dreaded, Is Now Desired," *New York Times*, May 17, 2020, p.1.

30 "Policies matter," concluded Allen Schick. "Wrong decisions in the 1980s condemned the nation to a decade of high deficits; right ones in the 1990s have liberated it from past budgetary misdeeds." "'A Surplus If We Can Keep It': How the Federal Surplus Happened," *Brookings Review*, 18, no. 1 (Winter 2000), p. 36. On the ripple effects through the economy of the 1993 plan and the market confidence it engendered, see Rubin, *Uncertain World*, pp. 122, 125.

31 Sinclair, *Unorthodox Lawmaking*, p. xii.
32 Barbara Sinclair, *Party Wars: Polarization and the Politics of National Policy Making* (Norman, OK: University of Oklahoma Press, 2006), p. 146. Cf. Sinclair, *Unorthodox Lawmaking*, chap. 6.
33 Norman Ornstein and Thomas Mann, *It's Even Worse Than It Looks* (New York: Basic Books, 2012), pp. xiii–xiv, 102. On the APSA report, see David E. Price, *Bringing Back the Parties* (Washington, DC: Congressional Quarterly Press, 1984), pp. 104–107. On its relevance to congressional reformers, see Daniel Stid, "Two Pathways for Congressional Reform," in William Connelly Jr., John Pitney Jr., and Gary Schmitt, eds., *Is Congress Broken? The Virtues and Defects of Partisanship and Gridlock* (Washington, DC: Brookings Institution Press, 2017), pp. 18–30; and James A. Thurber and Antoine Yoshinaka, "The Sources and Impact of Political Polarization," in Thurber and Yoshinaka, eds., *American Gridlock* (New York: Cambridge University Press, 2015), pp. 383–385.
34 Mann and Ornstein, *It's Even Worse Than It Looks*, p. xiv.
35 David R. Mayhew, *Partisan Balance: Why Political Parties Don't Kill the U.S. Constitutional System* (Princeton, NJ: Princeton University Press, 2011), p. 58.
36 Mayhew's basic argument is contained in *Divided We Govern: Party Control, Lawmaking, and Investigations, 1946–1990* (New Haven, CT: Yale University Press, 1991). Pertinent critiques include Mann and Ornstein, *It's Even Worse Than It Looks*, pp. 107–111; and Sarah Binder, "Polarized We Govern?" in Alan S. Gerber and Eric Schickler, eds., *Governing in a Polarized Age* (New York: Cambridge University Press, 2017), chap. 9. Binder quote at p. 239.
37 See the insightful discussion in James M. Curry and Frances E. Lee, "Congress at Work: Legislative Capacity and Entrepreneurship in the Contemporary Congress," in Lee and Nolan McCarty, eds., *Can America Govern Itself?* (New York: Cambridge University Press, 2019), pp. 194–203. "Leadership involvement does not necessarily mute committee influence....The leadership can also make it easier for committees to move their bills through the rest of the legislative process," p.202.
38 See Richard Fenno's classic accounts: *The Power of the Purse: Appropriations Politics in Congress* (Boston, MA: Little, Brown, 1966), esp. chap. 9; and *Congressmen in Committees* (Boston, MA: Little, Brown, 1973), pp. 83–94.
39 The account that follows draws on fuller versions in David E. Price, "After the 'Housequake': Leadership and Partisanship in the Post-2006 House," *The Forum*, 8 (2010); and "Response" to 'Fixing Congress,'" *Boston Review*, 36 (May/June 2011), pp. 27–30.
40 The term is David Mayhew's, who described the two committees (plus Rules) in 1974 as "delicately arranged to contribute to institutional maintenance." *Congress: The Electoral Connection* (New Haven, CT: Yale University Press), p. 149. Fenno noted that House appropriations bills were normally debated without a rule but did not treat this as a variable of any importance in determining the committee's influence or legitimacy. The Committee had many other ways to protect its bills on the floor (for example, the absence of roll call votes in the Committee of the Whole) and strong institutional norms working in its favor—most of which are weaker or nonexistent in the contemporary House. See *Power of the Purse*, chap. 9.
41 See Norman Ornstein, "GOP Members of Homeland Security Subcommittee Fail Key Test," *National Journal*, June 12, 2013.
42 Price, "Twilight of Appropriations?"
43 Paul Light, *Still Artful Work: The Continuing Politics of Social Security Reform* (New York: McGraw-Hill, 1995), pp. 2, 13, and passim.
44 Hamilton, "The Federalist," no. 65, in Clinton Rossiter, ed., *The Federalist Papers* (New York: Mentor, 1961), pp. 396–397.

45 The term is Mark Tushnet's. See the discussion by Jacob Hacker and Paul Pierson of "asymmetric" polarization and "intensifying" Republican violations of "established norms (without breaking legal restrictions) to gain partisan advantage"—the routinizing of the Senate filibuster, "hostage taking" with respect to debt ceiling increases, government shutdowns, mid-decade redistricting, voter suppression, and "the impeachment of President Clinton." "Confronting Asymmetric Polarization," in Nathaniel Persily, ed., *Solutions to Political Polarization in America* (New York: Cambridge University Press, 2015), pp. 59–61.

46 *Congressional Quarterly Almanac* 54 (1998), p. D13.

47 See Elizabeth Drew, "Why Clinton Will Be Impeached," *Washington Post*, September 23, 1998, p. A25; and Albert R. Hunt, "Unfit to Preside," *Wall Street Journal*, October 1, 1998, p. A23. Gingrich in April had basically declared the president guilty of obstruction of justice and had promised "never again, as long as I am speaker, [to] make a speech without commenting on this topic," Jackie Koszczuk, "Gingrich, Leading Attack on Clinton, Takes Off Gloves, Goes Out on a Limb," *CQ Weekly*, May 2, 1998, pp. 1127–1131.

48 On the committee's handling of the impeachment hearings, see Steven S. Smith and Sarah Binder, "Deliberation: Where, Oh Where Has It Gone?" *Washington Post*, weekly ed., December 21–28, 1998, p. 23.

49 See the discussions recorded by James Madison, Notes of Debates in the *Federal Convention of 1787* (New York: Norton, 1966) on July 20 and September 8, 1787. The words "against the state" were dropped by the Committee of Style, but with no intent to broaden the application of the terms.

50 "The Impeachment Bully," *New York Times*, December 6, 1998, pp. 4–18. For an analysis linking Republican tactics to their long years out of power, "uninvolved in managing the governmental process and free to lob grenades at the institutions that make it work," see Alan Ehrenhalt, "Hijacking the Rulebook," *New York Times*, December 20, 1998, pp. 4–13. "Having been lifted by the American electorate into a position of genuine power, they have continued to behave more like a party of insurgents, probing for cracks in the constitutional structure rather than taking its rules seriously and looking for ways to make them work."

51 The Republicans, the *Washington Post* editorialized, were "exercising power to prevent the very conscience they claim to be holding." "Censure and the Constitution," December 16, 1998, p. A30. Just before the House debate, Henry Hyde engaged in some mysterious backstairs maneuvers that were apparently intended to reopen the possibility of censure but came to naught. See Bob Woodwards' account in *Shadow: Five Presidents and the Legacy of Watergate* (New York: Simon & Shuster, 1999), pp. 483–489.

52 For both the complete and abbreviated statements, see *Congressional Record*, daily ed., December 18, 1998, pp. H11914–15.

53 On the asymmetry of the post-9/11 partisan truce, exemplified by the House Republicans' handling of the airport security and economic stimulus issues, see Jacob Weisberg, "Republicans Behaving Badly," *Slate*, November 9, 2001; and Michael Kinsley, "Bipartisan Etiquette," and E.J. Dionne Jr., "Back to Usual," *Washington Post*, October 26, 2001, p. A35.

54 Quoted in Charles Babington, "Scorched Earth Politics," *Washington Post*, weekly ed., January 5–11, 2004, p. 23.

55 Special Counsel Robert S. Mueller, III, *Report on the Investigation into Russian Interference in the 2016 Presidential Election* (Washington, DC, March 2019), vol. II, p. 182 and passim.

56 Ibid., vol. II, pp. 24–158.

57 Press release, August 13, 2019. See Ned Barnett, "A Wary Democrat Backs Impeachment Inquiry," Raleigh *News and Observer*, August 16, 2019.

58 Gil Cisneros, Jason Crow, Chrissy Houlahan, Elaine Luria, Mikie Sherrill, Elissa Slotkin and Abigail Spanberger, "These Allegations Are a Threat to All We Have Sworn to Protect," *Washington Post*, September 23, 2019.

59 "The American Crisis: XIII," in Nelson Adkins, ed., *Common Sense and Other Political Writings* (New York: Bobbs-Merrill, 1953), p. 67.

60 On September 24, the day after Pelosi's announcement, the White House declassified what Trump characterized as "an exact word-for-word transcript" of the July 25 call. It later became clear that the "transcript" was abridged, but it was nonetheless highly incriminating. The transcript is available at *CNN Politics*, September 24, 2019; see also Jonathan Chait, "Official Reveals Trump's 'Exact Call' with Zelensky Was Edited Down," *The National Interest*, October 29, 2019.

61 Sheryl Gay Stolberg and Nicholas Fandos, "Republicans Grind Impeachment Inquiry to Halt as Evidence Mounts against Trump," *New York Times*, October 24, 2019.

62 "Meet the Press," *NBC News*, November 24, 2019.

63 H. Res. 755, 116th Congress, pp. 2, 4, 6–8.

64 *Congressional Record*, daily ed., December 18, 2019, p. 12150.

65 See Ibid., pp. 12143 (Peter King—NY) and 12161 (Will Hurd—TX).

66 John F. Harris, "Donald Trump, You're No Bill Clinton," *Politico*, December 5, 2019.

67 *Congressional Record*, daily ed., December 18, 2019, p. 12137.

68 Quoted in Andrew Prokop, "Mitch McConnell's Impeachment Trial Strategy, Explained," *Vox*, January 24, 2020.

69 Fareed Zakaria, "How the Story of Impeachment Tells the Story of Polarization," *Washington Post*, January 30, 2020.

8   Venturing Abroad

Most members of Congress do not give top priority to international affairs. Even when strong constituency interests push them in that direction, the result is often sporadic or symbolic gestures (demonstrations of support for Taiwan, Israel, Greece, or India, for example, or blaming economic ills on trade agreements) rather than sustained, serious involvement.

My situation has been somewhat different, but not entirely. I was elected in a closely contested district with strong stakes in education, research, transportation, housing, health care, and other domestic policies. I thus gave priority to such matters in seeking committee and subcommittee assignments and in undertaking policy initiatives. From the beginning, however, I was predisposed to get involved in foreign affairs. This was rooted in my personal background and interests but also in the nature of my district: increasingly diverse ethnically, with relatively high levels of education and international exposure.

My involvement in foreign policy thus has increased over the years. It began with participation in exchanges with the German Bundestag and other European parliaments. I chaired the organization which arranges such visits, the Congressional Study Group on Germany, at the best possible time: 1990, the year of German reunification. By my third term, I was embarking on what would become my most sustained foreign policy involvements, which I will focus on in this chapter: supporting and strengthening representative institutions in emerging democracies, and promoting two-state diplomacy and nuclear nonproliferation in the Middle East.

I date my fascination with remote parts of the world to 1960, the summer before my senior year at UNC, when two friends and I drove through Mexico. We traveled from Nuevo Laredo to Merida via Guadalajara, Mexico City, and Tehuantepec, including 1,000 unpaved miles en route to the Yucatan peninsula. It was a totally new experience, which became more harrowing for my friends on their long drive back. I returned to the United States directly from Merida—my first plane trip—with an intermediate stop in Havana. We were briefly detained on the tarmac by revolutionary soldiers in fatigues before taking off on what turned out to be one of the last commercial flights before the U.S. embargo was imposed on Cuba.

This adventure left me with a lifelong interest in Mexico. Even more impactful was my first visit to Europe, Lisa's and my 1968 honeymoon trip, when we decided to include Prague, Budapest, and Ljubljana as well as the usual western capitals. As it happened, we landed in Czechoslovakia at the height of the Prague Spring, the ill-fated attempt by President Alexander Dubcek to liberalize communist rule and break free of Soviet domination. Through friends of Lisa's family, we looked up a young Czech plastic surgeon and artist, Jara Moserova, and her husband, who showed us around Prague while expressing the apprehension that "all this is too good to be true."

We have never been greeted as Americans the way we were that summer on the streets of Prague. But it was indeed too good to be true. Soviet tanks rolled into the city a few days after we left, and Czechoslovakia's experiment with "socialism with a human face" was extinguished for a generation. Our promise to keep up with our new friends largely came to naught.

It was thirty-five years later that Lisa and I again found ourselves in Prague, and in the company of Jara Moserova. I was a delegate to the NATO Parliamentary Assembly as a free and democratic Czech Republic prepared to claim full NATO membership! Jara, a lifelong friend of Vaclav Havel, had chaired his party, the Civic Forum, which led the 1989 Velvet Revolution. She was now a Czech senator, sitting on the front row as I prepared to address the assembly as our delegation's senior Democrat. My main topic was challenges confronting the alliance in the aftermath of the war in Iraq, but I had to steady my voice as I also acknowledged Jara's presence, recalled our 1968 visit, and reflected on the significance of the NATO Assembly's meeting in Prague at this historic juncture:

> Such memories remind us of how far we have come and what we have been through together. Remembering where we are and the momentous occurrences that have brought us to this point should put our present challenges in perspective and reinforce our commitment to the values and alliances and institutions that have made this day possible.

Parliament-to-Parliament: The House Democracy Partnership

Interparliamentary engagement, whether through bilateral exchanges or participation in organizations such as the NATO Parliamentary Assembly, is an important component of American diplomacy and a vital outlet for House members with an interest in foreign affairs. We have taken such engagements to a new level and linked them to democracy promotion through the House Democracy Partnership (HDP), distinctive both in the continuity of our interparliamentary relationships and in our focus on institution-building, beyond the bilateral issues of the day.

Launched in 2005, HDP saw itself as resuming and expanding the work of the Task Force on the Development of Parliamentary Institutions in

Central and Eastern Europe, founded in 1990 and chaired by then-Rules Committee Chairman Martin Frost (D-Texas), along with ranking member Gerald Solomon (R-New York). The Task Force was formed at a unique moment in history, as communist regimes simultaneously collapsed and showcase parliaments suddenly needed to function as governing institutions. The idea was to offer encouragement and colleagueship, technical and staff support, information resources and equipment to leaders and members as they established modern parliaments on the European model.[1]

House members traveled to the participating countries mainly to launch the projects and to promote ongoing cooperation. I joined delegations to Poland, Estonia, Latvia, and Lithuania in 1992 and to Hungary, Slovakia, and Albania in 1993. Staff members from the Congressional Research Service (CRS) of the Library of Congress and from House Information Systems went over for weeks at a time, delivering the equipment, assistance, and training necessary to establish modern library facilities and computer capabilities. The assistance we rendered depended in part on what equipment and personnel were already in place. Poland, Hungary, and the Czech Republic were ready for a fairly rapid takeoff, while in Albania our delegation delivered typewriters and a wall clock. The other countries were somewhere in between. The assignment was a political scientist's dream and a moving human experience as well, as we met with courageous democratic leaders—at a reception in the ambassador's residence in Tirana, we were told that the parliamentary leaders in the room had spent on average over twenty years in Albanian prisons—and saw what an inspiration the U.S. Congress, despite its flaws, was to them.

I returned to Bratislava as a former member after the 1994 election, joining with several European parliamentarians in an orientation program for new Slovakian legislators. Unfortunately, between the planning of the program and its execution, the "wrong" party—the authoritarian Movement for a Democratic Slovakia, led by Vladimir Meciar—staged a political comeback, producing as cold and unreceptive an audience as I have ever tried to address! (Fortunately, Slovakia turned the corner politically in 1998, and in 2004 attained membership in NATO.) In the meantime, the new Republican House leadership allowed the parliamentary assistance project to lapse—prematurely in my view. In 2004, Rep. Doug Bereuter (R-Nebraska), chairman of the International Relations Subcommittee on Europe, and I introduced a resolution (H.Res. 642) to authorize the renewal of the program. We expected to continue a focus on Central and Eastern Europe—former Yugoslav republics, Georgia, and other former Soviet and communist states if and when they developed freely functioning parliaments. But we also wanted to consider other struggling democracies worldwide, where member-to-member and staff-to-staff engagement would be welcome and mutually beneficial.

Bereuter had announced his retirement and identified passing this resolution as a priority before he left. John Lis, his Foreign Affairs Committee aide, whom I had gotten to know through work on the NATO Assembly, worked closely with us. But nothing happened. Finally, I decided that I would call Speaker Dennis Hastert (R-Illinois), my classmate from the class of 1986, personally, to make sure the request had actually gotten to him. It turned out that it had not, for reasons I could only speculate about. I received his return call on November 8, 2004, while on a NATO Assembly trip. I took the call in the living room of the U.S. Ambassador to Greece. Republican colleagues clearly wondered what was up when I was summoned from the room for a call from the Speaker. But Hastert heard me out, considered the proposal, and decided to push it forward. It was quite appropriate, I thought in retrospect, that the key conversation took place in Athens, the birthplace of democracy! Soon we were moving toward passage of the resolution, which occurred on March 5, 2005, shortly after the 109th Congress convened.

Speaker Hastert made the fortuitous decision to ask David Dreier (R-California) to sponsor the resolution in the new Congress and then to chair the commission. Dreier had a lively interest in international and inter-parliamentary affairs and wielded considerable influence in Republican leadership circles; like Frost, he was Rules Committee chairman. We agreed that John Lis should be our staff director and secured a staff slot for him on the Foreign Affairs Committee, which was maintained through agreement with the leadership of both parties until 2013. We were sometimes able to add a second Foreign Affairs staffer—usually by assessing our own and other offices to pay the salary—and were also aided by a series of detailees from USAID and the State Department. But we were always lightly staffed, and from the start Dreier and I both assigned members of our personal staffs to share in the substantive work of the Commission.

During HDP's first two years (our original name was the House Democracy Assistance Commission, later changed to more accurately reflect our approach), Dreier as chairman and I as ranking member set a pattern of bipartisan collaboration that has continued to this day. It is by far the most genuinely bipartisan undertaking I have been involved in as a House member. Dreier also established a pattern of cooperation with the Marine Corps liaison office on Capitol Hill, at that time led by Col. (later General) Paul Kennedy. The Marine office has gone far beyond the usual military escort role, helping plan and execute every one of our overseas missions.

As HDP got underway, we had an advantage that the Frost Commission had not: parliamentary development had become a more prominent empha-sis of U.S. foreign aid. Work was well underway in many promising situ-ations under the auspices of the National Democratic Institute (NDI), the International Republican Institute (IRI), and other non-governmental organizations under contract with USAID. We developed a close and fruit-ful partnership with these organizations. They saw that our Commission, with strong congressional involvement and regular reciprocal visits, could bring cachet to their programs and encourage member buy-in all around.

We came to understand that the consultation, technical support, and staff training that NDI, IRI, and similar programs offered could provide continuity between our own visits and the workshops for members and staff that we held, as well as day-to-day counsel and support on the ground. This greatly extended our reach and encouraged us to go beyond the Frost Task Force's emphasis on information technology and research capabilities.

Lis developed a process for choosing partner countries that drew on NDI, IRI, and other country and regional experts. Our staff typically assembled a team that spent a week in the country in question before making a recommendation as to how good the fit would be. We sometimes made visits to prospective countries while on trips to our partner countries; in several cases—Mali, Paraguay, Bangladesh, and Moldova—we decided that circumstances did not yet warrant a full partnership. Dreier faced a particularly hard decision when urged by a State Department official in the Bush administration to take on Morocco. We understood very well the importance of a strong parliamentary relationship with Morocco but had to explain that the country's parliament did not yet have sufficient independent powers to fully benefit from what we had to offer. We were seeking situations where the country had departed decisively from an autocratic past, where the parliament had demonstrated a desire and a capacity for more autonomy, and where our presence and support were welcome and could make a difference. In taking on partners such as Indonesia, Kenya, Colombia, and Peru, we were also aware of their regional strategic significance. The same was true of countries in and around major areas of conflict—Afghanistan, Pakistan, Iraq, Lebanon. But we also worked with several smaller, poorer countries for which our country felt a special responsibility: Kosovo, Liberia, Timor-Leste, Haiti. And we remained particularly attuned to the aspirations for self-determination and parliamentary democracy in post-communist states: North Macedonia, Georgia, Ukraine, Kyrgyzstan, and Mongolia.

I served four years as HDP chairman, during the 2007–2010 period of House Democratic leadership. We deployed eighteen congressional delegations (CODELs) over that period, visiting most of our partner countries at least twice. I led most delegations, with Donald Payne Sr. (D-New Jersey), Adam Schiff (D-California), Allyson Schwartz (D-Pennsylvania), Earl Pomeroy (D-North Dakota), and Mazie Hirono (D-Hawaii) leading others. We generally paid visits to the president and/or prime minister of our host country, but spent most of our time with parliamentarians: assembly officers, party and committee leaders, and often groups of special interest— women members, new members, reform commissions, and American-friendship caucuses, (see Figure 8.1). We usually had enough members to hold multiple simultaneous small-group discussions, and our staff—plus other staff we brought along from House committees, House administration, the Congressional Research Service (CRS), etc.—often had parallel meetings with their counterparts in the host institution.

Figure 8.1 House Democracy Partnership: with members of parliament in North Macedonia.

Photo courtesy of Asher Hildebrand.

Our careful selection process and our efforts to go "all in" once we had selected a partner produced sustained engagement in most of our partner countries. We experienced substantial difficulties, however, in the Middle Eastern theaters of war—Iraq, Afghanistan, and Pakistan. Security was often a barrier, and these parliaments were generally preoccupied by challenges that went far beyond how they were functioning day to day. The major exception, for a time, was Afghanistan. In general, during the presidency of Hamid Karzai (2004–2014), the Afghan parliament exceeded expectations and significantly strengthened its capacities as a coordinate branch of government.

We took four delegations to Kabul and welcomed dozens of members and staff to Washington. Many Afghan parliamentarians participated enthusiastically, focusing on how their institution was working despite the larger challenges and uncertainties that were never far from our minds. We particularly engaged with female legislators, most of whom had remarkable life stories and for whom we developed particular admiration. We also helped outfit a parliamentary library and initiate a research service.

There were, however, many reminders of the country's and the parliament's fragile security. During our first visit in 2006, the delegation was invited by Speaker Yunus Qanuni to lunch across the city in his heavily fortified residential compound. We were hastily evacuated when an alert was received and had a hair-raising ride through side streets back to our embassy. One poignant moment that has remained with me was witnessing three portraits on unoccupied seats in the chamber—and realizing that they memorialized recently assassinated colleagues.

As it turned out, the visit Dreier and I made to Kabul in 2012 was our last. Our discussions with members were no less enthusiastic, and we tried to sustain them through reciprocal visits that were increasingly difficult to arrange. But it became impossible for foreigners to visit the Afghan parliament safely. This lapse represented a huge lost opportunity and, unfortunately, indicated what Afghanistan faced as our military presence diminished. I almost succeeded in arranging a visit in early 2020 at a critical time for the parliament and the country, but the coronavirus intervened.

In addition to discussions with our parliamentary colleagues in their capitals, we tried to venture out to constituencies, accompanied by one or more local representatives—visiting district offices where they existed; local councils, agencies, and businesses; town meetings and other gatherings. Places like Buchanan and Tubmanburg, Liberia; Banda Aceh, Indonesia; Amboseli, Kenya; Negotino, North Macedonia; Arequipa, Peru; and Lviv, Ukraine had rarely seen congressional visitors and gave us insights beyond those we could gain through conversations with our hosts in their offices.

These trips also included memorable unscripted moments, such as a visit to Gorée Island during a transit stop in Senegal. I will never forget standing in the Door of No Return, the disembarkation point for untold thousands of captured slaves, with an African American colleague—the first visit for her, as it was for me. We had a joyous visit to Pristina one month after Kosovo's declaration of independence—the first congressional delegation to visit the world's youngest democracy! On four visits to Nairobi I was able to take a group of members into Kibera, the largest urban slum in Africa, and witness the remarkable work of Carolina for Kibera—an NGO started as a soccer club by a UNC-Chapel Hill student intern which now is a center for health services, microenterprises, and other community projects.[2] And we had a heartwarming return to Poland in 2010 as the parliament sponsored a commemoration of the 20th anniversary of the work of the Frost-Solomon Task Force. Task Force alumni from many Central and Eastern European parliaments came to Warsaw for a four-day conference, as did a number of members and staff from our HDP partner countries—a great celebration of parliamentary cooperation and reform.

The 2007–2010 period also featured nineteen "inbound" workshops in Washington for members or staffs of partner legislatures, typically administered by NDI or IRI. These week-long programs focused on topics such as committee operations, budget processes, defense oversight, and constituent relations. Presenters included HDP members and other colleagues, staff, and administrators from across the House. We also experimented with workshops based outside of Washington (Hawaii, Kenya, North Macedonia) for clusters of parliaments, and dispatched a number of staff or former staff as consultants to address needs in specific countries. On two occasions we organized delegations of former members, one to Kenya on parliamentary reform led by Martin Frost, the other to Georgia on defense oversight led by Martin Lancaster (D-North Carolina).

With the shift to Republican leadership of the House in 2011, Dreier again became HDP chairman. We maintained a full schedule of outbound and inbound activities but faced the necessity of transition as Dreier announced that he would not run for re-election in 2012. His suggestion to Speaker John Boehner that Peter Roskam (R-Illinois) be appointed to succeed him was a discerning one, but Dreier's level of personal and staff commitment was difficult to replace. We faced other challenges as well. HDP, like the Frost-Solomon Task Force before it, had always been an outlier in terms of House administration, dependent on the flexibility and favor of whoever was Speaker at the time. Boehner seemed to have little stake in HDP's work and certainly no reason to make an exception for us in terms of the overall reductions he imposed on House travel. Nor did he intervene when the new House Foreign Affairs chairman, Ed Royce (R-California) decided in 2013 to eliminate the position of John Lis, our only full-time staff member—a near-fatal blow.

Fearing for HDP's future, I worked with Roskam to recalibrate our program. We continued the tradition of bipartisan cooperation, and I assigned a senior member of my personal staff, Justin Wein, to take on much of what John Lis had been doing. We were not able to travel at all during the 113th Congress (2013–2014) but kept the flame alive through a continuing schedule of inbound member and staff workshops. We could not have done this without the extraordinary efforts of NDI and IRI, who further showed the value they placed on HDP by organizing a series of assessment visits to partner countries for staff and former members. These visits served not only to assess conditions in the parliaments but also to signal that our work would soon resume.

The CODEL Roskam led to Georgia and Ukraine in July 2015 confirmed that HDP was back in business. It occurred at a critical juncture for both countries—after the emergence of a new, but still pro-Western, governing party in Georgia, and after the Maidan revolution and installation of a heavily pro-Western but fractious parliament in Ukraine. Both faced severe pressure and the occupation of much of their territory by Russia.[3] On succeeding trips in 2015–2018, some led by Roskam and others by veteran HDP members Vern Buchanan (R-Florida) and Bill Flores (R-Texas), we managed to touch base in most of our partner countries as well as to initiate relationships with several new or prospective partners: Tunisia, Burma (Myanmar), Nepal, Sri Lanka, and Guatemala. We also returned to Poland, perhaps the Frost Task Force's most enthusiastic participant, for searching conversations with colleagues about the apparent reversal of democratic advances in that country. And we continued to hold member and staff workshops for clusters of parliaments, mostly in Washington but also in regional locations such as Estonia, North Macedonia, and Chile.

The schedule for our two-day program in North Macedonia, August 27–28, 2018, is typical of our CODEL engagements:

<u>August 27</u>
9:00 Embassy country team briefing
9:50 NDI briefing on state of parliament
10:15 Speaker Xhaferi and party whips
11:20 Parallel meetings with committee chairs on oversight
    A. Led by Rep. Flores
    Committees with corresponding ministries: Defense and Security, Foreign Policy, European Affairs, etc.
    B. Led by Rep. Price
    Committees without a corresponding ministry: Constitutional Issues, Civil Freedoms and Rights, Rules of Procedure, etc.
12:45 Lunch hosted by Speaker and other leaders
2:00 Parallel meetings with committee members
    A. Defense and Security
    B. Rules of Procedure
3:10 Women's Caucus
4:10 Reps. Flores and Price interview with Temla TV
5:30 Prime Minister Zaev and other ministers
6:30 Reception hosted by U.S. Ambassador

<u>August 28</u>
9:00 Civil Society Organization roundtable—good governance, election monitoring, young lawyers, etc.
10:45 Minister of Defense Shekerinska
12:30 Luncheon discussion of impending referendum on adopting new name of North Macedonia—with NDI and IRI program heads
1:15 Transit to Veles
2:00 Mayor and Municipal Council of Veles
3:30 Local MPs from Veles
5:10 Dinner with Peace Corps volunteers
8:00 Depart Skopje for Tunis

The 2018 elections brought Democrats back to House leadership and me back to the chairmanship of HDP. Peter Roskam lost his bid for re-election and was replaced as co-chairman by Vern Buchanan (R-Florida), a longtime HDP member who shared fully in our bipartisan ethos. Critically, Speaker Pelosi and Foreign Affairs Chairman Eliot Engel agreed to the restoration of our staff slot on the Committee, to which we appointed Derek Luyten, a veteran of numerous IRI assignments. My first CODEL in April 2019 focused on two longtime partners, Ukraine and Georgia. We had exploratory meetings in Armenia, which had recently experienced a democratizing "Velvet Revolution" and whose parliamentary leaders had expressed intense interest in working with us, laying the groundwork for an eventual partnership. We also looked in briefly on North Carolina's "partner" country, Moldova, talking with leaders of the three factions that were trying, with great difficulty, to form a governing coalition following parliamentary elections.

Our Ukraine visit was not ideally timed; the country was in the throes of the runoff election that would make Volodymyr Zelensky president. We nonetheless had substantive meetings with leaders of the parliamentary factions and with a group of reform-minded members. With us was our accomplished ambassador, Marie Yovanovitch. I remember thinking that I had seldom had better guidance in understanding to whom we were talking or what would be productive lines of discussion than what she provided. Little did we realize that she was already being subjected to a vicious smear campaign and in just nine days would be abruptly recalled to Washington, judged by President Trump to be an obstacle to his ongoing efforts to get the Ukrainian government to do his bidding. Yovanovitch would later be an important and wholly credible witness in the impeachment inquiry.

We took CODELs to Asia and Africa later in 2019, engaging with partner countries Indonesia, Timor-Leste, Kenya, and Liberia and undertaking exploratory conversations in Ethiopia and The Gambia, where changes that promised to enhance their parliaments' roles were underway. We also paid a memorable visit to the Dalai Lama and the Central Tibetan Administration in Dharamshala, India, engaging particularly with the Western-style Tibetan parliament-in-exile, (see Figure 8.2).

Figure 8.2 A memorable greeting from the Dalai Lama.

Credit: Photo courtesy of Tenzin Choenjor/Office of H.H the Dalai Lama.

Our ambitious plans for 2020 CODELs to Peru-Colombia-Ecuador and Mongolia-Kyrgyzstan-Tunisia were upended by the coronavirus. We were able to initiate online meetings with various groups of colleagues, beginning with Tunisia, Kosovo, Armenia, Peru, Georgia, and Ukraine. Our program of member and staff workshops and consultations, undertaken with the help of NDI and IRI, which we had stepped up considerably in 2019, were thrown into some uncertainty.

Fifteen years of experience with HDP have left a bipartisan cadre of House members and staff dedicated to the legislative-strengthening project. Martin Frost readily says this was the best idea he ever had while in Congress, and David Dreier says he values it more than anything else he did in the House. We are strongly supported, moreover, by collaborators in NDI, IRI, USAID, and others who have aided or complemented our efforts.[4] We still have a ways to go, however, in establishing our brand of institutional diplomacy as a priority for House leadership. We continue to work at securing the support we need, from staffing to workable travel rules, to function optimally, and at evaluating and improving our own operations. We must target our efforts, allocating scarce time and resources and our ability to travel, maintaining an effective balance between sustaining existing partnerships and taking on new challenges, and more accurately gauging our effectiveness.

Democracy Promotion: Remember the Legislatures

We have said it countless times: while free and fair elections are an essential component of democracy, it matters even more what happens *between* elections—when representative institutions must work effectively to represent diverse areas and interests, to address pressing policy challenges, and to gain legitimacy.

If promoters of democracy have often overestimated the potential of elections to ensure democratic development, so have we also often held impossibly high expectations for charismatic democratic leaders such as Viktor Yushchenko of Ukraine, Ellen Johnson Sirleaf of Liberia, and Aung San Suu Kyi of Burma. Even the best invariably disappoint, but even if they did not, the larger task is to develop vibrant institutions that will endure as leaders come and go and will give voice to the full range of interests in the society.[5]

Consider the case of Tunisia. In a persuasive analysis of the failure of the Arab Spring to produce successful democratic regimes, Amanda Taub notes the tendency of many to place the blame on the shortcomings of either the revolutionaries or the transitional leaders:

> The truth is that this was never a story primarily about individual heroes or villains. Rather it was about something much bigger and more abstract: the catastrophic failure of institutions.[6]

If you cannot make institutions work, Taub argues, "then your revolution is doomed." In most Arab Spring countries, the parliaments and other institutions had been "hollowed out" or destroyed under strongman rule; when the regimes fell, civil wars and struggles to reestablish order by force filled the vacuum.

Tunisia is the one democratic exception, albeit a fragile one. The revolution in Tunisia removed President Zine Ben Ali and his top lieutenants, but left other governing structures and the institutions of civil society relatively intact. The constitutional assembly and then the parliament assumed the task of bringing disparate forces together to draft a constitution and address the country's challenges legislatively. When the constitutional process faltered in 2013, a "national dialogue quartet" consisting of Tunisia's largest union and leading business, legal, and human rights organizations brokered talks among rival factions—for which the quartet was awarded the Nobel Peace Prize. At another critical juncture, after the presidential election of 2014, the staunch secularist who won the most votes and the leader of Ennahda, the country's dominant Islamist party, put their rivalry temporarily aside and formed a coalition government to promote accommodation and stability as the government continued to find its footing. Tunisia thus made a successful, if halting, transition both because of the relative strength of its surviving governmental and civil structures and because leaders from various sectors saw the importance of ensuring inclusion and otherwise strengthening the institutions of governance. These are the tasks to which HDP has also tried to contribute.

Democracy promotion is always a work in progress for two reasons: its end-product will never be perfectly realized, in our own country or any other, and it will always require adaptation and refinement in light of accumulated experience and changed circumstances. Its modern roots as a component of American diplomacy trace both to President Jimmy Carter's elevation of human rights as a foreign policy objective and President Ronald Reagan's embrace of democracy promotion in the context of the Cold War. Congress helped shape both initiatives, which initially focused on Latin America.

These approaches may appear complementary in retrospect, but they often contrasted and conflicted in practice. The Reagan administration, for example, conspicuously reversed the limitations Carter had placed on military aid to countries like Argentina, Chile, Guatemala, and El Salvador, despite serious human rights violations. But by 1982, Reagan, reflecting a structural and procedural more than a rights-based view of democracy, was laying the groundwork for the establishment of the National Endowment for Democracy and its constituent democracy-promoting organizations, including NDI and IRI.[7]

With the end of the Cold War, U.S. democracy promotion efforts shifted their focus to Central and Eastern Europe and quickly spread to developing nations worldwide. Congress, urged on by the Frost Task Force, approved aid to the parliaments of Poland, Hungary, and Czechoslovakia. President Clinton created a Democracy and Governance Office at USAID, which contracted with NDI, IRI, and other organizations to run programs aimed at ensuring fair elections and at strengthening legislatures, political parties, the rule of law, and the institutions of civil society. Appropriations for democracy assistance through USAID increased fourfold from 1990–2000, reaching a total of $539 million distributed among some 120 countries.[8]

Appropriations jumped again after the terrorist attacks of September 11, 2001, reaching a high of $1.13 billion by fiscal 2004, but with most of the increase going to the Middle East. The association of this aid with counterterrorism and military intervention, together with the intractability of governance challenges in Iraq and Afghanistan, led to skeptical questions about democracy promotion that still lingered as we began the work of HDP in 2005. After an assessment of the Afghan parliament's situation, we engaged there immediately. But we delayed our involvement in Iraq and Pakistan, concentrating instead on opportunities among post-communist states and other high-priority countries such as Indonesia and Kenya. And we took special pains to disassociate ourselves from the notion that democracy "could spring fully formed from the barrel of a gun."[9]

Barack Obama came to office critical of the Bush brand of democracy promotion, but within months was speaking in aspirational terms about the possibilities of democracy in the Middle East and elsewhere. In this, Thomas Carothers notes, he resembled other incoming presidents who, "intent on rigorous realism, ended up adopting democracy goals more than they had intended."

> One reason ... is that a sharp separation between foreign policy interests and values ... is an illusion. Once one descends ... to specific country cases, the fact quickly emerges that supporting democracy is often a useful way to advance "hard" economic and security interests.[10]

Still, democracy promotion was not the Obama administration's top foreign aid priority, and legislative strengthening in particular suffered considerable attrition. After the Haitian earthquake of 2010, we had only limited success in urging Secretary of State Hillary Clinton and her deputies to attend to the needs of the Haitian Congress, which was left in shambles, physically and otherwise. We sometimes were able to delay or prevent the premature termination of legislative strengthening efforts and, starting in 2015, inserted directives to USAID in Foreign Operations appropriations bills to give priority to programs that complemented HDP's efforts.

Donald Trump came to the presidency in 2017 denigrating support for human rights and democracy in favor of an "America first" foreign policy rooted mainly in military power. His proposed budgets slashed foreign aid in general and democracy assistance in particular. This coincided with my gaining membership on the State and Foreign Operations (SFOPS) Appropriations Subcommittee, where we obtained bipartisan support for doubling the administration's requests for USAID democracy support from $1.2 billion to $2.4 billion for fiscal 2019, for example. We were encouraged by the appointment of former Representative and IRI President Mark

Green as director of USAID and continued to press for the continuation or revival of legislative strengthening where we knew it was needed.

In this context, we must defend our work as well as constantly seek to improve it. But it is not a simple matter to measure or document "success." We have wrestled with the question of when a parliament should "graduate" from our program. In Europe, ascension to NATO or the European Union has often been taken as an indicator of parliamentary maturity, and in the case of countries such as Kenya, Indonesia, and Peru, our relationships have evolved to the point of collaboration in running regional workshops and working with other parliaments. USAID in 2015 made a significant effort to develop measures of effectiveness for legislative strengthening programs as part of ongoing reevaluation and reorganization of human rights, democracy, and governance support.[11] But because the end-point of legislative strengthening remains elusive and so many of our ongoing relationships have intrinsic value, we have hesitated to "drop" countries even as we have taken on more partners—five since 2015.

As the number of partner parliaments has increased and our ability to travel and engage intensively has declined, the practical effect has been to render our country-by-country relationships less uniform. We have prioritized certain countries, e.g., Ukraine and Tunisia, for more frequent visits, even as we have continued to involve members and staff from all partner countries in our Washington and regional workshops.

The need for continuous engagement remains a major lesson learned, however, and we are wary of spreading ourselves too thinly, or terminating programs too quickly. "Abandoning institutional strengthening efforts before the job is done threatens to squander multi-year investments and to take the wind out of the sails of reforms," we warned the incoming Obama administration, with mixed success.[12] This advice obviously applies not only to USAID but also to HDP, where we have often found ourselves countering narratives of American inconstancy (most dramatically in Pakistan) or of congressional inattentiveness to parliaments (which many CODELs, dropping in for a single day and calling only on the president or prime minister, unfortunately reinforce).

We have also learned, to the extent we did not understand it already, not to assume too much about the suitability and attractiveness of the American legislative model for export. Thomas Carothers noted some of the pitfalls in his 1999 critique of early legislative strengthening efforts; invariably, he said, they attempt to make these bodies "more independent of the executive branch, more concerned about exercising oversight of the executive, more engaged in public hearings, more open to outside lobbying, and more well equipped, with a large, powerful staff and a good library. In other words … [more like] the U.S. Congress."[13] To some of this I would plead guilty, arguing that such objectives often apply to representative institutions quite broadly and are aspired to by members in various legislative settings.

In fact, however, very few of our partner parliaments are organized on the American constitutional model; modified Westminster or mixed presidential models are much more common.[14] It is important to be sensitive to such distinctions in devising presentations and materials, and our discussions with colleagues often take note of what might or might not be applicable in their particular setting. But sometimes unfamiliar practices do take hold to good effect—an enthusiastically received town meeting in Buchanan, Liberia, for example, or a well-utilized constituency office in Arequipa, Peru, or parliamentary committees realizing the potential of oversight hearings in Kenya, Ukraine, North Macedonia, and Georgia.

We are restrained in the claims we make for the American system, acknowledging that in an era of polarization and gridlock, we have a great deal to be modest about. Neither we nor our partners take our 230-year history of representative government lightly, but it is hard to argue that most of them would be well served by a system that regularly produces divided party control of the major organs of government. We are not averse to discussing constitutional alternatives, but our main emphasis is on making existing structures effective and responsive—with an underling recognition, as we often say, that representative democracy remains a "work in progress" for all of us.

The most pressing challenge for many of our partner institutions is also one of the most difficult to address directly: corruption. We try to avoid self-righteousness, understanding that corruption is an endemic challenge for democratic governments, including our own. Our experience suggests that moralizing, hortatory approaches are often off-putting and ineffective. We have not hesitated to make the case for ethics rules and enforcement as integral to maintaining public trust. We have expressed support for such anti-corruption bodies as the KPK (Corruption Eradication Commission) in Indonesia and CICIG (International Commission Against Impunity) in Guatemala. But we also believe that much of what we do to professionalize legislative operations and to make them more transparent and accountable will have the collateral benefit of reducing the susceptibility of members and their institutions to corrupt practices.

We have also come to appreciate the relevance of our HDP experience for other areas of national policy. I have advocated on the SFOPS subcommittee, for example, not only for USAID democracy support but also for the continued prioritization of aid packages for such specific partner countries as Sri Lanka, Tunisia, and Georgia, cut or eliminated in Trump budget requests. We continue to push our colleagues to "remember the legislatures," in their CODELs and other international dealings. We often encounter the fact that democracy will have hard going if it cannot demonstrate economic success, and thus have become advocates for socioeconomic aid and enhanced trade and investment in our partner countries. And in the Trump era, we have often found ourselves cast as interpreters of American foreign policy more broadly. In particular, countries under threat from Russia and/or aspiring to NATO or European Union membership have looked to us for reassurance and support, which we have attempted to give on a truthful and non-partisan basis.

Legislative strengthening and democracy promotion are currently facing major headwinds. Comparative international studies have identified broad, interrelated trends toward a decline in the powers of legislatures, increased executive dominance, and the rise of authoritarianism. In 2019, for the fourteenth consecutive year, Freedom House found more countries suffering net declines in political rights and civil liberties than registering gains.[15] Earlier optimism about democracy's momentum has been dampened by backsliding and reversal, not only in the developing world but within the ranks of NATO and the European Union. Meanwhile, China, Russia, and other autocratic governments have steadily extended their international outreach. Particularly in Russia's case, this has included the encouragement of pushback against Western democracy promotion efforts—reflecting the view that states in their orbit face a zero-sum choice between Russia and the West.

Because HDP has concentrated on countries that have welcomed our partnership and have successfully navigated at least some democratic transitions (Iraq, Afghanistan, and Burma excepted, all of our partners are rated as free [4] or partly free [15] by Freedom House),[16] we are involved in a selective sample of more hopeful situations. Still, we have seen ample evidence of Russian-inspired pushback and, beyond that, are well aware that troubles in our own and other Western democracies have heightened doubts in some transitional countries as to "whether the keys to decisive governance and economic dynamism do not in fact lie down some path other than that of liberal democracy."[17]

The presence of headwinds, including those within our own executive branch, make it all the more important for HDP, and the democracy promotion effort to which it is the U.S. House's distinctive contribution, to continue. Added over the years to our conviction that the promotion of human rights and of responsive democratic governance is consistent with our values, universally shared, has been an identification with the struggles of colleagues who depend on us and our country's example. We are also aware of the costs and dangers of failure, if the countries with whom we are working were to revert to violent conflict, domination by hostile powers, or a collapse of governance. Extending colleagueship and sharing best practices with aspiring parliaments is a limited diplomatic niche, but one the HDP experience has convinced us to maintain and make ever more effective.

Supporting Middle East Diplomacy

Lisa and I first traveled to Israel in early 1990, midway in my second term, under the auspices of the Anti-Defamation League of B'nai B'rith (ADL). The trip made a powerful impression and left me with some political insights as well. One had to do with the diversity of Israeli political opinion on the Israeli-Palestinian question. The range was far wider than one would have assumed from the litmus-test positions (e.g., refusing ever to recognize or negotiate with the Palestine Liberation Organization [PLO]) urged on congressional candidates by the American Israel Public Affairs Committee (AIPAC) and allied groups. Another insight had to do with the potential quality of Palestinian leadership beyond the familiar figure of Yasser Arafat and the extent of the contacts our government had cultivated with moderate elements, mainly through our consulate in Jerusalem. I was struck by the widespread agreement on both sides as to what an eventual settlement might look like, as well as the formidable obstacles to getting there. I resolved to be more attentive to the issue and to seek avenues for positive engagement. Lisa, whose Jewish background sensitized her to the challenges faced by Israel and the region, supported such engagement fully.

Such opportunities greatly increased in the wake of the 1991 Madrid Conference, convened by the United States and the Soviet Union and attended by Israeli, Palestinian, Syrian, Lebanese, and Jordanian leaders, and the signing of the Declaration of Principles (the Oslo Accord) by Israeli Prime Minister Yitzhak Rabin and PLO chairman Yasser Arafat at the White House in 1993. Clearly, a continuing mix of American encouragement and pressure was essential if the successive steps envisioned in the Oslo Accord were to be taken. On returning to the House in 1997, I was drawn to the work of the Center for Middle East Peace and Economic Cooperation, an organization cofounded by Slim-Fast Foods chairman Daniel Abraham and former Rep. Wayne Owens (D-Utah), a friend from his days in the House. Sara Ehrman, whom I knew by virtue of Lisa's family ties, brought her expertise and advocacy skills to the Center as senior advisor. The Center had actively promoted the peace process behind the scenes since the run-up to the Madrid Conference. Owens was convinced that visits by members of Congress to the region were useful, not only in engaging and educating the members themselves but also in demonstrating American support for the peace process, nudging the participants along, and encouraging positive moves by political and business leaders in the region.

In late 1997, I set out with Abraham, Owens, and two House colleagues, Gary Ackerman (D-New York) and Jim Moran (D-Virginia) on the first of five trips I took with the Center. We visited Israel, the Palestinian territories, Jordan, Syria, Lebanon, Egypt, and Qatar. The experience convinced me that a small, independent, and creative organization could do significant work in this difficult environment and might have some advantages over formal delegations. We were not freelancing, however; we conferred with State Department officials before leaving and with our ambassadors in each country we visited. Our conversations ranged more widely and were more candid than those I had experienced in official settings. We benefited from the credibility and respectful relations Abraham and Owen had developed across the political spectrum in Israel, in the Palestinian community, and in most Arab states. We were almost always received by the head of state, and our conversations ranged from exchanging information and airing bilateral issues to exploring specific steps to strengthen regional support for negotiations.[18]

Despite the blow the peace process had suffered with the assassination of Prime Minister Yitzhak Rabin in 1995, in the context of hard-right opposition to Oslo, these were hopeful times. The Clinton administration increasingly focused on dual-track negotiations with Syria and the Palestinians, and in Israel a Labor government committed to negotiations, led by Prime Minister Ehud Barak, replaced Benjamin Netanyahu's Likud government in 1999. The timing also seemed right for Syria's ailing president Hafez al-Assad, who knew that time was running out on any hope he had that the Golan Heights, occupied by Israel since the 1967 war, would be returned to Syrian rule. Nonetheless, the process ran aground: the Syrian talks narrowly failed, as did the Palestinian talks at Camp David a few months later. There was ample blame to go around, but as Secretary of State Madeleine Albright observed, the "core failure was [Arafat's and] the Palestinians' obsessive focus not on how much could be gained but on the relatively little they would be required to give up."[19]

In any event, these opportunities would not recur. The situation rapidly deteriorated on all sides, and the American administration that came to power in 2001 was determined to disengage from proactive Middle East peacemaking.

My Middle East involvement was rooted in a dual commitment to the security and integrity of Israel and to justice and self-determination for the Palestinians—two goals that not only were consistent but were essential to each other. The disappointments of 2000 reinforced my conviction that the conflict was unlikely to be resolved without active American engagement. The quest for peace was then given a powerful additional rationale and new urgency by the terrorist attacks of September 11, 2001, and the need to mobilize internationally against al Qaeda and related groups. Osama bin Laden displayed little interest in the plight of the Palestinians until he used it in a post-attack bid for support, a fact well understood by most Arab leaders. Still, the continuing Israeli-Palestinian violence, given the widespread perception that the United States had not only disengaged from peacemaking but had taken a hands-off attitude toward the policies of Prime Minister Ariel Sharon (who had brought Likud back to power in 2001), fed anti-American sentiment in the Arab world. The festering conflict, featured as never before on satellite news outlets, made it more difficult and dangerous for friendly governments to ally themselves fully with our antiterrorism offensive.

The collapse of the peace process, along with the urgency of the war on terrorism, made for an altered mood and message in 2002, as I returned to the region with Sen. Dick Durbin (D-Illinois), Rep. Jim Davis (D-Florida), and Rep. Adam Schiff (D-California), again under the Center's auspices. We went to Egypt, Syria, Lebanon, Jordan, Kuwait, Saudi Arabia, Israel, and the Palestinian territories. Owens and I took a shorter trip in May focusing on Israel, Syria, and Lebanon; in December, Owens, Abraham, Davis, and I returned to most of the countries we had visited in January plus Oman and Qatar. We stressed that terrorism was no longer an abstraction for the American people and that our country was united in its determination to remove this threat. We expressed appreciation, where warranted, for cooperating with our military, sharing intelligence, and closing financial conduits to al Qaeda, and we expressed concern over failures to crack down on the terrorist groups wreaking havoc in Israel. We heard, in return, many complaints about sporadic, ineffectual efforts by the Bush administration to rein in Israeli-Palestinian violence and get the parties back to negotiations.[20]

Our January trip came at a time when the Israeli government was setting out, as Sharon put it, to "delegitimate" Yasser Arafat as a purveyor of violence with whom Israel no longer could deal. Our government, while frustrated with Arafat, still recognized him as the elected president of the Palestinian Authority, and our delegation scheduled meetings with him as well as other Palestinian leaders.

As we were driving into Jerusalem from Amman, we received word from our embassy that another group of House members would soon be holding a press conference to announce their refusal to meet with Arafat. While this was a tempting political course for some (AIPAC had asked members to boycott Arafat), it created concern among consular officials who had requested our meetings. Had our group also canceled, it would have been impossible for the other Palestinian officials on our agenda (including a future prime minister, Ahmed Qurei) to see us. After extensive discussion, we determined that Jim Davis and I would keep our appointment with Arafat; this allowed Consul-General Ron Schlicher to deliver to him personally our government's demand for a response to reports linking Palestinian leaders to a major arms shipment Israelis had just intercepted at sea. Davis and I reinforced that message and preserved our group's schedule with other Palestinian leaders, some of whom offered a promising counterweight to Arafat. AIPAC was not pleased: I had to contend with a Raleigh press report of the critical comments of their local representative, but the responses I received to the story were more favorable than not.[21]

Our December 2002 visit to Israel came in the midst of a crisis of another sort. Through members of my church, I knew of the work of the Hope Flowers School in Bethlehem, a school for children aged 5–14 that integrates principles of peace, democracy, and human rights into its curriculum. As access to the school was restricted in the wake of the Second Intifada, the settlement of Efrat encroached over a nearby hill, and Israel's separation fence was constructed nearby, I visited the school several times and worked through our Jerusalem consulate to avert various crises. But the 2002 threat was different: the school's headmaster had been arrested by the Israeli government on charges of harboring terrorists in his home (of which he was later cleared), and his home had been ordered to be demolished. As it happened, the demolition was occurring precisely on the day that our delegation was visiting with Prime Minister Ariel Sharon. We had notified Sharon's office that I would be raising the issue, and he assured me that due process would be followed. As we were leaving, however, I overheard one of our embassy personnel whisper to one of Sharon's aides, "You'd better be careful on this one." I later learned that the demolition had been halted at about the time of our meeting! It was a fortunate outcome for Hope Flowers, but hardly reassuring as to how such matters were ordinarily handled.

The December trip ended with a terrible personal blow, the death of Wayne Owens. After seven intense days of travel, Owens saw Jim Davis and me off at the Tel Aviv Airport. By the time we arrived at home, word was waiting that he had suffered a fatal heart attack while walking on the beach. Our shock and sorrow were acute, and the passing of this gifted, determined peacemaker left a tremendous gap to fill for the Center and those of us who collaborated with him.[22]

Owens's death brought the Center's member trips to the region to an end. By then, I was regularly involved in efforts to spur proactive engagement in Middle East peacemaking by the Bush, and later Obama, administrations and to build House support for such initiatives as the Bush administration's on-again, off-again "Road Map" plan. The Road Map was formulated in 2002 by the State Department, in concert with the "Quartet" partners: the United Nations, the European Union, and Russia. It envisioned reciprocal Israeli and Palestinian steps to end terror and violence, normalize Palestinian life and reform Palestinian institutions, freeze Israeli settlement building, and eventually undertake negotiations to produce an independent Palestinian state. But the administration delayed the introduction of the plan until after the onset of the Iraq war and temporized in pushing it thereafter. Those of us promoting the initiative in Congress faced a difficult environment, foreshadowing battles to come.

Majority Leader Tom DeLay was particularly unhelpful, speaking scornfully of the "Quartet of Appeasement" and muddling President Bush's message in a hard-line August 2003 speech to the Israeli Knesset.[23] It became increasingly clear that Republican leaders hoped to drive a wedge among Jewish voters, wooing them from their Democratic allegiance and forging an alliance with conservative Jews and fundamentalist Christians as the true supporters of Israel. This dynamic put Democrats under considerable pressure to endorse restrictive interpretations of the Road Map, encouraged by AIPAC, stipulating that no Israeli moves would be required before strict conditions were met on the Palestinian side.

A vast majority of House members signed a letter expressing this view, circulated by Chairman Henry Hyde (R-Illinois) and Ranking Member Tom Lantos (D-California) of the International Relations Committee in 2003. But I was convinced that many House members, especially Democrats, took a more balanced view toward Israeli and Palestinian responsibilities for fulfilling the Road Map conditions. I thus joined with Darrell Issa

(R-California) and Lois Capps (D-California) in organizing an alternative letter. Within three days we obtained forty-four names, including many who had also signed the Hyde-Lantos letter. We were encouraged when a group of prominent Jewish leaders, headed by Edgar Bronfman of the World Jewish Congress, sent an open letter to House and Senate leaders expressing similar sentiments—arguing that the Road Map could help Israel "escape the bloody status quo" and decrying the attempts of others to "sidetrack implementation."[24] The experience taught me that the failure of many House members to express a more balanced view of Middle East affairs was more attributable to the lack of an available alternative formulation than to a firm commitment to the Hyde-Lantos-AIPAC point of view.

Despite our efforts, as well as broad international support for the initiative, the Road Map proved fragile, and the administration's persistence did not outlast the predictable attempts at sabotage by terrorist groups and the resumption of the cycle of violence. On June 25, the House passed a resolution (H.Res. 294) that decried horrific acts of violence but managed in its ten "resolved" clauses to avoid any mention of the Road Map effort! The resolution condemned "the recent terrorist actions" and expressed "solidarity with the Israeli people." I voted for it, along with 398 other members, for I felt those sentiments as strongly as anyone; it had been barely a year since my visit to the site of a terrible Passover bomb attack in Netanya. But I found it baffling and regrettable that the resolution expressed no support for our country's major peacemaking initiative, and I said so on the House floor:

> We must condemn terrorism without qualification, and that is consistent with promoting the simultaneous accommodations by both sides which the Road Map envisions. We must affirm Israel's right to defend itself, but that is consistent with urging on Israel tactics and timing that do not undermine the Road Map initiative, as our President and our Secretary of State have recently articulated.[25]

This experience, like the Hyde-Lantos letter, underscored the dilemma members like myself faced. "I'm either going to vote for it and have to explain myself or vote against it and have to explain myself," I often said in frustration. But the way to escape the dilemma was to go on the offensive, to realize the power of doing the first draft and of seizing the initiative.

One such effort intersected with the House Democracy Partnership's efforts to strengthen the Lebanese parliament in the wake of the assassination of former Prime Minister Rafic Hariri and the ensuing Cedar Revolution. Along with Rep. Jim Leach (R-Iowa) and two others, I organized a 2006 letter urging the Bush administration to seek a cease-fire and otherwise to ensure that Israeli attempts to destroy Hezbollah did not at the same time disable the legitimate Lebanese government.[26]

Another 2006 effort illustrated the progress we were making but also how far we had to go. The "Palestinian Anti-Terrorism Act" (HR 4681) was sponsored by 294 House members, including the bipartisan leadership of the chamber and of the International Relations Committee. It expressed the consensus view that U.S. aid should not go to the Palestinian Authority (PA), over which Hamas had recently won control in the Palestinian legislative elections. But HR 4681 went farther, banning aid to non-governmental groups (e.g., the Hope Flowers School) doing educational and other humanitarian work in the West Bank and Gaza and denying visas for all PA and PLO members, including those with no connection, or opposed, to Hamas. "Isolating the Palestinian people and the NGOs working on the ground for peace will weaken Israel's security, damage our interests, and punish the wrong people," I declared in a "Dear Colleague" letter co-signed by Lois Capps (D-California), Ray LaHood (R-Illinois), and Earl Blumenauer (D-Oregon).

We also mounted a serious floor debate, led by Blumenauer. This seemed to surprise the bill's proponents, who were accustomed to members marching in lockstep on such occasions. The administration declared the bill "unnecessary" but did not actively oppose it. In the end, persuading thirty-seven members to vote "no" and nine more to vote "present" felt like real progress. We had made a telling argument and received expressions of gratitude and support from many more colleagues than were able to vote with us. Moreover, the Senate took note and fixed both the aid and visa provisions, producing a resolution I and my colleagues could support when it came back to the House.[27]

A noteworthy feature of the Palestinian aid debate was the increased prominence of pro-Israel organizations willing to counter AIPAC. One of these, Brit Tzedek v'Shalom (Jewish Alliance for Justice and Peace), had begun grass-roots organizing in Jewish communities around the country, including my district. In 2007, their work was picked up and carried forward by a new organization, J Street, which has since been a key ally and resource for members like myself who believe that "a two-state solution serves Israel's and America's interests and fulfills the legitimate national aspirations of the Jewish and Palestinian peoples."[28] Under the leadership of Jeremy Ben-Ami, the organization has grown steadily in support and influence. In the House this has not meant persuading members to alter their views as much as giving voice and legitimacy (and sometimes political cover) for views that members already held but were reluctant—or lacked opportunities—to express. In any event, the situation in the Democratic Caucus today is far different than it was in 2006, when we struggled to get thirty-seven "no" votes against a manifestly one-sided resolution opposing Palestinian aid. Positions on Middle East policy developed within the caucus are more balanced now, and there is a far greater willingness to question both AIPAC and right-wing Israeli governments.

Give Negotiations a Chance

As the Obama administration's efforts to engage diplomatically with Iran accelerated and ran into many of the same obstacles as the Road Map and other Israeli-Palestinian initiatives, I and several like-minded members turned our attention to building House support for a nuclear agreement. The HR 4681 playbook was largely replicated in 2012, as 278 House members, including the bipartisan leadership of the chamber and of the (renamed) Foreign Affairs Committee, cosponsored HR 4133, a wide-ranging measure to increase U.S.-Israeli military cooperation. The bill passed overwhelmingly, as did a related resolution (H.Res. 568) declaring the utter unacceptability of a "nuclear weapons-capable" Iran.

My floor statement on HR 4133 had a familiar ring: I would vote for the bill, but "with serious reservations about both [its] timing and its content ..."

> [The bill] gives little weight or emphasis to critical diplomatic and economic measures and at points comes perilously close to signaling intent or support for the military option. In fact, the timing of this legislation risks being taken as a vote of 'no-confidence' in our ongoing efforts [e.g., the upcoming resumption of talks between the 'P5 + 1' negotiating partners and Iran in Baghdad] to engage diplomatically with Iran.[29]

This time, however, I devised a counter-move. Within days, my HDP partner David Dreier (R-California) and I released a bipartisan letter to the president with seventy-one signatures (including twenty-one HR 4133 cosponsors) signaling congressional support for the diplomatic track. We welcomed the Baghdad talks, noted the "lengthened roster" of P5 + 1 partners (the five U.N. Security Council members plus Germany), and urged "continued diplomatic engagement."

The second of what became a series of Iran-related letters—this one coauthored with Rep. Charlie Dent (R-Pennsylvania) on July 17, 2013—helped head off congressional action that would have further downplayed and undermined diplomacy. Throughout early 2013 momentum was building for legislation that would impose additional crippling sanctions on Iran and stipulate in advance the contours of an acceptable final agreement. I watched with dismay as a sanctions bill moved toward passage in the House but detected a growing concern among colleagues that such actions, if unchecked, could do grave damage to the negotiations.[30]

Then, on June 14, Iran elected Hassan Rouhani, a former nuclear negotiator who had promised "constructive interaction with the outside world," as president. Dent and I seized the occasion to circulate a letter to President Obama to "test whether Dr. Rouhani's election represents a real opportunity for progress towards a verifiable, enforceable agreement." While acknowledging the uncertainty of the situation and the "mixed signals"

Rouhani himself had sent, we urged the utilization of "all diplomatic tools," including the careful calibration of sanctions to "induce significant and verifiable concessions from Iran ... in exchange for [the sanctions'] potential relaxation." We obtained 131 signatures, including eighteen Republicans, far more than we had anticipated.

Careful calibration was hardly what the authors of the anti-Iran resolutions had in mind. Israel's Prime Minister Benjamin Netanyahu denounced Rouhani at the United Nations as a "wolf in sheep's clothing" as he called for more and tighter sanctions.[31] AIPAC uncritically mirrored this view, but a number of the members who had earlier signed onto anti-Iran resolutions and letters also signed the Dent-Price letter. Minority Leader Nancy Pelosi reportedly cited that fact in resisting AIPAC's urging that another resolution be brought forward in December despite Iran's having just agreed to the interim Joint Plan of Action in Geneva. Subsequent efforts in the Senate also faltered, resulting in a "painful defeat" for AIPAC and a crucial victory for the Obama administration as talks on the final agreement began.[32]

Over the course of 2013, the administration had greatly intensified its efforts to secure congressional support for the negotiations. I helped lead an informal "Gang of Eight" House members—which could expand as needed for specific efforts—dedicated to promoting, and then protecting, the nascent agreement. We met regularly with White House aides, exploring ways to build support or head off threats. Emboldened by our success in turning back efforts that could have torpedoed the talks, Lloyd Doggett (D-Texas) and I next circulated a letter that unequivocally welcomed the Geneva agreement and opposed any "bill or resolution that risks fracturing our international coalitions or, worse yet, undermining our credibility in future negotiations and jeopardizing hard-won progress toward a verifiable final agreement."

"Give diplomacy a chance," we declared—"the first public statement from House [Democrats] en masse against [any new sanctions] measure and for diplomacy."[33] Doggett and I sent our letter to the president on February 12, 2014, with 104 signatures (including four Republicans), more than twice as many as we had thought we could obtain. We succeeded in shoring up those numbers on the Democratic side throughout 2014 as the negotiations lurched from deadline to deadline. But opposition hardened among Republicans, culminating in Speaker John Boehner's unprecedented invitation, without notifying the president or congressional Democrats, to Prime Minister Netanyahu to address a joint session of Congress on March 3, 2015, weeks before Israel's parliamentary elections were to be held.

Netanyahu's speech was full of unsubstantiated dire predictions—"The deal won't be a farewell to arms. It would be a farewell to arms control. And the Middle East would soon be crisscrossed by nuclear tripwires"— and his stunning show of disrespect likely shored up Democratic support of the president.[34] I listened to the speech in my office, joining fifty House Democrats who refused to recognize the legitimacy of the occasion in the

House chamber. Our Gang of Eight called a press conference after the speech, at which I explained my position further:

> Speaker Boehner should never have extended this invitation at this time, given the proximity of the speech to Israel's national elections and the fact that delicate international negotiations, which the Prime Minister wishes to upend, are hanging in the balance. And Prime Minister Netanyahu should never have accepted the invitation, which was extended without the usual consultation of bipartisan leadership or the normal notification and consultation with the president.... The invitation and speech set a dangerous precedent, whereby congressional leaders from one party can invite a foreign politician to publicly oppose the politics of the sitting president on the House floor. In doing so, we not only tarnish the grand tradition of the joint session; we also run the risk of politicizing diplomatic relationships—in this case, a very special one dedicated to Israel's security and prosperity.

Negotiations culminated in the announcement of a "framework" agreement, containing the basic elements of a final deal, in Lausanne on April 2, 2015. This brought to a head legislative efforts by critics of the negotiations to require congressional review of whatever agreement was finally reached and to provide a mechanism for disapproval. It also set the terms of my fourth letter and our Gang of Eight's most important effort: we had to secure 145 names—enough to ensure that, in the event a resolution of disapproval were passed, we would have enough votes to sustain President Obama's veto.

On May 7, 2015, Doggett, Jan Schakowsky (D-Illinois) and I sent a letter to the president with 152 signatures (all Democrats) commending the negotiating team for "significant progress" and urging the administration to "stay on course," turning the "framework" into a "long-term verifiable agreement." This went considerably beyond our earlier efforts in terms of our coordination with the White House—including the president himself—and the active involvement of Minority Leader Nancy Pelosi, who was essential in securing the last 20–30 names. Nor was our work over once the letter was sent. We formed a whip team over the summer, frequently checking on our colleagues, making certain there was no slippage right up until the final vote.[35]

Our numbers held firm: when the final vote on the resolution disapproving the Joint Comprehensive Plan of Action (JCPOA) came to the House on September 11, we lost only twenty-five Democratic members. In the meantime, Senate Democrats mustered forty-two votes to prevent the resolution from coming to the floor, so our ability to sustain a presidential veto was never put directly to the test.

The JCPOA focused almost exclusively on Iran's nuclear capacity, leaving the country's ballistic missile development, support of terrorism, violations of human rights, and other malign activity subject to continuing sanctions and future diplomatic efforts. I traveled to New York on two occasions (October 2, 2015 and September 23, 2016) for meetings organized by Senator Dianne Feinstein (D-California) with Iran's Foreign Minister, Javad Zarif, to explore possible areas of further cooperation—ranging from prisoner exchanges and aircraft sales to finding a basis for common action in Syria. A significant prisoner exchange involving four Americans held in Iran was executed in early 2016, but additional movement on ancillary issues was difficult to come by. The situation was complicated by a steady stream of Republican proposals on the House floor and then the advent of the Trump administration—which called U.S. fidelity to the agreement itself into question.

As the end of President Obama's term approached, Secretary of State John Kerry and the administration renewed their focus on two-state diplomacy. Prospects for a resumption of direct negotiations were bleak, but it was important to address situations on the ground and the positioning of relevant parties so as not to foreclose agreement in the future. Kerry thought, and I agreed, that a key element was for the United States to "set about drafting final status principles—international accepted terms of reference for direct negotiations."[36] On April 18, 2016, John Yarmuth (D-Kentucky) and I introduced a supportive resolution (H.Res. 686) encouraging the United States, as a way of creating "progress toward a negotiated two-state solution," to articulate "a non-binding vision of what a comprehensive final status agreement might entail."

Such language made AIPAC and its congressional supporters nervous. Their mantra was that a "durable and sustainable peace agreement" would "come only through direct bilateral negotiations between the parties."[37] While this was mainly meant to counter Palestinian efforts to gain United Nations or other international recognition, it was also intended to discourage administration proposals that might push the Israelis too far beyond their comfort zone. What Yarmuth and I were advocating, one colleague charged, would interject the United States into "sensitive and difficult issues" and risk "seriously setting back negotiations."[38] In reality, there were no negotiations underway and thus no risk of setting them back, and there were both ample precedents for offering final-status parameters and evidence they could be helpful. We obtained sixty-three sponsors for our resolution and helped vocalize congressional support for what Kerry had set out to do.

In the administration's final days, on December 23, 2016, it elected not to veto a United Nations resolution favored by the other fourteen Security Council members that called for a halt to Israeli settlement activity in the West Bank and East Jerusalem. This was consistent, as U.N. Ambassador Samantha Power stated, with "the United States' long-standing position that Israeli settlement activity ... harms the viability of a negotiated two-state outcome and erodes prospects for peace and stability in the region."[39]

But it broke a long-standing pattern of vetoing resolutions that were critical of Israel and provoked a predictable firestorm—and legislative overreach—in Congress.

The resolution (H.Res. 11) the Republican leadership brought to the floor on the third day of the new Congress provoked another firestorm, however—this time in the Democratic Caucus. Rep. Eliot Engel (D-New York), ranking member of the Foreign Affairs Committee and usually a reliable AIPAC ally, faced intense criticism for his cosponsorship of H.Res. 11, a resolution that was intemperate and inaccurate in its condemnation of the Obama administration's actions at the U.N. I and others from our Gang of Eight quickly amassed over 100 signatures, including Engel's, on our alternative resolution (H.Res. 23), which reaffirmed support for a two-state solution and advocated U.S. opposition to "one-sided and anti-Israel" resolutions at the U.N. without specifying whether the December 23 resolution fit that definition. Engel ceded to me most of the debate time on H. Res. 11 that he would have controlled, which we used to expose the resolution as "reckless and divisive ... designed solely to embarrass the outgoing administration."[40] Republicans denied us a vote on H.Res. 23, but we mustered eighty votes against H. Res. 11 (76 D–4 R) and mounted a debate that, as J Street noted in its newsletter, indicated "important changes in the political atmosphere on issues related to Israel in the Congress."

Donald Trump and his administration did grave and possibly fatal damage to both two-state diplomacy and the Iran nuclear agreement. We Democrats generally overcame past differences and united in opposition to policies that often lay outside the parameters of past debate. An early example was a letter Rep. Gerry Connolly (D-Virginia) and I formulated in the wake of the H.Res. 23 debate to "reaffirm the United States' long-standing, bipartisan commitment to supporting a just and lasting two-state solution to the Israeli-Palestinian conflict." Trump and Netanyahu had just held a press conference in which Trump had said he could "live with" either a one-state or two-state outcome—whatever the two parties "like the best." He had also just nominated David Friedman, a longtime supporter of the settler movement who was notorious for likening J Street to Jews who cooperated with Nazis during the Holocaust, as ambassador to Israel.[41] Connolly and I sent our letter affirming the two-state position to the president on March 24, 2017, with 191 signatures—virtually the entire Democratic Caucus but only two Republicans.

Similarly, Ted Deutsch (D-Florida) and I gathered support from 180 Democratic members, representing both sides of the vote on the Iran agreement, for an October 4, 2017, letter asking the president (accurately) to certify Iran's compliance with the JCPOA and to keep the United States in the agreement. This and other importunings largely fell on deaf ears, however. On May 8, 2018, a day I was inclined to see as the worst of the Trump administration, the president announced U.S. withdrawal from the Iran agreement. The administration subsequently undertook a "maximum pressure" campaign designed to cut off oil exports and otherwise squeeze the Iranian economy to the breaking point, which the European parties to the JCPOA attempted to counter with only limited success. But the pressure did not bring Iran back to the table to negotiate a "better deal," Trump's declared intent. Indeed, the administration had no diplomatic strategy—or demonstrated capacity—for achieving that result.

Instead, the situation continued to deteriorate, culminating in actions— a U.S. drone strike on January 3, 2020, that killed Major General Qasem Soleimani, commander of Iran's elite Quds Force, and retaliatory Iranian strikes on U.S. bases in Iraq that resulted in traumatic brain injuries for at least 100 service members and could easily have killed them—that brought the United States and Iran to the brink of war. For a time the Iranians, working with the Europeans, continued to adhere to the terms of the JCPOA. But in mid-2019, as the United States discontinued waivers that had permitted other countries to purchase Iranian oil, and again after the Soleimani assassination, Iran announced steps to reduce its compliance. The International Atomic Energy Agency continued its monitoring activities in Iran, however, and the possibility remained that, if the sanctions were pulled back, Iranian compliance could be restored.

There was little hope the Trump administration could or would take the necessary steps, although the situation was clearly far worse, with respect to both the prospect of a nuclear Iran and Iran's role in the region, than before Trump scuttled the agreement. The best hope was to wait out the November election, but even then, the prospects of putting the pieces of a viable agreement back in place would be daunting. I expressed the aspiration in a resolution I introduced with Barbara Lee and Jan Schakowsky favoring restoration of, and U.S. reentry into, the JCPOA. In the meantime, with the cosponsorship of the Gang of Eight, I was able to add an amendment to the 2020 defense authorization bill requiring the administration to report on the status of military-to-military and diplomatic "deconfliction" channels with Iran, designed to reduce the dangers of miscalculation and escalated conflict.[42]

Repeated blows to two-state diplomacy continued, ironically, as the administration prepared what Trump promised would be "the deal of the century" to resolve the Israeli-Palestinian conflict. "The administration has effectively abandoned dialogue with the Palestinian leadership and marginalized Palestinian concerns, embracing instead the agenda of the Israeli right," noted veteran diplomat William Burns. "In 3 1/2 decades of government service, I never saw an American president concede so much, so soon, for so little."[43]

"How is this supposed to work?" I asked Secretary of State Pompeo when he testified before our SFOPS subcommittee in early 2019:

> Outside the framework of any negotiations … this administration has made a series of [unilateral] moves. One: you moved the US embassy

from Tel Aviv to Jerusalem unilaterally, apart from the kind of broader agreement previous administrations have sought. Two, you closed the [de facto] Palestinian embassy in Washington, DC. Third, you shut down the US Consulate in Jerusalem ... the main interlocutor for communicating with the Palestinians. Four, you cut off all U.S. contributions to UNRWA [the United Nations Relief and Works Agency for Palestinian Refugees], closing schools in Gaza and exacerbating the severe humanitarian crisis there. Five, you cut off all assistance to the West Bank ... for things like food security, education for children with autism [a Hope Flowers School Program]....

So you're satisfied that this administration has reached out effectively to the Palestinians and has ensured them of your good faith ... and that the Palestinian reaction to this is somehow off-base?

"I hope they will view us as a fair arbiter." Pompeo said. But he attempted little defense beyond asserting: "What went before didn't work."[44]

The administration subsequently granted the Israeli right and Netanyahu additional items from their wish list: recognition of the Golan Heights, annexed in 1981, as Israeli territory, and a public rejection by Pompeo of the long-standing U.S. view that Israeli settlement activity in the West Bank was "inconsistent" with international law. Throughout the year, Netanyahu became increasingly explicit, in the context of Israel's protracted parliamentary elections, regarding his intention to annex the Jordan Valley and Jewish settlements on the West Bank. Every indication was that the Trump administration was prepared to bless such a move.

All of this added to apprehensions among Democrats as to what the Trump plan was likely to contain and the declining prospects of two-state diplomacy. We felt the need to take advantage of our House majority to affirm that at least one branch of the U.S. government and one of the country's major political parties were standing by the principles that had guided U.S. diplomacy since Oslo. Our legislative vehicle was a resolution, introduced by Rep. Alan Lowenthal (D-CA) and backed strongly by J Street, which affirmed congressional support for a negotiated two-state solution to the Israeli-Palestinian conflict and "discouraged" steps by either side that could put such a solution out of reach, including the unilateral annexation of territory.

Arduous negotiations within and beyond the Foreign Affairs Committee were required to gain consensus among Democrats as to both the content of the resolution and when to bring it to the House floor. AIPAC-oriented members not only objected to Lowenthal's wording—using the word "occupation," for example, to describe Israel's control of the West Bank—but also had trouble deciding when or if there was a "right time" to bring the resolution forward, given the twists and turns of Netanyahu's pronouncements and the ongoing Israeli elections (AIPAC declared its neutrality on the resolution, while hardly masking its lack of enthusiasm). I and others work-ing with Lowenthal grew impatient with the temporizing. We had originally wanted our resolution considered in tandem with a resolution expressing opposition to the Boycott, Divestment, and Sanctions (BDS) movement against Israel in July.[45] The Israeli elections, we felt, made it more rather than less important for us to make our position clear, as did the imminent release of the Trump plan. And we had some political wind at our back, reflecting the altered Middle East posture of the Democratic Caucus; some 200 members were cosponsoring the resolution, and most had supported the earlier, stronger version as well.

It was nonetheless important to take time to forge a unified Democratic position, which we did with the help of a couple of sweeteners: a reaffirma-tion of the 2016 Memorandum of Understanding pledging U.S. support for Israel's security needs, and a call for the resumption of U.S. aid to the West Bank and Gaza. The resolution, H. Res. 326, passed 226–188 on December 6, 2019, with every Democrat on board (except four from the party's left) and five Republicans. Noting that Congress had never before officially expressed its opposition to annexation, *Haaretz* described the resolution as a "watershed event."

> An overwhelming majority of the Democratic contingent in the House … including strong Israel supporters who had hitherto refrained from voicing any criticism whatsoever, highlighted the growing gap between the party and not only Netanyahu, but also Israel's right wing as a whole.[46]

Trump's plan, which he announced on January 28, 2020, with Netanyahu at his side, fully lived up to its negative billing. "The major problems with the president's plan," observed former U.S. Ambassador to Israel Daniel Shapiro, "result from having talked to only one side in the conflict—Israel."[47] The plan permitted Israel to annex the Jordan Valley and all Israeli settlements, while leaving the Palestinians disconnected enclaves that would not be viable as an independent state. It laid out governance capabilities that the Palestinians must meet in order to qualify for "statehood," but gave the Israelis the right to determine if those criteria had been satisfied. And so forth. The plan contrasted sharply with the terms of H. Res. 326, aban-doning "three decades of American diplomacy" aimed at two interdepend-ent goals: "self-determination for Palestinians and an Israel that is secure, democratic, and a homeland for the Jewish people."[48]

The Trump administration, despite Pompeo's claims, never seriously attempted to "arbitrate" the conflict. Trump also abandoned, Thomas Friedman noted, the role of "reality enforcer" played by previous presidents, which had helped both sides rein in their extremists. "Instead," Friedman argued, "Trump is pursuing a policy of steadily weakening the Palestinian Authority that governs the West Bank, while steadily lifting any restraints

on Israel's creeping annexation of the West Bank." Friedman termed this
the "existential threat" America poses to the Jewish state: "loving Israel to
death."

> By indulging ... Netanyahu in his quest for permanent Israeli control
> over the West Bank, Trump, the Congress, and the Israel lobby are
> going to create a situation whereby the Palestinian Authority ... will
> eventually collapse. The Palestinians thus will then say to Israel ...
> that they want Israeli citizenship. Israel will then find itself ruling over
> 2.5 million Palestinians with the choice of either sharing power with
> them on the basis of equality or systematically denying it to them....
> [This] will rip apart every ... Jewish institution in America, including
> AIPAC.... And [their] convention of 2022 will feature a panel it's never
> had before: "Who lost Israel?"[49]

Hyperbolic, perhaps, but not inconceivable. What does a preferable
strategy look like? The United States must again become both "arbiter" and
"reality enforcer," opposing settlement expansion and annexation schemes
on the Israeli side and rejectionism, terrorism, and incitement to violence
among Palestinians. We must resume two-state diplomacy. A buy-in by the
major Sunni states, the major missing element in the 2000 Camp David
effort, seems more likely now, but not without a more balanced solution
than the Trump administration has offered. The outlines of a viable settlement have not greatly changed—President Clinton's proposal at the Taba
Summit after Camp David came close, as did Secretary Kerry's final status
principles—however discouraging the situation on the ground might be.
The United States continues to have a huge stake in a fair and durable settlement and is the only country that conceivably has the ability to broker an
agreement and make it stick.

Members of Congress have a critical role to play in engaging a full
range of Middle Eastern leaders and constituencies and ensuring a robust
policy debate going forward. The initiatives that I and like-minded members undertook—often compensating for the inaction or even countering the positions of leaders of our own party—fostered, at least among
Democrats, a more balanced position on the Israeli–Palestinian conflict
and an appreciation of the diplomatic achievement the Iran nuclear agreement represented, along with a determination to protect it. Despite the
bitter disappointments of the Trump years, both efforts have left us in a
stronger position, under a Democratic president, for eventual progress. In
the meantime, as members of Congress we should not sell ourselves or our
country's interests short by disengaging or by engaging only reflexively,
signing letters or voting for resolutions when pressed to do so, taking the
path of least resistance. Short of presidential leadership, our diplomatic
capacities are limited, but members of Congress, even those without formal
leadership positions, have considerable ability to advocate and propose

and to encourage and support (or discourage and undermine) administration efforts. There is a pressing need, in our institution and in our country, for us individually and collectively to bring more energy and discernment to this task.

An "Article One" Moment

"This is an Article One moment," declared former Secretary of State Madeleine Albright in a conversation with our Democratic Policy Group on July 12, 2017, six months into the Trump administration. Her comment reflected both alarm at the direction being taken by the president in foreign affairs and a sense that the country's only recourse was for Congress to rise to the occasion, to assert itself in unaccustomed ways.[50]

The next three years gave me and others at the meeting many occasions to reflect on Albright's admonition. Sometimes it was literally a matter of protecting Congress's Article I prerogatives. Sometimes it was a matter of checking departures from the basic tenets that had governed American foreign policy and diplomacy—departures that became more extreme after National Security Advisor H.R. McMaster, Secretary of Defense James Mattis, and others who had sometimes exercised a restraining influence left government in 2018. By the time the House debated the Lowenthal two-state resolution in late 2019, I and others had come to see our efforts as far more than simply expressing policy differences; it was a matter of checking an errant executive branch:

> Mr. Speaker, this is an Article I moment. The president has sowed doubt about this country's historic commitment to two-state diplomacy.... It is extremely important for this Congress to assert itself as a coequal branch of government at a time when this historic commitment is being questioned and undermined.[51]

The U.S. Congress stands out among the world's legislatures for the extent of its constitutional powers. If the Constitution is designed to be a firewall against despotism and the abuse of power, then Article I, which defines the powers of the Senate and the House, is its keystone, keeping decisions over spending, taxation, and other major policies close to the people and out of the hands of any single ruler.

On matters of foreign policy, however, the picture is mixed. As presidential scholar Edward Corwin famously observed, the Constitution's "affirmative grants of power" set up an "invitation to struggle" between the branches for control of foreign policy.[52] In *The Federalist*, John Jay recognized the advantages the president would have in conducting foreign affairs—the unity of the office, its capacity for secrecy and "dispatch," and so forth—and Alexander Hamilton declared that "the direction of war" demanded "the exercise of power by a single hand."[53] Over time, the executive has come increasingly to dominate, not only in the conduct of war but in the projection of diplomatic and economic power as well.

And yet, at critical moments throughout our nation's history, Congress has asserted itself as an essential check on the President's foreign policy powers. Senate hearings on the Vietnam War played a decisive role in turning public opinion against the conflict and accelerating U.S. troop withdrawal. During Ronald Reagan's administration, Congress uncovered and reversed the President's policy of covert support for anti-leftist militias in Central America and delivered a bipartisan rebuke of his policy toward apartheid in South Africa. At other critical junctures, Congress led the way in reorganizing the Pentagon, achieving nuclear threat reduction in the former Soviet Union, and reforming the intelligence community. Generally, however, congressional oversight of foreign affairs has declined markedly since the 1990s, as has our capacity to pass State Department authorization bills.[54]

The Trump presidency represents, in its entirety, a "critical juncture" which has required not merely an assertion of congressional powers but the development of new legislative and oversight capabilities and of the political will to use them.

Within a few months of taking office, Donald Trump had pointedly questioned the principle of mutual self-defense that has formed the bedrock of our NATO alliance for six decades; expressed his disdain for the European Union and endorsed Great Britain's exit; withdrawn the United States from the most significant global climate agreement in history, which every other country in the world had signed or ratified; submitted a budget proposal to Congress that would have drastically cut diplomatic personnel, foreign assistance, and contributions to international organizations; and disparaged and marginalized the work of career diplomats and foreign policy experts, asserting that "I am the only one that matters" when it comes to America's international relations.[55]

As noted earlier in this chapter, Trump then unilaterally withdrew the United States from the Iran nuclear agreement and abandoned two-state diplomacy in the Middle East. He expressed and acted on an affinity for strongman dictators worldwide—deferring to Russia's Vladimir Putin to an inexplicable degree, for example; welcoming Viktor Orban, architect of democracy's demise in Hungary, to the Oval Office; and refusing to hold Saudi Arabia's Mohammed bin Salman accountable for his documented role in the murder of journalist Jamal Khashoggi. In the middle of the 2019 fiscal year, Trump abruptly cut off duly appropriated funds that were addressing the conditions driving migration in Central America and humanitarian and security needs in the West Bank and Gaza. He declared a national emergency in order to divert funds appropriated for other purposes to construct a wall on the Mexican border. He slapped tariffs on friend and foe alike, often with little connection to diplomatic processes, or even to clear objectives. The list could go on and on—it is long and alarming. Many of these actions flew in the face of the popular—and bipartisan—consensus regarding America's role in the world that had guided our foreign policy since the end of World War II. Far from "making America great again," they unsettled our allies, encouraged our adversaries, and undermined our moral authority. Many of the actions, in addition, flew in the face of congressional intent or took the president's discretionary powers to new and questionable lengths; they were far from merely routine policy disagreements.

Congress showed some signs of flexing its constitutional muscle, but with limited success. The House and Senate rejected President Trump's foreign affairs budgets nearly in their entirety in 2017 and subsequent years, restoring funding for functions ranging from global health to democracy promotion to diplomatic operations. Congress voted nearly unanimously in 2017 to limit the President's discretion to grant relief to Russia from sanctions related to their 2016 election interference, an injunction Trump objected to but honored. In 2019, however, Republicans successfully defended the administration's proposal to lift Ukraine-related sanctions on three Russian companies that had been imposed after Russia's military intervention in Ukraine in 2014 and beyond.

When Democrats assumed leadership in 2019, one of our first actions was to pass a bill (HR 676) affirming U.S. support of NATO and forbidding the use of funds for any actions related to possible withdrawal from the alliance. The bipartisan vote was 357–22, but the Senate never took up the bill. A few weeks later, both houses voted to end U.S. participation in Saudi Arabia's war in Yemen (S. J. Res. 7), but without enough Republican voters to override the President's veto. We tried again in early 2020 after the assassination of General Soleimani, passing a War Powers resolution (S. J. Res. 68) requiring congressional approval if military operations in Iran were to continue. As usual, the vote broke largely along party lines in the House. In the Senate, seven Republicans crossed over, enough to pass the resolution but not enough to provide the two-thirds majority that a veto override required.

As we have seen, Trump was inclined when he did not get his way through normal processes simply to declare a national emergency, an obvious threat to congressional prerogatives that was seldom effectively countered. After vetoing the resolution regarding U.S. military participation in Yemen, Trump doubled down on support for Saudi Arabia, invoking the emergency provisions of the Arms Export Control Act to proceed with arms sales without the prescribed period of congressional review. There was a considerable outcry, and both houses passed resolutions (S. J. Res. 36–38) to forbid the sales. But the override attempt nonetheless failed in the Senate.

Trump's extraordinary declaration of a national emergency in order to divert some $8 billion in appropriated funds to build his border wall also drew an immediate rebuke in the form of a resolution (H. J. Res. 46) to terminate the emergency declaration. In the Senate, the 59–41 vote for the resolution reached a high-water mark of twelve Republicans, but in the House only thirteen Republicans, not nearly enough, voted to override despite the clarity of the institutional challenge. We tried again in the Fall (S. J. Res. 54), focusing on the specific military projects that were being canceled or deferred, but with a similar result.

The president's withholding of appropriated military aid to Ukraine in mid-2019 was found by the Government Accountability Office (GAO) to violate the Nixon-era Impoundment Control Act. But of course his larger offense was to use the aid to pressure President Zelensky to do his political bidding, and the failure of impeachment in the Senate ended any possibility of holding the president accountable. Congress did not do much better in challenging the cutoffs of appropriated aid funds to the West Bank and Gaza and to the Triangle countries of Central America. We exercised vigorous oversight and wrote tightened directives in our funding bills for 2020, but the administration was defiant and the aid largely remained in suspension.

Trump's actions raised critical questions about the president's discretionary powers—often granted for good reasons historically but never subject to this kind of abuse. The case suddenly became much stronger for drawing boundaries around the president's ability to alter tariffs unilaterally, to withhold or divert appropriated funds, to fire independent Inspectors General throughout the government, or to unilaterally declare national emergencies that allowed him to act in disregard or defiance of congressional intent. These are serious questions of institutional powers and constitutional authority. While partisan considerations largely prevented their consideration during the Trump era, the day must come when measures like the Article One Act, drafted by House Budget Chair John Yarmuth (D-KY) in 2020, receive fair consideration. The proposal would tighten limits on the impoundment or reprogramming of appropriated funds, for example, and would strengthen Congress's role in the declaration of national emergencies and in the funding or defunding decisions made under such declarations.

It is also long overdue to determine that the Authorizations of the Use of Military Force (AUMFs) for Al Qaeda and Afghanistan (2001) and Iraq (2002) do not suffice for any and all military operations in the Middle East and beyond that administrations may wish to undertake. The Trump administration, in this instance extending the position of the Obama administration, rejected any limitations, going so far as to use the Iraq AUMF, the less expansive of the two, to justify its killing (on Iraqi soil, to be sure) of Iran's General Soleimani.[56] Members of Congress of varying persuasions have voiced support for terminating and replacing the 2001 AUMF, which has been used by three administrations to justify over forty military operations in some fourteen countries.[57] In a surprise development in 2017, we adopted an amendment to the defense appropriations bill in committee to end the 2001 AUMF within 240 days; the provision, authored by Rep. Barbara Lee, attracted diverse bipartisan support but was later dropped by order of the House leadership.

Admittedly, it is easier to get agreement on the proposition that Congress should claim its constitutional role in the instigation of armed conflict than it is to get agreement as to what renovated AUMFs should look like—how open-ended or how specific? limited in duration? subject to congressional approval or veto in specific applications? and so forth. But the failure of Congress to act or to counter the open-ended claims of successive administrations—together with difficulties in applying the War Powers Act or even knowing to which military actions it applies—have left the constitutional balance with respect to foreign and military affairs decisively tilted to the disadvantage of Congress.

Our Article One moment has also cast members of Congress in a more prominent role as interpreters of foreign policy and affirmers of basic American values and commitments. I described earlier how HDP visits took on this aspect after the 2016 election, particularly in Central and Eastern Europe where the American disposition toward NATO, the EU, and Russia were highly salient topics. The Munich Security Conference in early 2019 offered a bipartisan, bicameral group of over fifty legislators an opportunity, as one of them put it, "to show Europeans that there is another branch of government which strongly supports NATO and the trans-Atlantic alliance."[58] Similarly important were the decisions by the bipartisan congressional leadership to invite French President Emmanuel Macron and NATO Secretary General Jens Stoltenberg to address Joint Sessions on April 25, 2018, and April 3, 2019, respectively. Both addresses extolled multilateralism and the extraordinary success of the post-World War II transatlantic alliance.

Beyond the substance of foreign policy, Congress must address the hollowing out of our diplomatic capacity and the decline of the State Department. This requires adequate funding but also stepped-up oversight, scrutiny of administration nominees, and consultation with responsible officials once they are in place. The Trump administration was slow to fill many key positions and too often appointed unqualified loyalists to the senior positions that were filled. Trump's first Secretary of State, Rex Tillerson, undertook an internal reorganization that marginalized and demoralized top diplomats and other officials; this contributed to an exodus further fueled by disillusion with the president and his policies.

Secretary Mike Pompeo, who took office in mid-2018, at first was credited with filling senior positions and improving morale. It soon became clear, however, that he would not stand up to the president and was quite willing to be his "junior partner in undermining U.S. alliances and multilateralism."[59] The Department was consistently hampered by a White House that alternated between indifference and political meddling and by a president who often disregarded and disrespected official channels in favor of family members and other personal associates, made policy off the cuff and on Twitter, and was all too willing to bend foreign policy to his own personal and political ends.

In this admittedly difficult environment, Pompeo utterly failed to defend the Department and its personnel. He was aware of Trump's efforts to bypass diplomatic channels in order to get Ukraine to do his political bidding in 2019; he neither resisted the scheme nor defended Ambassador Marie Yovanovitch and others who had the fortitude to do so. The Department's Inspector General (IG) found in 2019 that numerous additional career staff had been subject to demotion and harassment by top political appointees based on their perceived political views or loyalties, and that Department leadership had failed to protect them.[60] This was the same IG, Steve Linick, who was fired by Trump at Pompeo's request in 2020, in the midst of his investigation of the contrived emergency declaration the president had used in 2019 to bypass congressional review of Saudi arms sales.

Stepped-up congressional engagement, as important as it is, can never fix all of this. There are many areas where Congress can never totally substitute for the executive branch, including the persistent and painstaking work of diplomacy. The "invitation to struggle" provided by our constitutional framers continues, and with it the inherent advantages of the executive in conducting foreign and defense policy. But the struggle has taken on a new urgency with the advent of a president who lacks the judgment, discernment, and integrity that the office requires, and with critical norms, policies, and institutions being laid waste. The challenge is profound with respect both to constitutional fidelity and to the core tenets of American foreign policy. Congress has not fully seized its Article I moment, but there can be no doubt that is exactly what it is.

Notes

1 See the final report of the Task Force: *Parliamentary Assistance Programs*, Congressional Research Service, Library of Congress, March 18, 1998. Cf. the assessment to two senior CRS specialists intimately involved in the project: William Robinson and Frances Miko, "Parliamentary Development Assistance in Central Europe and the Former Soviet Union: Some Lessons from Experience," in Lawrence D. Longley, ed., *Working Papers on Comparative Legislative Studies* (Appleton, WI: Research Committee of Legislative Specialists, International Political Science Association, 1994). Frost offers his account in Tom Davis, Martin Frost, and Richard Cohen, *The Partisan Divide: Congress in Crisis* (Campbell, CA: Premiere, 2014), pp. 227–230.

2 Rye Barcott, *It Happened on the Way to War: A Marine's Guide to Peace* (New York: Bloomsbury Publishing, 2011).

3 See the article Roskam and I wrote upon returning: "Political Reform Critical as Ukraine and Georgia Face Russian Offensive," *Roll Call*, August 4, 2015.

4 See the ten-year retrospective offered by IRI president Mark Green and NDI president Ken Wollack, "The House's Decade of Democracy Partnerships," *The Hill*, December 1, 2015.

5 See David Price, "Global Democracy Promotion: Seven Lessons for the New Administration," *The Washington Quarterly*, January 2009, pp. 159–170. Tommy Ross, my HDP aide at the time, did major work on this article.

6 Amanda Taub, "The Unsexy Truth about Why the Arab Spring Failed," *Vox*, January 27, 2016. See also Sarak Yerkes, "The Tunisia Model: Lessons from a New Arab Democracy," *Foreign Affairs*, October 2019.

7　Marian L. Lawson and Susan B. Epstein, "Democracy Promotion: An Objective of US Foreign Assistance," Congressional Research Service, Library of Congress, May 31, 2017, pp. 4–6; Daniela Huber, *Democracy Promotion and Foreign Policy* (New York: Palsgrave MacMillan, 2017), chap. 4; and Thomas Carothers, *Aiding Democracy Abroad: The Learning Curve* (Washington, DC: Carnegie Endowment for International Peace, 1999), chap. 2.

8　Dinorah Azpuru, Mitchell A. Seligson, Steven E. Finkel, and Anibal Perez-Linan, "Trends in Democracy Assistance: What Has the United States Been Doing?" *Journal of Democracy*, 19 (April 2008), pp. 150 ff. Funding totals are in 2000 dollars and include all appropriate USAID accounts but not direct appropriations for NED.

9　See Price, "Global Democracy Promotion," pp. 159–161.

10　Carothers, "Prospects for US Democracy Promotion under Trump," Carnegie Endowment for International Peace, January 5, 2017.

11　See John Lis and Gabrielle Plotkin, "Legislative Strengthening Evaluations and Their Implications for Future Programs," *USAID*, September 8, 2015.

12　Price, "Global Democracy Promotion," p. 168.

13　*Aiding Democracy Abroad*, p. 97. Cf. Carothers' later assessment of democracy assistance generally: "Democracy Aid at 25: Time to Choose," *Journal of Democracy*, January 2015.

14　John Hibbing and Samuel Patterson add a useful generic distinction between the U.S. Congress as a "transformative" institution that "consistently transforms proposals submitted by the executive" and most other parliaments as "arena-style" bodies where "executive proposals are debated but rarely modified." "The US Congress's Modest Influence on the Legislatures of Central and Eastern Europe," in Timothy Power and Nicol Rae, eds., *Exporting Congress?: The Influence of the US Congress on World Legislatures* (Pittsburgh, PA: University of Pittsburgh Press, 2006), p. 126.

15　See the case studies assembled and the causal factors identified in the symposium edited by Irina Khmelko, "The Decline of Legislative Powers and the Rise of Authoritarianism," *PS: Political Science and Politics*, 52 (April, 2019), pp. 267–280. Freedom House's 2019 estimate showed thirty-seven countries gaining and sixty-four losing ground. "Freedom in the World 2020: A Leaderless Struggle for Democracy," March 2020. Cf. Thomas Carothers and Richard Youngs, "Democracy Is Not Dying," *Foreign Affairs*, April 11, 2017.

16　"Freedom in the World 2020: Global Freedom Scores," March 2020.

17　Carothers, "Democracy Aid at 25."

18　After our early 2000 trip, for example, Rep. Robert Wexler (D-Florida) and I spearheaded a resolution of support for Kuwait's efforts to compel Iraq to account for prisoners taken during the Gulf War—H.Con.Res. 275, which passed the House on June 23, 2000—and helped persuade President Clinton to include an appreciative visit with Sultan Qaboos in Oman on the itinerary of his trip to India.

19　Madeleine Albright, *Madam Secretary* (New York: Miramax Books, 2003), p. 497. "I made a mistake in not accepting Clinton's deal," Arafat confided to John Kerry two years later. John Kerry, *Every Day Is Extra* (New York: Simon and Schuster, 2018), p. 453.

20　See the article I wrote after the January trip: "The Truth about Peace," *Middle East Insight*, March–April 2002, pp. 53–54.

21　See John Wagner, "Price Has Stern Words for Arafat; Meeting Questioned," *Raleigh News and Observer*, January 11, 2002, p. 15A.

22　David E. Price, "Owens' Commitment to Mideast Peace Should Inspire Others," *Roll Call*, January 29, 2003, p. 8.

23 Quoted in Jonathan Riehl, "Israel Supporters Warn Bush against Mideast Policy Shift," *Congressional Quarterly Weekly*, April 5, 2003, p. 832.

24 Letter from Edgar Bronfman, Larry Zicklin et al., dated April 29, 2003. On support and opposition among Jewish leadership, see M.J. Rosenberg, "A Firm 'Road Map,'" *Los Angeles Times*, April 6, 2003, p. M1; and Philip Weiss, "Big Jewish Leaders Tear the Road Map into Little Peaces," *New York Observer*, May 14, 2003, p. 1.

25 *Congressional Record*, daily ed., July 25, 2003, P. H5858.

26 See David E. Price, "U.S. Must Bolster Lebanon," *Atlanta Journal-Constitution*, August 8, 2006; and Price, "Lebanon for Lebanon's Sake," *Middle East Bulletin*, June 29, 2007.

27 See my remarks on the altered resolution, S. 2370: *Congressional Record*, December 7, 2006, p. H8914.

28 "Principles," *116th Congress Briefing Book*, J Street, 2018, p. 2.

29 *Congressional Record*, May 9, 2012, p. H2489.

30 The Nuclear Iran Prevention Act (HR 850), sponsored by Chairman Ed Royce and ranking member Eliot Engel of the Foreign Affairs Committee, passed the House on July 31, 2013. I was one of twenty members voting "no."

31 *CNN World*, October 2, 2013.

32 See the accounts in Connie Bruck, "Friends of Israel." *The New Yorker*, August 25, 2014, p. 60; and Mark Landler, "Potent Pro-Israel Group Finds Its Momentum Blunted," *New York Times*, February 3, 2014. On the outlook after adoption of the interim plan, see David E. Price, "Iran: An Opportunity We Must Pursue," *Charlotte Observer*, December 4, 2013.

33 Greg Sargent, "Another Big Blow to the Iran Sanctions Bill," *Washington Post*, February 3, 2014. See also Bruck, "Friends of Israel," p. 61.

34 See Secretary of State John Kerry's account: *Every Day Is Extra*, pp. 503–504. "The relationship between the two presidents never recovered," he notes. See also Peter Baker, "In Congress, Netanyahu Faults 'Bad Deal' on Iran Nuclear Program," *New York Times*, March 3, 2015; and Barak Ravid and Amir Ribon, "Netanyahu's Congress Speech Helped Iran Deal Gain Support, Democratic Congresswoman Says," *Haaretz*, October 24, 2017.

35 Greg Sargent, "The Odds of an Iran Nuclear Deal Just Got Better," *Washington Post*, May 7, 2015; Lauren French and John Bresnahan, "House Dems Whip Up Votes for Iran Deal," *Politico*, July 27, 2015, p. 1. See also David Price, Jan Schakowsky, and Lloyd Doggett, "Why We Will Vote for the Iran Deal," *Haaretz*, September 6, 2015.

36 Kerry, *Every Day is Extra*, p. 477. On the culmination of the process, a communique issued at an international conference in Paris in January 2017, see. p. 482.

37 H.Con.Res. 165, passed by the House on November 29, 2016. For my argument that such language should not "preclude the US from … offering a non-binding comprehensive framework to help bring the Israelis and Palestinians to the negotiating table," see *Congressional Record*, November 29, 2016, p. H6348.

38 "Dear Colleague" letter from Rep. Nita Lowey (D-New York), April 21, 2016. For an effective rebuttal, see Daniel Kurtzer, "A Case for the Yarmuth-Price Resolution," *The Hill*, April 27, 2016.

39 Text from *Haaretz*, December 24, 2016. On the context of the U.S. decision, see Kerry, *Every Day Is Extra*, pp. 480–482. At this point the settler population had surpassed 400,000, with 130 settlements and 101 illegal outposts. J Street, *Briefing Book*, p. 15.

40 See my floor statement, *Congressional Record*, January 5, 2017, p. H149.

41 Madeline Conway, "Trump Says He Can 'Live with' Either Two-State or One-State Solution for Israel," *Politico*, February 15, 2017; Matthew Rosenberg,

"Trump Chooses Hard-Liner as Ambassador to Israel," *New York Times*, December 15, 2016.

42 See H. Res. 495, 116th Congress, introduced on July 16, 2019; and H.R. 2500, passed on July 12, 2019.

43 William J. Burns, "The Doomed 'Deal of the Century,'" *Washington Post*, May 8, 2014, p. A21. See also Chris Van Hollen and Gerald Connolly, "Congress Cannot Afford to Ignore Netanyahu's Embrace of the Far Right," *Washington Post*, April 10, 2019.

44 "Fiscal Year 2020 Appropriations," *Hearing before the Subcommittee on State and Foreign Operations*, Committee on Appropriations, US House of Representatives, 116th Congress, March 27, 2019.

45 H. Res. 246, 116th Congress, passed the House on July 23, 2019, by a vote of 398–17.

46 Chemi Shalev, "House Resolution on Annexation Is a Wake-up Call for Israel and Netanyahu," *Haaretz*, December 7, 2019.

47 Daniel B. Shapiro, "Trump's Fundamentally-Flawed 'Vision' for Mideast Peace," *NPR*, January 30, 2020.

48 David Price, Andy Levin, Jan Schakowsky, Peter Welch, Alan Lowenthal, and Debra Halland, "A Disaster for Diplomacy and the Zionist Dream," *The Hill*, February 14, 2020. "We do not intend to abandon the position [expressed in H. Res. 326]," we declared, "and we anticipate that it may be reflected in the diplomatic posture of the next U.S. administration."

49 Friedman, "Loving Israel to Death," *New York Times*, March 25, 2019.

50 This section draws from a piece Albright and I later co-authored: "It's Time for Congress to Check Trump's Foreign Policy Powers," *CNN Opinion*, December 15, 2017.

51 *Congressional Record* (daily ed.), December 6, 2019, p. H9303.

52 Corwin, *The President: Office and Powers*, 4th ed. (New York: New York University Press, 1964), p. 171.

53 Numbers 64 and 74 in Clinton Rossiter, ed., *The Federalist Papers* (New York: Mentor, 1961).

54 Tommy Ross, "At a Crossroads, Part III: Reasserting Congress' Oversight Role in Foreign Policy," *War on the Rocks*, June 19, 2018; and Linda L. Fowler, "The Long Decline of Congressional Oversight," *Foreign Affairs*, November 15, 2018.

55 Jesse Byrnes, "Trump on Lack of Nominees: 'I Am the Only One That Matters,'" *The Hill*, November 2, 2017.

56 On my vote against the 2002 AUMF, and my work with Rep. John Spratt to develop a more limited alternative, see chapter 2 above and the third edition of this book, pp. 232–238.

57 Matthew Weed, "Presidential References to the 2001 Authorization of the Use of Military Force," Congressional Research Service, Library of Congress, February 16, 2018.

58 Sen. Jeanne Shaheen (D-New Hampshire), quoted in Steven Erlanger and Katrin Bennhold, "Rift between Trump and Europe Is Now Open and Angry," *New York Times*, February 17, 2019.

59 "Pompeo seems unwilling to apply any brakes on Trump's impulses and in fact seems willing to keep one foot on the accelerator—particularly when it comes to defending Trump's trade war with China and defending Saudi Arabia." Aaron David Miller and Richard Sokolsky, "Pompeo Might Go Down as the Worst Secretary of State in Modern Times," *CNN Opinion*, October 5, 2019.

60 Nahal Toosi, "State Department Watchdog Details Political Retaliation against 'Disloyal' Staffers," *Politico*, August 15, 2019.

9 Serving the District

This book has mainly focused on the aspects of my job that I share with 434 other members of the House of Representatives in Washington, D.C. I am only one of these strong-willed people trying to shape national policy outcomes. But as I often remind constituents in my community meetings, I am the *only* one of the 435 who is responsible for assisting individuals, organizations, and local governments in the Fourth District in their dealings with the federal government. The district-based aspects of the job are as important and demanding as the four days per week that I spend in Washington when the House is in session. Like most of my colleagues, I keep my main residence in the district and return there every weekend and every recess. I spend almost as many workdays there as in Washington, in and around the two district offices where almost half of my staff is based. And even in Washington, much of what my staff and I do is district centered, especially on Appropriations, but also in dealing with the policy concerns of local groups and correspondents.

Most successful members of Congress avoid tilting too far in either direction—"going Washington" and neglecting the home front, or "going local" and failing to find a serious policy role. In 2019, Alexandria Ocasio-Cortez (D-New York), a new member who had become a national sensation by defeating the Democratic Caucus chairman in a primary and attracting a massive social media following, polled her Instagram followers: "Would you rather have a Congress member with an amazing local services office, or one that leads nationally on issues?" Ocasio-Cortez's respondents apparently chose the national policy role, the *New York Times* reported, while noting that she was the only one of five new members from the state who had yet to open a local office three weeks after being sworn in.[1]

I would not have advised posing the question: in most districts, and probably in that one (where the previous member had handled 374 individual cases the year before), constituents do not expect to choose between national policymaking and local service. The roles do contrast, but representatives are expected to master both.

Keeping in Touch

Much of my time in North Carolina is spent traveling the district and maintaining an extensive schedule of public appearances. These include town meetings, some community-wide and others in workplaces or retirement community settings; civic club and chamber of commerce meetings; school and college classes and assemblies; visits to churches, synagogues, and temples; after-school programs and senior center gatherings; and tours of health centers, manufacturing plants, and research facilities. I often participate in ceremonial or holiday events—Veterans and Memorial Day services, Christmas and July 4th parades, the Indian community's Diwali celebrations, and Chinese New Year festivals (see Figure 9.1). One of the

Figure 9.1 Neighborhood July 4th parade in Durham.

Photo courtesy of Congressman Sam Farr.

pleasures of the job is to participate in groundbreakings and dedications of new or expanded businesses and laboratories, educational and health facilities, houses of worship, highways and train stations, and affordable housing developments. Especially with regard to transportation and housing dedications, I always say that, while we rightly celebrate the present accomplishment, our main goal should be to provide a reason for many more such occasions.

My community-wide town meetings are come one, come all affairs. We announce the sessions in the press and social media and often inform individual constituents through e-mail or otherwise. I then hold an open meeting on the date announced, giving a brief report on congressional activities and taking any and all questions from the floor. I also make staff available to assist attendees who may need casework attention. The meetings are normally scheduled in the early evening in a school, town hall, or county courthouse, and they generally draw 100–400 people, depending on what issues are hot at the moment. The openness of the meetings lets diverse groups of constituents attend and express themselves freely. The format also can be abused by those who wish to disrupt or by political opponents who wish to stage confrontations with their tape recorders or video cameras running.

As noted in Chapter 2, the tenor of my town meetings has been a remarkably reliable indicator of brewing political storms. As the turbulence increased in 1993–1994, we experimented with altering the format to give the meeting more focus on specific topics. Our success was quite limited. One evening, for example, I decided to start the meeting with presentations from a local textile plant manager and the dean of the College of Textiles at NC State University concerning the impact of federally funded research, which I had championed, on plant operations and job creation. But after my guests' articulate and appreciative presentations, the meeting erupted into the usual flood of congress-bashing questions and comments, channeling talk radio. The textile dean gamely sat through the entire two-hour ordeal, assuring me afterward that he would "never complain about a faculty meeting again!"

By the time the second such surge occurred, in 2009–2010, we were able to achieve a somewhat better result. The early 2009 meetings, soon after President Obama's election, could be brutal. But my staff and I never felt free to discontinue them, as much as they worried us. We did, however, alter the mix of community-wide meetings and those hosted by businesses and community organizations, which had the advantages of reaching people who would not likely come to a community-wide meeting and of avoiding domination by the extreme groups and individuals that sought out such meetings. We also were able to achieve better balance at the community-wide meetings. By the time of our largest ever such meeting—800 people coming onto the NC Central University campus during the 2009 August recess, at the height of the Affordable Care Act (ACA) debate—we were able to attract more proponents than opponents. We set up two microphones, lining up those for and against the ACA to alternate in speaking. The result was an orderly meeting, with advocates receiving greater audience support than detractors. This ensured our absence from national media, which had featured raucous town meetings throughout the month. This was confirmed by a national network stringer who informed me of his presence and then added: "Don't worry. Your meeting won't get covered unless it blows up."

The tables turned again in 2017–2018: it was impossible to exhaust the demand for town meetings. We scheduled ten community-wide meetings across the district and added four explicitly political gatherings under campaign sponsorship, normally attracting a younger crowd to a coffeehouse or brewery after hours. These meetings were the mirror image of those I experienced after the 1992 and 2008 elections, and they portended a similar political reaction. We had overflow crowds, overwhelmingly anti-Trump. The issues raised ranged widely, but we could usually anticipate personal accounts of what the Affordable Care Act had meant for at least one speaker and his/her family and of how devastating it would be to remove the protection the Obama administration had provided "Dreamers," young undocumented immigrants who had been brought to the United States as children.

Even before the coronavirus struck in 2020, holding town meetings by telephone, typically involving 2,000–3,000 constituents (at least at the beginning of the call), had become common for me and many members. When public meetings became impossible, telephone town halls became almost universal, along with meetings aimed at small businesses, nonprofits, party and issue activists, and other targeted audiences on Zoom and other social media platforms. These experiences seemed likely to change communications strategies in ways that outlasted the pandemic.

Town meetings are not the only way to maintain the appearance and the reality of accessibility to the entire community. At various times we have utilized "neighborhood gatherings"—meetings in the homes of friends who are asked to seek a diversity of participants; "neighborhood office hours"—setting up a card table in a well-traveled location, announcing my presence there in advance, and talking with anyone who comes by; and "neighborhood walks"—going door to door to seek out constituents' views, during non-campaign as well as campaign season. For years I also taped a monthly call-in show, *Keeping in Touch*, on cable television's local access channel. We featured clips from my recent House floor speeches and the like, but mainly conducted a town meeting of the air, focusing on the callers and my answers to their questions. Because the local cable outlets reran the shows frequently, channel surfers sometimes got an impression of my omnipresence. The show ended only when the cable system discontinued such public-service programming.

A familiar dilemma of scheduling is to strike a balance between invitations and requests that come from outside—which could easily fill up most available time—and proactive efforts to reach out to new groups and ensure a diversity of engagements. Some of the events we organize are of very long standing. The Farm Breakfast became a Fourth District tradition under my predecessor, Rep. Ike Andrews, but it has evolved as my district has become less rural and the mix of farms has changed from large dairy and tobacco operations to smaller farms focused on specialty crops and the organic market. The annual Veterans Breakfast, which we organize in conjunction with major veterans organizations, generally attracts about 125 to 150 on or around Veterans Day. We also sponsor a multidistrict small business procurement workshop, Marketplace, with the cooperation of our Small Business and Technology Development Center and the procurement offices at the Environmental Protection Agency (EPA) and National Institute of Environmental Health Sciences (NIEHS). The last time this workshop was held, we had booths for some fifty federal agencies, military bases, and prime contractors and some 450 business participants.

Every year we sponsor the Congressional Arts Competition for high school students, a national program that dates from 1982 which we use to engage students, teachers, and local arts councils from across the district. To this the Congressional App Challenge has been added in recent years, inviting students to design and pitch creative software applications. We organize receptions for everyone participating in both programs and their families, as we do for the thirty or so students I nominate for admission to the military service academies each year.

We also regularly organize roundtables to gather input on federal policy from groups such as affordable housing advocates, health care providers, nonprofit organizations, law enforcement representatives, veterans in area universities, and food security advocates. Sometimes these occasions provide an opportunity to interact with guests that I bring to town: for example, Rep. Adam Schiff (D-California) with high-tech entrepreneurs, Rep. Barbara Lee (D-California) with global health administrators and researchers, Rep. Anna Eshoo (D-California) with start-ups in a Raleigh business incubator, Federal Communications Commissioner Jessica Rosenworcel with stakeholders in net neutrality and media concentration, and Housing and Urban Development (HUD) Secretary Julian Castro with leaders in housing and community development.

Much of my proactive schedule consists of follow-ups to contacts I make as constituents contact me about issues or I move around the district. I am constantly learning about new businesses or health care organizations or nonprofits, and what follows is often an invitation to visit the organization and see its work first-hand. During 2017–2018, for example, I visited sixty-one businesses. These "biz tours" put me in touch with thousands of people I would not meet otherwise; we are almost always able to include town meetings with sizable groups of employees as well as the usual briefing and facilities tour.

The volume of incoming communications from the district has massively increased since the advent of e-mail and free long-distance calls. Numbers vary according to what may be in the news or on social media on a given day, but average about 1,600 calls, e-mails, and letters regarding policy issues per week. Fewer than five percent now come by postal mail, which is rendered brittle by the irradiation to which it has been subjected since the anthrax incidents that followed the 9/11 attacks.

My policy is to respond by letter or e-mail to every individual communication from a constituent, and, when possible, to those signing group appeals or petitions as well. Our greatest ongoing management challenge is to ensure that these letters and e-mails are on point and on time. There is a trade-off between speed and substance. Some offices achieve fast turnaround by sending responses that are little more than acknowledgments; we tend to take more time to make appropriate individual modifications to standardized letters and to include more information. My district is relatively demanding in terms of the volume, diversity, and sophistication of constituent contacts, and my staff and I devote a great deal of time to producing effective responses. It is a good problem to have, however, because it puts me in touch with thousands whom I would not otherwise reach and allows me to keep in touch with them proactively as legislative developments occur.

We initiate a great deal of communication ourselves. I maintain a website which contains recent speeches and press releases as well as basic information about me and my offices and how we can be of help. I communicate with constituents through ten or so district-wide electronic mailings per year, including newsletters, questionnaires, and issue pieces and announcements of general interest. Formerly, we sent (via postal mail) a couple of newsletters annually to every box holder in the district; now, a greater variety of pieces are e-mailed to a list of some 200,000 constituents assembled from the voter file and other sources. As before, these mass communications are subject to (somewhat nitpicking) approval by a "franking" commission, (franking refers to the practice, dating from the First Continental Congress, of mailing official communications at no cost) to ensure that they are not "political" in nature and otherwise conform with House ethics rules.

At least once each Congress, I include a lengthy multiple-choice questionnaire in a newsletter, giving constituents an opportunity to register their views on a number of major issues. Having been skeptical of the way some members asked loaded questions designed to elicit preferred responses, I have tried to word my questions straightforwardly. We usually get a good rate of response—5,000 questionnaires completed typically—and considerable interest when we disseminate the results.

Two other mass mailing categories are more targeted and also more flexible in that they do not require franking approval and can be sent during the ninety-day "blackout" periods that precede primary and general elections. "Subscriber" mail goes to constituents—in our case about 28,000—who have "opted in." These are not restricted in content and may be targeted according to indicated issues of interest. We sent out seventeen subscriber pieces in 2018. The other category is "499s," so-called because of the limit of 500 that applies to any proactive mailing during the pre-election period. We use these mailings year-round, usually to reach constituents who have expressed interest in a particular issue, whether or not they have placed themselves on our subscriber list.

My staff and I also try to maintain effective contact with the news media in the district. Members of the media, especially television, are often attracted to campaign fireworks, but it takes considerably more effort to interest them in the day-to-day work of Congress. We send television feeds and offer radio commentary to local stations from Washington and make me available for interviews on current topics when I am home. We provide a steady stream of press releases to newspaper, radio, and television outlets; most either offer news about my initiatives or interpret major items of congressional business, often relating them to North Carolina. We also furnish clips of my statements and speeches and let stations know when they can pick up my committee or floor appearances on C-SPAN.

Considerable ingenuity is required to relate the work of the Congress to local concerns in an informative and interesting way and to provide the "visuals" that television and Facebook videos require. In announcing a homeland security research grant to North Carolina State University, for example, we treated the local media to a "pyro-man" demonstration, showing how the protective clothing being developed enabled a mannequin to withstand intense flames. Announcing the introduction of my Teaching Fellows Act in the empty NCSU football stadium dramatized the number of teaching positions North Carolina needed to fill (see Chapter 5), just as announcing a school construction initiative in the midst of trailers serving as temporary classrooms furnished a striking visual image and reminded viewers of the local importance of the issue. In 2018, I staged a town hall meeting on "democracy reform," with panelists from three prominent reform organizations, to highlight my comprehensive "We the People" legislation (see Chapter 3).

Social media increasingly dominate the communications landscape. By 2018, 99 percent of House offices and all Senate offices were utilizing Facebook and Twitter, and YouTube was not far behind.[2] We regularly post photos and videos—many of them shot on an iPhone in my office or at events—on Facebook and Instagram. Twitter has become ubiquitous, with most members of Congress feeding the beast almost daily, including weekends. Tuesday, March 12, 2019, for example, was a busy day in Washington, and the six tweets I posted were fairly typical:

- Releasing a letter that, as Transportation-Housing and Urban Development (T-HUD) Appropriations Subcommittee chairman, I had written the Federal Aviation Administrator regarding the Federal Aviation Administration (FAA)'s delay in grounding Boeing's 737 Max 8 jets after a second fatal crash.

- Noting a Homeland Security appropriations subcommittee hearing I would be attending on disaster recovery.
- Announcing my cosponsorship of the reintroduced Development, Relief, and Education for Alien Minors (DREAM) Act.
- Inviting constituents to vote online for their favorite entry in the Congressional Arts Competition.
- Posting a picture of North Carolina Department of Transportation (NCDOT) Rail Division head Jason Orthner, a witness at my T-HUD hearing on passenger rail.
- Slamming the recently released Trump budget's "tired playbook" in the context of a Budget Committee hearing.

As congressional districts become more populous and go beyond existing community boundaries and as constituents become more reliant on media—conventional and social—and less on personal and party channels for their political information, members must develop extensive mail and media operations if they are to communicate effectively. There is no substitute for moving around the district personally; people like to see their representatives, and the closest personal tie many of them have to the federal government is their U.S. House member. But even the most energetic outreach program will miss thousands of people, while television, social media, and electronic mail offer manifold new possibilities for reaching them. Even those of us who regard ourselves stylistically as "workhorses" still have to pay far more attention to media and public relations than our predecessors ever did. The political landscape is littered with fallen members who assumed that their work in Washington would speak for itself and did not fully understand what effective communication under modern conditions requires. At its best, such communication conveys a sense of partnership, bringing constituents in on what is happening in Congress and what their representative is thinking and doing; it is a process of explaining and interpreting but also of listening and inviting reciprocal communications.

Media and mail operations obviously have the potential to improve a member's political standing, although the impact on one's standing among colleagues can be mixed. Just as we used to say wryly that "the most dangerous place to be in Washington is between Chuck Schumer and a TV camera," we now combine awe at some members' social media prowess with a sense that such endeavors have displaced member-to-member communications and investment in the institution in a regrettable way.

What of the charge that communications operations give an unfair advantage to incumbents? Media and mail unquestionably can be abused; I have seen members' newsletters that I thought went over the line, looking more like campaign brochures. Indeed, the line is hard to draw with precision, although the franking police try—limiting, for example, the number of photos and the number of times one can use "I" or "my" in a newsletter. House members invite public cynicism if we do not enforce the rules seriously and, more importantly, honor the spirit of the rules personally. But critics have a credibility problem of their own when they interpret efforts to communicate as nothing more than a crass attempt to gain political advantage. I have sometimes invited the critics to examine a newsletter or targeted mail piece and to judge whether it communicates useful information or self-promoting puffery. Members must be able to pass that test, but we are also responsible for making ourselves accountable, interpreting policy challenges to a wide audience, explaining and justifying our preferred solutions, and inviting constituents to put forward their own ideas. A good communications program will do all of those things, and its worth is not negated if it also turns out to be smart politics.

Casework

The staff members in my district offices spend much of their time on casework, assisting individuals and sometimes companies, organizations, and local governments in their dealings with the federal government. The most common areas of concern are Social Security, Medicare, veterans' benefits, tax problems, immigration and naturalization, and passports. Some of these services are routine, as when we expedite the issuance of passports or help people get tickets to visit the White House or U.S. Capitol; others involve convoluted disputes over benefits or entitlements that have been years in the making. We cannot tell an agency what to decide, but we can require answers if the resolution of a case has been delayed or the constituent has been given unclear or discrepant reasons for a decision. We seek to ensure timely and fair consideration and an explanation of the reasons for the agency's decision and what, if anything, the constituent can do about it.

It is impossible to please everyone. I remember a demonstration of this from my days on Senator Bartlett's staff. One day the senator received a plaintive letter from a young woman fearing that her boyfriend, who was stationed at a military base in Alaska, was about to be transferred out of the state. Could the senator do anything to help? While my friend who handled military cases was still pondering how to respond, a second letter came from the serviceman himself. Dear Senator Bartlett, he asked, could you please help me get transferred out of Alaska as soon as possible?!

Our interventions often result in the correction of an agency error or the rectification of an injustice. Sometimes our main contribution is to get the agency's attention and expedite the resolution of a matter that has dragged on for months or years. For example, the Social Security Administration withheld much needed disability payments for a constituent, based on information that she owned land in another state. Her family had furnished documents proving her local residency over a four-month period, but the matter was resolved in one week once my office got involved. In another instance, the widow of a veteran had applied numerous times for Veterans Administration (VA) survivor benefits for her daughter, but because of various bureaucratic snafus, the claim was never processed. Four days after my staff contacted the VA regional office, the benefits were started, and retroactive payments totaling $2,632 were sent.

Such cases can get quite convoluted. One constituent applied for a home loan guaranteed by the Federal Housing Administration (FHA) only to be told her name was on HUD's CAVIRS (Credit Alert Interactive Verification Reporting System) list of individuals defaulting on or owing debt to federal agencies. The loan in question was a Small Business Administration (SBA) disaster loan which had been discharged in bankruptcy years before. Although my constituent was correct, she was told by SBA and HUD that they could not remove her name from the list: each said it was the responsibility of the other. Only when my caseworker sent HUD's letter to the SBA and the SBA's letter to HUD was my constituent's name removed and her eligibility for a home loan restored.

A good number of cases involve small businesses. A local medical supply company, for example, was unable to pay its workers after Medicare withheld payments for over sixty days because of a mixup involving the firm's change of location. We were able to resolve the situation and get all the withheld payments restored. Another case involved a small business with considerable experience in specialized electronics work for the military. The firm was unable to bid on a particular job because military procurement officials had decided not to open the project to competitive bidding. Our inquiries revealed that the military had no defensible reason for this decision; subsequently, the bidding process was opened, and the local firm was able to pursue the contract.

The collapse of communism in the Soviet Union and Eastern Europe and the economic hardships that followed spawned numerous immigration cases involving my office—family reunification, the adoption of orphaned and abandoned children, and so forth. It opened up a remarkable family saga for a constituent of mine and set the stage for what still ranks as my most dramatic casework result. My constituent, who was Jewish, had fled from Poland in the 1930s as Nazism swept across Europe. He had heard secondhand that his brother and father had been killed early in the war and had presumed them dead for fifty years. Then in 1992, totally out of the blue, he received a letter from someone purporting to be his brother from the capital of one of the former Soviet states. He was excited but wary, fearing that someone was using his brother's name in an effort to get money or to leave the country. The constituent came to my office, asking for help in determining whether the correspondent was really his long-lost brother. My aide worked with the State Department on a plan whereby my constituent would write several questions to which only his brother would know the answers (What was our father's nickname? What color was his hair?—a trick question, for he had lost his hair early in life—and so forth). The brother was then called to the U.S. embassy, was asked the questions by an official, and answered them perfectly. The brothers were overjoyed to find each other, and my constituent brought his brother by my office for a memorable visit when he came to the United States a few weeks later.

Congressional casework often provides a kind of appeals process for bureaucratic decisions, a function that has sometimes been likened to that of the ombudsman in Scandinavian countries. It is not an ideal mechanism, and constituents vary considerably in their ability and inclination to use it. It would be preferable to have all comers receive fair and efficient service from the agencies in the first place, and congressional funding and oversight should be directed toward that end. Still, House members have a strong incentive not only to help constituents who present themselves but also to advertise the availability of their services and handle the cases in ways that inspire favorable comment. A reputation for good constituent service is an important political asset; party and ideological differences often mean nothing to a constituent who has been helped, just as they mean nothing to us as we perform the service. Helping people in these ways is inherently satisfying, and the results are frequently more immediate and tangible than in legislative work.

Casework experiences sometimes lead members to perceive broader problems and to seek fixes that go beyond individual cases. For example, during the 1990s we worked with several constituents with disabilities whose medical benefits were cut off once their condition improved enough to let them leave the house or take a job. This led me to seek more rational eligibility rules; I petitioned the Health Care Financing Administration (HCFA) and supported corrective legislation, which passed in 1999.

Another case alerted me to the possible adverse consequences of "joint consolidation" student loans, whereby married couples agreed to be jointly liable for repayment. Such loans proved to be problematic in the event of a divorce, and Congress wisely ended the program in 2006. But no provision was made for severing existing loans, even in cases of violence or abuse or an otherwise uncooperative partner. I introduced a bill with bipartisan, bicameral sponsors to allow loans to be split between former spouses under such circumstances. Blocked at first by a Republican committee chair, I succeeded in getting the provision included in the House Higher Education Act reauthorization in 2019 after the shift to Democratic control.

Difficult, often heart-wrenching cases most often cry out for broader policy changes in the area of immigration, particularly in the Trump era. Most of the initiatives I have taken or contributed to—targeting Immigration and Customs Enforcement (ICE) enforcement actions and insisting on prosecutorial discretion; lifting Trump's ban on immigrants from certain (mainly Muslim) countries and his virtual ban on refugees from most countries; preserving Temporary Protected Status (TPS) for immigrants from countries such as Haiti, Honduras, and El Salvador; protecting and providing a path to citizenship for "Dreamers"; fighting to preserve family reunification as an immigration criterion and a credible fear of family or gang violence as a criterion for seeking asylum; resisting the announced closing of most overseas

Citizenship and Immigration (CIS) intake offices—have been motivated and informed in large part by individual cases we have encountered. We have long dedicated most of the time of two district aides to immigration cases. The experience of recent years has left no doubt as to the human import of the work and the urgency of learning the right lessons from it—going beyond giving individual cases our best effort to making desperately needed changes in policy.

The coronavirus experience took casework into new areas and gave it a new urgency. The Coronavirus Aid, Relief, and Economic Security (CARES) Act, signed by the president on March 27, 2020, provided three avenues to economic relief: direct payments to individuals and families, administered through the Internal Revenue Service (IRS); federally enhanced unemployment benefits, administered through the state unemployment systems; and forgivable loans to small businesses and nonprofit organizations to enable them to maintain their payrolls, administered by lending institutions under a Small Business Administration program. All of these programs involved millions of claimants, many in desperate straits, delivery systems jammed and strained beyond capacity, and thorny questions of eligibility and entitlement. My staff, working from home, fielded a steady stream of inquiries for weeks from constituents reporting frustrations and seeking help in navigating the systems. We tried to anticipate such inquiries through virtual and telephone town halls featuring SBA, nonprofit, and financial institution representatives as well as public health and local government guests who could speak to the crisis. I also distilled the problems we saw into a number of policy and funding recommendations for the succeeding relief bills.

Appropriations and Grants

Local governments, agencies, organizations, and individuals often seek federal funding and ask for the help of their federal representatives in doing so. This may involve advising them as to possible sources of grant funds, backing up grant applications once made, and advocating for robust funding and favorable distribution formulae for the relevant appropriations accounts. Until 2011, when the Republican leadership disallowed congressionally directed spending, or earmarks, it also could mean writing a specific project into an appropriations bills (see Chapter 5).

I was able to secure favorable action on a number of proposed earmarks as a petitioner from outside the committee during my first two terms, often with the help of Bill Hefner, an Appropriations member from my state who had the distinct advantage of being a subcommittee chairman. But in 1991, as a new Appropriations member, I was able to lift my sights considerably. I consulted widely in the district and statewide, gathering the information I needed to defend an expanded list of projects but also winnowing through the growing number of requests my new position attracted. Sometimes I had to ask for help (e.g., from the state Department of Transportation and the NCSU central research office) in coordinating the flow of requests and setting priorities among them. I tried to ensure that every proposal I submitted had a solid justification and could demonstrate complementary funding from nonfederal sources, and I avoided pie-in-the-sky requests. Following these rules helped me attain a batting average well over .500, though I also experienced many disappointments.

I was especially pleased by early successes on my transportation subcommittee: a 75 percent federal share of a $1 million study of long-range transportation needs and possible mass-transit alternatives in the Research Triangle area, a grant to the city of Raleigh to purchase ten vans for an experimental suburban feeder service for the city's bus system, an earmarking of AMTRAK funds to support an additional intrastate train for North Carolina, $2.5 million to upgrade the instrument landing system at Raleigh-Durham Airport, and a directive to the FAA to permanently install the airport's experimental radar system on schedule.

Two early experiences demonstrated that appropriations are not merely about money: I wrote directives into appropriations bills after years of cajoling federal agencies to do right by my constituents. In the fiscal year 1995 Energy and Water bill, we ordered the Army Corps of Engineers to raise the height of the dam at Falls Lake, which contained most of Raleigh's future water supply, thus correcting a major shortfall from the lake's original intended capacity. And in the 1995 Veterans Administration-Housing and Urban Development (VA-HUD) appropriations bill, we directed that a portion of the VA's health care budget be used to fund a long-sought Veterans Center in Raleigh. The veterans population in Raleigh was among the largest of any city in the country without one of these centers, which offered counseling, group therapy, and other mental health services, particularly to Vietnam veterans.

I became more successful as I gained seniority and took on leadership positions on the committee. There were times when Democratic control helped—for example, funding a nutritional education center in Raleigh and NCSU's swine waste research operation, both from unconventional sources in the agriculture appropriations bill. On the other hand, my success in covering full construction costs for the EPA lab and establishing the secondary market pilot project at HUD (Chapter 5) left me singing the praises of appropriations bipartisanship.

The range of projects for which I secured funding in FY 2010, just before earmarking was disallowed, demonstrated the importance this funding had assumed—although it still accounted for only 1–2 percent of the federal budget—and the time and effort offices like mine put into processing the requests. My list included $350,000 for swine waste research at NCSU; $2.5 million for the national Food Animal Residue Avoidance Database (FARAD), operated by NCSU and other universities to monitor drug residues and contamination of livestock; $2.8 million for two national textile research consortiums; $2.4 million for a cybersecurity initiative among

NCSU, Red Hat, and other partners to devise protections for open-source software systems; $2.8 million for continuing development of a promising semiconductor material for use by the military; $3.8 million for Army Corps of Engineers dredging of Oregon Inlet; $6 million for Forest Service acquisition of a key parcel along the Appalachian Trail;[3] $400,000 for a Durham residential facility for recovering substance abusers; $300,000 for the NC Dental Health Fund's program of free dental care for low-income individuals; and so forth.

How have such efforts fared in the absence of earmarks? We have figured out how to fund some projects—FARAD, for example—as programmatic items, while others such as the textile research centers have struggled to find replacement sources. Forest Service land acquisitions have become much more difficult, and independent congressional judgment on funding levels for public works projects has become almost impossible to exercise through appropriations bills.

Our main recourse has been to direct those seeking funding toward federal grants. The most direct effort to establish a replacement fund for earmarks is the Defense Department's Rapid Innovation Fund (RIF), funded in recent years at around $250 million annually. Almost all of my Defense earmark requests were designed to get firms through the so-called "valley of death"—from the initial development of a technique or product, which may have had government or other startup support, to full readiness for procurement. I never included such a request without first confirming the Defense Department's interest in the project. Now, firms seeking such support apply to the RIF or to another grant program, perhaps a late-stage Small Business Innovation Research (SBIR) award.[4] Assuming such programs are adequately funded and are administered with openness to promising ventures, this may be preferable to Defense earmarking, which was sometimes erratic and lacking in clear criteria of merit. Moreover, as a practical matter, it is likely that when and if earmarks are resorted, they will be disallowed for private firms.

In most other areas, however, the end of earmarking has been a major loss, not only to the legitimate powers of the legislative branch and its members, but also to the access and prospects for support of countless agencies, organizations, and individuals in our communities. Like many members, I have redoubled my efforts in the intervening years to facilitate access to grants. But all too often, the grant categories do not offer a good fit for the need, and the applicants, particularly those with limited resources, find the application process difficult and daunting.

Earmarks thus played a vital role in getting federal seed money where it needed to go, and I strongly support their restoration, in an accountable and transparent fashion. Having said that, the bulk of discretionary (i.e., non-formula) federal funding always has been distributed through grants, and it will remain essential for members to understand the grant process and to help steer their constituents through it. We must also ensure adequate overall funding for programs for which localities and organizations may be entitled to receive a formulaic share (CDBG, HOME, HOPWA) or to compete for grants (Choice Neighborhoods, TIGER). This is also true of programs that have never been earmarked, where traditions of peer review and merit selection are strong, such as National Institutes of Health (NIH) and National Science Foundation (NSF) research grants.

Many of the organizations seeking my help with grant applications are already well versed in the funding process and simply ask me to register my support with the funding agency. But sometimes we need to help at the ground level. A staff member in my district office works with groups to identify possible funding sources and demystify the application process, and we periodically hold meetings and workshops to share information about funding opportunities, especially in the areas of housing and small business. Occasionally I need to work with an organization to ensure that its proposal is suitable for my support and/or agency approval. For example, I initially declined to endorse one of Raleigh's applications to HUD for a HOPE VI grant to demolish and replace dilapidated public housing because of the number of people it would displace and the lack of local consensus around the project. The city responded to feedback from my office and HUD, consulted more widely, revised its application, and eventually received a $36 million grant.

The ground rules for expressing support or advocating for a project to be funded or an administrative action to be taken at the discretion of a federal agency, generally after a process of professional review, are not always clear. Precedents and practices vary from program to program, although it is never appropriate to urge that established ground rules be violated or that political criteria override all others. In some cases, when asked by an applicant in whom I have confidence, I have simply dropped a note to the agency, flagging the application as one I hope will be given careful consideration. On other occasions my staff and I have gotten more directly involved, arguing strenuously for a Raleigh-Durham Airport/American Airlines London route application at the White House (with ample supportive data) and bringing U.S. Postal Service officials into high-growth communities to witness and assess the need for new facilities.

In one instance, I feared that unorthodox features of a funding application for Wake County's magnet schools might lead to a routine rejection. Consequently, I took pains to ensure that Department of Education officials understood the rationale for the unique features and gave the proposal individual attention. Occasionally I have intervened when trouble developed in what should have been a routine review and award process—as when a local university's grant for an engineering research center from the National Science Foundation got held up in an interagency dispute. I have paid special attention to TIGER (now BUILD) grants, stressing to the Department of Transportation (DOT) their intermodal character and their centrality to regional development. The strong case I and others made was rewarded with three complementary grants totaling $51 million from FY2012–2018 for Raleigh's Union Station and an adjacent bus facility. Such applications from local organizations and governments are more numerous than requests for direct appropriations ever were, and the procedures for handling them are far more routinized, located in another branch of government. Yet a member of Congress does well to follow them closely and can sometimes intervene with good effect.

Notes

1 J. David Goodman, "Ocasio-Cortez Builds a National Platform, but a District Office? Not Open Yet," *New York Times*, January 22, 2019.
2 Jacob R. Straus, "Social Media Adoption by Members of Congress: Trends and Congressional Considerations," Congressional Research Service, Library of Congress, October 9, 2018, p. 6.
3 I took particular satisfaction in protecting the Appalachian Trail, having grown up in Erwin, Tennessee, a "trail town," and having hiked the trail frequently since my high school years. See Jack Igelman, "For the Love of the Trail," *AT Journeys*, Spring 2020, pp. 30–32.
4 The Defense Department dispenses about $1 billion in SBIR grants annually, out of about $2.5 billion spread across eleven federal agencies. The program dates from 1982 and is overseen by the Small Business Administration. Participating agencies allocate some 3 percent of their extramural research budgets to small business projects in three stages—startup, expansion, and transition to the marketplace.

10 Religion and Politics

I had the good fortune to come of age politically in the early years of the modern civil rights movement—the years between the Montgomery, Alabama, bus boycott that brought Martin Luther King Jr. to prominence (1955–1956) and the passage of the landmark Civil Rights Act of 1964. I say good fortune because of the particularly challenging and positive kind of political experience this movement gave me and thousands like me in my student generation. Had we come along a few years earlier, I often thought, we would have faded into the blandness of the Eisenhower years. And the generation following ours had a far different political experience as the civil rights movement splintered into reformist and radical wings and the Vietnam War brought forth disillusionment, protest, and fierce political conflict. Many lost faith in politics as an instrument of positive change.

This contrasted markedly with the climactic moment of my own early political experience, which occurred on June 10, 1964, during my second summer as a junior staff member in a U.S. Senate office. On that day, I crowded into the Senate gallery to witness the decisive cloture vote on the Civil Rights Act. It could scarcely have been a more dramatic moment, as the dying Sen. Clair Engle (D-California) was wheeled into the chamber to cast this momentous vote.[1] It was a moment capable of convincing a young person that the system worked, that enough dedicated people, working together, could right ancient wrongs—a fitting climax to the formative political years that many in my generation experienced.

An important element in this experience for many of us was religion. Our religious backgrounds shaped our response to the civil rights struggle, and our religious outlook was challenged and broadened in turn. Religion had been central to my own upbringing; the Price family had been pillars of the First Christian Church of Erwin, Tennessee, ever since my grandfather's family had moved there in 1901. We were present whenever the church doors were open, including Sunday evening services and Wednesday night prayer meetings. Henry Webb, the minister there during my teenage years who also taught at nearby Milligan College, particularly influenced me. I went off to Mars Hill College intending to be an engineer, as befitted a member of the Sputnik generation, but with Webb's urging that I consider the ministry in the back of my mind.

Mars Hill, then a junior college, was identified with a Baptist regimen considerably stricter than my own upbringing. However, Robert Seymour, the community's young pastor who had trained at Yale Divinity School, helped me and many others move from a primarily individualistic understanding of our faith to appreciate its social and prophetic dimensions. Just before I transferred to the University of North Carolina, Seymour came to Chapel Hill to help found the Binkley Memorial Baptist Church, a progressive, racially inclusive congregation affiliated with the American as well as the Southern Baptist Convention.[2] This became my church home in Chapel Hill, as it still is today. And despite my lack of Baptist credentials, I was elected president of the Baptist Student Union at the University of North Carolina.

On campus the religious organizations took the lead in protesting discrimination and pressing for change. Many took to heart Martin Luther King's indictment of the church as a "thermometer that records the ideas and principles of popular opinion," rather than a "thermostat that transforms the mores of society."[3] And many of us saw in civil rights a challenge to translate the personal ethic of "love thy neighbor" into social terms.

One who has lived through such an experience is unlikely to make the mistake of assuming that the separation of church and state can or should mean a neat compartmentalizing of religion and politics. Indeed, the ensuing years have seen an increase in religiously oriented political movements. A number of those churches that King criticized for their "completely otherworldly religion [making] a strange, un-Biblical distinction between body and soul, between the sacred and the secular"[4] have been politically mobilized, though frequently in the service of an agenda markedly different from what King had in mind. As a result, the debate over the place of religion in politics has intensified. In the present chapter, I will reflect on how that debate has looked from Capitol Hill and how its terms might be clarified.

Religious Agendas

If I had not already been sensitive to the problematic relationship between religion and politics by virtue of my own religious background and divinity school training, my first campaign, against an incumbent identified with the religious right, certainly would have made me so. I have already described his "Dear Christian Friend" letter to prospective supporters, warning that he might be replaced by "someone who is not willing to take a strong stand for the principles outlined in the Word of God" (i.e., me). But that experience paled in comparison to what I encountered in 1994, with the Christian Coalition at the peak of its influence nationally and locally. People involved with or influenced by the coalition and like-minded organizations flooded our offices with calls and provoked confrontations in community meetings.

Churchgoers across the district found Christian Coalition scorecards giving me a zero rating on their windshields the Sunday before the election. A woman who snarled in my face at a North Raleigh polling place epitomized the onslaught for me: "You're a counterfeit Christian!"

As someone who thought, by virtue of my own religious background and involvement, that I would have something in common with almost anyone approaching politics from a perspective of faith, these negative experiences came as a rude awakening. The civil rights movement had taught me a powerful lesson in interfaith cooperation and had convinced me of religion's power to heal and unify, as people from diverse traditions found common ground in attacking injustice. What I have since confronted is religion's capacity to exclude and divide. Fortunately, I have had enough positive experiences to convince me that communication and even collaboration across religious boundaries are still possible. For example, our coalition in attempting to reverse the FCC media concentration rules in 2003 (see Chapter 5) included the Family Research Council and the Traditional Values Coalition.

I have continually engaged with local faith communities, meeting with clergy and other leaders and speaking to Sunday school classes, other religious forums, and occasionally from the pulpit. I have worshiped with dozens of African American congregations, which I have found especially welcoming (although many look askance at candidates who do not remain for the entire service or drop in only during campaign season). I began working with congregations and religious organizations on housing and social service initiatives (e.g., the construction of housing for the elderly under the HUD section 202 program) long before "faith-based initiatives" became a buzzword. Extra-congregational groups such as Bread for the World and Witness for Peace have been active in my district. Much of this demonstrates how the awakening of social concern and activism that I witnessed in the 1960s has continued to characterize American religious life.

Still, in my district and across the country, the religious right is a force to be reckoned with. During my early years in office, the issue that inspired the most communication and advocacy from religious communities was the Civil Rights Restoration Act of 1988—*against* the bill. I found this especially ironic and sad in light of my memories of the passage of the 1964 Civil Rights Act, which the 1988 proposal sought to protect from adverse judicial interpretations. To be sure, the mainline Protestant, Catholic, and Jewish bodies lined up in favor of the bill. But their efforts at grassroots mobilization were anemic compared to the thousands of letters and calls from the other side that kept the phones in all of my offices tied up for two weeks. "Grove City" (the bill's shorthand designation, taken from the Supreme Court decision it sought to reverse) was talked about among my staff for years, becoming the high-water mark against which all future floods of calls about flag burning, gun control, congressional pay raises, and the like, were measured.

Many of the calls were inspired by a widely circulated memorandum from Jerry Falwell, head of the Moral Majority, that described this rather modest bill as "the greatest threat to religious freedom and traditional moral values ever passed." The Civil Rights Restoration Act, he warned, could force churches "to hire a practicing active homosexual drug addict with AIDS to be a teacher or youth pastor."[5] My incredulity that people could ever believe such an absurd statement was overwhelmed by the mass of calls that we received, many from well-meaning, genuinely concerned people. In the end, however, Falwell and his allies did not succeed, and the White House operatives who had hoped the religious right could help them sustain President Reagan's veto of the bill had reason to doubt the utility of the alliance. It was a textbook case of a lobby over-reaching—using such outrageous tactics and such absurd misinformation that it became a point of honor with members not to be swayed. I particularly remember the statement of my North Carolina colleague Bill Hefner, a former gospel singer, on the House floor:

> I find reprehensible not those thousands of people who have made the phone calls, but ... the people that have instigated this misinformation.... If it means that I lose my position in the U.S. House of Representatives [if I do not] cave in ... and base my vote on what people believe to be true but what I know not to be true, I say to my colleagues this job is not worth that to me.[6]

In the end, the House voted to override the veto by 292–133, displaying remarkably little slippage from the original vote in favor of the bill (315–98).

By the time President Clinton took office in 1993, the Christian Coalition had replaced the Moral Majority as the vanguard of the religious right and wielded sufficient influence within the Republican Party to give issues like abortion and the status of gays and lesbians a prominent place on the opposition agenda. Clinton's proposal to lift the ban on gays in the military and his modification of several long-standing antiabortion policies deepened the antagonism of religious conservatives toward the administration and Democrats in Congress. By early 1994, the pattern was well established: every few weeks a flood of calls and letters would materialize on the current issue of choice. At one point, the focus was on the right to protest at abortion clinics, at another on (unfounded) accusations that the Equal Employment Opportunity Commission intended to forbid Bibles or religious objects in workplaces, or on alleged threats to home schooling from educational authorities.

The reauthorization of the Elementary and Secondary Education Act provided a cornucopia of opportunities for attack by religious conservatives and their allies. Consideration of the legislation continued intermittently for four weeks in early 1994; during that time, the House passed amendments eliminating any requirement that parents involved in home schooling be certified (a requirement the bill had never contained) and withholding federal money from school districts that prohibited voluntary prayer in school. Additional amendments, to make eligibility for federal funding dependent on the teaching of abstinence in sex education programs and to prohibit any programs "encouraging or supporting" homosexuality as a lifestyle (thus putting much counseling in jeopardy), were averted by the proposal and passage of Democratic alternatives.[7] Any doubts that such themes would figure prominently in the 1994 campaign were dispelled by this debate, most of which I witnessed directly by virtue of having been chosen by the Speaker to preside, and by the rising volume of calls and letters from my district.

As the 1994 elections approached and congressional Republicans attempted to bring down most of the remaining Democratic agenda, Newt Gingrich secured an alliance with the Christian Coalition to defeat the Lobbying Disclosure Act, a reform measure that had earlier passed the House and on which members from both parties had been working for eighteen months. With Rush Limbaugh fanning the flames daily on his radio show, Gingrich and the religious right network suddenly raised the specter of grassroots Christian lobbyists being "gagged," despite language in the bill that specifically excluded religious organizations from registration or reporting requirements. Gingrich, as minority whip, led the effort to defeat the conference report on lobbying reform on procedural motions. He took the floor to warn of "grassroots gag rules" and to suggest that "an administration that appoints Roberta Achtenberg" (an acknowledged lesbian whom Clinton had appointed HUD assistant secretary for Fair Housing and Equal Opportunity) should not be allowed to interpret freedom of religious communication. I vividly remember sitting in the chamber during the debate and thinking that I had never witnessed a more cynical performance. Gingrich's effort narrowly failed but left the conference report "easy pickings" for a Republican end-of-session filibuster in the Senate.[8]

The relationship between the religious right and the Clinton administration remained adversarial, culminating in the prominent role conservative religious leaders took in seeking the president's impeachment. Most of them warmly welcomed the advent of George W. Bush, who made it clear during the 2000 campaign that he was "one of them" personally and promised action on their major issues. One of his first moves after taking office was to reinstate the "Mexico City policy" that prohibited aid to any international family planning organizations that performed or provided information about abortions, even if they used their own funds to do so. He also withheld family planning appropriations from the U.N. Fund for Population Activities (UNFPA), accepting the allegations of antiabortion groups that such funds could indirectly aid forced abortions in China. In 2003, with a Republican majority in both houses, an eight-year crusade by social and religious conservatives culminated in the enactment of the so-called partial birth abortion ban. Twice vetoed by President Clinton, the measure placed federal restrictions on abortion procedures for the first time since the Supreme Court's 1973 *Roe v. Wade* decision.

In the meantime, President Bush established an Office of Faith-Based and Community Initiatives in the White House and pushed for a vast expansion of the "charitable choice" provisions Congress had added to scattered welfare and antipoverty programs during the Clinton administration. The idea was to enable religious organizations to receive federal funding to deliver social services without altering their religious practices or character. But the initiative foundered in the Senate on contentious issues such as the federal funding of sectarian activity and religious discrimination in hiring, and the president instead implemented its major provisions by executive order (nos. 13279–13280) in late 2002.

The elections of 2004 revealed the Republican advantage among voters attuned to such religious and cultural issues—the "God gap"—to be larger than ever, and prompted widespread soul-searching among Democrats. As E.J. Dionne described the lineup:

> There are Republican candidates and political operatives who assume that religious people live on the political right, care primarily about issues such as gay marriage and abortion, and will forever be part of the GOP's political base. There are liberals—although fewer than conservatives think—who buy this Republican account and write off religious people as backward and reactionary busybodies obsessed with sex.[9]

The percentage of self-described evangelicals supporting John Kerry for president was about 17 percent, down from Bill Clinton's 33 percent. Sixty-one percent of the four voters in ten who attended services once or more per week voted to reelect George W. Bush.[10] This was a major wake-up call, prompting renewed interest among Democrats, not only in reaching "faith voters" but also in figuring out how to relate our shared convictions and values more convincingly to politics. The high ground that many of us remembered from civil rights and the antiwar movement had to be reclaimed.

Discussions intensified among congressional Democrats, with groups such as Rosa DeLauro's dinner gatherings and even our Democratic Budget Group adding sessions on the faith-politics nexus. I revisited and extended my earlier thoughts on the subject and participated in numerous forums locally and nationally.[11] Minority Leader Nancy Pelosi formed a Faith Working Group in the Democratic Caucus, headed by Assistant Leader Jim Clyburn (D-South Carolina), to encourage outreach to faith communities.[12]

The quality of the discussion among Democrats was heightened by the fact that both of the contenders for the 2008 presidential nomination, Hillary Clinton and Barack Obama, demonstrated an unusual "ease and familiarity with religious language and communities."[13] National forums organized by Sojourners and CNN found both candidates addressing how people of faith could find common ground, demonstrating a discriminating understanding of church-state separation, and bringing religious and moral considerations to bear on poverty, global health, abortion, euthanasia, and torture.

The partisan gap among religious voters narrowed somewhat in the 2006 and 2008 elections, although it is difficult to separate these shifts from other forces taking these contests in a Democratic direction. On the whole, noted John Green of the Pew Forum, White evangelicals held firm for Republicans in 2006, but there were significant improvements for Democrats in many states where they "made a real effort to attract religious voters."[14] Faith outreach was more widespread in 2008, with twenty-two state Democratic parties adopting such programs and the Democratic Congressional Campaign Committee's incorporating it in many "Red to Blue" House campaigns.

Despite the success of these efforts, they were scaled back by subsequent Obama and Clinton campaigns in favor of other approaches. The post-2004 discussions still reverberate in the way Democrats talk about health care, food aid, and other aspects of the social safety net, immigration, equal rights, and discrimination. But the public conversations of 2008 have seldom been replicated, and Democratic efforts to reach religious voters, while still prominent in scattered campaigns, have faltered overall. Among many aspects of Hillary Clinton's 2016 loss, Democrats should ponder that she underperformed both Obama and John Kerry among White Catholics and evangelicals—against a candidate who, as Amy Sullivan noted, was "pretty much the human embodiment of the question 'What would Jesus *not* do?' "[15]

As the 2020 presidential campaign got underway, Pete Buttigieg and other candidates spoke of their own religious backgrounds and of the relation of faith to politics in a way not seen since 2008. Joe Biden testified convincingly as to how his faith had sustained him through personal tragedies, leading one commentator to speculate that might offer a connection to religious voters: "a Democratic candidate living an authentic faith juxtaposed with a Republican president just renting some religion." But it remained to be seen how prominently religious themes or outreach to religious voters would figure in the campaign.[16]

Meanwhile, the religious right had fragmented organizationally but solidified as a political force. The most familiar legislative efforts during Obama's presidency, as during Bill Clinton's, were oppositional. Efforts to defeat and then to repeal the Affordable Care Act utilized arguments that were more libertarian than theological; it was Democrats who were quoting Matthew 25 on the floor. But there were extensive arguments about whether the legislation could ever, however indirectly or remotely, subsidize abortion, and opposition in the name of religious liberty to its mandated contraceptive coverage. Obama's defense of LGBT rights and his eventual support of gay marriage also drew religious ire. He continued to reveal his theological seriousness throughout his presidency—most memorably in the eulogy he delivered on June 25, 2015, for Rev. Clementa Pinckney and other victims of the mass shooting at Emanuel AME Church in Charleston, South Carolina, an occasion I will never forget—but the accusations that he was waging a "war on religion" never diminished.[17]

Support for Donald Trump has often been justified by evangelical leaders in terms of political realism: judgments about the president's personal morality must give way to the need to secure conservative judges, policies that hinder abortion, and favored interpretations of religious liberty, all of which Trump promised to deliver. But columnist and former George W. Bush speechwriter Michael Gerson argues that this formulation will not do. Beyond grave questions of character—a proneness to "cruelty, bigotry, vanity, adultery, and serial deception"—the deeper problem is "the distinctly non-Christian substance" of Trump's core values:

> His unapologetic materialism. His tribalism and hatred for "the other." His strength-worship and contempt for "losers," which smack more of Nietzsche than of Christ.[18]

All of this, far from being merely a matter of personal morality, profoundly affects Trump's conduct as president. The contrast with any recognizable interpretation of the Christian faith is so stark as to raise questions as to what extent Christian beliefs are at work among evangelicals as opposed to a religious variant of identity politics. That is what evangelical writer Jonathan Martin suggests in contrasting Trump defender Jerry Falwell Jr. with his father: "There's a lot I didn't agree with him on, but I'm confident that it was important to [Falwell] Senior that he grounded his belief in scripture. Now the Bible's increasingly irrelevant. It's just 'us versus them.'" The result, Amy Sullivan concludes, is

> a malleable religious identity that can be weaponized not just to complain about department stores that hang "Happy Holidays" banners but more significantly in support of politicians like Mr. Trump ... and of virtually any policy so long as it is promoted by someone Fox evangelicals consider on their side of the culture war.[19]

This recent history helps explain why some have come to regard religion as an intrusive and dangerous presence in politics, easily manipulated. But that is not a satisfactory conclusion or, indeed, a realistic one, given the inseparability of religious faith and belief from the wellsprings of motivation across the political spectrum. The fact that the political applications of religious convictions may be opportunistic, offensive, or wrong does not justify avoiding or condemning all such expressions. But it does underscore the importance of thinking carefully about what the relation between religious life and the political order ought to be in a democracy.

Faith and Politics: The Passion for Justice

The relation of the sacred and the secular has inspired theological discussion for thousands of years. I will concentrate here on the Jewish and Christian faiths, which posit a profound tension between the kingdom of God and earthly kingdoms. But an analogous tension is present in Islam and in other world religions, and the questions I will raise can and should be considered in a broader interfaith perspective.

The contrast is stark in the earliest writings in the Hebrew scriptures: the desire of the people of Israel for an earthly king so as to "be like other nations" is portrayed as a rejection of divine rule.[20] That ambivalence about the political realm recurs in various forms throughout the Bible and subsequent religious history.

The various ways of relating the sacred and the secular, the religious and the political, were masterfully analyzed by H. Richard Niebuhr in *Christ and Culture*, which elaborated a "series of typical answers" to this "perennial Christian perplexity."[21] Some theologians have seen worldly kingdoms as a vehicle for divine law. Others have seen this world as virtually abandoned by God. Most theologians, however, have tried to keep those two views in tension. God's word has been interpreted as both a call and a guide to social involvement. Yet God's word remains transcendent, always imperfectly embodied in our institutions, always standing in judgment over them. In the remainder of this chapter, I will reflect on several elements of the relationship that may inspire, inform, and constrain our politics.

Surely the most powerful and compelling force is the prophetic call for justice that "rolls down like waters" (Amos 5:24). Yet this was not evident to many people of faith in the 1960s; one of the many contributions of the civil rights movement was to prompt a rediscovery of the Hebrew prophets. Many churches had come to embody a compartmentalization of the lives of the faithful; people who were loving and generous in their personal relationships often saw no contradiction in their support of social practices and laws that denied others their humanity. Such compartmentalization is ultimately untenable. Many in my generation found guidance in the writings of Reinhold Niebuhr, whose interpretation of the relation of the religious ethic of love to politics is still helpful today.[22] A love ethic can never be perfectly embodied in politics, he taught, but it nonetheless compels its adherents to seek justice as a proximate public expression of love. To fail to pursue justice in our common life is just as surely a betrayal of the ethic of love as it would be to reject a neighbor's need face to face.

William Lee Miller brought the point home in a gloss on Jesus's familiar parable of the Good Samaritan. The Samaritan came upon a man who had been robbed and wounded. He bandaged his wounds and took him to an inn for care and safekeeping, thus proving himself a true neighbor, in contrast to the priest and Levite who "passed by on the other side." What if the Samaritan had come by the same spot the next day and found another man robbed and wounded? And then suppose he met wounded and victimized travelers again and again. How long would it take him to conclude that his individual acts of kindness were not enough, that the road needed to be patrolled? "Would there not be something deficient," Miller asked,

> in the faith that never [sought] to prevent the attacks on travelers? What if the servant of God would give his last bread to a starving stranger in a bread line, yet never think to ask questions about the economic conditions that cause the bread line to exist?[23]

Rabbi Abraham Joshua Heschel, who worked closely with Martin Luther King, tellingly placed the call to social justice in the context of prayer, the most personal and "inward" of religious acts:

> Religion as an establishment must remain separated from the government. Yet prayer as a voice of mercy, as a cry for justice, as a plea for gentleness, must not be kept apart. Let the spirit of prayer dominate the world. Let the spirit of prayer interfere in the affairs of man. Prayer is private, a service of the heart; but let concern and compassion born of prayer dominate public life.[24]

This explains what Heschel said upon returning from the voting rights march in Selma in 1963: "I felt my legs were praying."[25]

The Faith and Politics Institute, a Capitol Hill-based organization with broad ecumenical and, increasingly, interfaith reach, appropriately makes a pilgrimage to major civil rights sites in the South the centerpiece of its annual program. The Institute was founded in 1991 by a North Carolina friend, Rev. Doug Tanner, and is unique in the range of pilgrimages, forums, retreats, and small "reflection groups" that it offers members and staff.[26] Lisa and I went on the 2005 pilgrimage to Selma, Montgomery, and Birmingham, led by civil rights pioneer and my colleague from the class of 1986, John Lewis (D-Georgia). We found the visits moving and evocative of the forces that had drawn both of us into political activism.

The pilgrimage is a unifying event in that it attracts and inspires broad bipartisan participation and suggests that we can indeed find common ground—at least if we look back forty to fifty years. I have often wished, however, that the homage paid to the pioneers could translate more readily into protecting their legacy—voting rights, fair housing, economic and social justice—in the present. And while civil rights remains a paradigmatic case, the prophetic imperative to "do justice and love kindness" (Micah 6:8) speaks to much of our political life, requiring us to ask what government is doing in our name—to subject military interventions to "just war" standards, for example, to bring moral criteria to bear on our treatment of immigrants and refugees (see Figure 10.1), and to evaluate budgets as statements of moral priorities.

Figure 10.1 Posting at the United Methodist Building on Capitol Hill, Spring 2018. The reference is to the words of Jesus in Matthew 25:35: "I was a stranger and you welcomed me."

Source: Twitter.

Engagement can take many forms stylistically and strategically. This is partly a matter of the skills protagonists bring to politics, partly what a given situation may permit or require. Our faith traditions recognize that people's different talents equip them to make diverse, but equally valuable, contributions to our common life (Romans 12:4–8).[27] Scripture particularly etches the roles of prophet and peacemaker. While the psalmist extols the blessings of "kindred living together in unity" (133:1), Jeremiah rebukes those whose desire for quiet leads to passivity in the face of evil. "From prophet to priest ... they have treated the wound of my people carelessly, saying 'Peace, peace' when there is no peace" (16:13–14). The life and teachings of Jesus display a similar tension, extolling "peacemakers" in the Sermon on the Mount but later warning his disciples, "I have not come to bring peace, but a sword" (Matthew 5:9; 10:34).

Martin Luther King's leadership stands out as a creative synthesis of the roles of peacemaker and prophet.[28] Such a synthesis, when it occurs, can surprise the world and lead to unexpected breakthroughs. It can also, as King, India's Mahatma Ghandi, Egypt's Anwar Sadat, and Israel's Yitzhak Rabin demonstrated, attract an assassin's bullet. The assumption of such roles takes place at all levels of political life. The first criterion, of course, should be faithfulness. But we should beware of judging too quickly. Our communities need prophets *and* peacemakers, agitators and conciliators, advocates and mediators, not all looking or sounding alike, sometimes challenging, sometimes complementing one another.

Neither is it always straightforward or simple to translate religious precepts into political action. In the years prior to World War II, for example, Reinhold Niebuhr challenged those who interpreted the love ethic to counsel nonresistance and pacifism. Such a view, he said, owed more to Enlightenment notions of human perfectibility than to a "Christian realism" that, in taking full account of human sin and the will to power, recognized "that justice [could] be achieved only by a certain degree of coercion on the one hand, and by resistance to coercion and tyranny on the other hand."[29]

Passion must also employ reason, even calculation. In the legislative arena, the anticipation of consequences is essential. I recall an early 2007 discussion in caucus of a Democratic proposal to put conditions and withdrawal deadlines on a supplemental appropriations bill on Iraq. One colleague stated that because the bill did not immediately and absolutely defund the war, he was not certain that he, as a former seminarian, could vote for it "in good conscience." This prompted me to say that I too was a former seminarian—the only time, I believe, that I ever played that card—and that I remembered the distinction from Ethics 101 between deontological and consequentialist theories of ethics (although of course I did not lay those exact terms on my colleagues!). What, I asked, if the result of joining Republicans in a "no" vote, because our proposal fell short of liberal members' notion of perfection, was to bring it down? What if the consequence was to forfeit the best chance we might have for some time to compel a change in war policy? What if the result was to show fatal weakness and divisions and thus to compromise our longer-term prospects for taking foreign policy in a new direction? It was *precisely* "conscience," I said, that required us not merely to measure our bill against an ideal standard but to count the costs and calculate the consequences of defeat.

Recall too the 2019 run-up to impeachment, recounted in Chapter 7. As the Mueller investigation continued, it was already clear that the president had committed grave, probably impeachable, offenses. I increasingly began to hear from constituents that it was a matter of conscience to immediately come out in favor of impeachment, or at least an impeachment inquiry. I particularly remember a discussion with some of my strongest hometown supporters at a June 6, 2019, fundraising reception. I expressed the apprehension that for the House to proceed to impeachment on the basis of what we already knew and were likely to learn from Mueller might well result in a successful vote in the House, albeit a difficult one for a number of swing-seat Democrats. But Republicans in the Senate would surely acquit, after which the president would take claims of a hyperpartisan process and his complete vindication into the 2020 election, with devastating political effect.

It turned out that many of my friends shared those apprehensions. A searching discussion ensued, which made it clear that those worrying about political and electoral consequences—a second Trump administration—were no less conscientious or principled than those who felt that the need to act immediately on Trump's offenses overrode such calculations. Of course, with the revelation in September of Trump's attempts to extort Ukraine's president, the balance of considerations shifted radically. These allegations were so serious and so clearly involved impeachable conduct that the imperative to pursue an inquiry was overwhelming. The predictions regarding Senate acquittal and Trump's electoral use of the episode still held, but additional likely consequences entered the picture, ranging from the constitutional precedent we would set to the reactions of our own voters. The calculations shifted, in other words, but not the need to weigh trade-offs and consequences.

Passion and conviction are compatible with seeking common ground with those who come to politics from varied backgrounds of perspectives—indeed, they often require it. The happy experience of the civil rights movement and of many movements since is that one can bring one's deepest convictions to political advocacy and at the same time ally with people whose theological and philosophical perspectives differ greatly and sometimes do not have conventional religious roots at all. This will often involve going beyond a specifically religious frame of reference, invoking the commonly held values and shared aspirations of the wider community. It also requires a willingness to "reason together," as opposed to viewing our religious convictions as debate-stoppers.

Religious conservatives sometimes portray the search for common ground as requiring them, as one of my colleagues put it, "to check my Christian beliefs at the public door." There is also a tendency to see the invoking of universal values as producing a mere "common denominator" that lacks specificity or force.[30] That, I believe, greatly underestimates the power of the fundamental principles of our constitutional democracy, which have deep religious roots but also find broader resonance. Certainly it would have come as news to Frederick Douglass and Martin Luther King, as they invoked the Declaration of Independence to combat slavery and segregation, that making a universalistic appeal diluted their passion or the force of their argument.[31]

What if such common ground is not to be found? Obviously, there are sectarian rules and observances that individuals and communities regard as binding, with no thought of extending them to the broader community. But the boundaries delineating how and to what degree religious convictions may legitimately be taken into the public arena are neither clear nor uncontroversial. Some politicians, for example, including many who are personally opposed to abortion on religious or moral grounds, argue against "imposing" such beliefs on society. Other abortion opponents regard that position as unjustifiably preempting legitimate policy debate. Still others bring to the debate a positive defense of the Supreme Court's *Roe v. Wade* decision in moral and religious terms.

Our religiously inspired judgments as to what is moral and our political judgments as to what can and should be embodied in law are related, but they are not the same thing. The complexity of the relationship is compounded in a pluralistic setting, where multiple religious and ethical traditions flourish. We should move cautiously indeed in enshrining in civil law moral precepts that lack substantial support beyond a specific religious tradition. The U.S. Constitution, former New York governor Mario Cuomo acknowledged, "guarantees my right to try to convince you to adopt my religion's tenet as public law.... The question for the religious public official then [becomes] ... *Should* I try?" Cuomo's suggested criterion for crossing that threshold was the presence of consensus, or the "plausibility of achieving that consensus," on the basis of convictions shared in the community at large.[32]

How do such considerations apply to the abortion issue? It surely is an area where consensus is lacking, but while the arguments made for government restrictions are mostly moral and religious, they are not always narrowly sectarian. We cannot simply declare them "off limits" for political debate. We must engage—within religious and other institutions of civil society as well as in the political arena. We would do well to consider Cuomo's prudential counsel: in a pluralistic setting where ethical common ground cannot be found, we generally should refrain from placing specific religious and moral precepts in civil law, rather leaving the individual and communal expression of conscience free. But we also engage in terms of countervailing values such as personal liberty, self-determination, and the health and well-being of women and families, and a theologically grounded understanding of the voluntaristic character of religious obedience. The desire to embody morality in the law must be tempered by a recognition of the deficiencies and dangers—not least, to religious liberty—of using the authority of the state to enforce any group's disputed concept of moral behavior.

Many additional questions surround the agenda for engagement—not only what issues are best left free of government prescription, but also how to prioritize the wide range of issues with implications for faith and morality. Religious communities often seem to talk past one another. Conservative groups focus on matters such as abortion and gay marriage, while liberals stress questions of economic justice and war and peace. We should welcome convergence where we find it, on issues ranging from human trafficking to global health and hunger to environmental stewardship. But all would do well to guard against the human tendency to address only those questions and heed only those teachings that we find convenient or comfortable.

There is no escaping selective judgment, however, whether we are dealing with the codes of Leviticus or the admonitions in the Sermon on the Mount. Much depends on how we read and understand the Bible—referencing scriptural commands, for example, as opposed to heeding the admonitions throughout the prophets and the New Testament to attend less to the minutiae of the law and more to its "weightier matters … justice and mercy and faith," (Matthew 23:23). Relating faith and politics is not merely a matter of personally obeying commands; it requires ongoing efforts to mine the riches of our religious traditions and to apply them to new and challenging circumstances across our society.

These efforts will determine the way we relate to our community and our country, our politics, and our patriotism. William Sloane Coffin, a powerful, prophetic preacher who was chaplain at Yale during all of my years there, had a striking formulation. There are three kinds of patriots, he said, two bad and one good. The bad ones are the "uncritical lovers" of their country and the "loveless critics." But good patriots "carry on a lover's quarrel with their country, a reflection of God's lover's quarrel with all the world."[33] Indeed, this is the kind of patriotism—loyalty to our country, coupled with a determination to mend its flaws—on which America continues to depend. It is not a monopoly of the people of faith, but neither is it a mere option: people of faith have a solemn obligation to seek justice, mercy, and peace in a sinful world.

Faith and Politics: Humility and Constraint

Even as our faith prompts passionate engagement in the political arena, it also raises warnings and suggests constraints on the form and content of our advocacy. Two constraints written into the U.S. Constitution—checks and balances among the major organs of government, and the First Amendment's twin prohibitions of the "establishment" of religion or the prevention of its "free exercise"—have deep religious roots and continuing significance in terms of our understanding of human nature and religious liberty.

Why constraints? While our faith traditions reject cynicism and the placing of arbitrary limits on our aspirations, they also provide a realistic view of human nature and the pervasiveness of sin and self-interest in society. We should have no illusions about the evils of which human beings, individually and collectively, are capable. Our task in politics therefore becomes not only to utilize power for the common good but also to check the abuses of power that will inevitably occur. Reinhold Niebuhr's most quoted line is pertinent here: "Man's capacity for justice makes democracy possible; but man's inclination to injustice makes democracy necessary."[34] No policy or program, even the most well intentioned, can escape the taint of self-interest and self-seeking. Consequently, the task of democracy is not only to realize our positive aspirations but also to provide a check against miscarriages of justice and abuses of power.

The framers of the Constitution believed that no governmental power could safely go unchecked. They therefore "contriv[ed] the interior structure of the government [so] that its several constituent parts [might], by their mutual relations, be the means of keeping each other in their proper places." James Madison's reflections on these arrangements revealed a persistent streak of Calvinism among these heirs of the Enlightenment:

> It may be a reflection on human nature that such devices should be necessary to control the abuses of government. But what is government itself but the greatest of all reflections on human nature? If men were angels, no government would be necessary. If angels were to govern men, neither external nor internal controls on government would be necessary. In framing a government which is to be administered by men over men, the great difficulty lies in this: You must first enable the government to control the governed; and in the next place oblige it to control itself. A dependence on the people is, no doubt, the primary control on the government; but experience has taught mankind the necessity of auxiliary precautions.[35]

Thus do we draw on our religious traditions in recognizing the distortions and dangers to which the exercise of political power is liable and in protecting ourselves against them.

This view, interpreted by Reinhold Niebuhr as a landmark expression of "Christian realism," must be distinguished from the more simplistic antipower ideology that persistently rears its head in American politics. Government is hardly the only realm in which power exists or can be abused; in fact, political power can be used to counter or control economic, military, or other kinds of power. Realism requires that we not only attend to the dangers of strengthening a given organ of government but also to the powers and interests that might fill the vacuum if it is weakened. There is nothing automatically efficacious about checkmated governmental institutions; a simplistic distrust of power is sometimes a poor guide to what is required to make institutions function accountably and effectively. What the realism rooted in our religious traditions offers is, rather, an awareness of the presence of self-interest and self-seeking in all human endeavors, the necessity of using power deliberately as we pursue the common good, and the need for checks and safeguards as we recognize the vulnerability of power in all realms to distortion and abuse.

The First Amendment's dual provisions also have religious roots and also constrain our politics. Government is neither to establish religion nor prohibit its free exercise. There are to be no state-sponsored religious exercises and no religious tests, formal or informal, for political participation or election to office. At the same time, the state is not to discriminate against religion or place undue burdens on religious practice. By no means do these precepts require a "privatization" of faith; the separation of church and state does not require the separation of faith and politics. But there are ground rules for engagement; far from being a secular imposition, those ground rules have deep and firm religious roots. Rogers Williams and other early proponents of church-state separation were far more focused on the liberty of the believer and the integrity of the church than they were on the state's prerogatives. What was and still is at stake is not only civil liberty but also religious faithfulness.

Maintaining a delicate and judicious balance between the antiestablishment and free exercise principles is a continuing challenge for our country. Occasionally, advocates have presumed that they might improve on the First Amendment. One such effort, the so-called Religious Freedom Amendment to the Constitution, fell considerably short of the required two-thirds vote in the House of Representatives in 1998. This amendment, a project of the religious right, went considerably beyond the school prayer amendments of years past, relaxing the barriers to state-sponsored religious exercises and to government aid for sectarian institutions.[36] An impressive alliance of mainline religious organizations worked to defeat the amendment, and it was significant how many of the members opposing it spoke not only of protecting constitutional democracy, of which freedom from religious coercion is a cornerstone, but also of protecting freedom *for* the unimpeded expression of religious faith and conviction.

Establishment clause debate has continued over such issues as federal funding for religious schools, government-sponsored religious exercises, religious displays on public property, and government support of religiously sponsored programs or projects. The boundaries of the latter have been tested by state and federal "faith-based initiatives." The George W. Bush administration pushed (and exceeded) the limits, but the Democratic response left much to be desired as well.

Religious organizations and congregations had long utilized federal funding to construct and operate housing for the elderly and the disabled, shelter and feed the homeless, deliver hot meals to elderly shut-ins, and provide other services. They normally carried out these activities through affiliated but legally distinct entities—often called 501(c)(3) organizations from the relevant section of the tax code—which prevented federal funds from being used for religious worship or proselytization and ensured nondiscriminatory practices in hiring and the choice of beneficiaries. This is what Bush sought to change. His legislative proposals and the executive order he ultimately issued weakened the barriers to the funding of sectarian activity and removed them with respect to discrimination in hiring.

From the perspective of my district, where faith-based initiatives had flourished for years, this had the appearance of "fixing" a system that was not broken. But many Democrats overreacted, seeming hostile to the very idea of facilitating the work of religious groups. By contrast, I thought we should have said, "Welcome to the cause, Mr. President! We've been doing this right all along, consistent with the First Amendment. Where have you been?"

The free exercise clause has provoked even more controversy in recent years. Religious liberty is not an absolute, but it has been given strong deference by the courts and by Congress—particularly by the Religious Freedom Restoration Act of 1993, which increased the burden of proof facing any law that restricted free exercise. What are the appropriate limits? Sometimes when the establishment clause itself comes into play, as when religious exercises are performed in the public square. Sometimes it is when third-party harm is threatened, as when parents deny blood transfusions or vaccinations to their children. Sometimes public health and safety may be at stake. A particularly misguided application arose in 2020 amid the coronavirus pandemic, as scattered judges ruled that churches should be exempted from the limits on the size of indoor gatherings that states adopted. In a 5–4 ruling that "should have been unanimous," the Supreme Court rejected this interpretation of the free exercise clause.[37]

Increasingly, religious liberty arguments have been used to justify the denial of liberties or rights to others. Should providers of public accommodation be allowed, by virtue of their religious convictions, to deny services to LGBTQ individuals or others of whom they morally disapprove? Should corporations, in offering health insurance coverage to their employees, be able to claim a religious exemption to the Affordable Care Act's requirement that contraceptive services be covered? The Supreme Court decided in the 2014 *Burwell v. Hobby Lobby* case, by a 5–4 vote, that the answer to the latter question was "yes," and the controversy continues to reverberate.[38]

Such disputes remind us that, as much as we might look to constitutional or other principles to guide and constrain us as we relate faith to politics, they remain open to interpretation and misinterpretation, to use and abuse. We must exercise discerning judgment, and we should do so with some humility and wariness of the pretensions of others.

Such a posture comes from deep within our faith traditions, yet it can be a heavy lift indeed. Few virtues seem as out of fashion nowadays as humility. In-your-face assertiveness is in vogue, and uncertainty or even reflectiveness—to say nothing of willingness to admit error or change one's mind—are often equated with weakness, a lack of moral fiber, or a fatal lack of confidence. It is jarring in this context to realize that the apostle Paul regarded people's tendency toward prideful self-glorification to be the very essence of sin.

Interpreting the Pauline view, Reinhold Niebuhr saw particular danger in *spiritual* pride, "when our partial standards and relative attainments are explicitly related to the unconditional good, and claim divine sanction." The worst form of intolerance, he went on, "is religious intolerance, in which the particular interests of the contestants hide behind religious absolutes. The worst form of self-assertion is religious self-assertion, in which under the guise of contrition before God, [God] is claimed as the exclusive ally of our contingent self."[39]

Niebuhr did not issue these warnings as a secularist, skittish about the influence faith might have on public affairs. His was a prophetic faith, leading him to a lifetime of engagement in the struggle for justice. But integral to that faith is the recognition that people are inclined to a kind of idolatry whereby they identify their own interests or ideologies with God's sovereign will. That will remains transcendent and is only imperfectly reflected in human endeavors, which are invariably subject to the taint of self-seeking and the will to power. "We must not regard any human institution or object as being an end in itself," wrote Rabbi Heschel. "Man's achievements in this world are but attempts, and a temple that comes to mean more than a reminder of the living God is an abomination."[40]

The American statesman who best understood these matters was Abraham Lincoln. Recall the words of his second inaugural address, all the more remarkable for being uttered after almost four years of civil war:

> Both [sides] read the same Bible, and pray to the same God; and each invokes His aid against the other. It may seem strange that any men should dare to ask a just God's assistance in wringing their bread from the sweat of other men's faces; but let us judge not, that we be not judged. The prayers of both could not be answered—that of neither has been answered fully.[41]

Niebuhr once wrote that this passage "puts the relation of our moral commitments in history to our religious reservations about the partiality of our moral judgments more precisely than, I think, any statesman or theologian has put them."[42]Lincoln expressed the moral commitment against slavery in uncompromising terms, along with his determination to "finish the work we are in." But there followed the religious reservation, the recognition that ultimate judgment belonged to God alone, the refusal, even in this extreme instance, to presume an absolute identification between his own cause and God's will.

On another occasion, responding to a clergyman who expressed the hope that the Lord was on the side of the Union, Lincoln reportedly said, "I know that the Lord is always on the side of the right. But it is my constant anxiety and prayer that I and this nation should be on the Lord's side."[43]We are too quick to claim that God is on our side, to claim divine sanction for the program that we are promoting or the power that we seek, and sometimes to demonize our opponents. "As all 'God-fearing' men of all ages," Niebuhr warned, we "are never safe against the temptation of claiming God too simply as the sanctifier of whatever we most fervently desire."[44]The crucial question is the one that Lincoln asked: are we on the Lord's side? We ought never to lose that sense of God's transcendence and of the fallibility of all our human efforts, political and otherwise. This is the ultimate reason for rejecting the political pretensions and religious arrogance of those who equate their own program with God's will. Here too we look not only to the tenets of pluralism and the U.S. Constitution but to the deepest insights of our religious traditions themselves. For these traditions counsel a kind of religious humility, a sense that our own strivings are always subject to God's judgment.

The imperatives of faith will continue to require and inspire political action. The fact that others may put a religious label on policies too easily, quickly, or opportunistically does not make the imperative of faith any less compelling. But there are good reasons, rooted not only in democratic experience but also in the theology of divine transcendence and human sinfulness, for refusing to identify any particular ideology or political program with the will of God and for rebuking those who presume to do so. "For my thoughts are not your thoughts, neither are your ways my ways, says the Lord."[45]

Notes

1 See Colin Son, "Clair Engel and the Brain Tumor That Almost Derailed the Civil Rights Act," *Neurosurgical Focus*, 39 (July 2015), p. 1–4.

2 Seymour gives an account of his ministry, particularly as it concerned the struggle for racial justice, in *"Whites Only": A Pastor's Retrospective on Signs of the New South* (Valley Forge, PA: Judson, 1991).

3 Martin Luther King Jr., "Letter from Birmingham Jail," in Herbert J. Storing, ed., *What Country Have I? Political Writings by Black Americans* (New York: St. Martin's, 1970), p. 128.

4 King, "Letter," p. 127.

5 Rev. Jerry Falwell, "Special Memorandum to Pastors," March 7, 1988.

6 *Congressional Record*, daily ed., March 22, 1988, p. H1041.

7 Debate on this latter amendment occasioned the most vicious personal attack I ever witnessed on the House floor. Representative Steve Gunderson (R-Wisconsin), who had acknowledged that he was gay, spoke in opposition to the amendment. He was immediately attacked by Rep. Robert Dornan (R-California): "He has a revolving door on his closet. He's in, he's out, he's in, he's out, he's in. I guess you're [now] out because you went up and spoke at a huge homosexual dinner." The manager of the bill, Rep. Bill Ford (D-Michigan), demanded that Dornan's words be "taken down" because of the personal and demeaning nature of the attack. As presiding officer, I was astounded by the viciousness of the attack and needed considerable guidance from the parliamentarian in handling the situation. After a few minutes, Dornan withdrew his words, stopping the process short. For this reason, the text remaining in the *Congressional Record* (March 24, 1994, p. 6560) does not reflect the full exchange.

8 *Congressional Record*, daily ed., September 29, 1994, pp. H10277–H10278; and *Congressional Quarterly Almanac* 50 (1994), p. 42.

9 E. J. Dionne Jr., *Souled Out: Reclaiming Faith and Politics after the Religious Right* (Princeton, NJ: Princeton University Press, 2008), p. 1. On the historical backdrop of the 2004 outcome, see Amy Sullivan, *The Party Faithful: How and Why Democrats Are Closing the "God Gap"* (New York: Scribner, 2008).

10 Dionne, *Souled Out*, p. 52; Nancy Gibbs and Michael Duffy, "Leveling the Praying Field," *Time*, July 21, 2007. Dionne noted, however, that even at this "high point" of religious polarization, this was "not the whole story"—noting the interactive impacts of race and ethnicity, class, and religion (pp. 50–61).

11 See David E. Price, "Faith Engaging Politics: Passion and Constraint," *Reflections* (magazine of Yale Divinity School), 94 (Fall, 2007), pp. 65–68; and "Faith Informing Politics: Pitfalls and Promise," lecture delivered at the Walter H. Capps Center of the Study of Ethics, Religion, and Public Life, University of California–Santa Barbara, June 1, 2008.

12 For Clyburn's reflections on the 2004 losses, marked by Democrats' failure to speak "in terms of morality and fundamental values," and the formation of the Faith Working Group, see his *Blessed Experiences: Genuinely Southern, Proudly Black* (Columbia, SC: University of South Carolina Press, 2014), pp. 245–247.

13 Amy Sullivan, "The Dems' Delicate Dance on Faith," *Time*, April 15, 2008. See especially Obama's keynote address at the Call for Renewal's 2006 Conference, *New York Times*, June 28, 2006.

14 Laurie Goodstein, "Religious Voting Data Show Some Shift, Observers Say," *New York Times*, November 9, 2006. For a fuller account of Democratic campaign efforts, see Sullivan, *The Party Faithful*, chapter 7.

15 Sullivan, "A Very Merry War on Christmas," *New York Times*, December 17, 2017. See Gregory Smith and Jessica Martinez, "How the Faithful Voted: A Preliminary 2016 Analysis," Pew Research Center, November 9, 2016.

16 Rob Stutzman, "Trump Is a Religious Poser: That Gives Biden an Opportunity," *Washington Post*, May 31, 2019. See also Emma Green, "Democrats Have to Decide Whether Faith Is an Asset for 2020," *The Atlantic*, April 5, 2019.

17 See Adelie M. Banks, "The Obama Presidency: 'War on Religion' or 'Amazing Grace'?" *Religion News*, January 9, 2017.

18 Michael Gerson, "Evangelical Christians Found Their Own Goliath," *Washington Post*, January 4, 2019; and Gerson, "Trump Evangelicals Have Sold Their Souls," *Washington Post*, March 13, 2018. On Trump's "unholy outburst" at the 2020 National Prayer Breakfast, which included a disavowal of Jesus's command to "love your enemies," see Gerson, "The Negation of the Christian Ethic," *Washington Post*, February 7, 2020, p. A23.

19 Sullivan, "War on Christmas." By "Fox evangelicalism" Sullivan means the "emerging religious worldview … preached from the pulpits of conservative media outlets like Fox News [that] imbues secular practices like shopping for gifts with religious significance and declares sacred something as worldly and profane as gun culture."

20 1 Samuel 8:20.

21 H. Richard Niebuhr, *Christ and Culture* (New York: Harper, 1956), p. 2.

22 See Harry R. Davis and Robert C. Good, eds., *Reinhold Niebuhr on Politics* (New York: Scribner's, 1960), chaps. 12–14.

23 W.L. Miller, *The Protestant and Politics* (Philadelphia, PA: Westminster, 1958), p. 24. See Luke 10:29–37.

24 Abraham Joshua Heschel, "On Prayer," in Susannah Heschel, ed., *Moral Grandeur and Spiritual Audacity* (New York: Noonday, 1996), p. 261.

25 Quoted in Arthur Waskow, "'My Legs Were Praying': Theology and Politics in Abraham Joshua Heschel," *Conservative Judaism*, volume L, number 2–3 (Winter–Spring 1998), p. 144.

26 For an account of the Institute's work and how it enriched her congressional service, see Lois Capps, *Keeping Faith in Congress* (Minneapolis, MN: Fortress Press, 2018), chap. 7.

27 "We have gifts that differ according to the grace given to us: prophecy, in proportion to faith; ministry, in ministering ; the teacher, in teaching … the compassionate, in cheerfulness" (vv. 6–8).

28 See, for example, King's characterization of nonviolent resistance: "Not passive non-resistance to evil [but] active nonviolent resistance to evil … directed against

forces of evil rather than against persons who happen to be doing the evil."
Stride toward Freedom (New York: Ballantine Books, 1958), p. 82.

29 Davis and Good, eds., *Niebuhr on Politics*, p. 148.

30 See Mark Souder, "A Conservative Christian's View on Public Life," in E. J.
Dionne Jr. et al., eds., *One Electorate under God?* (Washington, DC: Brookings
Institution Press, 2004), p. 21. See my rejoinder at p. 168. Souder objects to
limitations both on the issues that are appropriate for debate in the public sphere
and on the arguments regarded as admissible.

31 "What does July Fourth mean to the slave?" Douglass thundered in 1852. "To
him your celebration is a sham; your boasted liberty, an unholy license; your
national greatness, swelling vanity ... your shouts of liberty and equality, hollow
mockery; your prayer and hymns ... with all your religious parade and solemnity,
are to him, mere bombast, fraud, deception, impiety, and hypocrisy—a thin veil
to cover up crimes which would disgrace a nation of savages." Philip S. Foner,
ed., *Frederick Douglass: Selections from His Writings* (New York: International
Publishers, 1964), pp. 52–53. Compare Amos 5:21–24: "I hate, I despise your
feasts, and I take no delight in your solemn assemblies.... But let justice roll
down like waters, and righteousness like an ever-flowing stream."

32 Mario Cuomo, "In the American Catholic Tradition of Realism," in E. J. Dionne
et al., eds., *One Electorate under God* (Washington, DC: Brookings Institution
Press, 2004), pp. 14–15. "As I understood my own religion," Cuomo said of his
Catholicism, "it required me to accept the restraints it imposed in my own life,
but it did not require that I seek to impose all of them on all New Yorkers," (p.
14).

33 William Sloane Coffin, *Credo* (Louisville, KY: Westminster John Knox Press,
2004), p. 84.

34 Davis and Good, eds., *Niebuhr on Politics*, p. 186.

35 James Madison, "The Federalist," no. 51, in Clinton Rossiter, ed., *The Federalist
Papers* (New York: Mentor, 1961), p. 322.

36 The text of the proposed amendment was as follows: "To secure the people's
right to acknowledge God according to the dictates of conscience: Neither the
United States nor any State shall establish any official religion, but the people's
right to pray and to recognize their religious beliefs, heritage, or traditions on
public property, including schools, shall not be infringed. Neither the United
States nor any State shall require any person to join in prayer or other religious
activity, prescribe school prayers, discriminate against religion, or deny equal
asset to a benefit on account of religion" (House Joint Resolution 78, 105th
Congress). My floor statement on the proposal may be found in *Congressional
Record*, daily ed., June 4, 1998, pp. H4074–H4075; also see the statements of
Reps. Vic Fazio and Bill Hefner, pp. H4093–H4094.

37 *South Bay United Pentecostal Church et al v. Gavin Newsom et al*, 590 US ____
(2020). See Linda Greenhouse, "The Supreme Court, Too, Is on the Brink," *New
York Times*, June 7, 2020, p. SR-2.

38 573 US 682 (2014).

39 Niebuhr, *The Nature and Destiny of Man* (New York: Charles Scribners' Sons,
1949), I, pp. 200–201.

40 Abraham Joshua Heschel, *God in Search of Man* (New York: Octagon, 1972),
p. 415.

41 Philip Stern, ed., *The Life and Writings of Abraham Lincoln* (New York: Modern
Library, 1940), p. 841.

42 Quoted in William Lee Miller, *President Lincoln: The Duty of a Statesman* (New
York: Alfred A. Knopf, 2008), pp. 403–404. I am drawing here on Miller's
insightful exegesis. For further exposition of the Second Inaugural as "almost

a perfect model of the difficult but not impossible task of remaining loyal and responsible toward the moral treasures of a free civilization on the one hand while yet having some religious vantage point over the struggle," with an application of the model to the post–World War II conflict with communism, see Niebuhr, *The Irony of American History* (New York: Scribner's, 1952), pp. 171–174.

43 Francis B. Carpenter, *Six Months at the White House with Abraham Lincoln* (New York: Herd & Houghton, 1867), p. 282.

44 Niebuhr, *Irony*, p. 173.

45 Isaiah 55:8.

11 Public Service in Moral Perspective

As a member who came to the Congress in 1987 from a teaching career that included work in ethics and public policy, it seemed strange to me to hear talk of an "ethics craze" in government and to witness a recurring preoccupation with ethical matters, centered around the troubles of House Speakers Jim Wright and Newt Gingrich but by no means limited to those episodes.

My first assignment on joining the Duke University faculty in 1973 was to devise an ethics course to be required as a component of the graduate public policy curriculum. Over the next decade, I worked with a growing group of academics and practitioners across the country, holding workshops, writing papers, attending conferences—promoting the study and teaching of professional ethics while developing its intellectual content and broadening its applications. I thus stepped into the swirling waters of ethical agitation and debate in the House with considerable background in the subject, but that background often seemed to have precious little relevance to what passed for ethical discussion there.

I say that not in criticism of the fields of political and public policy ethics as they have developed in academia. I am more inclined to be critical of prevailing public and congressional conceptions of ethics, what I will somewhat disparagingly term "ethics committee" ethics. This does not mean that the ethics committees and the congressional code of conduct should appreciably broaden their domain. The point, rather, is that the implications of ethical reflection and analysis for the Congress—for the policies it makes and how its members function—go far beyond what can or should be contained in a code or enforced by a watchdog committee. It is that broader conception of ethics and its relevance to legislative life that I will explore in this chapter.

Numerous colleagues and I had examined the ethical content of the legislator's role as part of a major Hastings Center project in the early 1980s.[1] What I encountered as a member was an intensifying ethical concern in Congress itself, which was partly but not entirely a defensive reaction to the willingness of Newt Gingrich and others to wield ethics charges as weapons in partisan warfare. This concern led to the appointment of the House Bipartisan Task Force on Ethics and the passage of the Government Ethics

Reform Act of 1989, which embellished ethics committee ethics considerably without significantly broadening the terms of discussion and debate.

A readiness to believe the worst about the motives and the integrity of public officials has characterized American political culture from the beginning. Historians like Bernard Bailyn and James Sterling Young documented the prevalence of a strong anti-power ideology in the revolutionary and subsequent generations, a conviction that those with political power would invariably abuse it and that corruption and self-aggrandizement were endemic to government.[2] Young attributed the disabilities and demoralization of the early congresses in large measure to the tendency of the members to internalize the dominant public view of "power-holding as essentially a degrading experience.... The power-holders did not, in their own outlook, escape a culturally ingrained predisposition to view political power and politics as essentially evil."[3] Such cynicism and the mistrust of officeholders and public institutions have been heightened in recent years by highly publicized scandals and by the growing inclination of the modern mass media to publicize and dramatize the foibles and failings of politicians.

For most of their first two centuries, the House and Senate had no written codes of behavior but dealt sporadically and often inconsistently with discrete acts of wrongdoing. I came across one such instance in researching a brief bicentennial piece on those who preceded me in representing my district in North Carolina. I discovered that one of my predecessors, a Reconstruction congressman named John Deweese, had resigned his seat in 1870 one day before he and two other members were censured for selling appointments to the military academies. Progressive era reform sentiments and various election scandals led to a series of federal campaign practices statutes beginning in 1907. After World War II, Congress finally moved to adopt more general codes of conduct for its members. The first was a government-wide aspirational code, adopted in 1958 in the wake of the Sherman Adams–Bernard Goldfine scandal in the Eisenhower administration. Widely publicized congressional scandals a decade later involving Sen. Thomas Dodd, Senate majority secretary Bobby Baker, and Rep. Adam Clayton Powell led both chambers to form standing committees on ethics and to adopt their first formal codes of conduct. These were toughened considerably in 1977 and again in 1989.[4]

The 1989 changes, passed after the resignation under fire of Speaker Jim Wright and packaged with a major increase in congressional pay, tightened limits on outside income and eliminated speaking fees (honoraria), strengthened financial disclosure requirements, enjoined members from converting campaign funds to personal use on retirement, and prohibited lobbying by members and staff for one year after leaving their positions. These reforms, rightly portrayed as "sweeping" relative to earlier efforts, attempted to address growing anti-institutional turbulence.[5] But they were comprehensive only in relation to the already defined domain of congressional ethics.

The same was true of the establishment in 2009 of the House Office of Congressional Ethics (OCE), which nonetheless made significant changes in the ethics process. OCE receives and reviews complaints from the public regarding alleged misconduct by members and, when appropriate, refers findings of fact to the Committee on Ethics. I served briefly on the task force that proposed the new office, convened by Speaker Nancy Pelosi as Democrats assumed leadership and ably chaired by Rep. Michael Capuano (D-Massachusetts). The OCE addressed long-simmering complaints about the pitfalls of Congress's policing itself and provided a more accountable means of dealing with charges from sources outside the institution.[6] But some members, although eventually exonerated, found that the OCE process subjected them to damaging exposure and large legal expenses.

The 1985 Hastings report acknowledged that a code of official conduct should be only "one element in a well-rounded effort to inspire the conduct of legislators as well as to engender trust on the part of the public in those legislators." Nonetheless, it still was critical of the limits of existing codes: "They are generally narrow in scope, short on aspirational statements, and fail to deal with the full range of representative or legislative functions."[7] The report proposed three touchstones for legislative ethics: autonomy (the "obligation to deliberate and decide, free from improper influence"), accountability (the "obligation to provide constituents with the information and understanding they require in order to exercise responsible democratic citizenship"), and responsibility (the "obligation to contribute to the effective institutional functioning of the democratic legislative process").[8] Existing codes address the first two principles in their conflict of interest and financial disclosure provisions, but they still construe autonomy and accountability quite narrowly and barely deal with responsibility.

The Hastings report suggested that a more adequate code of legislative ethics might contain aspirational elements and espoused ideals as well as precisely defined rules of conduct.[9] It probably underestimated the difficulty of reaching consensus on aspirational maxims and did not suggest what kind of enforcement mechanisms, if any, might be appropriate in this realm. But it was correct in noting the severe limitations of ethics committee ethics. Using that as my point of departure, I want to look beyond personal and official probity and ask what further ethical dilemmas and challenges confront legislators as they define and carry out their jobs. I will begin, however, with an account of some of the intellectual tools—historical, ethical, analytical—that have proved most valuable in gaining a perspective on my job and the decisions I confront.

Education for Public Life

When I am asked how I first got into politics, my inclination, as noted in Chapter 2, is not to describe my party chairmanship or even my first congressional campaign, but to go back to my formative years in the 1960s, when the civil rights movement pricked the country's conscience and our collective sights were lifted as to what politics and policy might achieve. There, my political course was set.

Similarly, when asked about academic preparation for a career in politics or public service, I'm inclined to stress broad exposure to the arts, humanities, and social sciences rather than more narrow or specialized kinds of training, at least in my undergraduate years. As an advisor to students, I always suggested a basic course in economics and courses that developed writing skills, regardless of their career goals. I also regard the growing popularity of internships and study abroad as promising developments. But my own career experience—as well as the strengths and deficiencies I have observed in working with colleagues and staff—have made me more convinced than ever of the value of a liberal arts education. That is the main reason I have gladly co-chaired the House Humanities Caucus and helped commission and propagate the work of the American Academy of Arts and Sciences' Commission on the Humanities and Social Sciences.[10]

I will illustrate by citing three specific "connections" between what I have read, researched, and taught in the humanities and what our country has experienced—and I have needed to understand and interpret—during my period of service. The first concerns what might be called the "antifederalist moment" we have been experiencing in American politics—ideas and attitudes about government that have hobbled our country's response to the COVID-19 pandemic and may or may not be altered in its aftermath.

I used to tell my students that if they wanted to understand our constitutional history they should read *The Federalist*, but if they really wanted to understand American politics, they should read the antifederalists. American revolutionary thought, as Bernard Bailyn and others have pointed out, was distinctive in its juxtaposing of power and liberty—with little sense that power might serve or expand liberty, or that governmental power might counter power in other realms. The inclination rather was to see the power of government and the liberty of citizens as fundamentally opposed. This proved to be problematic as a governing principle, and after six perilous years under the Articles of Confederation, the drafters of the Constitution sought to strike a new balance between what they called "energy in government" and the checks and balances that would keep that government within its proper bounds.

The antifederalists were having none of it. In considering the proposed government, one of them wrote to a Boston newspaper, we "ought to look upon those who are to put it in motion as our enemies—to be careful what we give, to see what use it is to be put to, and where to resort for a remedy if it is abused."[11] The antifederalist legacy has major positive aspects, most obviously the addition of the Bill of Rights to the Constitution. But the extreme anti-governmental strain's continuing impact is decidedly mixed— often leading to a misdiagnosis of whose power we should be concerned about and throwing up ideological obstacles to the practical and judicious use of governmental power. Tea Party libertarianism is only antifederalism's latest manifestation, ironically posing as the defender of Federalism and the Constitution. Understanding the historic power of antifederalist themes in American thought can help us understand the appeal such ideas have to a major segment of America's population and how, at least for now, they have gained sway over one of our major political parties. And for those of us who find such ideas inadequate to our present reality, understanding how deeply rooted they are will underscore the importance of challenging them with a compelling counter-narrative.

The second connection also hearkens back to a recurring strain in American political thought, a "communitarian" tradition that has often provided a counterpoint or corrective to the dominant themes of liberal individualism and self-determination. Communitarianism highlights the dependence of our sense of self—identity, loyalty, moral responsibility—on the communities that nurture us and in which we situate ourselves. Communitarian thought has Puritan and Transcendentalist roots but received its fullest articulation in the Progressive era, with thinkers ranging from philosopher Josiah Royce to pioneer sociologist Charles Horton Cooley, to political theorists Herbert Croly, W.E.B. DuBois, and John Dewey. These thinkers caught my attention early on and led me to make the late nineteenth–early twentieth century the centerpiece of my teaching and writing in American political thought.[12] David Brooks and E.J. Dionne have recently revisited the tradition with striking results.[13]

Communitarian values and assumptions exist in tension with those central to the American liberal tradition: interdependence alongside autonomy; responsibilities as well as rights; identity, solidarity, and obligation as well as freedom and voluntarism. They thus have serious implications for how we think about moral obligation, our common life, and public policy. And as I will elaborate later in this chapter, they illumine our relationships to public and private institutions. It is common to criticize such institutions and proudly to assert our independence of them. But institutions also shape and channel our loyalties and enable us to achieve collectively what we cannot achieve by ourselves. The failure of institutions can be catastrophic. We thus have an obligation to contribute to their health and effectiveness.

The third connection involves what also must be regarded as a dissenting strain of thought, a sensibility at odds with prevailing views, although it is enshrined in Lincoln's iconic Second Inaugural: the sense of individual and collective fallibility that we bring to politics. We may express this awareness, and our relationship to the powers and purposes larger than ourselves, in theological or non-theological terms. But as noted in Chapter 10, the sensibility—the warning against pride and self-righteousness and the awareness that we are never totally in control—is surely rooted in our religious traditions. It counsels a kind of humility in political life whereby we decline to claim ultimate sanction for our own ideology or political cause and reject the pretensions of those who do make such claims. The relevance to today's politics could hardly be clearer.

A good social science education likewise provides insights—often counterintuitive—as to how the world works. Pioneering theories of collective action, for example, produced a shock of recognition in me as a student in the 1960s, after which I never saw the world in quite the same way. Despite the ultimate value that our society places on individual freedom, we are increasingly faced with challenges before which policies that set out simply to maximize freedom will be not only inadequate to our shared objectives but actually destructive of freedom itself. Garrett Hardin's classic "The Tragedy of the Commons" considers the paradigmatic situation of villagers grazing their cattle on a common pasture. Each farmer, exercising his freedom and seeking to maximize his gain, adds an animal to his herd, then another, and another. But as others do the same, the result is overgrazing and destruction of the resource. "Freedom in a commons brings ruin to all."[14]

Freedom must thus be regulated and constrained; the question in a modern democracy is not whether, but how. Political scientist Jane Mansbridge has noted how many pressing national and international needs take this form: "how to coerce ourselves into giving up what we need to give up in order to stop global warming ... how to stop nuclear proliferation ... how to tax ourselves sufficiently to keep our infrastructure from crumbling, or how to pay for the rising medical costs of an aging population," or how, she now surely would add, to contain and counter a pandemic. In fact, Mansbridge concludes, "solving collective action problems is the most significant reason for government, particularly as society becomes more complex and interdependent." But while such ideas have "swept through the social sciences," their "full implications have still not been assimilated into general knowledge."[15]

In the meantime, what Mansbridge calls the "resistance tradition"—antifederalism, libertarianism—often dominates our politics. Today, however, she concludes "the challenge of creating legitimate coercion is at least as great as the challenge of resisting illegitimate coercion."[16] The challenge is also one of interpretation. When I confront questions in a town meeting about why the Affordable Care Act's individual mandate—the requirement that all participate in the insurance pool—should not be dropped in the name of individual freedom, I'm unlikely to delve directly into the logic of collective action. But devising and interpreting such policies does depend on an understanding, at some level, of these ideas—for both those making the policies and those being asked to accept them as necessary and legitimate.

A comparable challenge is posed by macroeconomic policy, particularly the need for countercyclical stimulative measures during an economic downturn. The relevant theory, mainly associated with John Maynard Keynes, was counterintuitive in the 1930s, but is now a staple of introductory economics classes—"about as controversial in the economics profession as antibiotics in the medical profession," noted Christina Romer, President Obama's first chair of the Council of Economic Advisers, referring to the 2009 Recovery Act.[17]

Republicans drew on the theory in devising their own stimulus plans in 2008, albeit with a preference for tax cuts over increased spending as the main stimulative device. But when they lost the election and had to deal with Obama's stimulus plan—a mix of tax cuts and spending measures—they reverted to a pre-Keynesian proposal to slash spending, making the improbable argument, in an economy with deficient demand, that such cuts would spur confidence and growth. It was clear that many Republicans knew better, since they had earlier put forward their own countercyclical proposals, but they formulated a message of absolute opposition that exploited a lack of basic economic knowledge among their members and the public they were trying to convince. As a result, Michael Grunwald recounts in his insightful history of the episode, "Obama struggled to explain the counterintuitive Keynesian insight that government needs to loosen its belt when families and businesses are tightening theirs."[18] That it was such a struggle raises important questions as to what sort of civic education our era requires for policymakers and informed citizens alike.

Finally, understanding that public policy choices are, among other things, choices of value, places a premium on understanding the historical, philosophical, and theological grounding of our concepts of liberty, justice and fairness, community, and the public interest. How do such concepts complement or contradict one another, and what are their implications for specific questions of policy?[19]

For years I taught a course called Ethics and Public Policy based on the assumption that policymakers and the policy process would benefit from more careful and critical reflection on our inherited notions of human well-being and the public good, coupled with more explicit efforts to discern the implications of these ideas for particular policies and institutions. Much of what I have experienced during my time in the U.S. House has strengthened that assumption. Although the ethical assessment of policy among practicing legislators seldom takes the same form that it does in the academy, our notions of social value come into play as we develop, justify, and press our policy positions.[20] And one element in the viability of a legislative proposal or policy critique is its resonance with widely held notions of justice or the public good.

Competing concepts of social value often arise with particular clarity in the areas of housing and community development. How, for example, should funds for housing rehabilitation be targeted? I used this issue as a textbook case in my class on ethics and public policy, and it is still debated from time to time in congressional committees. One's sense of justice (reinforced in my class with a reading of John Rawls's *A Theory of Justice*) might lead one to give priority to the poorest neighborhoods, to those most in need.[21] But broader utilitarian calculations might lead one to a different conclusion, at least as long as total community development funding does not greatly exceed its present level. Rehabilitation projects can halt deterioration and help turn a marginal neighborhood around at a relatively low cost per unit, providing benefits that extend far beyond those persons directly assisted. In the poorest neighborhoods, by contrast, such funds might likely sink without a trace. Other types of housing programs are needed in the poorest areas, of course, but it would be a mistake to target rehabilitation funds too narrowly in this direction; the money should be used where it can be effective and do the most good for the most people.

A related dilemma concerns the mix of income levels that should be accommodated in affordable housing developments. At the time I joined the Banking Committee, "federal preference" rules in public housing required that priority be given to those who paid more than 50 percent of their income in rent, were involuntarily displaced, or were living in substandard housing. "At face value," the director of the Greensboro Housing Authority told the Subcommittee on Housing and Community Development at the hearing we convened in Raleigh, "these rules suggest fairness, providing that scarce housing resources go to the most needy."[22] But she went on to describe how the rules were requiring the authority to replace the working families who had left public housing with multi-problem families and individuals who could not function independently. These were people who frequently placed a great strain on the inadequate network of community services (such as budget counseling, job training, and tutoring) and aggravated community drug and security problems. What was being lost was the socioeconomic mix that had given public housing projects stability and had provided indigenous role models and leadership. The obligation to assist the most destitute obviously stood in tension with the need to promote the well-being of those already in the project, ensure the viability of the project as a whole, and enable it to function as a community.

It has now become standard practice to provide for a mix of income levels in HOME-funded projects and to replace concentrated, often dilapidated public housing complexes with less dense and more diverse developments. I've had extensive experience with HOPE VI (now called Choice Neighborhoods) projects that take a comprehensive approach to redeveloping distressed neighborhoods—including one, as recounted in Chapter 9, that had to be recalibrated to lessen the displacement of those most in need. As the supply of subsidized housing lags far behind demand and urban development squeezes out more and more poor residents, our ability to accommodate those most in need while maintaining community viability will depend not only on striking the right balance but also on increasing the overall housing supply.

The idea of community and the communitarian strain in American political thought often provide a perspective on policy questions distinctive from those formulated in terms of individual liberty, social utility, or distributive justice.[23] This notion gained currency in the 1990s with the founding of a "communitarian" movement, complete with a quarterly journal and a platform recognizing "both individual human dignity and the social dimension of human existence," under the leadership of sociologist Amitai Etzioni and ethicist William Galston, who later served as President Clinton's deputy assistant for domestic policy. Communitarian ideas helped shape the agenda of the Democratic Leadership Council and Clinton administration initiatives in areas ranging from National Service to family and tax policy and community development.

For two of the efforts described in Chapter 5, I framed much of my argument in explicit communitarian terms. The Teaching Fellows Act drew on the values of community service and reciprocal obligation and focused on collaborative learning and an extensive support system as means of strengthening professional identity. In these latter ways it differed markedly from simply awarding a scholarship to a student or forgiving a loan. The attempt to roll back Federal Communications Commission (FCC) media concentration rules was an even better fit. "The key value at stake," I told the unofficial hearing that Commissioner Michael Copps convened in Durham,

> is *community*, a value partly but not entirely addressed when we speak of 'localism' as a public interest goal.... The term 'media' suggests ... communication within or across a locality or region whereby isolated 'consumers' of media have their identities as members of the community strengthened, their knowledge increased, and their participation enhanced.... If the day comes—and I'm afraid it's fast approaching—when local media are merely a conduit for nationally generated information and entertainment, we will have lost a critically important component of community life.[24]

On questions of war and peace, the most familiar evaluative framework is "just war" theory, rooted in Catholic moral philosophy going back to Augustine and in secular seventeenth- and eighteenth-century systems of international law. In discriminating between the post-9-11 offensive against al Qaeda and the Taliban and the 2002 invasion of Iraq, I and others drew on and adapted just-war concepts such as the proportionality of means to ends and war as a last resort, whether we directly acknowledged it or not. I cited the eminent just-war theorist Michael Walzer in arguing against the rush to war in Iraq and aspired to the kind of moral discrimination that the tradition, at its best, exemplifies.[25] Walzer later elaborated his argument that the necessity of invasion was never established: "Even given the knowledge available at the time, the risks of war should have looked greater than the risks involved in sustaining the containment regime. And there were means available to increase the severity and forcefulness of [that] regime."[26]

In the context of the Bush administration's penchant for unilateralism and preventive wars—to say nothing of the Trump administration's narrow nationalism and disregard for critical alliances—just-war thinking is likely to counsel discrimination and restraint. But nations, like individuals, may commit sins of omission as well as commission, failing to do the good that they can and should do. The genocidal massacres in Rwanda in 1994 offer a drastic and troubling example, as do the atrocities, including chemical warfare, committed by the Assad regime in Syria during the Obama administration. One of the cardinal obligations in the just-war tradition is preventing the slaughter of innocents. Here too rational and prudential calculations are required; not all innocents can be protected nor all tyrannies removed. But looking back, it is impossible to justify the failure of the United States and other nations to intervene as the mass killings in Rwanda and Syria proceeded. Former Secretary of State Madeleine Albright termed the failure in Rwanda her "deepest regret" from her years in public service. Effective action, she argued, "would have required a heavily armed, almost certainly U.S.-led coalition able to deploy quickly, intimidate extremists, arrest leaders, and establish security." While noting the likelihood that such a course would have been rejected by Congress and the public, she regretted her failure to advocate it and wondered aloud if the United States or the world would muster the political will to respond differently next time.[27]

In thinking about war and peace, the perspective offered by our religious traditions (see Chapter 10) is indispensable. Reinhold Niebuhr considered just-war theory vastly superior to pacifism, which he regarded as a simplistic application of the love ethic to politics, and to the moral skepticism he associated with Lutheran theology. But even just-war thinking, he warned, is susceptible to the distortions and blind spots of self-interest and the will to power. There is good reason to be wary of leaders who speak in absolute terms of good and evil or identify the nation's cause with God's will. We must recognize mass murder, dehumanizing ideologies, and brutal tyrannies for what they are, assess the threat they pose, and realistically consider the full range of means that may be required to stop them. We must realize that even peacemaking—if we seek durable peace that goes beyond the mere dominance of the strongest—sometimes requires coercive, violent means. But we must understand the limits and perils of military force and make discriminating judgments about the efficacy and morality of alternative means. And we must be acutely aware, for ourselves as for others, of the dangers of denying one's fallibility or absolutizing one's own cause.

What Sort of Member Shall I Be?

I now want to look at the legislator's responsibility from a different perspective, moving beyond the ethics of policy choice to the role he or she assumes as a member of an ongoing institution. Legislators must define themselves in relation to forces impinging on them from outside and from within the legislature and in terms of their responsibility for the institution's collective performance. Dilemmas of role definition and institutional responsibility depend, in the specific form they take, on the character of the legislative system and the possibilities it offers its members. I will therefore highlight some critical features of the U.S. Congress as it currently operates before focusing on specific dilemmas of role and responsibility that arise in this setting.

Portrayals by leading congressional scholars of members in their institutional environment have shifted significantly since the 1960s, reflecting changing fashions in social science research as well as changes in Congress itself. A sociologically based emphasis on member adaptation to well-defined norms and procedures gave way in the 1970s and 1980s to a portrayal of them as purposive agents in a fluid organizational setting, utilizing assumptions more characteristic of the economist. In the former category, Richard Fenno's landmark studies of the Appropriations Committees stand out, as does Donald Matthews's portrayal of the Senate, centering on the "folkways" of the institution, "its unwritten rules of the game, its norms of conduct, its approved manner of behavior," just like, as one senator put it, "living in a small town."[28] Consider, by contrast, the premise of David Mayhew's pivotal *Congress: The Electoral Connection* (1974). "I have become convinced," Mayhew wrote, "that scrutiny of purposive behavior [of individuals] offers the best route to an understanding of legislatures—or at least of the United States Congress."[29] Mayhew therefore assumed that members of Congress were "single-minded seekers of reelection" and found a close fit between the behavior such an assumption led one to predict and actual congressional performance.

A number of developments made an individualistic portrayal of Congress an increasingly plausible one. Folkways such as the expectation that members would serve an extended period of apprenticeship before taking an active role in committee or on the floor eroded significantly. Members still valued specialization and expertise, but they became less hesitant to get involved in areas beyond their committee assignments. Introducing bills and issuing pronouncements on a wide variety of subjects, formerly the hallmark of a few mavericks, became widely practiced and tolerated, and members were less concerned to maintain a facade of committee or party unity as they took their causes or their amendments to the floor.

These changes were rooted to a considerable extent in an altered electoral environment: the decline of party as a determinant of public perceptions or assessments of politicians; reduced party control over the means of communicating with and mobilizing voters; and the rise of television, direct mail, and other technologies that promised unmediated contact with voters while offering opponents the same possibility. Increasingly on their own electorally and eager to gain visibility and leverage earlier in their congressional careers, members chafed at the traditional folkways and pressed for the dispersal of power and prerogatives within the institution. As already noted, this led to subcommittee proliferation and expanded opportunities for entrepreneurship and participation. It also prompted a strengthening of House party leadership, first as a counterweight to committee oligarchs and then as a corrective to the problems decentralization posed for mobilizing the chamber and realizing members' policy goals.

The centralization of leadership power since the mid-1980s, particularly since the advent in 1995 of Republican control—as well as the "nationalization" of House elections in partisan terms—have exceeded what most students of the "electoral connection" anticipated, leading to academic portrayals of the House as a party-centered institution. By most accounts, however, party government remains "conditional," dependent on homogeneity and agreement within the parties as well as disagreement and polarization between them.[30] The current electoral environment maximizes both of these factors, and party organizations in the House have found effective ways of reinforcing loyalty and discipline. Members nonetheless have numerous conflicting pulls in terms of electoral incentives, group and constituency pressures, and personal beliefs and preferences, and they have considerable leeway in determining what roles they assume.

What shape do decisions regarding role and responsibility take, and what is their ethical significance? I will focus on five questions every legislator must face. The electoral and institutional constraints on members vary considerably in character and severity. In posing these questions I do not assume that members can blithely disregard the profit-and-loss calculations related to maintaining their electoral viability and preserving their place in the institution. I also assume, however, that a broad range of legislative strategies and activities are compatible with, and can be supportive of, self-interest in these senses. Most members of Congress, most of the time, have considerable latitude in defining their roles and what kind of job they wish to do. If they do not have the latitude, they can often create it, for they have a great deal of control over how their actions are perceived and interpreted. Consequently, I conceive of these ethical dilemmas as choices a politician makes within the bounds of political "necessity."

First, *to what range of values and interests should I be responsive?* I may believe that I am being properly representative and responsive if I give a respectful hearing to groups that present themselves on a given issue and then reach a reasonable accommodation among them. Such an assumption finds support in the pluralist school of political science, which assumes that those most intensely interested and directly affected will usually make their voices heard on a given policy question. "Normally," we are assured, "people are not slow to protest when a policy looks like worsening their condition."[31] Public officials, such analysts conclude, generally feel constrained to be attentive to these groups and strike some sort of balance among them. Perhaps that is an acceptable operationalization of representative government under contemporary conditions.

But perhaps not. A number of analysts have argued persuasively that politically active organizations or constituencies that are prepared to press their views on a given question are likely to be a highly selective sample of all those whose interests and values are affected.[32] Furthermore, one cannot assume that all affected interests will find ready access to the political arena. Some lack the organizational or other resources to make their voices heard. Others may be frozen out by the ties that exist between dominant groups and clientele-oriented committees and agencies. Broader, more diffuse interests generally have more difficulty mobilizing their constituencies and developing effective organizational structures than more narrowly based interests whose stakes are more immediate and tangible.

A responsible legislator takes the initiative in looking to poorly organized or nontraditional interests that the system might exclude and to broad, shared public interests and values that are inadequately mirrored in the "pressure system." Many of the features of our politics discourage such an approach—the prominence of organized interests in lobbying and campaign finance, the growth of self-styled "grassroots" organizations that can flood legislators with calls and emails on a moment's notice, the fragmentation and special-interest orientations of committees and subcommittees, and the parties' uncertain roles as mediators between interest groups and public officeholders, because of either incapacity or overidentification with certain group agendas. But taking a broader view of one's representative role need not be seen as self-sacrificial behavior, at least most of the time. Legislators often find it politically profitable to cultivate new constituencies or appeal over the heads of contending groups to a broader public concerned with one issue or another. Such strategies do not succeed automatically. Legislators must work at increasing the salience and attractiveness of their policy stances. To transcend the brokering role and make such moves politically viable and attractive to their colleagues, members must shore up supportive groups, cultivate the media, and broaden the terms of debate.

Responsible representation does not require a dark view of any and all collaboration with "the interests." But neither does it permit a sanguine view of representation as a mere balancing of pressures or an expectation that competition among the interests that are best organized and most vocal in a given area will ensure an equitable outcome. It is important to take account of the biases and exclusions of the group system and of the full range of values and interests a policy question entails.

Second, *to what extent and in what fashion will I contribute to the work of the legislature?* It is often said, by both observers and members, that we legislators are very thinly spread. However, such complaints may miss the mark in accounting for institutional performance. The real problem is the erosion of inducements to engage seriously in the work of Congress. Pulling one's weight in committee and developing a substantial area of expertise are still serviceable strategies for members who desire the esteem of their colleagues. But weakening norms of apprenticeship and specialization, together with the pressures for self-promotion created by the media-dominated electoral environment, have made show horse behavior more profitable and less costly than it was in the past. Members still have strong incentives to latch onto a piece of policy turf, gain control of a subcommittee, and cultivate an image of policy leadership. At the same time, their incentives to engage in the painstaking work of legislative craftsmanship, coalition building, and mobilization may actually be weaker. Incentives to seek out serious discussions and to do one's homework may pale before the pressures of fundraising and the lure of social media. Moreover, the public is only sporadically attentive. This may make the electoral payoffs for merely taking a position, introducing a bill, touting one's loyalty to the party team, or, alternatively, claiming independence of all such ties, greater than those that reward more extensive or consequential efforts.

To stress the importance of serious legislative work is not to denigrate the nonlegislative aspects of the job. Constituent communication and service are worthwhile and necessary. Moreover, they can support the member's legislative efforts in important ways—enhancing the two-way, representative relationship and giving the member the kind of leeway he or she needs for flexible and cooperative legislative involvement.[33] But alterations in the electoral environment and the congressional ethos have made it thinkable, perhaps even profitable, for a number of members to engage almost exclusively in constituency- or media-cultivation activities to the detriment of legislative and oversight tasks. And when members do turn their attention to policy, their involvement is too often superficial and fleeting.

This sort of position taking can be just as deceptive and manipulative as other forms of self-promotion. "Appearing to do something about policy without a serious intention of, or demonstrable capacity for, doing so," as Richard Fenno stressed, "is a corruption of the representative relationship."[34] Such behavior robs the legislative institution of the energy and persistence needed to make it work. Congress still contains many skilled and persistent legislators (more, I think, than Mayhew's model would lead one to predict), and some have managed to make their legislative power and productivity a substantial electoral asset. The institution still depends on members assuming such roles and adopting such priorities, but this behavior is currently more dependent on the choices and proclivities of the members themselves and less on institutional pressures and constraints than it was in the past.

Third, *what responsibilities do I bear for the functioning of the committee and party systems and of Congress as an institution?* Political philosopher Edmund Burke made the classic case for legislators to subordinate their individual ambitions and pretensions and, for the sake of collective effectiveness, to associate and cooperate under the standard of a party:

> No man, who is not inflamed by vain-glory into enthusiasm, can flatter himself that his single, unsupported, desultory, unsystematic endeavors, are of power to defeat the subtle designs and united cabals of ambitious citizens. When bad men combine, the good must associate; else they will fall, one by one, an unpitied sacrifice in a contemptible struggle.[35]

This view squares imperfectly with individualistic notions of moral autonomy to which Americans typically repair—a "Lone Ranger" ethical bias—and which they often bring with them into public service. Sen. Jacob Javits (R-New York) anticipated and no doubt received his readers' applause as he recalled: "In this clash of loyalties—loyalty to constituents, loyalty to party, and loyalty to myself—my constituents and I had to prevail."[36] But we should be wary of imputing ethical superiority to the loner. If the committees and the parties play a legitimate and necessary role in developing and refining measures, aggregating interests, and mobilizing the chamber, should not the member who would violate the comity and the discipline necessary to their successful functioning bear some burden of justification?

The American founders regarded individual virtue—civic virtue, the willingness to forgo private advantage for the sake of the commonwealth—in citizens and in those chosen to govern, as essential to the health of the new republic. They were, however, unwilling to rely on virtue alone or to trust human nature to its own devices. On the contrary, they believed government must be structured in a way that not only anticipated self-serving behavior but turned it to good account. "Ambition must be made to counteract ambition," wrote James Madison in *The Federalist*:

> This policy of supplying, by opposite and rival interests, the defect of better motives [is] particularly displayed in all the subordinate distributions of power, where the constant aim is to divide and arrange the several offices in such a manner as that each may be a check on the other—that the private interest of every individual may be a sentinel over the public rights.[37]

It can be argued, analogously, that certain organizational features of Congress have structured the pursuit of political advantage and turned it to the institution's account. The committee system, for example, accommodates the aspirations of disparate members but also represents a corrective of sorts to congressional individualism—a means of bringing expertise and attention to bear on the legislature's tasks in a more concerted fashion than the free enterprise of individual members could accomplish. The committee system channels members' desires for leverage and status into activity that serves the institution's needs and builds its policymaking capacities. Members are not bound to defer to committee decisions any more than they are bound to contribute to their own committee work product, but in both instances they should give due weight, in assessing their own responsibilities, to what committees contribute to the institution.

I realize that counseling a due regard for the health and effectiveness of congressional structures and processes represents a challenge to our tendency to regard moral responsibility in individualistic and nonconformist terms. The U.S. Congress in fact often serves as an unvarnished example of what Yuval Levin terms our "tendency to think of institutions not as molds of character and behavior but as platforms for performance and prominence."

> Rather than work through the institution, [many members of Congress] use it as a stage to elevate themselves, raise their profiles and perform for the cameras in the reality show of our increasing culture war.[38]

But if in fact we depend on institutional means to translate our individual efforts into positive achievement—to say nothing of checking abuses of power—we bear some responsibility for facilitating institutional performance.

This is not to counsel, I hasten to add, simply marching in lockstep. Nor is it to deny that conflicts with party or committee leadership should sometimes be resolved in favor of one's personal convictions regarding constituency interests or the public good. Certainly no leader has the right to demand action based on deception or distortions of the truth. In fact, the ethical pitfalls of party regularity have become more evident as polarization has advanced and party discipline has tightened, including the possibility that the demands of party may contravene broader institutional responsibilities. But what is still needed is a conscientious balance between autonomy and accommodation, between individual initiative and team play. More than most of the world's parliaments, the U.S. Congress places the responsibility for striking such balances on legislators themselves.

It is important, finally, to subject parties, committees, and institutional practices themselves to ethical scrutiny. They may supply "the defect of better motives" and enhance the institution's capacities, but they are hardly ethically neutral. The norms and structures that gave inordinate power to committee chairs (mainly southern Democrats) in the 1950s, for example, had a distinctive policy impact, inhibiting overdue changes in civil rights, education, and other areas. More recently, the Republican Conference's attempts to adhere to the "Hastert rule"—whereby legislation was not advanced until it had majority support within the Conference—was implemented in ways that alternately paralyzed the institution and gave inordinate leverage to those at the ideological extremes.

The effective, legitimate functioning of the Congress demands strong, resilient, and accountable party structures that are open to broad participation, responsive to member needs, respectful of the roles of committees, committed to fair treatment of the opposition, and ultimately able to overcome fragmentation and govern. It calls for a credible budget process that is responsive to policy priorities but honest in its assumptions and projections. And it requires committees with the skill and will to gather information, aggregate interests, foster initiatives, and build consensus in ways that produce effective and attractive legislation. Members should spend as much or more time ensuring that these structures function well as they do asserting their independence of them when the need (or temptation) arises.

Fourth, *what responsibility do I have to assert and protect the constitutional role of Congress and the rule of law?* Tellingly, I have added this question in this book's current edition. Members who regard themselves as "institutionalists" have always valued the place of Congress as the Article One branch of government and have regarded the robust exercise of its powers as an essential buttress of that position. Moreover, all modern presidents have utilized various tools—executive orders, signing statements, statements on pending bills, recess appointments—to compensate for congressional inaction or to shape policy to their liking.[39] But Donald Trump's actions—ranging from harsh denunciations of judicial, investigative, and security agencies, to attempts to block or discredit investigations into his own conduct, to executive orders, "emergency" declarations and diversions of funds that fly in the face of congressional prerogatives—have exceeded those of his predecessors in degree and in kind.

"I have an Article II," Trump told a student audience in 2019, "where I have the right to do whatever I want as president," and in William Barr he had an attorney general who forcefully defended that position.[40] Such claims of unchecked and uncheckable presidential authority were used to justify Trump's complete refusal to cooperate with the House's impeachment proceedings and reached an apogee during the COVID-19 pandemic. "When somebody's the president of the United States, the authority is total," Trump declared at one of his raucous press brieings. "That's the way it's got to be. It's total." Vice President Mike Pence, ever the enabler, offered his support: "The authority of the president of the United States during national emergencies"—which presidents themselves declare—"is unquestionably plenary."[41]

Such claims demand of Congress and its members forthright rebuttal and whatever actions are required to protect the constitutional balance of powers and the rule of law. The responsibility particularly falls on members of the president's own party: when he oversteps constitutional, legal, or moral bounds, they must be willing to say so and to place institutional over party loyalties in calling him to account.

The five-week partial government shutdown in early 2019 raised pointed questions as to what an appropriate institutional defense on the part of Senate Majority Leader Mitch McConnell (R-KY) would have been.[42] President Trump precipitated the shutdown by demanding a $5.6 billion appropriation for a border wall—reversing earlier signals as to what kind of bill he would sign, after the fiscal year had already begun and the government was running on continuing resolutions. Senate Republicans acquiesced, with McConnell insisting that the Senate would not write or vote on a funding bill without prior approval from the president. Then, when the shutdown—the longest in U.S. history—finally ended and a conference committee (on which I served) produced a bill to fund the balance of the year, Trump again balked. McConnell persuaded him to sign, but at a significant constitutional price: he agreed to support a declaration by Trump that the border situation constituted a national emergency, freeing him to fund his wall independent of congressional appropriations. So much for institutional defense!

For those in the party opposite from the administration, constitutional fidelity and the rule of law must be given special status, apart from the broader pursuit of viable alternatives to the president's policies. Those alternatives, too, are often rooted in moral convictions and defended in principled terms. But not every moral and political difference implicates constitutional principles and the rule of law. Those have a foundational importance which one recognizes as a citizen and a federal representative, not as a partisan. Certainly impeachment, as I argued in Chapter 7, should proceed on no other basis. When members of the opposition party call out an errant president, they have a special responsibility to distinguish conduct and claims that threaten constitutional principles from disputes and differences of other sorts.

Fifth, *how should I present myself in relation to the workings of the legislature and the overall performance of government?* Throughout this book I have stressed the member's role as interpreter—of his or her own votes and positions, of realistic possibilities for action, of the historical, political, and moral context. The price of a failure to interpret accurately and persuasively can be high: reduced credibility and trust, vulnerability to group pressures and opposition attacks, lost opportunities to inspire and mobilize.

Here I turn to another facet of interpretation: how members portray Congress and the government of which they are a part. Richard Neustadt, finding that American mistrust of government had reached proportions "truly and continuously damaging for timely innovation in governmental programs, for thoroughgoing implementation of them, and for realistic expectations about them," placed much of the responsibility on politicians themselves. They feed the mistrust, not only by their ethical lapses and policy failures but as a matter of deliberate political strategy: "Mistrust is of proven use in stalling or unraveling unwanted programs, and also in diverting public anxiousness from unmet needs. If mistrust were unfunctional from every point of view, contemporary politicians and reporters would be fighting it, not feeding it. And feed it they do."[43]

Richard Fenno, traveling with House members around their districts, found them constantly polishing their "individual reputation[s] at the expense of the institutional reputation of Congress":

> In explaining what he was doing in Washington, every one of the eighteen House members took the opportunity to picture himself as different from, and better than, most of his fellow members in Congress. No one availed himself of the opportunity to educate his constituents about Congress as an institution—not in any way that would "hurt a little." To the contrary, the members' process of differentiating themselves

from the Congress as a whole only served, directly or indirectly, to downgrade the Congress.

This was in the mid-1970s, before Newt Gingrich began his systematic effort to condemn the institution as "corrupt" and "despotic," and when Congress-bashing by advocacy groups and in the media was still relatively subdued. "We have to differentiate me from the rest of those bandits down there in Congress," Fenno heard a member say to a campaign strategy group. "'They are awful, but our guy is wonderful'—that's the message we have to get across."[44]

The solution is not to defend Congress uncritically or to ignore its failings. Indeed, members have an obligation to assess the institution's workings critically and to press for improvements. But there is a line to be drawn between constructively criticizing practices and performance and undermining the legitimacy of the institution itself. Although it is often tempting to pose as the quintessential outsider, carping at accommodations that have been reached on a given issue as though problems could simply be ignored, cost-free solutions devised, or the painful necessities of compromise avoided, it is also deceptive and irresponsible. Responsible legislators will not only communicate to their constituencies the assembly's failings but also define fair and reasonable expectations, suggest what accommodations they would be well advised to accept, and so forth. In the past, a misplaced civics-text reverence sometimes assumed that whatever the constitutional process produced must be acceptable. But self-righteous, anti-institutional posturing is no better. The moral quixotism to which reelection- or media-minded legislators are prone too often serves to rationalize nonproductive legislative roles and perpetuate public misperceptions of the criteria that can reasonably be applied to legislative performance.

Although it may be politically profitable to "run for Congress by running against Congress," the implications for the institution's effectiveness and legitimacy are ominous. As Fenno concluded,

> The strategy is ubiquitous, addictive, cost-free, and foolproof.... In the short run, everybody plays and nearly everybody wins. Yet the institution bleeds from 435 separate cuts. In the long run, therefore, somebody may lose.... Congress may lack public support at the very time when the public needs Congress the most.[45]

Service on the House Democracy Partnership has given me some perspective on this interpretive challenge. As indicated in Chapter 8, we make it clear in working with partner legislatures that we do not assume that our constitutional design is ideal in their situations, nor do we hesitate to acknowledge the ways our institution's performance is falling short. This sort of modesty and candor opens the way for mutually beneficial exchanges. But it is entirely compatible with the pride we take in our institution's 230-year history and the desire of our international colleagues to emulate this achievement. It is often touching to realize the esteem in which our country and its democratic institutions are held, despite our uneven progress and obvious flaws. Our response, I believe, should be both to honor the legacy and to proceed resolutely to mend the flaws. I will turn to that challenge in the concluding chapter.

Notes

1 Bruce Jennings and Daniel Callahan, eds., *Representation and Responsibility: Exploring Legislative Ethics* (New York: Plenum, 1985); and Daniel Callahan and Bruce Jennings, *The Ethics of Legislative Life* (Hastings-on-Hudson, NY: Hastings Center, 1985).
2 Bernard Bailyn, *The Ideological Origins of the American Revolution* (Cambridge: Belknap, 1967), chap. 3; and James Sterling Young, *The Washington Community, 1800–1828* (New York: Harcourt, Brace, and World, 1966), chap. 3.
3 Young, *Washington Community*, pp. 56, 59.
4 A useful overview is provided in Richard Allan Baker, "The History of Congressional Ethics," in Jennings and Callahan, *Representation and Responsibility*, chap. 1. See also Jacob R. Straus, "House Committee on Ethics: A Brief History of Its Evolution and Jurisdiction," Congressional Research Service, Library of Congress, February 1, 2017.
5 Representative Vic Fazio (D-California), *Congressional Record*, daily ed., November 16, 1989, p. H8745.
6 See Jacob R. Straus, "House Office of Congressional Ethics: History, Authority and Procedures," Congressional Research Service, Library of Congress, June 6, 2018.
7 Callahan and Jennings, *Ethics of Legislative Life*, pp. 53, 55.
8 Callahan and Jennings, *Ethics of Legislative Life*, pp. 34–42. This framework was first developed by Amy Gutmann and Dennis Thompson, "The Theory of Legislative Ethics," in Jennings and Callahan, *Representation and Responsibility*, chap. 9; also see Thompson, *Ethics in Congress: From Individual to Institutional Corruption* (Washington, DC: Brookings Institution, 1995), pp. 19–24.
9 Callahan and Jennings, *Ethics of Legislative Life*, p. 55. Note the aspirational character of most of their suggested "next steps," pp. 60–62. For a more cautious view, see John D. Saxon, "The Scope of Legislative Ethics," in Jennings and Callahan, *Representation and Responsibility*, chap. 10.
10 See the report of the Commission, *The Heart of the Matter*, 2013. The passages that follow are adapted from my remarks upon receiving the North Carolina Humanities Council's Caldwell Award: *North Carolina Conversations*, Winter/Spring 2012, pp. 2–5.
11 Cecelia Kenyon, "Introduction" in Kenyon, ed., *The Antifederalists* (Indianapolis, IN: Bobbs-Merrill, 1966), p. lxii.
12 See David E. Price, "Community and Control: Critical Democratic Theory in the Progressive Period," *American Political Science Review*, 68 (December, 1974), pp. 1663–1678.
13 E. J. Dionne, *Our Divided Political Heart: The Battle for the American Idea in an Age of Discontent* (New York: Bloomsbury USA, 2013); and David Brooks, *The Second Mountain: The Quest for a Moral Life* (New York: Penguin Random House, 2019).

14 Garrett Hardin, "The Tragedy of the Commons," *Science*, 162 (1968), pp. 1243–1248. See also Mancur Olson Jr., *The Logic of Collective Action* (New York: Schocken, 1965).

15 Jane Mansbridge, "What Is Political Science For?" *Perspective on Politics*, 12 (March 2014), pp. 8–10.

16 Ibid., p. 9.

17 Quoted in Michael Grunwald, *The New New Deal: The Hidden Story of Change in the Obama Era* (New York: Simon and Schuster, 2012), p. 426.

18 Ibid., p. 15. Tellingly, presidential contender Mitt Romney proposed a stimulative mix of tax cuts and spending increases in 2008 but later deleted any suggestion he had favored such an approach from the 2011 edition of his book, *No Apologies*. "The politics of stimulus had shifted," notes Grunwald, "and so had Mitt Romney," (p. 450).

19 The terms in which we conceptualize a problem may determine the solutions to which we are drawn. Consider, for example, the implications of conceiving of affirmative action policy in terms of social utility or the public interest rather than individual fairness; see David E. Price, "Assessing Policy," in Joel L. Fleishman et al., eds., *Public Duties: The Moral Obligations of Public Officials* (Cambridge: Harvard University Press, 1981), pp. 151–155.

20 See Dennis Thompson's discussion in *Political Ethics and Public Office* (Cambridge: Harvard University Press, 1987), chap. 4.

21 Rawls's theory of justice places a burden of proof on social and economic arrangements: do they maximize the well-being of the "least advantaged" members of society? This might not always require giving first priority to those most in need, but assistance to other groups would depend on whether it improved the lot of those who were worst off in the long run. John Rawls, *A Theory of Justice* (Cambridge: Harvard University Press, 1971), chap. 13 and passim.

22 Testimony of Elaine T. Ostrowski, *Affordable Housing*, field hearing before the Subcommittee on Housing and Community Development, Committee on Banking, Finance, and Urban Affairs, U.S. House of Representatives, 101st Congress, January 26, 1990, p. 97.

23 Price, "Assessing Policy," pp. 155–167.

24 See David E. Price, "On Recruiting Teachers: A Communitarian Approach," *Responsive Community*, 11 (Fall 2001), pp. 4–8; and Sasha Polakow-Suransky, "When Corporate Media Giants Call the Shots: How New Rules from the FCC Will Squeeze Out Community," *Responsive Community*, 13 (Summer 2003), pp. 34–41.

25 See *Congressional Record*, daily ed., March 11, 2003, pp. H1739–H1741, citing Walzer, "What a Little War in Iraq Could Do," *New York Times*, March 7, 2003, p. A27.

26 Walzer, "Can There Be a Moral Foreign Policy?" in E.J. Dionne Jr. et al., eds., *Liberty and Power: A Dialogue on Religion in an Unjust World* (Washington, DC: Brookings Institution, 2004). Walzer also claimed a just-war defense for multilateralism: "In a system of sovereign states, multilateral action is preferable to the action of single states, since it protects those acted upon from imperial ambition and state aggrandizement.... On balance, over time, arrogance, zeal, and ignorance are more likely to be curbed than furthered by alliances, treaties, and international organizations."

27 Madeleine Albright, *Madam Secretary* (New York: Miramax Books, 2003), pp. 147, 154–155.

28 Donald R. Matthews, *U.S. Senators and Their World* (New York: Vintage, 1960), p. 92. Fenno likewise drew heavily on concepts from functionalist social science—role, function, integration, and adaptation—terms suggesting that

members conformed to the institutional environment more than they shaped it. See Richard Fenno, "The House Appropriations Committee as a Political System: The Problem of Integration," *American Political Science Review*, 56 (June 1962), pp. 310–324; Fenno, *The Power of the Purse: Appropriations Politics in Congress* (Boston, MA: Little, Brown, 1966).

29 David R. Mayhew, *Congress: The Electoral Connection* (New Haven, CT: Yale University Press, 1974), p. 5.

30 For a succinct account that explicitly references Mayhew's assumptions, see John H. Aldrich and David W. Rohde, "Lending and Reclaiming Power: Majority Leadership in the House Since the 1950s," in Lawrence C. Dodd and Bruce I. Oppenheimer, eds., *Congress Reconsidered*, 11th ed. (Washington, DC: Congressional Quarterly Press, 2017), pp. 33–35.

31 David Braybrooke and Charles E. Lindblom, *A Strategy of Decision* (New York: Free Press, 1963), pp. 185–186. In chapter 10, these analysts treated "disjointed incrementalism"—the free contending of interests—as a tolerable substitute for (and in some ways an improvement on) utilitarianism's felicific calculus.

32 Early critics include Robert Paul Wolff, *The Poverty of Liberalism* (Boston, MA: Beacon, 1968), chap. 4; E. E. Schattschneider, *The Semi-Sovereign People* (New York: Holt, Rinehart & Winston, 1960), chap. 2; Theodore J. Lowi, *The End of Liberalism*, 2nd ed. (New York: Norton, 1979), chap. 3; and Olson, *Logic of Collective Action*, chap. 5.

33 On this latter point, see Richard F. Fenno Jr., *Home Style: House Members in Their Districts* (Boston, MA: Little, Brown, 1978), pp. 240–244.

34 Fenno, *Home Style*, p. 243.

35 Edmund Burke, "Thoughts on the Cause of the Present Discontents," in *Works*, 3rd ed. (Boston, MA: Little, Brown, 1871), 1:526.

36 Jacob K. Javits, *Javits: The Autobiography of a Public Man* (Boston, MA: Houghton Mifflin, 1981), p. 134.

37 James Madison, "The Federalist" no. 51, in Clinton Rossiter, ed., *The Federalist Papers* (New York: Mentor, 1961), p. 322.

38 Yuval Levin, "How We Lost Faith in Everything," *New York Times*, January 19, 2020, p. SR-4.

39 See David E. Price, "Congressional-Executive Balance in an Era of Congressional Dysfunction," *PS: Political Science and Politics*, 49 (July 2016), pp. 487–488.

40 Quoted in *Business Insider*, July 25, 2019. On Barr's "fierce advocacy of unchecked presidential power," see Donald Ayer, "Why Bill Barr Is So Dangerous," *The Atlantic*, June 30, 2019.

41 Charlie Savage, "Trump's Claim on Total Authority in Crisis Is Rejected across Ideological Lines," *New York Times*, April 14, 2020. "Separation of powers and federalism" commented Georgetown law professor Neal Katyal, embody "our founders' desire to divide and check power— not vest 'total' authority in one person, no matter how wise that person may be." "It's the Worst Possible Time for Trump to Make False Claims of Authority," *New York Times*, April 14, 2020.

42 Adam Jentleson, "How Mitch McConnell Enables Trump," *New York Times*, February 19, 2019.

43 Richard Neustadt, "The Politics of Mistrust," in Joseph S. Nye Jr. et al., eds., *Why People Don't Trust Government* (Cambridge: Harvard University Press, 1997), pp. 180–181.

44 Fenno, *Home Style*, pp. 164, 166. For an analysis of the behavior Fenno described and an account of historical antecedents, see Kenneth R. Mayer and David T. Canon, *The Dysfunctional Congress? The Individual Roots of an Institutional Dilemma* (Boulder, CO: Westview, 1999), pp. 31–32, 57–59.

45 Fenno, *Home Style*, pp. 168, 246.

12 Concluding Reflections

This book has portrayed a Congress—and hence a congressional experience—in significant transition. The transition entered another, unanticipated phase in early 2020 as I was concluding work on the current edition and the COVID-19 pandemic closed in. The immediate effects on the functioning of Congress were without precedent, as it became impossible to meet, deliberate, and vote in the normal congregate fashion. It also seemed possible, though by no means certain, that political thought and practice, including many of the ideological and political developments touched on in this book, would be significantly altered. It was hard to denigrate government and expertise within government when the nation so clearly depended on both. It was hard to maintain political polarization and prosecute the cultural wars when the nation so clearly needed to get past both in addressing a deadly threat and pursuing the common good. The pandemic required a serious, well-functioning democracy, able to bring science and intelligence to bear on a mortal threat and to gain public trust and confidence in doing so. The prolonged crisis put political folly and failings, as well as how a legitimate and responsive government needed to perform, in sharp relief—thus shaping and reshaping political beliefs and expectations going forward.

Even before the coronavirus, however, the volatility and norm-shattering character of the Trump presidency made it difficult to sort out the enduring from the transitory (and possibly reversible) aspects of the transformations it wrought. Earlier chapters have highlighted the extent of Trump's deviancy, from the realms of personal character and constitutional fidelity to long-held assumptions about America's commitment to democracy and its role in the world. Trump's dominance of the Republican party in Congress steadily increased, taking it in new or more extreme directions with respect to trade and immigration policy, the pursuit of two-state diplomacy in the Middle East and the cultivation of democracy worldwide, and commitment to our post-World War II network of alliances. His assertions and abuses of power went far beyond his predecessors in both parties: firing independent Inspectors General across government, withholding and diverting billions in appropriated funds, refusing cooperation with congressional hearings and investigations.

It was not all new, however. In fact, Trump and Trumpism in most instances built on foundations laid long before—Richard Nixon's "Southern Strategy" to attract segregationist White voters, Ronald Reagan's sweeping denigration of government, George W. Bush's unilateralism in foreign affairs, and decades spent casting Republicans as champions of "salt-of-the-earth American patriotism" and Democrats as "locked in an embrace with foreign elitism and timidity."[1]

In Congress, the Republican transformation was rooted in Newt Gingrich's House insurgency of the 1980s. In retrospect, Gingrich's refusal to back the 1990 bipartisan budget agreement on the basis of a rigid anti-tax ideology was a harbinger of what was to come, as were the rebellion of House Republicans, stoked by talk radio, against bipartisan immigration reform in 2007, and the attempts in 2013–2016 of future Secretary of State Mike Pompeo (R-Kansas) and other House Republicans to block and then destroy the Iran nuclear agreement.

Trump's 2017 tax cut, mainly benefiting corporations and the wealthy, came right out of the 1981 and 2001–2003 Republican playbook, while his annual budgets bore the distinctive mark of his Office of Management and Budget (OMB) director, former congressman Mick Mulvaney (R-South Carolina), a founder of the House Freedom Caucus. For all of his populist bombast, Trump "fully morphed into a supply-side conservative" and governed in most respects—erratically to be sure—as a standard-issue right wing Republican.[2]

In earlier chapters, I have suggested that increased partisan polarization, including the asymmetric rightward lurch of the Republican party, is the dominant, if not exclusive, factor in the transformation of American politics—and with it the Congress—over the past thirty years. "Party unity" voting scores in both parties regularly exceed 90 percent. Policy entrepreneurship has become less and less a matter of introducing a bill and shepherding it through committee, often with bipartisan input, and more a matter of latching onto some omnibus vehicle. The policy process is far more centralized and leadership-driven, and the committees less autonomous and free-wheeling, than when I first arrived. Major authorizations often lapse and are renewed sporadically or not at all. Appropriations has changed less than most committees, but the appropriations process is often swamped by larger partisan forces; funding bills are almost always late and require agreements negotiated between the parties before they can be stitched together and finally cleared.

When I first came to the House, the incentives to "learn the ropes," master my assigned policy areas, and work within the committee and party systems were stronger than they now seem to be for many members. I had more opportunities to take on projects and initiatives and was less defined by my party affiliation than is now the case. Still, as I stressed in Chapter 11, members have a good deal of leeway in how they relate to the congressional environment and how they answer the question, "What sort of member shall I be?"

I have become accustomed, especially during the Trump presidency and the post-2010 years of House Republican control, to having constituents ask me solicitously, "How can you stand it?" My usual response is to remind them that I *asked* for the job! Given a bit more time, I suggest that the fireworks they see on C-SPAN are not the whole story. Admittedly, in casting my lot with the Appropriations Committee and the House Democracy Partnership, I exercise leadership in relatively cooperative arenas. When need be, I can display the "D" on my jersey with determination and pride. But while such occasions are more frequent than they used to be, they still only define a fraction of our work, despite the polarized environment.

I have, in fact, enjoyed and taken great satisfaction in my sixteen terms of service in the House of Representatives. I did indeed ask for the job, repeatedly, and I am grateful to my constituents for almost always responding positively. In this book I have tried to convey some of the lessons I have learned—some joyfully, some painfully—about the resilience and resolve politics requires, the promise and the perils of taking on challenges and proffering solutions, the necessity of team play alongside the dangers of partisan excess, the interplay of personal and institutional responsibility. Overall, the job has gotten harder, no doubt, in terms of both individual and collective performance. But producing good policy in the American institutional and constitutional context has always been akin, in Max Weber's memorable phrase, to the "strong and slow boring of hard boards."[3] The challenge, to use another apt metaphor, is to navigate the shifting currents represented by public sentiments and electoral outcomes, successes and failures of political leadership, and the lineup of affected interests to find workable remedies. Such efforts will be more successful if Congress is functioning in an orderly and responsive way; the goal of congressional reform should be to make it so.

My own job satisfaction and sense of effectiveness have waxed and waned over the years, clearly related to the realities of partisan control, the increasingly polarized environment, and the opportunities that come with seniority and committee leadership. I took great satisfaction in the policy advances that the two periods of unified party control with a Democratic president, 1993–1994 and 2009–2010, made possible. But Chapter 5 documents major successes during periods of Republican or divided control—launching the House Democratic Partnership (HDP), for example, and completing Environmental Protection Agency (EPA) laboratory construction—as well as other projects that proved difficult to deliver no matter who was in control! And it leaves no doubt of the personal and policy leverage that came with accession to the Homeland Security and Transportation-HUD appropriations leadership, as ranking minority member and certainly as chairman.

I have thus had enough successes to keep me going, even in the worst of times—to say nothing of the unvarying importance of the work I and my staff do in servicing our district and the satisfaction that provides. Still, the sense of institutional failure looms large, the conviction that the collective response of Congress has often been inadequate to our country's needs.

This is not to say a clear or consensual idea of what an "adequate" response would be is always at hand. The 1990s, for example, featured two relatively systematic partisan efforts to take on the country's challenges: the Democratic experiment of 1993–1994 under President Clinton's leadership, and the Gingrich revolution of 1995–1996, with its attendant effort to govern the country from the House of Representatives. The political result? "Two neat piles of rubble," as E.J. Dionne put it.[4] As one who participated in the first experiment and helped reverse the second, I am well aware of the shortcomings of both. But the collapse of these ambitious efforts was not solely a matter of personal and political failings. Public opinion was divided and sometimes contradictory, demanding action but resisting the imposition of costs. Most people resisted unsettling change, whether it was revamping workplace-based health insurance by the Clintons in 1994 or Gingrich's 1995 Medicare cutbacks; a strong, supportive consensus for major new departures in policy was difficult to come by. Popular divisions were reflected not only in divided control of government but also in the tenuous balance between the parties in Congress and the intraparty factionalism both were at pains to avoid. In neither 1994 nor 1995 was there a consolidation of views within Congress or in a skeptical and hostile public, although a modus vivendi of sorts was reached in the remaining years of the Clinton administration.

Such divisions have not lessened in the Obama and Trump eras, and for the parties as currently configured to somehow, someday meet in the middle seems increasingly unlikely (and probably undesirable). My hope for the post-Trump era is, first of all, that the end of Trumpism comes quickly, and secondly, that it involves the gathering of a broad center-left coalition on the Democratic side, with Republicans regrouping as an authentic center-right conservative party. It is conceivable that the wrenching coronavirus experience may move us in that direction. In any event, mainstream Democrats need to overcome factional divisions for the sake of the larger goal of defeating Trump and Trumpism, forming a workable governing coalition, and taking the country in a positive direction, internationally and at home.

In urging such a course before our Democratic Policy Group on March 11, 2020, E.J. Dionne quoted commentator Mark Shields to the effect that political, like religious, movements sometimes have to decide whether they are going to seek converts or hunt heretics.[5] This is not a time to accentuate differences and apply litmus tests, but rather to unite and inspire the disparate political forces that can come together to oppose Trumpism and the extreme rightward course of the modern Republican party. The 2018 midterm elections and the emergence of Joe Biden as the

2020 presidential nominee offered hopeful evidence that the lesson was being learned.

Where does this leave congressional and political reform? Nothing on the reform agenda matches the importance of the political agenda I have just outlined as a means of changing the country's direction. Having said that, however, failures of reform, particularly in areas such as legislative and congressional districting, money and politics, and the right to vote, discussed in Chapter 3, bear considerable responsibility for the ideological extremism, polarization, and unresponsiveness that have come to characterize our politics. And the way Congress as an institution is able to function will determine the degree to which positive political change, when it comes, will translate into policies that actually make a difference.

I will thus conclude this book with a look at the reform agenda—promising measures, as well as bromides to be avoided.[6] What Congress actually produces will still depend on the vision, skill, and political will members and leaders bring to the legislative process. But reform is basic, as the placement of HR 1 on the 2019 agenda suggested, in protecting both the ground rules of democracy and the functionality and legitimacy of Congress and other institutions responsible for translating the popular will into public policy.

Reform Agendas

In writing the first edition of this book, I decided not to call it *A Political Scientist Goes to Washington*. In some ways, it would have been an apt title, for my training and work as a political scientist have helped shape my perceptions of my congressional experience and certainly my recounting of it here. But I did not like the connotations. "Political scientist" was only one of several identities I brought to Washington, and my primary purpose in coming was certainly not to study. Moreover, in bringing to mind *Mr. Smith Goes to Washington*, Frank Capra's classic film, the title might have suggested that I wished to perpetuate a stereotype of Washington as a den of conspiracy and corruption or that my academic background had prepared me poorly for the harsh realities I encountered. Neither was the case.

Being cast as a kind of academic Mr. Smith, however, is something I have occasionally had to endure. One wizened senior member took to calling me "Professor" soon after I arrived, which I did not take to be a compliment. "I'll bet you're discovering it's not like they say in the textbooks!" people sometimes say, or they ask, "How are you finding things in the *real* world?" To such remarks I often think but seldom respond: "If you think academe is never-never land, you should try politics for a while!" The congressional studies of my generation, on which I was trained and to which I made a modest contribution, were based on close, sympathetic observation of the institution and provided an accurate picture of its workings—a view that went beyond the personality-centered, episodic accounts often rendered by journalists and members themselves. The experience of being a member is very different, in terms of what one learns and how one feels, from being an academic observer. But for an orientation to the place, I could have done far worse.

As a young political scientist, however, I found that the hands-on style of contemporary congressional research, often based on member interviews, along with the functionalist framework into which scholarly analysis was often cast, threatened a loss of critical distance from the institution.[7] The policy frustrations and failures of the early 1960s suggested the need for a performance-based critique of Congress—a need that was lessened but not removed by the post-1964 spate of congressional productivity. Books with titles like *Obstacle Course on Capitol Hill* and *House Out of Order* underscored the point.[8] It was therefore with a great deal of anticipation that I, along with a dozen other young academics, agreed to spend the summer of 1972 with Ralph Nader's Congress Project in Washington. As the scholarly arm of the enterprise, we were to combine solid research on the workings of congressional committees with a critical assessment of institutional performance and specific suggestions for reform. To some extent, we realized this goal, although I have never experienced as many frustrations and difficulties with a publishing project before or since.[9] What we received in the meantime, however, was an introduction to the kind of Congress bashing that came to full flower in the 1980s.

Nader apparently decided in midsummer that our studies were not moving fast enough and were not likely to attract sufficient attention. As a result, he put three of his in-house writers to work on a volume that, despite our protests to the contrary, presumed to anticipate and summarize our findings. *Who Runs Congress?* dealt with Congress's substantive policy failings only incidentally and instead highlighted such topics as "Who Owns Congress?" and "Lawmakers as Lawbreakers." Some attention was given to the distribution of power within Congress, but the idea was to highlight instances of arbitrariness and abuse rather than distinguish dysfunctional concentrations of power from those that might enhance congressional performance. In one area—portraying Congress as "overwhelmed by the vastly greater forces of the presidency"—the Nader critique differed from what was to come.[10] In fact, it often seemed that a subservient legislative branch was precisely what the Congress bashers of the Reagan era, often highly partisan, had in mind. But in most respects, *Who Runs Congress?* anticipated the themes of modern congressional criticism and represented an unfortunate departure from the older but still important performance-based critique.[11]

The increasing din of Congress bashing powerfully reinforced the tendency of members to run for Congress by running against Congress. This mode of criticism, with its withering cynicism about all things congressional, encouraged a defensive detachment from the institution on the part of members, an exposé mentality on the part of the press, and increasing public distrust and alienation. What tended to get crowded out was any serious attempt to understand how Congress actually worked, as well as the sorts of proposals for change that could improve institutional performance. Indeed, the relentless trashing of the institution helped prevent positive change. Instead of considering what distributions and concentrations of power would make the institution work effectively, the critics tended to stigmatize all exertions of power as personal aggrandizement. Instead of asking what sorts of support services Congress needed to function efficiently, the critics often regarded such accoutrements indiscriminately as "perks." Although members' incentives to contribute to the work of the institution needed to be strengthened, the critics often viewed legislative machinations with a jaundiced eye and encouraged a righteous aloofness. All of this suggested that many of the critics were aiming (some deliberately, some inadvertently) not for a more assertive, competent institution but for the opposite. And they were contributing to an indiscriminate distrust of government that hobbles us to this day.

Most critiques of the 1960s and early 1970s, by contrast, aimed at a stronger, more democratic Congress turning out more coherent and responsive legislation. This strain of reform helped produce both enhanced participation and opportunities for initiatives down through the ranks and increased ability for leadership to overcome obstruction and produce a policy product. The House Rules Committee was reined in; leadership control over committee assignments, bill referrals, and floor operations was strengthened; a measure of accountability by committee chairs to the party caucus was instituted; and Congress's budgeting capacity was improved (see Chapters 6–7). These efforts did not always succeed in balancing their multiple objectives, and from the vantage point of three decades of increasing polarization, it is clear that leadership centralization and partisan mobilization can assume their own dysfunctional forms. But the early reformers were often asking the right questions.

The harsh institution-bashing that arose in the 1980s took reform in less productive directions. Proposals such as the line-item veto and term limits, emanating from the most vociferous critics of Congress and masquerading as congressional reform, gained wide currency, as I often learned in my community meetings. It was an agenda that helped Newt Gingrich and the Republicans win control of the House, but it offered them little help (and sometimes proved a burden) as they actually tried to run the institution.

Some positive changes were made, in part as a reaction to the critics. Measures such as banning honoraria and restricting other outside income, prohibiting the conversion of campaign funds to personal use, controlling the frequency and the content of franked mailings, and clarifying the limits of appropriate advocacy on behalf of constituents before regulatory bodies were moves in the right direction, in some cases considerably overdue. A law subjecting Congress to the same workplace laws and standards that govern the private sector was passed in 1995 as the first item in the Contract with America. Republicans were quick to claim credit, although an almost identical bill had passed the House 427 to 4 in 1994, only to be blocked by Senate Republican leaders.

The Contract with America featured both term limits and the line-item veto. The proposal to give the president the authority to veto individual items in appropriations bills, touted as a way to restrain spending, was more likely to have the opposite effect, since presidents more often than not ask for *more* overall spending than Congress is willing to appropriate. Given the leverage the line-item veto would give presidents in pressuring individual members to accede to their spending requests, the line-item veto might be expected to lead to more, rather than less, spending over time. An institutionalized line-item veto could radically alter the constitutional balance of power and the dynamics of congressional policymaking. Members would likely focus less on working together to craft a balanced legislative product and more on securing the acquiescence of the president, item by item.

A short-lived experiment with the line-item veto began in 1996 when Republicans pushed through an "enhanced rescission" bill. Budget lines rescinded by the president could be restored only by vote of a veto-proof majority of both chambers. President Clinton, who as governor had found the Arkansas line-item veto serviceable, eagerly signed the enhanced rescission bill.

Clinton used his new powers sparingly during the 105th Congress, but the discussions I had with administration officials to ensure that several of my research provisions would not be deleted from the agriculture funding bill gave me a glimpse of how appropriations might work in the future. Republicans began to regret handing this power to a Democratic president, and both chambers voted overwhelmingly in 1998 to override Clinton's veto of $287 million in military construction projects. Few objections were heard from either side of the aisle when the Supreme Court struck down the law as a violation of the "presentment clause" (Article 1, Section 7) of the Constitution.[12]

Term limits, even more than the line-item veto, would weaken Congress, making its members—the one group of actors in the federal system who regard themselves as representatives of local communities and ordinary citizens—less knowledgeable, less seasoned, less confident, and hence more dependent on staff, lobbyists, and bureaucrats for information and guidance. Term limits proponents often seem to think that serving effectively in Congress requires no particular experience or expertise. Perhaps I have said enough in this book to indicate otherwise. I have heard members of the Intelligence Committee say that it took them four years simply to know how to ask the right questions of career people who were accustomed to revealing only what they wished, and I confess that I sometimes felt the same way on the Banking Committee. To arbitrarily expel all members after a short period of service would mean for the Congress, as it would for any business or other organization, a damaging loss of institutional memory, stature, and staying power. The slack would surely be taken up by the executive establishment, which makes term limits a particularly puzzling cause for conservatives (those erstwhile critics of bureaucracy and concentrated presidential power) to embrace.

None of this is to deny that Congress, like most institutions, needs periodic infusions of new blood and needs to replace aging or ineffective leaders. One does not always have to agree with voters' decisions (for some members, as I often note in community meetings, *one* term may be too many) to observe that they are owed deference in a democratic system and that they already produce substantial turnover. New members normally come into the House at a rate of 10–18 percent (and sometimes much higher) each election cycle. The 1992 and 1994 elections together replaced almost half of the House membership; the Republican landslide of 2010 replaced almost one-fourth of the House in a single year.

These influxes of new members did not necessarily strengthen the case for term limits. As Tom Mann and Norm Ornstein observed in the wake of 2010:

> Populist Tea Party members fit almost perfectly the profile of citizen legislators that term-limit advocates favor.... If anything, their determination to stick to their principles has reinforced partisan polarization in Congress and further weakened its deliberative capacity. What is most lacking in Congress today are members with institutional pride and loyalty, who understand the essential and difficult task of peacefully reconciling diverse interests through processes of negotiation and compromise.[13]

About half the states placed term limits of some sort on legislators, but the Supreme Court ruled such efforts unconstitutional for federal representatives in 1995.[14] Republican leaders dutifully trotted out a term limits constitutional amendment for House votes in 1995 and 1997, but it fell short of the requisite two-thirds both times. Some members of the class of 1994 who had come into office promising to leave after three terms kept their promise, but others decided to seek reelection anyway, hoping not to fall victim to the voter cynicism that they had exploited six years before. This drama is still repeated each election cycle, but by a dwindling number of members; term limits has largely lost its luster as a reform mantra.

Is there a stronger case to be made for the imposition of term limits on committee leaders? Republicans imposed three-term limits on all their committee and subcommittee leaders in 1992 and wrote the limits into House rules when they assumed control in 1994. As 2001 approached, the date when most chairmanships were set to expire, unanticipated consequences became apparent, as some disestablished chairs elected to retire and others engineered swaps of committee and subcommittee positions in order to stay in power. In fact, given the authority Speaker Gingrich assumed to name chairmen, often bypassing seniority claims, it could hardly be argued that term limits were necessary to move along leaders who needed to be replaced. But these rules remain in place and continue to be a major factor in the retirement rate among senior Republicans.

Democrats never adopted term limits for committee leaders and removed them from House rules after assuming leadership in 2007 and 2019. However, rules adopted in the mid-1970s gave the Democratic Caucus the power to disapprove sitting chairmen and then, in a subsequent ballot, to choose among multiple alternatives. The process has been utilized sparingly to replace (or try to replace) leaders judged infirm or out of step with the Caucus. In recent years it has become easier procedurally to unseat a sitting chairman, but Democrats have only rarely done so—the successful challenge of Energy and Commerce chair John Dingell by Henry Waxman in 2008 being a glaring exception. On the other hand, it has become fairly common, when a committee chairmanship or ranking minority member position is vacant, to have a competitive race and to choose someone other than the most senior member. In the 116th Congress, among the exclusive committees, Appropriations and Ways and Means are not chaired by their most senior members. Energy and Commerce is, but the chair Frank Pallone (D-New Jersey) was strongly challenged (by Anna Eshoo [D-California]) when he first ran to succeed Waxman as ranking member in 2014.

The Democratic Speaker (or Minority Leader) often weighs in on the selection of committee leaders (as in the Waxman and Eshoo cases above), but without the degree of control Republican leaders typically exercise. There is still a presumption in favor of seniority, partly because of the support of the Black Caucus and other groups who feel that it protects their interests. That may change as these groups produce their own cadre of younger members who wish to challenge long-entrenched leaders. At present, however, the Democratic system errs on the side of leaving too many committee chairs in place for too long.

Republican-style term limits would be a cure worse than the disease, turning out committee leaders on a rigid timetable, regardless of the quality of their service and how it fits committee or party needs. Republicans have coupled term limits with a devaluation of seniority and a dominant role for the Speaker (or Minority Leader) in naming committee leaders. Term limits reinforce this centralization of power, while creating a less collegial and stable working environment within committees and arbitrarily depriving the institution of the contributions experienced members could make, sometimes pushing them to early retirement.

The impact of the 1994 Republican victory and the Gingrich speakership on House operations—"the most sweeping overhaul … in almost fifty years"—superseded by far any and all reforms advertised in the Contract with America.[15] Congress bashing, in fact, became less prevalent in the media and campaign rhetoric, mainly because those who had fanned the flames were now trying to run the institution. The official reform agenda, which had never been as coherent or compelling as that spawned by the critiques of the 1960s and early 1970s, largely fizzled. But the changes in the distribution of power in the House and the way it was run were nonetheless profound—and, as it turned out, enduring. They involved some important changes in House or Republican Conference rules, such as placing term limits on committee chairs, but the driving force was Gingrich's assertion of control over everything from the appointment of committee members and leaders to the legislative agenda and its execution (see Chapter 6).

These were matters with which Democrats had previously grappled. The reforms of the mid-1970s devolved authority and resources from committee chairs upward to party leaders and downward to subcommittee chairs and individual members. A widespread feeling developed during Tom Foley's speakership (1989–1994) that the balance needed further adjustment in order to facilitate development of a unified Democratic agenda, early intervention to ensure that bills were reported by committees in a form that most Democrats could support, and improved party discipline. I participated throughout 1992 as a member of the Committee on Organization, Study, and Review (OSR) in discussions of reform proposals, many of which involved an enhanced leadership role in defining and coordinating the legislative agenda and to some extent anticipated the Republican changes of 1995. It became clear in the course of these discussions how resistant committee chairs would be to any process or structure that impinged on their authority and how disinclined Foley was to take them on. The sort of enhanced leadership many of us were looking for would be difficult to "legislate" through altered rules and structures and would rely more on the entrepreneurship and personal assertiveness of the leaders themselves. In any event, the package approved by the Democratic Caucus at the beginning of the 103rd Congress did not strengthen leadership prerogatives significantly, and the agenda-setting panel of members it established, the Speaker's Working Group on Policy Development, "quickly faded into obscurity, lacking the formal powers and political support to bind the committee chairs to a caucus- or speaker-driven policy agenda."[16]

Speaker Foley was probably correct in 1992 when he concluded that there was not a sufficiently strong consensus in the Democratic Caucus on policy issues or institutional reform to underwrite a major redistribution of power, particularly considering the opposition of the committee chairs and the anticipation of policy leadership to come from a new Democratic administration. But as I wrote from the perspective of the 2004 edition of this book, "that same judgment need not and should not hold if and when Democrats retake the chamber. It will be a time to revisit the questions of leadership prerogatives and committee autonomy and to adjust the balance between them to ensure a coherent agenda and enhance collective performance."[17]

Nancy Pelosi and other Democratic leaders did indeed "revisit" these questions in 2007, seeking to strike a balance between Gingrich's top-down leadership and the former committee-centric model (see Chapter 6).

I suggested in 2004 that Democrats could "learn from Republican organizational successes just as Gingrich learned from Jim Wright," but hopefully could avoid the "pitfalls" associated with Gingrich's role: "the deterioration of deliberation and debate, particularly in committees; inordinate deference to favored groups and restricted opportunities for member input; bitter partisanship and interpersonal acrimony."[18] At the onset of another period of Democratic leadership in 2019–2020, I would say we have moved toward a more workable balance. The pressures toward centralization are pervasive, however. They transcend the impulses of any single leader and are rooted in the challenges posed by a treacherous and polarized political environment. They are also a function of constantly legislating under *crisis*, not just natural or public health or economic disasters, but also the man-made, preventable crises created by ideological extremism, polarization, and budgetary collapse.

As my account in Chapter 7 suggests, the remedies for fiscal and budgetary dysfunction lie more in the realms of political leadership and the modulation of partisan extremism than in rules changes or institutional tinkering. Having said that, there are two changes that are sufficiently obvious to have gained the consensual approval of the Congressional Reform Task Force, a broadly based group of scholars assembled by the American Political Science Association (APSA) in 2019 to advise the Select Committee on the Modernization of Congress.

The first recommendation is to no longer require congressional approval for increases in the debt ceiling, a vote that "creates opportunities for political brinksmanship with little evidence that it provides any fiscal constraint."[19] It is almost inconceivable that Congress would take the country into default, depriving the U.S. Treasury of the ability to raise sufficient funds to meet the country's obligations. But requiring a vote on a statutory debt limit nonetheless poses that possibility and creates the context for extortion by extreme elements in Congress. The most extreme recent example is the standoff between President Obama and House Republicans in 2011 that begat the Budget Control Act and sequestration.

The second recommendation is to lift the ban on congressionally directed spending, or earmarks. The task force argues correctly that eliminating earmarks has neither reduced spending nor rendered funding decisions less "political"; it has merely shifted the locus of project-level decisions from legislators to agency officials.[20] As I have argued in Chapters 5 and 9, earmarked projects, large and small, rank among the most significant things I have been able to do for the people of the Fourth District. The earmark ban is an affront to members' ability to serve their district and state, to say nothing of Congress's constitutional power of the purse. The restoration of earmarks in a transparent and accountable form should be a high priority. I have no doubt that most members from both parties agree. But as efforts to restore earmarking on a targeted basis in 2020 demonstrated, it will not happen without a bipartisan, bicameral agreement to defend the action publicly and to discourage and refute its exploitation by opposition campaigns.

For good reason, the Task Force could not reach agreement on another proposed reform, which I put in the "bromide" category but nonetheless has some vocal defenders: biennial budgeting. As I noted before another reform panel in the previous Congress, I have been testifying against proposals to move appropriations to a two-year cycle for more than twenty years. Most notably, this included a successful bipartisan effort to defeat a plan backed by the House Republican leadership in 2000.[21] Understandably, perhaps, some witnesses to missed budget and appropriations deadlines, repeated continuing resolutions, and threatened shutdowns are attracted to the idea of at least cutting the chaos by half. But moving to a two-year cycle would do nothing to address the underlying problems and would introduce a host of new issues.

Annual appropriations are the best instrument Congress has for keeping government responsive to emerging needs and accountable, line by line, for the responsible execution of programs and expenditure of funds. To expect executive agencies to put forward a budget request for the second year of a two-year cycle as much as 28 months in advance would require an unrealistic level of planning and foresight, given the uncertainty of revenue and expenditure projections and the constantly evolving challenges governments must tackle. Additional supplemental appropriations bills would surely be required to address unmet or unanticipated needs—bills that too often are sporadic, rushed, and heavily controlled by leadership.

What of the argument that biennial budgeting would "free up" the appropriations committees in the off-years to conduct enhanced oversight? That claim is supremely ironic, for the most careful and effective oversight Congress conducts is through the annual appropriations process, when an agency's performance and needs are reviewed in detail. Off-year oversight would be less effective, not more, because it would be "toothless," removed from actual funding decisions. Congress's leverage would thus be greatly reduced.

The fact that a number of recent presidents from both parties have favored biennial appropriations should not surprise (or convince) anyone. If this suggests that the proposal is not a *partisan* issue, it warns that it is indeed an *institutional* issue. It is understandable that presidents might welcome relief from an annual process that is time-consuming, exacting, and sometimes threatening—just as they have often supported the line-item veto, a ban on earmarks, and other measures that would weaken Congress's authority vis-a-vis the executive branch. But that is hardly an argument for congressional assent.

The argument against biennial appropriations does not necessarily apply to multi-year budget agreements of the sort that helped achieve fiscal balance in the 1990s. Nor does it apply to the two-year budget resolutions that avoided the worst consequences of the Budget Control Act (BCA) after

2012 and allowed annual appropriations (belatedly) to proceed. In the post-BCA world there may still be a need for multi-year budget parameters, but they must leave the annual appropriations process intact.

The Select Committee on the Modernization of Congress, chaired by Derek Kilmer (D-Washington) and Tom Graves (R-Georgia), which the APSA Task Force was set up to advise, concentrated its early work on upgrading technology, expanding bipartisan orientation and other interactive activity, and centralizing and strengthening human resources operations.[22] Hopefully, the Select Committee will give the House the opportunity to address *staffing* needs—to reverse the declines in staff resources in individual offices and on committees, to increase compensation and training opportunities, to broaden staff diversity, and to improve the workplace climate. We regularly stress to HDP partners the centrality of staff to independent and effective legislative operations; the application of these exhortations needs to begin at home.

The key litmus test for any congressional reform should be whether it will leave the Congress stronger and make it a more competent and effective institution, able to produce better policy. This suggests a couple of caveats, drawing on themes developed in chapters 10–11. The first is to abjure a simplistic distrust of power. Congressional reform has reduced and should reduce the power attached to certain persons or positions when it is abused or when it hinders institutional performance. But it is not enough to scatter power and resources around and leave it at that; effective congressional reform will attend to the need for effective (albeit accountable) concentrations of power. The second caveat is to be wary of the Lone Ranger ethical bias, the tendency to idealize independence and autonomy. Congressional effectiveness requires strengthening the means of collective action and instilling in members a sense of responsibility not only for their personal integrity but for the performance of the institution.

It is important to recognize the limits of reform. This too is a critical lesson from earlier chapters. The strength and quality of the leadership of various Speakers was less dependent on their formal powers or the rules under which they operated than on their personal ambition, skill, and temperament and their political base of support. Policy entrepreneurship among members could be facilitated or hindered by conditions in committees, the chamber, and the external environment, but the main ingredients were the motivation, ability, and energy of the entrepreneurs themselves. Budget breakdowns and failures were often less indicative of flawed procedures or machinery than of an absence of public consensus, political will, and responsible leadership. Rules and structures do matter; pay-as-you-go (PAYGO) and other process changes in the 1990 budget agreement, for example, greatly facilitated later deficit reduction efforts. But the fact remains: the main concern of those who would move the institution forward should not be endless tinkering with rules and structures but rather mustering the leadership, discipline, energy, and initiative to take advantage of the opportunities the system already offers.

Finally, it is important to see congressional reform as part of the broader challenge to repair and preserve our democracy. The Trump presidency has underscored that it may matter little how fairly and smoothly Congress is functioning if the institution is sidelined by exorbitant claims of executive power and privilege. In the face of repeated "Article One moments," the defense of the institution and its constitutional prerogatives become an overriding reform imperative, and one that should transcend party lines.

The same is true with respect to the workings of our broken electoral system. The maladies identified in Chapter 3—extreme partisan gerrymandering; the dominance of unaccountable, unlimited big money in elections; widespread voter suppression and other barriers to the straightforward translation of votes into seats and responsive politics—are directly linked to many of the congressional dysfunctions identified throughout this book. Both extreme partisan gerrymandering and the campaign role of "independent" groups espousing extremist ideologies, for example, have encouraged members to tend only to their own electoral bases and to eschew cooperation and compromise. This, in fact, goes farther toward explaining budget brinksmanship and breakdown than do the rules or the design of the budget process. Reform of our electoral system thus promises not only to increase the integrity and legitimacy of congressional elections but also to free up the institution to operate more cooperatively and effectively.

Governance, Legitimacy, and Citizenship

In our House Democratic Partnership's discussions with parliamentary colleagues, we often share the results of a survey some years ago that found regular viewers of C-SPAN—the citizens most likely to have an up-front, relatively unfiltered view of Congress—actually have a *less* favorable view of the institution than those who were less attentive.[23] There are invariably chuckles and bemused nods of recognition around the table. Legislatures are among the least-admired institutions worldwide, even when the alternative, as is literally true for some of our partner governments, is fighting in the streets.

This is not to say that media coverage reliably offers a more nuanced or balanced view; Thomas Patterson and other analysts have found that it regularly features "self-interested officials and dysfunctional institutions," treats the legislative process in terms of its machinations more than its substance, and frequently attributes a manipulative or deceptive intent to politicians.[24] With or without media filters, however, "the vagaries of interpersonal politics and policy-making are ... on continuous public display—the clashing egos, the sharp controversies, the self-serving rhetoric, the very messiness of it all."[25]

John Hibbing and Elizabeth Theiss-Morse concluded in an important study that people often do not "distinguish between essential modern democratic processes and perceived abuses of those processes.... [They] want it both ways ... democracy and no mess." As Hibbing further explained:

> Even if Congress were reorganized and reoriented, even if the media covered issues, not fluff, in mind-numbing detail, even if Congress hired the best public relations firm on the planet, and even if people cared about substance more than scandals, the modern Congress would still be suffering from public disapprobation. Why? Because the public does not like to witness conflict, debate, deliberation, compromise, or any of the other features that are central to meaningful legislative activity in a polity that is open, democratic, heterogeneous, and technologically sophisticated.[26]

This poses a tremendous challenge to the responsible legislator who chooses neither to exploit public mistrust nor to be victimized by it but to convey an honest and realistic sense of what constituents should expect from the legislative process.[27]

It is probably too much to expect Congress ever to be loved by the public, but we should strive for understanding and respect, the underpinnings of public legitimacy. As members we contribute (or detract) by the way we conduct ourselves in office—the priorities we set, the initiatives we take, the results we achieve—and by how we interpret that work and portray the institution to the various audiences we address.

Much of this communication takes place in a campaign context, which often provides a stark contrast to the realities of governing. I examined in Chapter 4 the transition that a successful candidate must make from one arena to the other. But it is to the campaigning more than the governing that the media and the public most often attend. And the advent of social media has made campaign-style communication a year-round proposition.

It is the nature of political campaigns to oversimplify and polarize, but my years in politics—which, after all, began in the shadow of Jesse Helms and the National Congressional Club—have seen a great increase in distortions and personal attacks and a more and more tenuous link between what candidates say in their campaign ads and the decisions they make once in office.

The growing gap between campaigning and governing both draws on and feeds public alienation and cynicism. Voters complain about the nastiness and irrelevance of campaign advertising, and such tactics can sometimes be turned against an opponent (see Chapter 2). My "Stand by Your Ad" provisions help voters identify those responsible for tactics of which they do not approve. But voters who find little to encourage or inspire them in politics are tempted to vote in anger or protest, inclinations that modern campaign advertising exploits effectively. As E.J. Dionne suggests, the decline of the "politics of remedy" (i.e., politics that attempt "to solve problems and resolve disputes") has created a vicious circle.

> Campaigns have become negative in large part because of a sharp decline in popular faith in government. To appeal to an increasingly alienated electorate, candidates and their political consultants have adopted a cynical stance which, they believe with good reason, plays into popular cynicism about politics and thus wins them votes. But cynical campaigns do not resolve issues. They do not lead to "remedies." Therefore, problems get worse, the electorate becomes more cynical—and so does the advertising.[28]

If modern campaigns reveal a dangerous decline in democratic accountability, so does modern governance, but not always in the way one might think. Ironically, the result of the campaigning–governance gap often is not governance in disregard of the popular will but a *failure* of governance, based on a sensitivity (sometimes, but not always, exaggerated) to opponents' anticipated use of difficult policy decisions. This accounts for much of the skittishness surrounding tax and budget measures and is illustrated by the difficulty of fending off "hang 'em high" amendments to crime bills, "gotcha" votes designed to cast members as soft on illegal immigration, and the like. A Republican primary in the district next to mine in 2016, necessitated when two incumbents were drawn into the same district, featured a litmus test of votes on which the winning candidate accused his opponent of being insufficiently conservative. On closer inspection, these votes proved to be not instances when the member voted with Democrats but occasions when she voted with her own Republican leadership, often on end-of-session budget compromises necessary to keep government running.

Members often feel stronger electoral pressures to avoid difficult tasks or votes than to be active and productive in areas of positive concern. This is not to say we must succumb to these pressures. All of us feel occasionally that "I'd rather vote against this than to have to explain it," but we should worry if we find ourselves taking this way out too often or on matters of genuine consequence. It is our job not only to make difficult decisions but to interpret and explain them. With sufficient effort, we can usually do so successfully.

Narrowing the campaigning–governance gap does not require dull or soft-pitch campaigns. On the contrary, it is our duty to arouse people's concern and anger about areas of neglect, to convince them that we can do better, to inspire them to contribute to the solution. Most people believe that politics and politicians ought to have something constructive to offer in the realms of education, housing, health care, economic security, environmental protection, and other areas of tangible concern. Our challenge is to get to work on these major issues in both campaigning *and* governing in a credible way that inspires confidence and enthusiasm. By so doing, we can expose hot-button attack politics for the sham it is.

How do we handle disappointment and failure, as often we must? Our ideas and initiatives may not compel widespread agreement, and even if they do, we operate in a system with many veto-points, designed more to prevent abuses of power than to enable its efficient exercise. Still, it is often harder to get important work done than it should be, and the difficulties have increased considerably over the three decades that I have witnessed directly. The "messiness" has increased, and the institution has paid a heavy price in legitimacy and respect. I have in this volume traced the increase of severe partisan polarization, the centralized leadership it has brought forth, the dysfunction and deadlock it has produced. I have provided examples of working around the obstacles but, I hope, have also left no doubt that our institution's performance could be enhanced by diminished ideological polarization and by a range of electoral and institutional reforms.

I suggested in Chapter 10 that the patriotism our country needs is neither uncritical love nor loveless criticism but a posture of love and loyalty combined with a determination to repair and reform. The same posture applies to the Congress, for members and citizens alike. There is much about the design of the institution and its performance over 230 years that deserves respect. But there is much that is dangerously flawed. This has sometimes resulted in a breakdown of the most basic functions of government and often in serious underperformance in addressing the country's basic needs and in living up to our Article One constitutional responsibilities. As members, we should be accountable for our efforts to be "a part of the solution" in the way we do business personally and in our efforts to promote needed institutional change.

This does not call for the kind of posturing that purchases respect for oneself at the expense of the institution. Members are not merely institutional critics or gadflies; it is our responsibility to actually make the institution work in ways that serve our democracy and gain legitimacy and respect. That is the point of the questions I suggested members should ask themselves (Chapter 11). What is my responsibility to assume a productive role within the legislature, to contribute to the functioning of the committee and party systems, to assert Congress's constitutional prerogatives, and to promote public understanding of how representative democracy works? None of this requires uncritical or unqualified defense of the institution, but neither does it permit posing as the perpetual outsider. What is called for is a kind of *institutional* patriotism, combining an appreciation of democratic structures and processes with a determination to deal with their failings and renovate them for the future.

It is important, finally, for elected officials and citizens alike to see our expectations and demands with respect to Congress and other democratic institutions in the context of our *citizenship*. In politics, we expect people and groups to express their wants and interests vigorously, and public officials expect to be judged on how effectively they respond. But our democracy requires something more, what the founders recognized as civic virtue: the ability and willingness to make the common good one's own. Each of us is simultaneously a private individual pursuing our own ends and a citizen with an obligation to attend to the well-being of the community.[29] We must bring an understanding of this balance to the demands we make of representative institutions and the assessments we make of their performance. Until we do that, and citizens and officials alike assume greater responsibility for the common good, our politics is likely to feature unproductive standoffs and to breed cynicism and disillusionment.

To assume this broader stance is likely to heighten rather than weaken the critique conscientious citizens bring to Congress and the way it works. Certainly, it is not a formula for removing conflict from politics: good citizens will still find plenty to debate about. But our country needs a broader, more visionary debate about how all of our people are faring and about how to secure our common future. We are unlikely to frame that debate satisfactorily or meet our challenges decisively unless and until we recapture a strong sense of citizenship.

This need is especially acute for public officials. A central part of my job is to become aware of the interests of my variegated constituents and to respond in appropriate ways. I expect the individuals and groups who approach me to express what they want unequivocally. They are especially likely to gain my respect if they show some awareness of legitimate competing views and formulate their requests with due regard for the good of the whole. But whether they do or not, that is the context into which I am obligated to place them.

Members of Congress are not entirely on our own in seeking and promoting this broader view. We are part of an institution; at their best, deliberative processes are not merely hurdles to clear but means of tempering biases and oversights. However, just as members have a wide latitude in how we define our jobs, so are we responsible for how we define and how vigorously we pursue the good of the community. The job has many satisfactions and challenges but none greater than the opportunity it daily affords to act on the imperatives of citizenship.

Notes

1 E.J. Dionne Jr., *Code Red: How Progressives and Moderates Can Unite to Save Our Country* (New York: St. Martin's Press, 2020), p. 65.
2 E.J. Dionne Jr., Norman Ornstein, and Thomas Mann, *One Nation after Trump* (New York: St. Martin's Press, 2017), p. 133.
3 Max Weber, "Politics as a Vocation," in H.H. Gerth and C.W. Mills, eds., *From Max Weber: Essays in Sociology* 3rd edition (New York: Oxford University Press, 1946), p. 128.
4 Dionne, *They Only Look Dead: Why Progressives Will Dominate the Next Political Era* (New York: Simon and Shuster, 1997), p. 327.

5   See Dionne et al., *One Nation*, p. 282. "Democrats must become a 'fusion' party, to use a term once popular among urban reformers, ... [whereby] narrow partisanship [gives] way to a larger and more urgent cause" (pp. 280–281). See also Dionne, *Code Red*, especially chap. 10.

6   See the varied list of "bromides" critiqued by Thomas Mann and Norman Ornstein: third-party strategies, a balanced budget constitutional amendment, term limits. *It's Even Worse Than It Looks* (New York: Basic Books, 2012), chap. 4.

7   I expressed some of this in an otherwise appreciative review of Richard Fenno's *Congressmen in Committees*, in *American Political Science Review*, 71, no. 2 (June 1977), pp. 701–704.

8   Robert Bendiner, *Obstacle Course on Capitol Hill* (New York: McGraw-Hill, 1964), is an account of frustrated efforts to pass aid to education legislation; Richard Bolling, *House Out of Order* (New York: Dutton, 1965), is a brief for reform by a prominent House member. See also Morris K. Udall's newsletters from the 1960s, reprinted in *Education of a Congressman*, ed. Robert L. Peabody (New York: Bobbs-Merrill, 1972), especially chapters 19–22.

9   The study that I directed, *The Commerce Committees* (New York: Grossman, 1975), although completed in a few months, was published almost three years later as one of a set of six volumes.

10 Mark J. Green, James M. Fallows, and David R. Zwick, *Who Runs Congress? The President, Big Business, or You?* (New York: Bantam, 1972).

11 The high (or low) point of the progression was reached in a 1989 *Newsweek* piece that Rep. David Obey dubbed "the worst example of institution trashing that I have seen in my twenty years here." In the space of six pages, readers were informed, without benefit of documentation, that most congressional staff members were employed "to enhance re-election"; that it was now "theoretically possible for a lawmaker to spend virtually his entire working day on the air" (although admittedly no one had done it); that "trading votes for money or pleasure is just another day at the office"; and that campaign money "allows members to live a virtually expense-free existence" (my wife and I were especially intrigued by that one). The article simultaneously condemned Congress as a "fortress of unreality, its drawbridges only barely connected to life beyond the moat" and took members to task for "commuting home for four-day weekends!" Jonathan Alter et al., "The World of Congress," *Newsweek*, April 24, 1989, pp. 28–34. Obey's comments were made in an address to the Center for National Policy on May 10, 1989, p. 5. For a later elaboration of many of these themes, see Obey's extended comments on the House floor in the *Congressional Record*, daily ed., November 5, 1991, pp. H9377–H9383.

12 *Clinton v. City of New York*, 524 U.S. 417 (1998).

13 *It's Even Worse*, pp. 125–126.

14 *U.S. Term Limits, Inc. v. Thornton*, 514 U.S. 779 (1995).

15 C. Lawrence Evans and Walter J. Oleszek, *Congress under Fire: Reform Politics and the Republican Majority* (New York: Houghton Mifflin, 1997), p. 84.

16 Ibid., p. 55.

17 David E. Price, *The Congressional Experience*, 3rd ed. (Boulder, CO: Westview Press, 2004), pp. 306–307.

18 Ibid., p. 307. Foley expressed some bemusement and envy at Gingrich's "luxury of being King John without the barons." He concluded, however, that "while I might have envied the new Speaker's ability to curb the independent agendas of committee chairmen relative to the leadership, [the] price was too high." Jeffrey R. Biggs and Thomas S. Foley, *Honor in the House: Speaker Tom Foley* (Pullman, WA: Washington State University Press, 1999), pp. 199, 270. For a

more positive though mixed assessment of the Republican changes and a prediction that reversion to Democratic control probably would not lead to their "systematic reversal," see Evans and Oleszek, *Congress under Fire*, pp. 172–179.

19 *Report of the Congressional Reform Task Force*, American Political Science Association, October, 2019, p. 25.

20 Ibid., p. 26.

21 *Testimony before the Joint Select Committee on Budget and Appropriations Process Reform*, 115th Congress, June 27, 2018. See also Price, "Biennial Budgeting Is Not the Answer," *Roll Call*, March 6, 2000, p. 38; and floor proceedings of May 16, 2000: *Congressional Record*, daily ed., pp. H3108–H3128.

22 The House approved an initial set of recommendations (H. Res. 756) by a vote of 395–13 on March 10, 2020.

23 Thomas E. Mann and Norman J. Ornstein, introduction to *Congress, the Press, and the Public* (Washington, DC: American Enterprise Institute/Brookings Institution, 1994), p. 10.

24 "Ingrained cynicism, rather than knee-jerk liberalism, is the media's real bias," Patterson concluded. "Bad News, Period," *P.S.: Political Science and Politics*, March 1996, p. 19. See also Mark J. Rozell, *In Contempt of Congress: Postwar Press Coverage on Capitol Hill* (Westport, CT: Praeger, 1996).

25 Roger H. Davidson, "Congress and Public Trust: Is Congress Its Own Worst Enemy?" in Joseph Cooper, ed., *Congress and the Decline of Public Trust* (Boulder, CO: Westview Press, 1999), p. 66.

26 Hibbing and Theiss-Morse, *Congress as Public Enemy: Public Attitudes toward American Political Institutions* (New York: Cambridge University Press, 1995), pp. 147–148; Hibbing, "Appreciating Congress," in Cooper, ed., *Congress and the Decline of Public Trust*, p. 53.

27 It also poses a challenge to civic education. "The public's distaste for the core features of any real-life democracy—disagreement, debate, compromise, all probably at a measured pace—must be addressed by a totally restructured educational process. Schooling on constitutional and institutional niceties desperately needs to be accompanied by schooling on unavoidable democratic realities." Hibbing and Theiss-Morse, *Congress as Public Enemy*, p. 160.

28 E.J. Dionne Jr., *Why Americans Hate Politics* (New York: Simon & Schuster, 1991), pp. 16–17. Dionne borrowed the concept of democratic politics at its best as "the search for remedy" from Arthur Schlesinger Jr.

29 See the formulation in Joseph Tussman, *Obligation and the Body Politic* (New York: Oxford University Press, 1960).

Index

Note: Numbers in *italics* refer to figures.

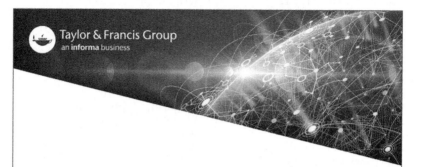

Made in the USA
Las Vegas, NV
24 April 2021